THE EUROPEAN INTEGRATED BORDER MANAGEMENT

What are the human rights obligations of Frontex and its Member States at the borders of Europe? Who is responsible when the rights of people crossing those borders are breached? Those are the main questions that this book addresses while exploring the evolution of the European integrated border management (EIBM).

The mode of administration of European borders has become a complex and polymorphous affair involving multiple actors working at different levels, with different competences and powers. In this context, borders are no longer lines on a map but enmeshed in a tapestry of different actors and technologies. This evolution not only tests the relationship between territory and public power, it also requires a different understanding of the responsibility for the exercise of that power by a panoply of actors.

This book addresses the challenges related to the implementation of the EIBM and the human rights responsibilities that it can trigger. It entwines two separate but interlaced discourses: the first being a reflection on the concept of EIBM and its human rights impact; the second being the question of the attribution of international responsibility for violations that occurred in the implementation of the EIBM.

Volume 120 in the Series Modern Studies in European Law

Modern Studies in European Law

Recent titles in this series:

The Architecture of Fundamental Rights in the European Union
Šejla Imamovic

The EU and its Member States' Joint Participation in International Agreements
Edited by Nicolas Levrat, Yuliya Kaspiarovich, Christine Kaddous and Ramses A Wessel

The UN Convention on the Rights of Persons with Disabilities and the European Union: The Impact on Law and Governance
Carmine Conte

EU Criminal Law, Second Edition
Valsamis Mitsilegas

The EU as a Global Digital Actor: Institutionalising Global Data Protection, Trade, and Cybersecurity
Elaine Fahey

Exporting the European Convention on Human Rights
Maria-Louiza Deftou

Judicial Authority in EU Internal Market Law: Implications for the Balance of Competences and Powers
Vilija Velyvyte

The Changing European Union: A Critical View on the Role of Law and the Courts
Edited by Tamara Capeta, Iris Goldner Lang and Tamara Perisin

The Structural Transformation of European Private Law: A Critique of Juridical Hermeneutic
Leone Niglia

The Future of EU Constitutionalism
Edited by Matej Avbelj

The Changing Role of Citizens in EU Democratic Governance
Edited by Davor Jancic

The EU and the Baltic Sea Area
Edited by Allan Rosas and Henrik Ringbom

The Evolving Governance of EU Competition Law in a Time of Disruptions: A Constitutional Perspective
Edited by Carlo Maria Colombo, Kathryn Wright and Mariolina Eliantonio

The European Integrated Border Management: Frontex, Human Rights, and International Responsibility
Giulia Raimondo

For the complete list of titles in this series see www.bloomsbury.com/uk/series/modern-studies-in-european-law/

The European Integrated Border Management

Frontex, Human Rights, and International Responsibility

Giulia Raimondo

•HART•

OXFORD • LONDON • NEW YORK • NEW DELHI • SYDNEY

HART PUBLISHING

Bloomsbury Publishing Plc

Kemp House, Chawley Park, Cumnor Hill, Oxford, OX2 9PH, UK

1385 Broadway, New York, NY 10018, USA

29 Earlsfort Terrace, Dublin 2, Ireland

HART PUBLISHING, the Hart/Stag logo, BLOOMSBURY and the Diana logo are trademarks of Bloomsbury Publishing Plc

First published in Great Britain 2024

A catalogue record for this book is available from the British Library.

A catalogue record for this book is available from the Library of Congress.

Library of Congress Control Number: 2023949150

ISBN: HB: 978-1-50996-454-3
ePDF: 978-1-50996-456-7
ePub: 978-1-50996-455-0

Typeset by Compuscript Ltd, Shannon

To find out more about our authors and books visit www.hartpublishing.co.uk. Here you will find extracts, author information, details of forthcoming events and the option to sign up for our newsletters.

L'obligation est efficace dès qu'elle est reconnue. Une obligation ne serait-elle reconnue par personne, elle ne perd rien de la plénitude de son être. Un droit qui n'est reconnu par personne n'est pas grand-chose.

Simone Weil, *L'Enracinement* (Paris, Gallimard, 1943).

ACKNOWLEDGEMENTS

This book reflects many years of interest in migration and in how international law collimates or responds to the ethical intuitions that dominate the way we think about the movement of people across borders. It originates from my doctoral research at the Geneva Graduate Institute and was revised during my time as a postdoctoral researcher at the University of Luxembourg. Along the way, I was lucky enough to meet many people who encouraged me during those inevitable times when everything seemed a bit too much or too nonsensical.

I conducted this research under the direction of Professor Vincent Chetail, who provided vital guidance and rigorous feedback. Over the years, I have learned a great deal from him, and for that I am sincerely grateful. I am also grateful to the members of my PhD jury, Professor Andrew Clapham, whose sharp insights and optimism kept challenging and motivating me throughout this journey, and Professor Violeta Moreno-Lax, whose expertise, thoroughness and generosity are true sources of inspiration, within and much beyond this book.

I should also like to extend my gratitude to the Swiss National Science Foundation for supporting a research visit to the University of Oxford, and to Professor Mary Bosworth who made it possible. Beyond refining the arguments put forward in this study, that research visit showed me how academia – despite restless competition – could be a great collective effort to understand something about the world together. My time at the University of Luxembourg's Faculty of Law, Economics and Finance reinforced this conviction, not least because of the collegiality and insightful conversations shared with many colleagues and friends.

As with many academic endeavours, this research originates in the personal background of its author. The border is part of my life. When I was born, my young father worked as a border guard on a bridge deep in the Alps between Italy and Switzerland. No other place in Italy would have been farther away from his home, Sicily. The mountains were solitary and wild – perhaps more than he would have wished or expected. Yet, those mountains became home, and he ended up staying, because of family, because of love. I grew up at the border, and I was always fascinated by its symbolic value. I remember the visits to the border crossing as a child. It was a strange place, and I would ask time and again: 'Where is the border?' – I could not see it – 'And why do we need guards on both sides of the frontier?' Everyone knew each other and the community to which we all belonged, irrespective of borders and accents. I decided to research borders in another border place, Geneva, a strip of Switzerland inside France. I continued this study in Luxembourg, where my family is now split across borders – because of love.

In a somewhat genre-breaking move, I would also like to acknowledge the places where this book has been conceived, researched and written. Beyond my curiosity about the border, I am grateful for the serenity I found at my parents' house, with its mountains and memories. Spending hours in the silence of my room was a privilege for which I will always be grateful. I'm also grateful for the long and (literally) pregnant walks in Oxford University Parks and for the hospitality of my partner's office in Geneva.

This work grew amid a lot of silence and a lot of love. I should thank both silence and love, which often intersect. Over the years, many people have made the silence less solitary, and I thank them for their presence but also for knowing how to be there without being there, which is sometimes more complicated. In a little valley across the Swiss border, my roots, my family and friends kept me grounded and motivated. Thank you for understanding how important this work was to me and for supporting me despite my absences.

Every day, everywhere, Thierry is my companion, best opponent, most reliable co-driver, and my safe place. He patiently listened to my monologues about border politics, read drafts, challenged my ideas and gave me the time and the space I needed to think through my rants – all this while we were becoming parents together. If it were not for his confidence in me, I would never have had the courage nor the energy to muddle through any academic endeavour after my PhD defence, even less so if that involved moving with a two-year-old to a different country. The completion of this work would have been immensely harder without his constant support and care. Thank you for all that you are for us.

Finally, this book is dedicated to two women in my family who, each in her own way, have experienced how borders can bridle our lives. These women are my grandmother, Rosanna, who found hospitality behind the Swiss border during the Second World War, and her great-granddaughter – my daughter – Mathilde, who was born behind that same border in a moment fraught with different challenges. This work is for them, and for those who experience borders – and the inequalities they structure – in a much more violent and unjust way.

TABLE OF CONTENTS

LIST OF ABBREVIATIONS

ACHPR	African Charter on Human and People's Rights
ACHR	American Convention on Human Rights
AFSJ	Area of Freedom Security and Justice
ArCHR	Arab Charter on Human Rights
ARIO	Articles on the Responsibility of International Organizations
ARS	Articles on Responsibility of States for Internationally Wrongful Acts
CEAS	Common European Asylum System
CFI	Court of First Instance
CFR	Charter of Fundamental Rights of the European Union
CFSP	Common Foreign and Security Policy
CJEU	Court of Justice of the European Union
CoE	Council of Europe
CRC	Committee on the Rights of the Child
CSDP	Common Security and Defence Policy
EBCG	European Border and Coast Guard
ECA	European Court of Auditors
ECOSOC	UN Economic and Social Council
ECHR	European Convention on Human Rights (also, 'Convention')
ECommHR	European Commission of Human Rights
ECtHR	European Court of Human Rights
EEAS	European External Action Service
EEC	Treaty Establishing the European Economic Community
EIBM	European Integrated Border Management
EU	European Union

Euratom	European Atomic Energy Community
ExComm	Executive Committee (UNHCR)
FRA	Fundamental Rights Agency
FRM	Fundamental Rights Monitors
FRO	Fundamental Rights Officer
GAMM	Global Approach to Migration and Mobility
GCM	Global Compact for Safe, Orderly and Regular Migration
HRC	Human Rights Committee
ICC	International Criminal Court
ICCPR	International Convention on Civil and Political Rights
ICERD	International Convention on the Elimination of All Forms of Racial Discrimination
ICESCR	International Convention on Economic, Social and Cultural Rights
ILC	International Law Commission
ICRMW	International Convention on the Protection of the Rights of All Migrant Workers and Members of Their Families
Inter-AmCtHR	Inter-American Court of Human Rights
MRCC	Maritime Rescue Co-ordination Centre
OLAF	European Anti-Fraud Office
OPLAN	Operational Plan
SBC	Schengen Borders Code
SCIFA	Strategic Committee on Immigration and Frontiers
TEU	Treaty on the European Union
TFEU	Treaty on the Functioning of the European Union
UN	United Nations
UNGA	United Nations General Assembly
UNHCR	United Nations High Commissioner for Refugees
UNSC	United Nations Security Council
VCLT	Vienna Convention on the Law of Treaties

TABLE OF INSTRUMENTS

International Treaties

Regional Treaties

African Union

Council of Europe

European Union

EU Law and Selected Agreements

Regulations

Directives

Frontex Status Agreements with Third Countries

Organisation of American States

League of Arab States

Bilateral Treaties

Memoranda of Understanding

TABLE OF CASES

International Case Law

Permanent Court of International Justice

International Court of Justice

International Tribunal for the Law of the Sea

International Criminal Tribunal for the Former Yugoslavia

UN Committee on the Rights of the Child

UN Human Rights Committee

Regional Case Law

African Commission of Human and Peoples' Rights

European Court of Justice and Court of Justice of the European Union

European Court of Auditors

European Commission and Court of Human Rights

European Court of Human Rights

Inter-American Commission on Human Rights

Inter-American Court of Human Rights

National Case Law

Italy

The Netherlands

United Kingdom

United States

Introduction

I. How to Navigate a Maze?

In the early hours of 26 February 2023, an overcrowded boat, which left Turkey a few days before, capsized 150 metres from the Italian coast. The night before the incident, the European Border and Coast Guard Agency (Frontex) spotted the vessel and alerted the Italian authorities, which sent two patrol boats to intercept the ship, in accordance with the terms of Frontex joint operation Themis. The Italian coast guard did not intervene. The search and rescue capacity of other law enforcement authorities was limited. Misunderstandings and delays resulted in the death of more than 90 people, and more than 30 went missing. Whilst the victims' bodies were still being recovered at sea, the many authorities involved started to shift the blame among themselves. Italy criticised Frontex for not having signalled the distress situation of the boat; Frontex replied that Italy had the primary responsibility for the search and rescue operations. In turn, the Italian authorities started investigating the coast guard in charge of search and rescue activities. The Italian minister of the interior then implied that migrants brought tragedy on themselves by attempting dangerous journeys,[1] and that Greece's containment strategy pushed them on such journeys.[2] In the same context, he also referred to the lack of 'responsibility' underlying migrants' decision to embark on these crossings.[3] But whose responsibility, precisely?

Beyond the obscenity of blaming the victims and criminalising them, this situation illuminates the intricate network of legal, administrative and enforcement powers governing border management in Europe. European borders are increasingly integrated and managed by a panoply of actors with different mandates and pertaining to different jurisdictions and legal frameworks. Lack of clarity in the nature and scope of their obligations towards migrants has a number of repercussions. On the one hand, it impacts the very performance of relevant obligations. Ambiguity as to who owes which duties to whom, and under which conditions, undermines compliance. The same ambiguity impairs the position of the victims,

[1] *Meloni, Piantedosi 'slap' for shipwreck victims* (ANSA, 27 February 2023) www.ansa.it/english/news/politics/2023/02/27/meloni-piantedosi-slap-for-shipwreck-victims-msf_e79d48c6-9562-4487-b4fd-d3a7e941d4ca.html.

[2] *Greece's policies may affect migrant sea routes to Italy – Italian minister* (Reuters, 1 March 2023) www.reuters.com/world/greeces-policies-may-affect-migrant-sea-routes-italy-italian-minister-2023-03-01/.

[3] Angelo Picarello, *Meloni scrive alla Ue. Le opposizioni all'attacco di Piantedosi* (Avvenire, 28 February 2023) www.avvenire.it/attualita/pagine/meloni-scrive-alla-ue-urgente-intervenire-le-opposizioni-allattacco-di-pia.

who must identify each actor, their contribution to the harm suffered and the circumstances under which this is legally relevant for responsibility to arise. Frontex joint operations offer a perfect illustration of the complexity and the opacity surrounding multilateral cooperation in the field of border control, where the respective responsibilities of multiple actors involved are difficult to individuate.

As I write these lines, we assist to the same scene in Greece, where a fishing boat capsized, taking with it, to around 5000 metres under the water, the vast majority of the 750 persons on board. While Frontex aerial surveillance spotted the overcrowded boat and transmitted the information to the Greek and Italian authorities, rescue activities were delayed and inadequate. The role of these national and supranational actors in the shipwreck is still to be determined.[4] The conditions that render these shipwrecks possible are not only delays and misunderstandings but also the very structure of the laws and policies governing the administration of European borders, in the interstices of which 'legal black holes' are forged to evade responsibility whenever a violation is revealed.[5]

The European integrated border management (EIBM) and its implementation by Frontex and the Member States challenge common assumptions regarding borders, human rights and the responsibility that their violation entails. This book is concerned both with the cooperation of states and the European Union (EU) in managing the external borders of the Schengen area of free movement – and with the legal challenges their concerted action can pose. It will explore the evolution of the EIBM and how it is implemented by Frontex. It will then identify the content and scope of international obligations binding the agency and the Member States participating in concerted border management activities. Finally, it will address the question of international responsibility for migrant rights violations that may occur during the implementation of integrated border management activities.

The overall goal is to offer a guided tour of the legal labyrinth framing the administration of EU borders using the compass of international law. The study moves from the fundamental hypothesis that international law can provide some significant answers to questions arising from the diffusion of responsibility inherent to multi-actor situations such as the EIBM. Yet, the analysis also unfolds some of the limitations of the current legal framework structuring the predicament of people caught in the meshes of the EIBM.

II. The EIBM, Frontex and the Changing Nature of Borders in Europe

The European project has brought the image of national borders into perspective in various ways. On the one hand, the creation of an area of free movement implicated

[4] Frontex, Frontex statement following tragic shipwreck off Pylos (16 June 20223) https://frontex.europa.eu/media-centre/news/news-release/frontex-statement-following-tragic-shipwreck-off-pylos-dJ5l9p.

[5] Itamar Mann, 'Maritime Legal Black Holes: Migration and Rightlessness in International Law' (2018) 29 *European Journal of International Law* 347.

the growing inconsequentiality of internal borders; on the other hand, the duty to control the external borders of Europe shifted to its periphery. The abolition of internal border checks entrained a common effort to control the external borders of Europe.[6] The progressive integration of the European border administration aims to ensure harmonisation and burden-sharing among the Member States. However, the external borders of the Schengen area remain the borders of the Member States and therefore are controlled by national border control authorities. In this context, the concept of European integrated border management emerged to ensure the coordination of various domestic border control authorities and the application of common standards with a view to establishing 'open, but controlled and secure borders'.[7]

A dual logic underlies the EIBM, a logic of openness and closure. The EIBM attempts to reach a greater level of security while maintaining fluidity in the movement of goods, capital, services and (preselected) people. Technological advances facilitate the achievement of this dual objective, with many different actors involved in a complex dynamic of securitisation through digital and military tools. In turn, the EIBM expands the reach of European border controls. The EIBM rests on a 'four-tier access control model' comprising measures taking place in neighbouring and third countries, border control measures at the EU external borders, risk analysis, measures within the Schengen area and return activities.[8] Enforced through this model of diffused control, the European borders fulfil their exclusionary purposes even before the beginning of the migration journey and well beyond the territories of Member States. European borders are therefore both increasingly integrated, yet shifting in space, time and in how they are experienced. These concomitant tendencies challenge the orthodox conception of borders.

In the common imagination, borders, like lines or fences, identify and protect the community they comprise. The symbolic force of this image reflects the modern conception of the sovereign right to control who enters the national territory. The European border integration process scatters this traditional idea of the border as both a stable line demarcating territorial boundaries and a defence technology. At the same time, it does not contradict the assumption according to which states have the right to control the entry of non-nationals into their territory.[9]

Borders are no longer exclusively represented by stable physical frontiers. They can take the form of paper walls, virtual fences or controls performed in countries of origin and transit. As such, borders can shift in time and space, following

[6] Here and in the following pages, I will use the term Europe as a synonym for the Schengen area, including the EU Member States and Schengen-associated countries.

[7] Commission, Guidelines for Integrated Border Management in the Western Balkans, 2007, 76; European Commission, EU Guidelines for Integrated Border Management in European Commission External Cooperation, European Commission, 2010, 23.

[8] Recital 11, Regulation (EU) 2019/1896 [2019] OJ L 295.

[9] See most notably: ECtHR, *Abdulaziz, Cabales and Balkandali*, Appl No 9214/80 9473/81 9474/81, 28 May 1985, para 67.

the journeys of migrants, both before their departure and after their arrival.[10] These shifting patterns directly concern the conception of Europe and its borders. Borders are also no longer imagined solely as technologies of *state* power. They are controlled and secured by multiple authorities at various levels – national and supranational, public and private, direct and vicarious. Specialised agencies and private actors increasingly undertake immigration control functions previously dominated by state authorities. Moreover, third countries have become critical actors in implementing EU extraterritorial border controls.

The European Border and Coast Guard Agency, better known by its acronym Frontex (from the French *frontières extérieures*), plays a pivotal role in the complex network of actors, practices and techniques constituting the EIBM. Frontex strengthens the control of the external borders by implementing the integrated management of Member States' external borders.[11] Its actions are meant to complement those of member states, to ensure the effectiveness and efficacy of the EU's migration policy.

The creation of Frontex was a compromise: while Member States retain the primary responsibility to control their respective borders, the agency reinforces, assesses and coordinates their border control activities. However, since its inception – and despite its coordinative and technical role – Frontex has rapidly gained momentum and accumulated powers. The agency was created in 2005 with a budget of around six million euros.[12] Seventeen years later, the agency's budget has risen to more than 754 million euros.[13] Beyond its growing financial resources, Frontex's technical and operational powers have grown rapidly and consistently. Today, its role goes far beyond the ancillary position originally assigned. The most recent revision of Frontex's founding regulation establishes a standing corps of 10,000 border guards, including Frontex's own staff, entrusted with the exercise of executive powers on the ground.[14]

With these expanding powers, Frontex has become the fulcrum of the EIBM. In implementing it, the agency and the Member States have committed to fully respecting fundamental (human) rights.[15] Yet situations at the external borders of Europe often illuminate the disjunction between abstract commitments and their concrete implementation. The EIBM, in general, and Frontex's activities in particular, disclose a variety of human rights implications. Over time, Frontex has

[10] The literature on the topic is vast. For a recent appraisal, see most notably: Ayelet Shachar, *The Shifting Border: Legal Cartographies of Migration and Mobility: Ayelet Shachar in Dialogue* (Manchester, Manchester University Press, 2020).

[11] Art 1, Regulation (EC) 2007/2004 [2004] OJ L 349/1.

[12] Frontex, Management Board Decision, Budget of the Agency for 2005, 30 June 2005. The following year, when the agency was fully operational, it had a budget of around 19 million EUR. Frontex, Management Board Decision, Budget of the Agency for 2006.

[13] Frontex, Management Board Decision 70/2022 adopting the Single Programming Document 2023–2025 including the Multiannual Programming 2023–2025, the Work Programme 2023 and the Budget 2023.

[14] Art 55(7) and Annex V, Regulation 2019/1896.

[15] Art 1, Regulation 2019/1896.

attracted as much scholarly attention[16] as criticism for its lack of human rights compliance.[17] There have been frequent and severe criticisms, notably concerning violations of the prohibition of torture and *refoulement* and the holding of migrants in detention facilities in deleterious conditions.

The ubiquitous nature of border controls, performed remotely through an arsenal of new technologies and cooperative tactics, challenges the traditional notion of human rights jurisdiction linked to physical control over a territory or a person. The extraterritorial scope of many Frontex operations further entails serious legal challenges to hold the agency or the states it coordinates responsible for potential human rights violations.[18] The agency's operations encompass the cooperative action of multiple state and non-state actors. In the event of a human rights violation, these actors shield themselves behind the veil of legal uncertainty created by such cooperation. Frontex aims to buttress cooperation among domestic border control authorities and foster harmonisation of border control procedures. Yet, the agency magnifies existing challenges in allocating responsibility for the potentially harmful consequences of the operations it coordinates and supervises.

The post-national shift of border control practices at the European level not only puts to test the relation between territory and public power, but also requires a different understanding of the responsibility ensuing from the exercise of that power by a panoply of different actors. This study highlights the potential disjunction between the changing functions and shapes of borders and the protection of migrant rights, focusing on the legal implications of such a mismatch.

III. Objectives and Structure of the Study

The mode of administration of European borders has become a composite, heterogeneous and polymorphous affair involving multiple actors working at different levels with different competences and powers. It is thus necessary to account for

[16] Among the numerous and diverse scholarly contributions, two monographs were specifically devoted to the many legal issues that Frontex arises: Roberta Mungianu, *Frontex and Non-Refoulement: The International Responsibility of the EU* (Cambridge, Cambridge University Press, 2016); Melanie Fink, *Frontex and Human Rights: Responsibility in 'Multi-Actor Situations' under the ECHR and EU Public Liability Law* (Oxford, Oxford University Press, 2018).

[17] Eg: CoE, Parliamentary Assembly, *Frontex: Human Rights Responsibilities*, Recommendation 2016 (2013) 25 April 2013; OLAF, Final Report on Frontex, Case No OC/2021/0451/A1, 3 Mai 2021; European Parliament, Report on the fact-finding investigation on Frontex concerning alleged fundamental rights violations, 14 July 2021.

[18] Anneliese Baldaccini, 'Extraterritorial Border Controls in the EU: The Role of FRONTEX in Operations at Sea' in Bernard Ryan and Valsamis Mitsilegas (eds), *Extraterritorial Immigration Control: Legal Challenges* (Leiden, Martinus Nijhoff, 2010); Melanie Fink, 'A "Blind Spot" in the Framework of International Responsibility? Third Party Responsibility for Human Rights Violations: The Case of Frontex' in Thomas Gammeltoft-Hansen and Jens Vedsted-Hansen (eds), *Human Rights and the Dark Side of Globalisation: Transnational Law Enforcement and Migration Control* (Abingdon, Routledge, 2016).

such complexity, not least because it creates a potential dispersion of responsibility; this study attempts to tackle this complexity using the vocabulary of international law.

This book integrates the discussion about Frontex's human rights responsibilities in the broader context of the European border integration process. What is the human rights impact of the European integrated border management implemented by Frontex and the Schengen Member States? What international obligations do the EU and its agency Frontex hold towards migrants attempting to cross the EU borders? Is it possible to hold Frontex and the Schengen Member States accountable for human rights violations occurring when they implement the EIBM? If it is, how should responsibility be distributed among them? These are some of the specific questions this book addresses and that continue to generate lively debates. The underlying theoretical question animating this study concerns how international responsibility is understood in an interdependent global society where borders are legitimised and operationalised in a post-national fashion. This crucially emerges from the evolution of the EIBM, an evolution that challenges traditional notions of border controls, as well as the principle of independent and exclusive responsibility in international law.[19]

Respectively, human rights violations occurring during Frontex operations implicate the personnel and equipment of both the agency and various states. In this complex situation, numerous actors are involved with different de iure mandates and de facto capabilities. In cases of migrant rights violations, these actors hand responsibility off to one another, blaming each other for the harmful consequences of their collective action (or inaction) at Europe's borders. On the one hand, the public discourse often focuses on Frontex as the main actor of the EIBM. This shifts the blame to Frontex, distracting attention from member states' role and their responsibility for any human rights violation at borders.[20] On the other hand, the agency has often diverted any human rights concerns towards the Member States, which retain primary responsibility for managing their sections of the external borders.[21]

When the actors controlling the European borders abuse their powers, and the rights of those subject to their coercive action are violated, three legal issues become crucial. First is the scope of these actors' international obligations; second, the content of these obligations; and third, the distribution of responsibility among the various actors involved in wrongful conduct.

This work does not assume that human rights violations generally occur during Frontex activities, nor does it try to prove that this is the case in concrete instances.

[19] Art 1, Articles on Responsibility of States for Internationally Wrongful Acts, with commentaries, Yearbook of the International Law Commission, 2001, vol II, Part Two; Art 1, Articles on Responsibility of International Organizations, with commentaries, Yearbook of the International Law Commission, 2011, vol II, Part Two.

[20] Jorrit J Rijpma, 'Frontex: Successful Blame Shifting of the Member States?' [2010] *Análisis del Real Instituto Elcano (ARI)* 1.

[21] Art 7, Regulation 2019/1896.

Instead, it explores the legal framework governing the agency's actions to appraise its conformity with the international obligations of the EU and its Member States. EU law, international human rights and refugee law constitute the prism through which this work examines the challenges of Frontex activities. Accordingly, it delineates the pluralist legal framework on which these activities rest. Part of the study, therefore, consists of 'mapping' the legal labyrinth encompassing the integrated management of European borders.

The elements outlined thus far determine the scope of this book. First, it focuses on the international responsibility of Frontex and the Member States for potential migrant rights violations that may occur during the implementation of the EIBM, in particular in the context of Frontex joint operations. Other breaches of international law (for instance, the law of the sea, or international criminal law) will be mentioned when relevant but will not receive detailed analysis. In this respect, a terminological caveat is in order. As this book will show, migrant rights derive from many different sources at various levels. To reflect the broad scope of the analysis, the term 'migrant rights' is used to capture the rights of people on the move under both human rights and refugee law.[22] In addition, the responsibility that derives from their violation is here understood in its narrow legal sense, as the legal principle governing the determination of the legal consequences ensuing from the violation of an international obligation.[23] That notwithstanding, this study will also offer a broader reflection on the accountability of public institutions in the performance of border control activities.

Second, and related, this book will explore these questions from the perspective of the legal responsibility of Frontex (and the EU) and the Member States for human rights violations at their borders. Therefore, it will not cover the human rights responsibility of private actors; but it will, incidentally, consider their inextricable influence on border control activities enforced by public actors. Third,

[22] To be sure, migrant rights and refugee rights are human rights. However, the interaction between human rights and refugee law remains a vast and complex topic. While some authors recognise the Refugee Convection as a human rights treaty; others treat the former as a *lex specialis*, as opposed to the *lex generalis* of human rights law. See respectively: Jane McAdams, *Complementary Protection in International Refugee Law* (Oxford, Oxford University Press, 2006) 1; James C Hathaway, *The Rights of Refugees under International Law* (Cambridge, Cambridge University Press, 2021) 158. However, the dichotomy between human rights and refugee rights has been questioned both normatively and descriptively. For a systematic appraisal of the interaction between the two regimes, see: Vincent Chetail, 'Are Refugee Rights Human Rights? An Unorthodox Questioning of the Relations between Refugee Law and Human Rights Law' in R Rubio-Marin (ed), *Human Rights and Immigration* (Oxford, Oxford University Press, 2014) and references included therein. The debate about the value of the distinction between refugee and migrant rights has recently resurfaced with the adoption of the Global Compact on Refugees (GCR) and the Global Compact for Safe, Orderly and Regular Migration (GCM). See: Pia Oberoi, 'Words Matter. But Rights Matter More' (2018) 11 *Anti-Trafficking Review* 129; Cathryn Costello, 'Refugees and (Other) Migrants: Will the Global Compacts Ensure Safe Flight and Onward Mobility for Refugees?' (2019) 30 *International Journal of Refugee Law* 643; Annick Pijnenburg and Conny Rijken, 'Moving Beyond Refugees and Migrants: Reconceptualising the Rights of People on the Move' (2021) 23(2) *International Journal of Postcolonial Studies* 273.

[23] PCIJ, *Case Concerning the Factory at Chorzów*, (Jurisdiction) 26 July 1927, PCIJ Reports Ser A No 9, 21.

the main judicial fora addressed by the present study are the European Court of Human Rights (ECtHR), the Court of Justice of the European Union (CJEU) and the national courts of Member States, as far as they apply relevant rules of EU and international law.

The book proceeds in two steps. First, it sets the scene by exploring the evolution of the EIBM and introduce Frontex, its main actor. It analyses the development and functions of the agency in relation to its activities' impact on migrant rights. Second, the study explores the question of international responsibility for potential human rights violations occurring during border control activities implemented by Frontex and its Member States.[24]

Accordingly, chapter one provides an overview of the EIBM, its origin, development, legal basis and its main logics and functions. The chapter introduces all the relevant actors operating in the intricate web of the EIBM and situates Frontex in the broader picture of the border integration process. After a bird's-eye view of the EIBM and its manifold implications, chapter two zooms in on Frontex, the 'anchor stone' of the EIBM.[25] It closely analyses Frontex's role in assembling the actors, practices and techniques constituting the EIBM. Along with Frontex's legal framework, this chapter explores the agency's main tasks and functions to identify the human rights implications of its activities.

Against this background, the following chapters, respectively, address the content of the international obligations binding Frontex and the Member States in implementing the EIBM, their scope of application and the distribution of responsibility for their violation. Chapter three explores the pluralistic legal framework within which Frontex and the Member States operate. The analysis of the law applicable to their activities will prepare the ground for their evaluation through the prism of international law. The interplay of international refugee law, human rights law and EU law illuminates the impact of Frontex activities on people on the move towards Europe. Chapter four then defines the scope of application of the legal framework previously discussed. It focuses particularly on the extraterritorial reach of EIBM measures implemented by Frontex and the Member States, with a view to determining the jurisdictional limits of their international obligations under EU and international law.

Last, chapter five addresses the question of attribution of responsibility in the complex situation of Frontex operations and maps the different 'levels' of responsibility for human rights violations occurring during the management of the European borders by the agency, its Member States and third countries cooperating with them. The aim is to define whether the sharing of competences among various actors participating in these operations can lead to their shared responsibility for human rights violations.

[24] Various states participate to different extents in Frontex's activities. As there are states who contribute to the agency's activities which are not EU or Schengen-associated states, in the following analysis I will generally refer to them as 'Frontex and its Member States'.

[25] See eg: Frontex' Programme of Work 2009, 14; Frontex' Programme of Work 2011, 15.

By way of conclusion, the study summarises its findings and draws some lessons learned for border control activities. Yet, the result will not constitute a 'how-to book' on allocating international responsibilities in complex situations, using Frontex operations as a case study. Instead, I propose a reflection on the limits and potential of the regime of international responsibility in the context of complex organisations. Ultimately, this study cannot and will not find unique and compelling answers to all the questions that it raises, but – I hope – it will offer more insight and understanding of the many paths that can be taken in the quest for responsibility in complex situations like those at the borders of Europe.

1

The European Integrated Border Management

I. Introduction: Boundaries, Frontiers and Borders in Europe

In common speech, the words 'frontier' and 'boundary' are generally used almost interchangeably. It does not take much reading in relevant literature to discover that a distinction exists, however, and it is quite significant.[1] For the present purposes, the word 'frontier' implies what it indicates etymologically: that which is 'in front'.[2] The frontier as a political institution can be described as a defence line.[3] In this sense, the couple 'frontier' and 'control' cannot be divorced. The word 'boundary', on the other hand, immediately points to its principal function, which is to establish the limits (the bounds) of a given political or social unit. An internal bond fastens everything within a boundary, and this is the final aim of boundaries: ensuring internal unity. The concept of border pairs these two dimensions: it epitomises the limits of territorial sovereignty and, at the same time, it represents a 'marker of identity' of national communities. Boundaries produce

[1] It would be impossible to give a complete account of all the works devoted to boundaries and frontiers. It suffices to mention here some of the works that lawyers, geographers, anthropologists and philosophers dedicated to this question over the years: Paul de Geouffre de La Pradelle, *La Frontière: Étude de Droit International* (Paris, Editions Internationals, 1928); Samuel Whittemore Boggs, *International Boundaries: A Study of Boundary Functions and Problems* (New York, Columbia University Press, 1940); Charles De Visscher, 'Problèmes de Confins en droit international public' (1970) 56 *Bulletins de l'Académie Royale de Belgique* 70; JR Victor Prescott, *Boundaries and Frontiers* (Abingdon, Taylor & Francis, 1978); Didier Bigo, Riccardo Bocco and Jean-Luc Piermay, 'Logiques de Marquage : Murs et Disputes Frontalières' (2009) *Cultures & Conflicts* 7; David Miller and Sohail H Hashmi, *Boundaries and Justice: Diverse Ethical Perspectives* (Princeton, Princeton University Press, 2001); Seyla Benhabib, 'Borders, Boundaries, and Citizenship' (2005) 38 *PS: Political Science and Politics* 673; Daniel-Erasmus Khan, 'Territory and Boundaries' in Anne Peters and Bardo Fassbender (eds), *The Oxford Handbook of the History of International Law* (Oxford, Oxford University Press, 2012); Giuseppe Nesi, 'Boundaries', in Marcelo G Kohen, Mamadou Hébié and Giuseppe Nesi (eds), *Research Handbook on Territorial Disputes in International Law* (Cheltenham, Edward Elgar, 2018).

[2] Kristof D Ladis, 'The Nature of Frontiers and Boundaries' (1959) 49 *Annals of the Association of American Geographers* 269.

[3] Didier Bigo, 'Frontières, territoire, sécurité, souveraineté' (2011) *CERISCOPE Frontières.*

forms of inclusion and exclusion that affect the enforcement and materialisation of borders, which themselves contribute to the reproduction of boundaries.[4]

Traditionally, international law recognises borders as the perimeter of territorial sovereignty. State sovereignty, and the equality that flows from it, rests on the notion of exclusive authority over discrete portions of territory delimited by territorial boundaries. Borders represent the dividing lines between one sovereign entity and another.[5] The delineation of territorial boundaries is therefore the essential framework within which states' interests are expressed and concerning which they interact and collide.[6] In a world of equal and independent states, stable borders are coterminous with a stable international legal system.[7] At the same time, borders have become more and more permeable to international law. Most notably, international human rights law pierces states' borders and requires states to account for the treatment of people within their territory. That notwithstanding, the whole rhetoric of 'permeability' supports the notion of borders as predetermined physical barriers, a notion that, as the following pages will reveal, has been overhauled by the current reality of delocalisation of border controls.[8]

Modern states monopolised the legitimate means of movement across spaces.[9] By drawing a distinction between nationals and non-nationals, borders legitimate states' exclusion of aliens from their territories. This is still reflected in human rights law and its failure to fully recognise a right to freedom of movement across countries.[10] The European project has challenged the conventional understating of borders.[11] Under EU law, border checks on the movement of goods, persons, services and capital among Member States have been eliminated to buttress the EU internal market.[12] The realisation of a European area of freedom of movement has brought the representation of national borders into perspective in two different ways. First, this area of freedom of movement strives

[4] Carolin Fischer, Christin Achermann and Janine Dahinden, 'Revisiting Borders and Boundaries: Exploring Migrant Inclusion and Exclusion from Intersectional Perspectives' (2020) 17 *Migration Letters* 477.

[5] ICJ, *Frontier Dispute (Benin v Niger)*, Judgment of 12 July 2005, ICJ Reports 90, para 124.

[6] Malcolm N Shaw, 'The Heritage of States: The Principle of Uti Possidetis Juris Today' (1997) 67 *The British Yearbook of International Law* 75, 75.

[7] ICJ, *Corfu Channel Case*, Judgment of 9 April 1949, ICJ Reports 4, 35; UN GA, Declaration on Principles of International Law concerning Friendly Relations and Cooperation among States in accordance with the Charter of the United Nations, A/RES/2625(XXV), 24 October 1970.

[8] Alison Kesby, 'The Shifting and Multiple Border and International Law' (2007) 27 *Oxford Journal of Legal Studies* 101.

[9] John C Torpey, *The Invention of the Passport: Surveillance, Citizenship and the State* (Cambridge, Cambridge University Press, 2018) 6–8.

[10] See ch 3, s IV.D.

[11] Elspeth Guild, *Moving the Borders of Europe*, Inaugural lecture (Nijmegen, University of Nijmegen, 2001).

[12] Art 3, Treaty on European Union (Treaty of Maastricht), OJ C 191, 7 February 1992 (entry into force: 1 November 1993) as subsequently amended.

to trigger a new post-national identity, which can be summed up in the concept of European citizenship. Second, freedom of movement has been set above the control of national borders.[13]

Yet, the free movement of people was not conceived to challenge traditional notions of borders. The right of free movement under EU law can be assimilated to the right to free movement within a state's borders under international law.[14] What has brought the concept of borders as material barriers into question is their operationalisation by multiple authorities enforcing them in different places and at different times. The transfer of prerogatives from the states to the EU created a situation where concurrent entities have certain powers over the same territory.

Borders are no longer imagined solely as technologies of *state* power. They are controlled by a multiplicity of different authorities at various levels – national and supranational, public and private, direct and vicarious. Borders are also no longer represented exclusively as stable physical frontiers. They can take the form of paper walls, virtual fences or controls performed in countries of origin and transit. As such, borders can shift in time and space, following the journeys of migrants, both before their departure and after their arrival. These shifting patterns directly concern the representation of the borders of Europe.

This chapter outlines the process of European border integration to contextualise the concerted border control activities of the European Border and Coast Guard Agency (Frontex) and the Member States. In so doing, it explores the changing nature and functions of borders arising from the juxtaposition of various intertwining authorities exerting control over European borders. I begin, therefore, with an overview of the gradual integration of border management in Europe (Section II). This is followed by an elucidation of the functions of the European border integration process, underlining the pivotal role played by Frontex (Section III). The analysis culminates in a reflection on how this process has influenced how European borders are conceived, controlled and experienced (Section IV). Apart from introducing the concept of integrated border management, this chapter seeks to offer a bird's-eye-view of the multiplication of European borders and the implications of their pervasive control for people crossing them.

II. The Europeanisation of Border Controls

Before World War I, the European continent did not know systematic border controls.[15] During the late nineteenth century, travellers needed a *carte de visite*

[13] Elspeth Guild, *The Legal Elements of European Identity: EU Citizenship and Migration Law* (Alphen aan den Rijn, Kluwer Law International, 2004) ch 2.

[14] ibid 25.

[15] The most notable exceptions to this general rule were the borders with the Russian and Turkish empires.

rather than a passport.[16] In the aftermath of World War II, the first moves were made to lessen the controls introduced in the wake of both conflicts. With the implementation of the Schengen Agreements,[17] their extension to most EU Member States, and their incorporation in EU law with the Treaty of Amsterdam,[18] the late nineteenth-century situation in Europe seemed almost to be re-established.[19] Yet, the gradual development of an area of free movement and the suppression of internal border checks implied their transfer to the external borders of the Schengen area.[20] As internal border checks were abolished within the Schengen area, controls at the external borders were needed to safeguard internal security and prevent illegal immigration.[21]

The Schengen *acquis* comprises a set of rules enabling the proper functioning of the Schengen area. It is now codified in the Schengen Borders Code (SBC), which constitutes the legal framework for the control of the external borders of the Schengen area.[22] The Schengen area comprises all EU Member States, except for Denmark and Ireland – and formerly the UK[23] – as well as non-EU countries (Norway, Iceland, Switzerland, Lichtenstein). Moreover, the complete lifting of internal border checks between Schengen Member States has been postponed with regard to Bulgaria, Cyprus and Romania.[24]

[16] Kees Groenendijk, 'Reinstatement of Controls at the Internal Borders of Europe: Why and Against Whom?' (2004) 10 *European Law Journal* 150.

[17] Agreement between the governments of the States of the Benelux economic union, the Federal Republic of Germany and the French Republic on the gradual abolition of checks at their common borders, 14 June 1985 (Schengen Agreement); Convention implementing the Schengen Agreement of 14 June 1985 between the governments of the States of the Benelux economic union, the Federal Republic of Germany and the French Republic on the gradual abolition of checks at their common borders, 19 June 1990, OJ L 239, 22 September 2000.

[18] Treaty Amending the Treaty on European Union, the Treaties Establishing the European Communities and Certain Related Acts of 2 October 1997 (Treaty of Amsterdam), OJ C 340/1, 10 November 1997, entry into force: 1 May 1999.

[19] Under Art 77(1)(a), Treaty on the Functioning of the European Union, (Consolidated version) 7 June 2016, OJ C202/1.

[20] Among the vast literature, see in particular: Guild (n 11); Bigo Didier and Guild Elspeth, *Controlling Frontiers: Free Movement into and Within Europe* (Farnham, Ashgate, 2005).

[21] Art 17, Schengen Agreement.

[22] Regulation (EU) 2018/1240 [2018] OJ L 236/1.

[23] TFEU, Protocol No 22 on the position of Denmark, Art 4. Protocol No 21 on the Position of the United Kingdom and Ireland in Respect of the Area of Freedom, Security and Justice, annexed to the TFEU [2016] OJ C202. With regard to the UK, alongside the 2019 Withdrawal Agreement, the UK and the EU adopted a Political Declaration where the parties committed to 'cooperate to tackle illegal migration, including its drivers and its consequences, whilst recognising the need to protect the most vulnerable'. This would be achieved through cooperation with Frontex and Europol. See, Political declaration setting out the framework for the future relationship between the European Union and the United Kingdom, OJ C 384 I/178, 12 November 2019, para 114; Agreement on the withdrawal of the United Kingdom of Great Britain and Northern Ireland from the European Union and the European Atomic Energy Community, 17 October 2019.

[24] This is stipulated by the respective Act of Accession. Nonetheless, a simplified regime for the control of persons at the external borders of these countries was introduced. See: Decision No 565/2014/EU, OJ L 157, 27 May 2014.

The gradual integration of the management of the EU external borders has been regularly presented as a necessary corollary for abolishing internal border checks. Member States, however, remain responsible for their respective sections of the external borders.[25] The progressive Europeanisation of border management has been principally realised through minimum harmonisation, mutual recognition and operational cooperation. This soft integration method has been put to the test in recent years, when the ideal of a 'Europe without borders' appeared to be crumbling under the pressure of security threats, the 2015 migration crisis and the COVID-19 pandemic.[26]

A. The Integration of Border Controls as a Shared Competence

The abolition of internal border checks between Member States triggered the expansion of the EU's control over external borders. Article 77 of the Treaty on the Functioning of the European Union (TFEU) is the current legal basis for EU competence in the area of border management.[27] Accordingly, the EU is mandated to ensure the efficient control of external borders and the absence thereof within the Schengen area,[28] as well as to gradually introduce the integrated management of external borders.[29] To this end, the Union adopts 'any measure necessary for the gradual establishment of an integrated management system for external borders'.[30]

EU policies on border checks, asylum and immigration are covered by the scope of the EU area of freedom, security and justice. The EU and its Member States exercise a shared competence in this area.[31] Member States are free to decide on the volume of admission of migrants within their territories.[32] However, the EU has enlarged its competence in establishing a common immigration policy. As a result, today, almost every aspect of migration governance – outside and within Europe – has a supranational dimension.

The EU and the Member States may legislate and adopt legally binding acts in shared competence areas.[33] This situation may change inasmuch as the Union exercises its competence to exhaustively regulate a matter, for the Union's action excludes

[25] Art 7, Regulation (EU) 2019/1896 [2019] OJ L 295.

[26] See: Jorrit J Rijpma and Melanie Fink, 'The Management of The European Union's External Borders', in Philippe De Bruycker and Lilian Tsourdi (eds), *Research Handbook on EU Asylum and Migration Law* (Cheltenham, Edward Elgar, 2022).

[27] Treaty on the Functioning of the European Union (Consolidated version) [2016] OJ C202/1 (TFEU).

[28] Art 77 (1)(a)(b), TFEU.

[29] Art 77 (1)(c), TFEU.

[30] Art 77 (2)(d), TFEU.

[31] Art 4 (2)(j), TFEU.

[32] Art 79 (5), TFEU.

[33] Art 2 (2), TFEU.

the power of Member States to compete in the same field of legislation. This constraint on Member States' competence derives from the principle of sincere cooperation, according to which the Union and Member States 'shall refrain from any measure which could jeopardise the attainment of the Union's objectives'.[34] In sum, the shared competence initially allows the Union and Member States to regulate various matters in tandem;[35] when the Union takes action and legislates comprehensively in a given field, Member States are prevented from adopting inconsistent legislation on the same matter. It follows that the competence of the Union has an expanding potential that depends on the timing and modalities of its exercise.[36] Conversely, achieving shared objectives relies significantly on the will of Member States.[37]

Initially, Member States were reluctant to unify external border management and partially delegate their border control powers. Such operations have generally been perceived as practically complex, given the multitude of national border control agencies, and politically problematic, as the control of national borders is a symbol of national sovereignty. The Treaties, therefore, include several 'counter-constraints' to the exercise of the Union's competences. These limits, established under Article 4(2) Treaty on the European Union (TEU) and Articles 72 and 73 TFEU, mainly concern maintaining law and order and safeguarding the internal security of EU Member States. The Union is prevented from regulating these policy areas, which are profoundly related to border control, and to the very idea of territorial sovereignty.

In such a context, the European integrated border management (EIBM) is implemented as a shared responsibility of the national authorities responsible for border management and Frontex, the European Union Border and Coast Guard Agency.[38] Member States are the primary responsible for managing their external borders, in their interest and in the interest of all other Member States. Frontex supports the Member States in implementing EIBM measures by 'reinforcing, assessing and coordinating' their actions.[39] That notwithstanding, the idea of a 'shared responsibility' of Member States and Frontex emphasises how controlling the external borders is a common interest that requires an appropriate legal and institutional framework.

B. The (Dis)Integration of Internal Border Controls

In 2015, 30 years after the signing of the Schengen Agreement, several EU Member States reintroduced controls at their internal borders. This decision was dictated

[34] Art 4 (3), TFEU.

[35] The list of shared competences included in Art 4 (2) TFUE is not exhaustive.

[36] Allan Rosas, 'Exclusive, Shared and National Competence in the Context of EU External Relations: Do Such Distinctions Matter?' [2014] *The European Union in the World* 17, 22.

[37] Miguel Angel Acosta Sánchez, 'An Analysis of Integrated Management of the External Borders of the European Union' [2020] *Paix et sécurité internationales: Journal of International Law and International Relations* 121, 126.

[38] Art 7, Regulation 2019/1896.

[39] Art 7(4), Regulation 2019/1896.

in the specific case of France by the state of emergency created by terroristic threats and in all the others by the migratory pressures and the serious deficiencies in external border controls in the wake of the so-called '2015 refugee crisis'. Underlying the decision to introduce and then prolong internal border checks, one finds a discourse based on the threat to public order and internal security that irregular migrants allegedly represent for the whole EU system.[40]

Articles 25 and 26 of the SBC provide Member States with the faculty to temporarily reintroduce internal border controls in exceptional situations, in cases of serious threat to public policy or internal security.[41] Article 29 of the SBC further provides for a specific procedure applicable as extrema ratio when the overall functioning of the Schengen free-movement area is at risk 'as a result of persistent serious deficiencies relating to external border control'. This provision allows Member States to introduce internal border checks for an additional six months, which can only be renewed three consecutive times for similar six-month periods. The EU Member States, however, reintroduced and prolonged border controls more than 300 times since 2006.[42] Yet the reintroduction and prolongation of border controls should in principle be an exceptional measure of last resort, whose use and abuse has been sanctioned by the CJEU.[43]

Faced with the endogenous problem of Member States re-establishing border controls and the exogenous challenge of increasing migratory pressure, the Union could not remain idle. It has elaborated a composite strategy of emergency and long-term measures mainly focused on border controls and securitisation.[44] On many occasions, the Commission has recognised the importance of framing a common policy on asylum, immigration and external border control based on solidarity between Member States and fairness to third-country nationals. However, the need for a systematic approach to migration phenomena has yet to lead to a genuinely European asylum system, with uniform international protection status and a common procedure across the Union.[45] On the contrary, the first action

[40] Council Implementing Decision setting out a Recommendation for prolonging temporary internal border control in exceptional circumstances putting the overall functioning of the Schengen area at risk, 13979/16, 11 November 2016.

[41] Regulation (EU) 2016/399 [2016] OJ L 77/1 (Schengen Borders Code).

[42] For a full list of notifications of the temporary reintroduction of border control at internal borders pursuant to Article 25 et seq of the SBC, see: https://home-affairs.ec.europa.eu/policies/schengen-borders-and-visa/schengen-area/temporary-reintroduction-border-control_en#:~:text=The%20Schengen%20Borders%20Code%20(SBC,public%20policy%20or%20internal%20security.

[43] Joined Cases C-368/20 and C-369/20, *NW v Landespolizeidirektion Steiermark*, ECLI:EU:C:2022:298, 26 April 2022. See also: Stefan Salomon and Jorrit Rijpma, 'A Europe Without Internal Frontiers: Challenging the Reintroduction of Border Controls in the Schengen Area in the Light of Union Citizenship' (2023) 24 *German Law Journal* 281.

[44] Communication from the Commission, *Back to Schengen – A Roadmap*, COM(2016) 120, 4 March 2016.

[45] For further analysis see: Philippe De Bruycker, Francesco Maiani and Vincent Chetail (eds), *Reforming the Common European Asylum System: The New European Refugee Law* (Leiden, Martinus Nijhoff, 2015).

was to protect the external borders. The road to harmonisation was paved with increased efforts in the domain of external border control.[46]

In the aftermath of the so-called 'European refugee crisis', the reintroduction of internal border controls by various EU Member States may be interpreted as sovereign resurgence – a measure to resist the supranational assault. A different interpretation would describe the situation as 'a crisis of borders', mainly due to a 'federalist deficit' in the edifice of the Union.[47] According to this view, the incomplete spoliation of Member States' competences over border management has impeded the EU's promise to create an area of freedom, security and justice. The creation of an integrated administration of EU borders is therefore regarded as indispensable for the European area of free movement. Along these lines, in 2017 and 2021, the Commission proposed to amend the SBC to better address 'the shortcomings in the Union's management of the external borders'.[48]

Meanwhile, migration management practices obstruct, complicate and prolong the migration trajectories to and across the EU, exposing migrants to violence and fundamental uncertainty. The Mediterranean Sea has become one of the world's deadliest and most dangerous migration routes, especially for women and children;[49] on the mainland, pushbacks, collective expulsions and violence too regularly ending in fatalities have become the norm;[50] and transit spaces, such as hotspots, railways, informal camps or detention centres have become the site of increasingly coercive policies.[51]

Against the dark background of migrants' necropolitical experiences,[52] and despite the reticence and resistance of Member States, the control over national borders – the last bastion of national sovereignty[53] – has gradually been corroded in the sense of supranational management of borders at the EU

[46] Communication from the Commission, *Back to Schengen – A Roadmap*, COM(2016) 120, 4 March 2016.

[47] Mario Savino, 'La Crisi Dei Confini' [2016] *Rivista trimestrale di diritto pubblico* 739.

[48] See, European Commission Proposal for a Regulation of The European Parliament and the Council amending Regulation (EU) 2016/399 as regards the rules applicable to the temporary reintroduction of border control at internal borders, COM(2021) 891 final, 14 December 2021.

[49] See, among various sources: UNICEF, *A Deadly Journey for Children the Central Mediterranean Migration Route*, February 2017; OHCHR, *Unsafe and Undignified: The Forced Expulsion of Migrants from Libya*, May 2021.

[50] ECtHR, *M.H. and Others v Croatia*, Appl Nos 15670/18 and 43115/18, 18 November 2021; Report of the Special Rapporteur on the human rights of migrants, Felipe González Morales, *Report on means to address the human rights impact of pushbacks of migrants on land and at sea*, A/HRC/47/30, 12 May 2021; Report of the Special Rapporteur on the human rights of migrants, Felipe González Morales, *Human rights violations at international borders: trends, prevention and accountability*, A/HRC/50/31, 26 April 2022, paras 27–39.

[51] Leonie Ansems de Vries and Elspeth Guild, 'Seeking Refuge in Europe: Spaces of Transit and the Violence of Migration Management' (2019) 45 *Journal of Ethnic and Migration Studies* 2156.

[52] First introduced by Achille Mbembe, the notion of 'necropolitics' refers to the brutal forms of oppression in colonial spaces. Here, I use it to mark the (neo)colonial violence of the EU border practices. Achille Mbembé, 'Necropolitics' (2003) 15 *Public Culture* 11.

[53] Catherine Dauvergne, 'Sovereignty, Migration and the Rule of Law in Global Times' (2004) 67 *The Modern Law Review* 588.

level. The underlying logic is an attempt to find strength in the Union against unfathomable 'external threats'.[54]

C. Bounded Solidarity at the EU External Borders

While much disagreement exists on the solidaristic protection of refugees, Member States agree on the necessity to protect the EU external borders and prevent the threat of irregular migration. The perception of an immigration-related threat may simultaneously destabilise and unify a community.[55] It can spread a disruptive sense of fear of the other, while improving the narrative of shared identity and concrete cooperation against the perceived external danger. The securitisation of the European external borders emerges as the result of a widespread sense of fear. A fear that may be politically manipulated in societies where the majority of individuals live in precarious socio-economic situations, where the other is seen as an enemy or, at best, an unwelcome competitor.

The idea of a Union against an external threat, with its external borders functioning as a *cordon sanitaire*, underlies the COVID-19 travel restrictions.[56] In the wake of the COVID-19 global pandemic, Schengen Member States took different and uncoordinated border control measures, including the reintroduction of temporary internal border controls, travel restrictions or entry and exit bans.[57] As a response to incoherent action by the Member States, the Commission stressed the importance of maintaining the functioning of the internal market and that internal border checks should be introduced only in extremely critical situations, in accordance with the SBC.[58] Internal border checks should be justified only for reasons of public policy or internal security proportionate to the health of the individual concerned, and they should guarantee the principle of non-discrimination between EU citizens, who cannot be refused entry in a Member State but should be granted access to appropriate health care.[59]

[54] See Recitals 1 and 9, Regulation 2019/1896.

[55] See Denis Duez, 'L'Europe et Les Clandestins: La Peur de l'autre Comme Facteur d'intégration?' [2008] *Politique européenne* 97.

[56] On the compatibility of these restrictions with international law, see: Vincent Chetail, 'Crisis Without Borders: What Does International Law Say About Border Closure in the Context of Covid-19?' (2020) 2 *Frontiers in Political Science*; Carla Ferstman and Andrew Fagan (eds), *Covid-19, Law and Human Rights: Essex Dialogues* (Colchester, University of Essex, 2020); Alessandra Spadaro, 'COVID-19: Testing the Limits of Human Rights' (2020) 11 *European Journal of Risk Regulation* 317.

[57] For a complete reconstruction of all the measures adopted by Member States, see: Sergio Carrera and Ngo Chun Luk, 'Love Thy Neighbour? Coronavirus Politics and Their Impact on EU Freedoms and Rule of Law in the Schengen Area' (CEPS 2020) No 2020-04.

[58] Commission, COVID-19: Guidelines for border management measures to protect health and ensure the availability of goods and essential services, C(2020) 1753 final, 16 March 2020, para 18.

[59] ibid, paras 11 and 19–25.

Yet, with regard to the control of the EU's external borders, Member States can refuse entry to third-country nationals if they are considered a threat to public health.[60] Furthermore, Member States were granted wide flexibility regarding the reception conditions of asylum seekers during the pandemic.[61] This prompted the use of 'quarantine ships' in Italy and Malta, with several harmful consequences for the migrants held on these vessels.[62] While any refusal-of-entry decision should be proportional and non-discriminatory, the Commission also recommended the European Council adopt a 'Temporary Restriction on Non-Essential Travel to the EU' for application in the EU+ area.[63] The core idea behind this Temporary Restriction was that the EU's external border should act as a 'security perimeter for all Schengen states'.[64]

The same 'circumstantial unity'[65] stemming from converging interests in protecting borders and containing migrants was the main driver of the Union's policy response to the exodus of refugees in the aftermath of the 2022 Russian invasion of Ukraine. The activation of the Temporary Protection Directive as a reaction to this exceptional situation has been widely portrayed as an expression of unprecedented solidarity.[66] Nonetheless, this generous approach was limited to Ukrainian nationals and refugees residing in Ukraine.[67] Europe's double standard for admitting and treating refugees is well-documented and heavily criticised.[68] Yet again, this 'unequal solidarity',[69] and the creation of a hierarchy of refugees that it implies, reflects the deterrence paradigm ordinarily performed by the EU and its Member States and aimed at containing undesirable migratory movement. The Russian invasion of Ukraine risks destabilising the EU's power and security structures. The Union had no alternative but to open its borders to secure its unity against an external existential threat.

[60] ibid, para 15.

[61] See: European Commission, Communication from the Commission COVID-19: Guidance on the implementation of relevant EU provisions in the area of asylum and return procedures and on resettlement 2020/C 126/02, OJ C 126, 17 April 2020.

[62] See, Lorenzo Tondo, *Death of teenage boy on Italian 'quarantine ship' being investigated* (The Guardian, 7 October 2020).

[63] See Communication from the Commission to the European Parliament, The European Council, the Council, COVID-19: Temporary Restriction on Non-Essential Travel to the EU, COM(2020) 115 final, 16 March 2020.

[64] ibid 1.

[65] Eleni Karageorgiou and Gregor Noll, 'Receiving Ukrainian Refugees in the EU: A Case of Solidarity?' (ASILE, 3 June 2022) www.asileproject.eu/receiving-ukrainian-refugees-in-the-eu-a-case-of-solidarity/.

[66] Council Implementing Decision (EU) 2022/382, OJ L 71/1, 4 March 2022.

[67] For a detailed analysis, see: Daniela Vitiello, 'The Nansen Passport and the EU Temporary Protection Directive: Reflections on Solidarity, Mobility Rights and the Future of Asylum in Europe', European Papers, 7 (2022) 15.

[68] Lorenzo Tondo, 'Embraced or pushed back: on the Polish border, sadly, not all refugees are welcome' (*The Guardian*, 4 March 2022); UN Special Rapporteur on contemporary forms of racism, 'Ukraine: UN expert condemns racist threats, xenophobia at border', 3 March 2022.

[69] Sergio Carrera, Meltem Ineli Ciger, Lina Vosyliute and Leiza Brumat, 'The EU grants temporary protection for people fleeing war in Ukraine Time to rethink unequal solidarity in EU asylum policy', CEPS Policy Insights No 2022-09, March 2022.

The predominant deterrence practice to counter a threat of irregular immigration through immobilisation can rapidly morph into facilitation of mobility of certain groups of migrants if a larger geopolitical threat so requires.[70] The administration migration movements are enacted not only by obstructing legal admission and enforcing detention, but also by facilitating (what is perceived as good) mobility. This corroborates the idea of the EU external borders as boundaries that produce differentiated forms of inclusion and exclusion to ensure internal unity and maintain the status quo.

III. The EIBM: Evolution of a Multifaceted Concept

The EIBM has a relatively short history, but a broad spectrum of implications. It developed progressively from a system of intergovernmental exchange to one of enhanced supranationalisation.[71] The idea of integrated border management is not unique to the EU. In many parts of the world, it equates to greater efficiency in border control cooperation at the domestic level.[72] Yet elsewhere in the world, it has been developed at the national level or within a closed circle of border and customs administrations. In contrast, the composite structure of the EIBM requires coordinating different authorities at the local, national and supranational levels. The main complexity of the EIBM originates in the special nature of the EU, which is neither a federation of states nor an ordinary international organisation.[73] The EU borders are divided into many national segments controlled by an even greater number of authorities with different powers and mandates.

The European Border and Coast Guard Agency (Frontex) was precisely conceived in response to the fragmented border services controlling the external borders of the Schengen area. It plays a pivotal role in the gradual integration of European borders.[74] At the same time, however, its coordinative and supervisory functions magnify the complexity of the EIBM, raising questions about whether this composite network of border enforcement actors complies with EU and international law – and about its responsibility for the (mis)management of the EU borders. Most notable is the fragmentation in Frontex operations of

[70] Karageorgiou and Noll (n 65).

[71] Violeta Moreno-Lax, *Accessing Asylum in Europe: Extraterritorial Border Controls and Refugee Rights under EU Law* (Oxford, Oxford University Press, 2017) 13–45; Sergio Carrera and Ngo Chun Luk, 'Love Thy Neighbour? Coronavirus Politics and Their Impact on EU Freedoms and Rule of Law in the Schengen Area' (CEPS 2020) No 2020-04.

[72] Giulia Raimondo, 'Integrated Border Management' in Vincent Chetail (ed), *Elgar Concise Encyclopedia of Migration Law* (Cheltenham, Edward Elgar, forthcoming).

[73] For further discussion, see ch 3, s II.A.

[74] See Daniela Vitiello, 'Agencification as a Key Component of the EU Externalisation Toolkit. Observations on a Silent Escape from the Rule of Law' in Sergio Carrera and others (eds), *The EU External Policies on Migration, Borders and Asylum in an Era of Large Flows: Policy Transfers or Intersecting Policy Universes?* (Leiden, Brill Nijhoff, 2019).

law-enforcement powers among multiple authorities belonging to different legal orders at various levels; it can present serious challenges in attributing a given conduct and its harmful consequences to every actor involved. We will discuss the attribution of responsibility issue later in this work. For the moment, I shall stress that this multiplicity of actors contributing to the EIBM to different extents implies significant difficulties in reconciling their standards, functions and methods.

A. Genesis and Structure of the EIBM

The multifaceted concept of integrated border management started circulating in EU policy documents in the early 2000s, most notably in the EU Schengen Catalogue, collecting recommendations and best practices for border controls.[75] It included the so-called 'integrated border security model' encompassing all aspects of the EU border policy and characterised by a logic of diffused control.[76] This precursor of the EIBM anticipated the idea of articulating border controls along a pattern of concentric circles, or levels of control, starting with pre-border measures in countries of origin and transit, supported by bilateral and international cooperation; continuing with measures at external borders; followed by further activities inside the territory of Schengen states.[77]

The emphasis on border *security* rather than border *management* underlines the main goal of the model: 'to safeguard internal security'.[78] Moreover, differences between Member States regarding the interpretation and implementation of the Schengen rules have led the Commission to advocate the establishment of a 'coherent legal framework' to avoid security deficiencies and 'enhance the fight against illegal immigration'.[79] The imminent EU enlargement and the risks related to potential deficiencies in applying Schengen standards in new Member States also preoccupied EU institutions. It is precisely the need for harmonising those standards to ensure securitisation of external European borders that prompted the establishment of Frontex, the European Border and Coast Guard Agency.

The first formal step towards the establishment of the EIBM can be traced back to the Laeken European Council of December 2001, where the Council prompted that 'the Union's external border controls will help in the fight against terrorism, illegal immigration networks and the traffic in human beings' and asked the EU institutions 'to work out arrangements for cooperation between services

[75] EU Schengen Catalogue, External borders control, Removal and readmission: Recommendations and best practices, February 2002.

[76] ibid 11.

[77] ibid 11–15.

[78] ibid.

[79] See: European Commission, Communication from the Commission to the Council and the European Parliament, A community immigration policy, COM(2000) 757 final, 22 November 2000, 17; European Commission, Communication from the Commission to the Council and the European Parliament, A common policy on illegal immigration, COM(2001) 67, 15 November 2001, 5.

responsible for external border control and to examine the conditions in which a mechanism or common services to control external borders could be created'.[80] The following year, the Commission proposed the development of a common policy on the management of the EU's external borders, with five mutually interdependent components: a common corpus of legislation; a common co-ordination and operational cooperation mechanism; common integrated risk analysis; staff trained in the European dimension and inter-operational equipment; and burden sharing between Member States in the run-up to the creation of a European Corps of Border Guards.[81]

Nonetheless, a clear definition of the EIBM and how it was supposed to function was lacking. EIBM rules were spread across a number of legal and administrative instruments and, therefore, could not straightforwardly be located within just one legal instrument. It was only in 2006 that the Council described for the first time the EIBM as a multidimensional concept.[82] One of the fundamental components of the EIBM was the establishment of a 'common corpus of legislation' governing the movement of persons across borders.[83]

With the Lisbon Treaty, 'the gradual introduction of an integrated management system for external borders' has been codified in primary EU law.[84] The diffused control paradigm underpinning the EIBM has been transposed into the TFEU to the extent that the EU is to develop

> a common immigration policy aimed at ensuring, at all stages, the efficient management of migration flows, fair treatment of third-country nationals residing legally in Member States, and the prevention of, and enhanced measures to combat, illegal immigration and trafficking in human beings.[85]

Frontex ensures the implementation of this common policy. As further detailed below, the agency plays a fundamental role in the design and execution of the EU border integration strategy. Not surprisingly, the developing definition of the EIBM traces the constant reform of Frontex's legal mandate.

The 2016 reform of Frontex's regulation included a legal definition of the EIBM comprising its various functions.[86] This definition was further refined in Article 3 of Regulation 2019/1896.[87] The provision constructs the EIBM as a crescendo of measures to be implemented, starting from within the Schengen area, continuing

[80] European Council, Presidency Conclusions Laeken, 14–15 December 2001.

[81] Communication from the Commission to the Council and the European Parliament, Towards integrated management of the external borders of the member states of the European Union, COM/2002/233 final, 7 May 2002; see, also, European Council, Plan for the management of the external borders of the Member States of the European Union, 14 June 2002.

[82] Council of the European Union, Justice and Home Affairs, 2768th Council Meeting, Brussels, 4–5 December 2006, Press Release, 15801/06, 27.

[83] ibid 26.

[84] Art 77 1 (c), TFEU.

[85] Art 79, TFEU.

[86] Art 4, Regulation (EU) 2016/1624 [2016] OJ L 251.

[87] Art 3(1), Regulation 2019/1896.

at its borders, and expanding beyond them. First, the EIBM centres on border control measures to facilitate legal migration and counter security threats at the EU's external borders, while individuating migrants in need of protection.[88] Second, it encompasses activities undertaken within the Schengen area, such as analyses of security risks; information sharing and cooperation between Member States, EU agencies and other bodies or institutions; research and innovation in the field of border control technology, including large-scale information systems; a vulnerability assessment of border management in the Schengen area; and a solidarity fund.[89] Third, it involves measures to be implemented outside the Schengen area, such as search-and-rescue activities performed in the context of Frontex's border-surveillance operations; return operations; and cooperation with third countries, in particular neighbouring countries and those identified as 'countries of origin or transit for illegal immigration'.[90] Lastly, fundamental rights, education and training of border guards, as well as research and innovation, are overarching components of the EIBM structure.[91]

The EIBM rests on a 'four-tier access control model'[92] reflecting the diffused control paradigm already present in the EU Schengen Catalogue.[93] This model comprises measures in neighbouring and third countries, border control measures at the external borders, risk analysis, measures within the Schengen area and return.[94] The same logic of diffused border control permeates the proposal for a New Pact on Migration and Asylum that the European Commission tabled in September 2020.[95] Effective border controls are presented as indispensable to the safeguarding of the Schengen area of free movement and the formation of a comprehensive migration policy.[96] When presenting the Pact, the Commission's vice-president compared it to a house with three floors.[97] On the ground floor, the external dimension of EU migration policy, centred around strengthened partnerships with countries of origin and transit, supports the whole building; on the second and third floors, respectively, a 'robust management' of external borders and 'firm but fair internal rules' ensure the stability and functioning of the Schengen area of free movement. Despite the constant use of new narratives,

[88] Art 3(1)(a), Regulation 2019/1896.
[89] ibid, Art 3(1)(c)(d)(e)(f)(h)(i)(j)(k)(l).
[90] ibid, Art 3(1)(b)(g).
[91] ibid, Art 3(2).
[92] Recital 11, Regulation 2019/1896.
[93] EU Schengen Catalogue, External borders control, Removal and readmission: Recommendations and best practices, February 2002, 11.
[94] Recital 11, Regulation 2019/1896.
[95] European Commission, Communication from the Commission to the European Parliament, the Council, the European Economic and Social Committee and the Committee of the Regions, on a New Pact on Migration and Asylum, COM(2020) 609 final, 23 September 2020.
[96] European Commission, Communication on a New Pact on Migration and Asylum, 11; See also: Recital 87, Regulation 2019/1896.
[97] European Commission, Speech by Vice-President Schinas on the New Pact on Migration and Asylum, 23 September 2020 https://ec.europa.eu/commission/presscorner/detail/en/speech_20_1736.

the Pact largely traces the old logic of diffused control already present in embryonic versions of the EIBM. The aim is to manage migration 'at all stages',[98] thereby ensuring the constant and ubiquitous control of people on the move towards and within Europe.[99]

The EIBM pursues a multilevel control paradigm that comprises the activities of multiple actors following diverse logic. A dense network of controls displaces the border, both inward and outward, detecting and following people's movements and predicting future migratory trajectories. The physical border becomes, therefore, increasingly distant and yet persistent.

B. A Multilevel EIBM Strategy for a Plurality of Actors

The implementation of the EIBM is a shared responsibility of Frontex and the national border control authorities.[100] Member States retain the primary responsibility for their sections of the EU external borders. They do so in their own interest and in the interest of all Member States.[101] This common interest is secured by Frontex, which is mandated to reinforce, coordinate and assess Member States' actions. The process that led to the creation of Frontex will be discussed in more detail in the next chapter; here, it seems worth stressing the pivotal role the agency plays in the European border integration process. Frontex epitomises the composite nature of the EIBM. At the same time, the agency is a prominent security force and the leading actor ensuring the practical harmonisation of border control standards. Accordingly, it should ensure the coherence of the EIBM by facilitating and rendering the application of Union measures relating to border management more effective.[102]

In practice, however, an increasing number of actors – both public and private, national and supranational – are involved in border management activities in the EU. More than 50 national authorities are involved in border control activities,[103] and more than 300 national authorities hold coast guard functions in the EU.[104] Each of these domestic actors has a different mandate and corresponding powers pertaining to various ministries, including interior, finance, fisheries and defence.[105] This results in an uneven involvement of civil, paramilitary and military actors, depending on each Member State.

[98] Art 79 (1), TFEU.
[99] See generally: Moreno-Lax (n 71) ch 2.
[100] Art 7, Regulation 2019/1896.
[101] ibid Art 7(3).
[102] ibid Art 5.
[103] See: European Commission, Update of the list of national services responsible for border controls as referred to in Article 16(2) of the Schengen Borders Code [2018] OJ C 345/05.
[104] See Sergio Carrera, Steven Blockmans, Jean-Pierre Cassarino, Daniel Gros and Elspeth Guild, *The European Border and Coast Guard: Addressing Migration and Asylum Challenges in the Mediterranean?* (Brussels, CEPS, 2017) 26.
[105] ibid.

In addition to Member States' authorities, the border services of third countries are also involved in the EIBM, in a complex surveillance network and intelligence exchange. Frontex supports and coordinates the action of Member States' authorities and cooperates with third states, as well as with other non-state actors. While international organisations have gained a significant role within the EIBM, regularly collaborating with Frontex,[106] but also taking critical stances, non-governmental organisations are often contributing to shaping the EIBM through lobbying or contestation.[107] Beyond public authorities, the EIBM also involves private actors, such as carriers or private security companies to which certain border control services are outsourced.

The large number of actors involved in the EIBM requires a common strategy, ensuring their coherent and concerted action. To this end, regulation 2019/1896 introduces a 'multiannual strategic policy cycle for European integrated border management'.[108] With a duration of five years, the strategic policy provides guidance on how to implement the EU border control and return policies in a 'coherent, integrated and systematic manner'.[109] The EU strategic policy aims at identifying long-term goals, available means and necessary improvements.

Frontex and the Member States adopt complementary strategies to implement the EU strategic policy. Frontex establishes a technical and operational strategy operationalising the objectives identified by the EU strategic policy.[110] The Member States, in turn, adopt their own national strategies, which should be consistent with both the EU strategic policy and Frontex's technical and operational strategy for the EIBM. Finally, an integrated planning process for border and return management, involving the preparation of operational, contingency and capability development plans at both the EU and the national level, ensures the coherence of these strategies.[111]

This multilevel approach aims to guarantee that national authorities and Frontex have a common understanding of their different roles and responsibilities in implementing the EIBM. In developing, implementing and evaluating their strategies for the EIBM, Frontex and the Member States should comply with fundamental rights. In this respect, while Frontex has elaborated its fundamental rights strategy,[112] the Member States' national strategies should include

[106] Art 68(2), Regulation 2019/1896 includes a list of the international organisations cooperating with the agency.

[107] Leila Giannetto, 'CSOs and EU Border Management: Cooperation or Resistance? The Case of Frontex Consultative Forum' [2019] *American Behavioral Scientist* 0002764219882988.

[108] Art 8, Regulation 2019/1896.

[109] Art 8(2), Regulation 2019/1896.

[110] Frontex, Technical and Operational Strategy for European Integrated Border Management, 2019, 10.

[111] Art 9, Regulation 2019/1896.

[112] Management Board Decision 12/2021 adopting the Fundamental Rights Strategy, 14 February 2021.

specific procedures and guidelines to ensure the respect of fundamental rights standards in all stages of border management.[113]

C. Conceptualising Border Integration

The main goal of the EIBM is to manage the external borders efficiently and effectively.[114] Yet, the precise content of border integration and how it will be achieved can only be implied from the concrete measures listed in Article 3 of Regulation 2019/1896.

The gradual integration of European border controls can be observed from various perspectives, underlying different yet interlaced integration models.[115] The European border integration can be related to the process of the securitisation of the European space, especially after 9/11.[116] In this sense, the EIBM serves a preventive function linked to intelligence and surveillance technologies.[117] By extension, the EU border integration is centred on increasing border authorities' technical and operational capacities at the external borders. This involves not only national border control authorities, but also EU agencies, institutions and bodies, as well as other actors involved, to varying extents, in border management activities, such as border check and surveillance, search-and-rescue operations, predictive risk assessments and return operations. These activities are supported by advanced technologies, dedicated Union funding instruments and appropriate training. At the same time, the integration of European borders further underlines the necessity of administrative cohesion along the perimeter of the EU, where a growing variety of national and supranational authorities manage external borders. From this angle, the emergence of the EIBM highlights the importance of harmonised legal and operational standards for border practices among different Member States.[118]

The evolution of the EIBM reflects the constant tension between openness and closure,[119] paradigmatic for institutionalised forms boundary work.[120] While

[113] European Commission, Annex I to the Commission Implementing Decision establishing the report of 2019–2020 thematic evaluation of Member States' national strategies for integrated border management, C(2020) 8000 final, 17 December 2020, 22.

[114] See Recital 1, Regulation 2019/1896.

[115] See Moreno-Lax (n 71) 27–28; Sánchez (n 37); Otwin Marenin, *Challenges for Integrated Border Management in the European Union* (Geneva, DCAF, 2010).

[116] Didier Bigo, 'The Möbius Ribbon of Internal and External Security(Ies)' in Mathias Albert, David Jacobson and Yosef Lapid (eds), *Identities, Borders, Orders* (Minneapolis, University of Minnesota Press, 2001); Jef Huysmans, *The Politics of Insecurity: Fear, Migration and Asylum in the EU* (Abingdon, Routledge, 2006); Christina Boswell, 'Migration Control in Europe After 9/11: Explaining the Absence of Securitization' (2007) 45 *JCMS: Journal of Common Market Studies* 589.

[117] Moreno-Lax (n 71) 28.

[118] Andrew W Neal, 'Securitization and Risk at the EU Border: The Origins of FRONTEX' (2009) 47 *JCMS: Journal of Common Market Studies* 333.

[119] Gerard Delanty, 'Borders in a Changing Europe: Dynamics of Openness and Closure' (2006) 4 *Comparative European Politics* 183.

[120] Fischer, Achermann and Dahinden (n 4).

global collectives are becoming increasingly mobile, they are also more concerned with potential security risks. This has led to the emergence of a border architecture that seeks to respond efficiently to the apparently competing demands of mobility and security. The EIBM is the product of such a dualistic logic; it attempts to reach a greater level of security while maintaining fluidity of movement of goods, capital, services and (preselected) people.[121] On the one hand, it aims to detect irregular migrants and potential threats associated with cross-border crimes; on the other hand, it requires legitimate travellers to be identified as quickly as possible to facilitate mobility and trade. Meanwhile, technological advancements are changing the traditional practice of border control, with many different actors involved in a complex dynamic of securitisation through digital and military tools.

Ultimately, the European border integration is a flexible instrument articulating border controls around different degrees of mobility, facilitating the free movement of certain people, while reducing – or even blocking – that of others.[122] The fundamental objective of this integration process is to ensure the efficient and effective management of people's movements so that European borders are 'open, but well controlled and secure',[123] in 'full respect for fundamental rights'.[124] This work is precisely concerned with this last requirement.

IV. The Multiplication of European Border Controls

The multifaceted design of the EIBM reflects the changing infrastructure of EU borders. No longer the simple management of legal admission at the physical frontiers of Member States, border controls are now performed by multiple actors and diffused within and beyond the territory of Schengen states.[125] The European border initiates its exclusionary purpose before the beginning of the migration journey.[126] Pre-border controls are achieved through formal and informal cooperation with countries of origin and transit. Combined with various pre-border measures, this cooperation expands the enforcement of European borders beyond the territories

[121] Thomas Spijkerboer, 'The Global Mobility Infrastructure: Reconceptualising the Externalisation of Migration Control' (2018) 20 *European Journal of Migration and Law* 452.

[122] See European Commission, Annex to the Commission Implementing Decision establishing the report of 2019–2020 thematic evaluation of Member States' national strategies for integrated border management, 17 December 2020, C(2020) 8000 final, 6–7.

[123] See European Commission, Guidelines for Integrated Border Management in European Commission External Cooperation, 2010, 14.

[124] Recital 1, Regulation 2019/1896.

[125] See extensively: Elspeth Guild, 'Danger – Borders under Construction: Assessing the First Five Years of Border Policy in an Area of Freedom, Security and Justice', in J de Zwaan and F Goudappel (eds), *Freedom, Security and Justice in the European Union: Implementation of the Hague Programme* (The Hague, Asser Press, 2006).

[126] See extensively: Moreno-Lax (n 71).

of Member States.[127] Border controls are further outsourced to private actors and enforced with an arsenal of military and digitalised technologies.[128]

The complex EIBM infrastructure is the result of the concomitant and interlaced dynamics of de-localisation, digitalisation, securitisation and privatisation of border controls.[129] The EIBM underlines the process of delocalisation of border controls beyond and within the frontier lines of Member States. On the one hand, information exchange and cooperation with third countries reinforce the externalisation of border controls.[130] On the other hand, technical and operational measures within the Schengen area contribute to spreading these controls inside the territories of Member States.[131] With the most recent amendment to Frontex legal mandate, for example, the agency is now able to detect and report 'unauthorised secondary movement of third-country nationals'.[132] The aim is to ensure 'situational awareness' and produce risk analyses about the secondary movement of irregular migrants within the Schengen area.[133]

Their increasing digitalisation further reinforces the delocalisation of border checks and surveillance. The increased use of large-scale information technology has become a constitutive element of the EIBM, producing a distinctive sort of virtual borders.[134] These virtual borders represent a 'buffer zone' administratively connecting the EU and neighbouring third countries through a dense information exchange network.[135] This not only determined the proliferation of new data systems,[136] but also prompted their 'enhanced interoperability' cutting across border control and counter-terrorism domains.[137] The interoperability of

[127] Among the vast literature on the topic, see most notably: Violeta Moreno-Lax and Mariagiulia Giuffré, 'The Rise of Consensual Containment: From "Contactless Control" to "Contactless Responsibility" for Forced Migration Flows' in Satvinder S Juss (ed), *Research Handbook on International Refugee Law* (Cheltenham, Edward Elgar, 2019); Thomas Gammeltoft-Hansen, 'International Cooperation on Migration Control: Towards a Research Agenda for Refugee Law' (2018) 20 *European Journal of Migration and Law* 373; Thomas Gammeltoft-Hansen and James C Hathaway, 'Non-Refoulement in a World of Cooperative Deterrence' (2014) 53 *Columbia Journal of Transnational Law* 235.

[128] See Sarah Léonard and Christian Kaunert, 'The Securitisation of Migration in the European Union: Frontex and Its Evolving Security Practices' (2020) 48 *Journal of Ethnic and Migration Studies* 1417; Daria Davitti, 'Beyond the Governance Gap: Accountability in Privatized Migration Control' (2020) 21 *German Law Journal* 487.

[129] This subdivision is inspired by: Moreno-Lax (n 71) ch 2.

[130] Art 3(1)(d)(g), Regulation 2019/1896.

[131] ibid, Art 3(1)(h).

[132] ibid, Recital 40 and Art 24(1)(a).

[133] ibid, Sections 4 and 5.

[134] Dimitri Van Den Meerssche 'Virtual Borders: International Law and the Elusive Inequalities of Algorithmic Association' (2022) 33(1) *European Journal of International Law* 171.

[135] Luisa Marin, 'The Cooperation Between Frontex and Third Countries in Information Sharing: Practices, Law and Challenges in Externalizing Border Control Functions' (2020) 26 *European Public Law* 157.

[136] Regulation (EC) 1987/2006 [2006] OJ L 381/4; Regulation (EC) No 767/2008 [2008] OJ L 218; Regulation (EU) No 603/2013 [2013] OJ L 180; Regulation (EU) 2017/2226 [2017] OJ L 327; Regulation (EU) 2018/1240 [2018] OJ L 236/1.

[137] Regulation (EU) 2019/817, [2019] OJ L 135.

EU databases is a key element of this virtual borders infrastructure.[138] To illustrate, with the European Border Surveillance system (EUROSUR),[139] Frontex and Member States' border control authorities are now interconnected within a 'common information sharing environment'.[140] This multipurpose system aims to enhance cooperation between Frontex and national authorities 'to improve situational awareness and increase reaction capability for the purposes of border management'.[141] Significantly, EUROSUR provides an integrated framework for information exchange and operational cooperation not only at the external borders but also within the Schengen area and in the pre-frontier zones.[142]

The enhanced interoperability of these databases raises concerns beyond the indirect harm that transmitting sensible information might cause. Machine learning systems are essential to integrate disconnected silos of data, thereby predicting and classifying potential risks. The elusiveness inherent in machine learning, entails serious difficulties in identifying the ultimate duty bearer or the cause of the harm occurring as a result of the cross-checking these databases.

This network of virtual borders is ultimately operationalised by military tools and equipment, such as drones, radar, unmanned aerial vehicles (UAVs) or firearms used for border surveillance purposes.[143] The EU and Member States are supporting the development of 'dual-use' technologies, for both civil and military purposes, to track, identify and control the movements of people. Frontex, for instance, has been testing various drone technologies in the Mediterranean and Aegean for the surveillance and interdiction of migrants' vessels hoping to reach European shores.[144] While the impact of these technologies on migrants' rights is manifest, their actual effectiveness and the purportedly increased security they are supposed to provide remain disputed.[145]

The synergies between civil and military policies and practices reveal the growing role of the defence industry in the design and the transformation of border controls in Europe. Military and security corporations are contributing to the design of European border management through lobbying pressures, regular

[138] Philip Hanke and Daniela Vitiello, 'High-Tech Migration Control in the EU and Beyond: The Legal Challenges of "Enhanced Interoperability"' in Elena Carpanelli and Nicole Lazzerini (eds), *Use and Misuse of New Technologies: Contemporary Challenges in International and European Law* (New York, Springer, 2019).

[139] Regulation (EU) 1052/2013, [2013] OJL 295/11.

[140] European Commission, Working document accompanying COM(2008) 68 final, impact assessment, SEC(2008) 151.

[141] Art 18(1), Regulation 2019/1896.

[142] ibid Recital 34.

[143] ibid Art 19 and Annex V.

[144] Report of the Special Rapporteur on contemporary forms of racism, racial discrimination, xenophobia and related intolerance, UN Doc A/75/50289, 10 November 2020, para 12; Petra Molnar, 'Technological Testing Grounds: Migration Management Experiments and Reflections from the Ground Up' (EDRi and the Refugee Law Lab, 2020).

[145] Raluca Csernatoni, 'Constructing the EU's High-Tech Borders: FRONTEX and Dual-Use Drones for Border Management' (2018) 27 *European Security* 175.

interactions with the EU agencies and by influencing the overall research and development agenda of border management technologies.[146] The expansion of security technology emerges clearly in Frontex's partnerships with the security industry. Every year, Frontex hosts an 'industry day', with private companies sharing the latest technological developments related to border control with Member States' border authorities and Frontex experts.[147] The agency has the power to directly acquire border management equipment,[148] making it an important potential customer.[149] For example, the agency recently signed a contract with two private companies concerning the operation of a long-term maritime drone surveillance service for the Mediterranean Sea.[150] Importantly, rather than purchasing the surveillance technology directly, Frontex is contracting services from private companies that will manage the drones and provide operational support.[151] Images taken by drones are live-streamed to Frontex headquarters in Warsaw, fed into the EUROSUR and evaluated by the competent national authorities.[152]

The synchronous de-localisation, digitalisation, securitisation, and privatisation of border controls led to the development of a legal architecture entailing significant delegation of power, heedless deference to new technology and unresolved accountability issues. Multiple actors, representing different legal orders and exercising different powers, control the external borders of Europe. The blurred lines of their respective mandates obfuscate their responsibilities for the harm they might directly or indirectly occasion. Further, border enforcement activities are vicariously performed by third states and private actors and increasingly dematerialised within a range of interoperable databases. The diffusion of border controls across various territories, institutions and technologies thus results in the diffusion of responsibility for potential human rights violations.

[146] Martin Lemberg-Pedersen, 'Private Security Companies and the European Borderscapes', in *The Migration Industry and the Commercialization of International Migration* (Abingdon, Routledge, 2012); Chris Jones, *Market Forces: The Development of the EU Security-Industrial Complex* (Statewatch and TNI, 2017).

[147] See eg Frontex, Invitation to Frontex Industry Days, 21 September 2020, https://frontex.europa.eu/research/invitations/invitation-to-frontex-industry-days-bzcBF7#:~:text=Frontex%2C%20the%20European%20Border%20and,will%20be%20held%20on%2Dline.

[148] Art 63, Regulation 2019/1896.

[149] Csernatoni (n 145).

[150] Airbus, *Frontex selects Airbus and its partner IAI for Maritime Aerial Surveillance with Remotely Piloted Aircraft Systems (RPAS)*, 20 October 2020, www.airbus.com/newsroom/press-releases/en/2020/10/european-border-and-coast-guard-agency-frontex-selects-airbus-and-its-partner-iai-for-maritime-aerial-surveillance-with-remotely-piloted-aircraft-systems-rpas.html.

[151] Frontex applied the same model to its return operations by signing a framework contract with several private companies in order to operate its 'emergency return flights'. See: https://etendering.ted.europa.eu/cft/cft-display.html?cftId=5405.

[152] Frontex, *Tender Specifications – Annex I, Remotely Piloted Aircraft Systems (RPAS) for Medium Altitude Long Endurance Maritime Aerial Surveillance*, Frontex/OP/888/2019/JL/CG, 14 October 2020, 23.

V. Conclusion: The EIBM Assemblage

Originating in intergovernmental cooperation over border control, the EIBM is increasingly integrated into a supranational structure. It relies on a vast array of different technologies and actors to ensure the constant and diffused control of European borders. Migration management is enforced not only on the physical frontiers of the Schengen Member States, but also beyond their territories – not only at the time of arrival but also before departure. Moreover, the basic infrastructure supporting the EIBM consists of multiple relationships among various actors and institutions operating at different levels and within different legal systems. These relationships are flexible: the same actors and institutions may be entangled in different ways in more than one legal, economic or political framework.

The plurality of border control actors involved in the EIBM, their manifold purposes and expanding functions conjure the image of an assemblage.[153] This term offers the possibility of grasping how entities as heterogeneous as the various actors, technologies and logics underlying management of Europe's borders hold together in an integrated whole without necessarily ceasing to be heterogeneous.[154]

The European borders are increasingly integrated, yet shifting in space, time and how they are experienced.[155] From this perspective, European borders are not predetermined and stable entities. Their management cannot be captured through a centralised governing structure. Rather, they are intertwined in a continuum of surveillance and coercive practices distributed within a plurality of interactions. All coalesce in a sort of 'surveillant assemblage'[156] whose aim is to contain migratory movements by expanding and deepening the reach of European border controls.[157]

This assemblage of border control practices entails several legal challenges. First, multiple actors being involved in the management of European borders

[153] I use the concept of assemblage in a descriptive sense to illuminate the complexity of the EIBM. However, many scholars have developed sophisticated theories around the term assemblage. Most notably, Gilles Deleuze and Felix Guattari articulated the concept of *agencement* (loosely translated as assemblage) to suggest that collective entities cannot be reduced to stable and predetermined unities; instead, they are dynamic and precarious phenomena that depend on the interrelations of their parts. Gilles Deleuze and Felix Guattari, *A Thousand Plateaus: Capitalism and Schizophrenia* (Minneapolis, University of Minnesota Press, 1987). This central idea has been applied to various fields, including geography, sociology and architecture. See most notably: Bruno Latour, *Reassembling the Social: An Introduction to Actor-Network-Theory* (Oxford, Oxford University Press, 2007); Saskia Sassen, *Territory, Authority, Rights: From Medieval to Global Assemblages* (Princeton, Princeton University Press, 2008); Kim Dovey, *Becoming Places: Urbanism / Architecture / Identity / Power* (Abingdon, Routledge, 2009); Manuel DeLanda, *A New Philosophy of Society: Assemblage Theory and Social Complexity* (London, Bloomsbury, 2019).

[154] John Allen, 'Powerful Assemblages?' (2011) 43 *Area* 154.

[155] Ayelet Shachar, *The Shifting Border: Legal Cartographies of Migration and Mobility* (Manchester, Manchester University Press, 2020).

[156] Kevin D Haggerty and Richard V Ericson, 'The Surveillant Assemblage' (2000) 51 *The British Journal of Sociology* 605.

[157] Loren B Landau, 'A Chronotope of Containment Development: Europe's Migrant Crisis and Africa's Reterritorialisation' (2019) 51 *Antipode* 169.

means that multiple legal regimes are applicable to their (collective) actions. This implies a complex interplay of different norms and institutions. Second, the shifting nature of border control poses serious questions regarding the scope of the applicable legal framework – questions about the extraterritorial jurisdiction of the various actors involved in the EIBM. Third, both the multiplicity of border enforcement authorities and the extraterritorial reach of their activities contribute to diffusing the responsibility for any harm caused by their cooperative action or inaction. The next parts of this study will address these interlaced issues in an attempt to determine the responsibility for potential human rights violations occurring during border controls performed by Frontex and the Member States implementing the EIBM.

Before delving into these issues, the next chapter will take the reader to the operational centre of the EIBM and offer a closer look at Frontex, 'the spider in the web' of the EIBM.[158] Frontex emerges both as a property of the EIBM assemblage and the technical architect of the underlying multi-layered control structure. Its creation was crucial to the gradual integration of border-management standards and services across Europe. The agency is a crucial enabler of diffused border control practices underlying the EIBM. Not only it contributes to the transformation of European border control practices, but it also significantly influences the policies it is mandated to implement. Frontex is thus an indispensable element of the subsequent parts of this study. The next chapter will clarify the agency's role within the EIBM, outlining its main functions and mandate. What follows will then address, respectively, the question of the law applicable to EIBM measures as implemented by Frontex and the Member States (chapter three), the jurisdictional reach of their obligations (chapter four) and the attribution of responsibilities for their violation (chapter five).

[158] Rijpma and Fink (n 26).

2

Frontex and the Implementation of the European Integrated Border Management

I. Introduction: Frontex and the EIBM

This chapter focuses on the operational centre of the EIBM: the European Border and Coast Guard Agency, better known as Frontex.[1] The following analysis will explore how the idea of a European border agency developed and how it found expression in Frontex. It will offer an overview of the agency's main tasks and functions to identify the main human rights implications of Frontex's activities.

As seen in the previous chapter, a large part of Europe today represents a single area of free movement of people, where 26 states have reciprocally abolished their border controls. The effective control of the external borders of the Schengen area is generally presented as a 'necessary corollary' to the free movement within it and an 'essential component' of EU migration policy.[2] While Member States retain the primary responsibility to manage their external borders, they do so in the interest of all the Member States of the Schengen area.[3] Yet, the financial, administrative and operational onus of controlling the external borders of the common area of free movement lies with only a few Member States, generally depending on their geographical location.[4] Frontex was established to respond to this uneven distribution of responsibilities without directly displacing Member States' power to control entry into their territories.[5]

The agency's actions are meant to complement those of Member States to ensure the effectiveness and efficacy of the Union's migration policy. Frontex strengthens the control of external borders of the Member States by implementing the European integrated border management.[6] It is therefore not surprising that

[1] Regulation 2019/1896 [2019] OJ L 295.

[2] Recitals 1 and 87, Regulation 2019/1896; See also: European Commission, Communication on a New Pact on Migration and Asylum, 11.

[3] ibid, Recital 12.

[4] European Commission, Communication from the Commission to the Council and the European Parliament, Towards integrated management of the external borders of the Member States of the European Union, COM/2002/233 final, 7 May 2002, para 46.

[5] Melanie Fink, *Frontex and Human Rights: Responsibility in 'Multi-Actor Situations' under the ECHR and EU Public Liability Law* (Oxford, Oxford University Press, 2018) 39–41.

[6] Art 1, Regulation (EC) 2007/2004 [2004] OJ L 349/1.

even before the formal legal definition of the EIBM, Frontex labelled itself 'the anchor stone of the European concept of integrated border management'.[7]

Frontex is a crucial player in the assemblage of actors, practices and techniques constituting the EIBM. It combines harmonising and technocratic facets with a more general security-driven approach to managing borders and immigration. In line with the 'four tiers access control model' underlying the EIBM, Frontex operates at the external borders of Member States and beyond, orchestrating a system of anticipatory controls enforced with the support of military tools and surveillance technologies. Since its inception – and despite its coordinative and technical role – the agency has rapidly gained momentum and power. Frontex's role today goes far beyond the merely ancillary position it was originally assigned. A clear account of its structure, functions and powers is essential to better understand the distribution of responsibilities in Frontex's activities.

This chapter will first discuss the agency's evolution (Section II), structure (Section III) and functioning (Section IV); it will then examine the legal status of the agency under EU and international law to elucidate its capacity to bear responsibility for human rights violations that might occur during its activities (Section V). Next, the chapter will focus on Frontex's main operational activities and their human rights implications in light of the most recent developments in its legal framework (Section VI). It will then consider the mechanisms that Frontex currently has in place to respond to potential human rights violations (Section VII) and the available venues for public scrutiny over the agency's action (Section VIII). Last, I will conclude with a reflection on Frontex's role within the EIBM (Section IX).

II. A Genealogy of Frontex

The unceasing tension between national sovereignty and the enhancement of supranational powers over the management of European borders is reflected in the origin and evolution of Frontex. The agency's creation was characterised by political tensions between Member States demanding more integration in the domain of border management and those rejecting the idea of conceding more powers at the supranational level in a field (border control) with a substantial symbolic value. This tension accompanied the evolution of the agency, which emerged as a compromise between two opposing views on the supranational management of EU borders.[8]

[7] See eg: Frontex General Report, 2009, 2; Frontex Programme of Work 2009, 14; Frontex Programme of Work 2011, 15.

[8] Roberta Mungianu, *Frontex and Non-Refoulement: The International Responsibility of the EU* (Cambridge, Cambridge University Press, 2016) 15; Violeta Moreno-Lax, *Accessing Asylum in Europe: Extraterritorial Border Controls and Refugee Rights under EU Law* (Oxford, Oxford University Press, 2017) 157.

Frontex's creation can thus be interpreted as one of the compensatory measures accompanying the Schengen area of free movement[9] or as a political reaction to critical events such as the terrorist attacks of the early 2000s and the prospect of the EU's enlargement.[10] Frontex synthesises the dialectic between emergency politics and technocratic solutions to risk management.[11] A compromise between these two rationales underlies the creation of an agency endowed with emergency and risk-prevention functions.[12] At the same time, Frontex's mission was to foster cooperation between Member States, reducing transaction costs and contributing to the formation of a set of common standards with regard to border control policies.[13]

The contradiction between Frontex's increasing powers and the merely coordinative role envisioned in its founding regulation reveals the political objectives behind the agency's creation. Despite a certain reluctance of Member States to give up their sovereignty over border control issues, EU institutions were determined to build a genuinely supranational border police capable of elaborating its own strategic and operational plans while exercising the correlated coercive powers. This political drive toward creating a supranational border police places Frontex under a permanent reform process, progressively increasing its operational autonomy.[14]

A. The Origins of the European Border and Coast Guard Agency (Frontex)

The European Agency for the Operational Cooperation at the External Borders of the Member States of the European Union, also known as Frontex, was established in 2004 and became operational in 2005.[15] Under the Frontex aegis, border guards from each Member State and states associated with the EU are made available for deployment in the surveillance operations organised by the agency.

In 2007, Frontex was mandated to deploy Rapid Border Intervention Teams to assist Member States facing urgent and exceptional migratory pressure at their

[9] Andrew W Neal, 'Securitization and Risk at the EU Border: The Origins of FRONTEX' (2009) 47 *Journal of Common Market Studies* 333.

[10] Sarah Léonard, 'EU Border Security and Migration into the European Union: FRONTEX and Securitisation through Practices' (2010) 19 *European Security* 231; Sarah Léonard and Christian Kaunert, 'The Securitisation of Migration in the European Union: Frontex and Its Evolving Security Practices' (2020) 48 *Journal of Ethnic and Migration Studies* 1417.

[11] Giuseppe Campesi, 'European Border and Coast Guard (Frontex): Security, Democracy, and Rights at the EU Border' [2018] *Oxford Research Encyclopedia of Criminology and Criminal Justice*.

[12] Moreno-Lax (n 8) 157.

[13] Giuseppe Campesi, 'Frontex, the Euro-Mediterranean Border and the Paradoxes of Humanitarian Rhetoric' (2014) Vol. II *South East European Journal of Political Science (SEEJPS)* 126.

[14] Giuseppe Campesi, *Polizia della frontiera: Frontex e la produzione dello spazio europeo* (Rome, DeriveApprodi, 2015) 109–11.

[15] Regulation (EC) No 2007/2004 [2004] OJ L 349/2; Frontex, General Report, 2005.

external borders.[16] The agency's operational power was further strengthened in 2011 with an amendment to Frontex regulations. The agency gained reinforced organisational power, especially during joint operations and pilot projects; this included the possibility of deploying European Border Guards Teams to support national authorities under the supervision of a Frontex Coordinating Officer.[17]

The 2011 Regulation required the inclusion in the periodic evaluation of the agency's activities of an analysis of 'the needs for further increased coordination of the management of the external borders of the Member States, including the feasibility of the creation of a European system of border guards'.[18] In accordance with that disposition, the Commission mandated Unisys, a private information technology company, to elaborate a study on the possibility of creating a European System of Border Guards to control the external borders of the Union.[19]

The study envisaged a gradual transition from national to supranational management of borders, achieved through a phased approach comprising three stages. The first stage was concerned with the structural reinforcement of the agency through the optimal use of existing instruments. The second stage proposed a shared responsibility between the EU and Member States on border management. The third and final stage, to be reached by 2030, envisages the full integration of European border management, coupled with legal amendments to the provisions of the TFEU limiting such complete supranational integration.

To some extent, the Unisys study preluded the agency's evolution. In 2016, after the so-called EU 'migration crisis', Frontex's mandate was reformed entirely.[20] Frontex changed its name to the European Border and Coast Guard Agency. The agency, with the national border and coast guard authorities, formed the European Border and Coast Guard. Most importantly, the new legal framework increased the agency's regulatory and operational capacities and level of independence.[21] Regulation 2016/1624 incorporated into EU law a fully developed definition of the EIBM.[22] Yet, while Member States favoured suggestions of further EU cooperation with third countries and shared responsibilities, they received the idea of direct delegation of competencies over border controls with caution.

[16] Art 1, Regulation (EC) 863/2007 [2007] OJ L 199/30.

[17] Art 1, Regulation (EC) 1168/2011 amending Council Regulation (EC) No 2007/2004 [2011] OJ L304/1.

[18] ibid, Art 33 (2a).

[19] Unisys, Final Report for European Commission, DG Home, *Study on the feasibility of the creation of a European System of Border Guards to control the external borders of the Union*, 16 June 2014.

[20] Regulation (EU) 2016/1624 [2016] OJ L 251.

[21] Jorrit Rijpma and Melanie Fink, 'The Proposal for a European Border and Coast Guard: Evolution or Revolution in External Border Management?', European Parliament, Study for the LIBE Committee, March 2016; Francesca Ferraro and Emilio De Capitani, 'The New European Border and Coast Guard: Yet Another "Half Way" EU Reform?' [2016] *ERA Forum* 1; Philippe De Bruycker, 'The European Border and Coast Guard: A New Model Built on an Old Logic' (2016) 1 *European Papers: A Journal on Law and Integration* 559.

[22] Art 4, Regulation 2016/1624.

Despite the suggestive renaming, several political and legal obstacles still impeded the complete and concrete Europeanisation of external border management. Fulfilling this objective became a definite possibility with the 2019 agency's legal framework reform. The 2016 regulation did not confer any executive power independent from Member States to Frontex officers, but this has changed with regulation 2019/1896.[23]

B. New Powers Perpetrating Old Logics?

Three years after the agency's last reform, on 4 December 2019, the new regulation on the European Border and Coast Guard Agency came into force. Frontex's new mandate resulted from an uncommonly rapid legislative process involving some critical developments.

Most notably, with the enhancement of Frontex's financial, technical and operational capacities, the agency will be able to establish a standing corps of 10,000 operational staff exercising executive powers and operating with its equipment, including service weapons.[24] Conferring executive powers to Frontex's operational staff may stretch the boundaries of the primary law provisions that regard Member States as ultimately responsible for their internal security and external border management.[25] This is why Article 82(2) specifies that the exercise of executive powers should 'be subject to the authorisation of the host Member State on its territory' as well as to applicable Union, national or international law, as described in the operational plans.[26] Importantly, Article 82(8) adds that the host Member State can authorise members of the border management teams, including the agency's statutory staff, 'to perform tasks during a deployment that requires the use of force, including the carrying and use of service weapons, ammunition and equipment, and shall be subject to the consent of either the home Member State or, for statutory staff, the Agency'.[27] Annex V to Regulation 2019/1896 adds specific rules loosely defining situations where the use of force is allowed. This might increase the possibility of finding the host state responsible in the event of human rights violations committed by its staff.

In addition to establishing a permanent body of European border guards, Regulation 2019/1896 enhances at least three other components of the previous legal framework. First, the agency's new mandate reinforces Frontex's role in data collection and information sharing; second, it expands its operational reach in the territories of third countries; third, it enhances Frontex's role concerning return procedures. These changes are interlinked and reinforce one another.

[23] Art 82, Regulation 2019/1896.
[24] ibid, Art 55.
[25] Mungianu (n 8) 29.
[26] Art 82(2), Regulation 2019/1896.
[27] ibid.

With the new regulation, the agency becomes the concrete administrator of an integrated surveillance framework, comprising EUROSUR and a set of national and EU databases, to increase the efficiency of the European integrated border control system.[28] The agency is charged with elaborating a European situational picture that should provide national authorities and the Commission with 'effective, accurate and timely information and analysis, covering the external borders, the pre-frontier area and unauthorised secondary movements'.[29] Thus, Frontex's monitoring function extends beyond the external borders and pervades the Schengen area.

While it ensures the interoperability of surveillance systems, Frontex can exchange information with EU agencies[30] and third countries.[31] The overall increase of its prerogatives regarding data processing makes Frontex an 'information hub' placed at the centre of a data processing and information exchange system.[32] In this context, Frontex should operate following the applicable standards regarding data protection.[33] Yet, the 2019 regulation does not identify the specific purpose of the agency's data processing. In particular, Frontex's increased information competences, coupled with the enhanced interoperability environment in which it operates, contribute to blurring the lines between migration management and internal security.[34]

Another major challenge concerns the implications of Frontex's increased cooperation with third countries for data collection and retention purposes.[35] Information processing and exchange are central elements of every working arrangement concluded between Frontex and third countries.[36] The information gathered by Frontex is put at the service of pre-emptive border controls, often implemented in the territories of third countries.[37] Frontex may also deploy liaison

[28] Recital 33 and Art 18, Regulation 2019/1896.

[29] ibid, Art 26.

[30] ibid, Art 3(e)(f) and 12.

[31] ibid, Art 75.

[32] As observed by the European Data Protection Supervisor, this trajectory was already clear in the 2016 regulation. See: EDPS' Recommendations on the Proposed European Border and Coast Guard Regulation, Opinion 2/2016, 18 March 2016, 3.

[33] The applicable legal framework for Frontex is Regulation (EU) 2018/1725 [2018] OJ L295/39, while for Member States the General Data Protection Regulation applies; however, when they share information in the context of the fight against crime, Directive 2016/680 [2016] OJ L 119 applies. Regulation (EU) 2016/679 (General Data Protection Regulation) [2016] OJ L 119.

[34] See: Formal comments of the EDPS on the Proposal for a Regulation on the European Border and Coast Guard and repealing Council Joint Action 98/700/JHA, Regulation (EU) 1052/2013 of the European Parliament and of the Council and Regulation (EU) 2016/1624 of the European Parliament and of the Council, 30 November 2018.

[35] Luisa Marin, 'The Cooperation Between Frontex and Third Countries in Information Sharing: Practices, Law and Challenges in Externalizing Border Control Functions' (2020) 26 *European Public Law* 157.

[36] The only exception is Frontex cooperation with the Federal Security Service of the Russian Federation, which covers only operational and technical cooperation. The list of working agreements concluded by Frontex is available at: https://prd.frontex.europa.eu/.

[37] Regulation 2019/1896 clarified that the extraterritorial reach of these operations was not limited to neighbouring countries but to any third countries more generally. Cf, Art 54(3)–(4), Regulation 2016/1624; Art 73(3), Regulation 2019/1896.

officers and establish antenna offices on the territory of third countries to coordinate and support the agency's activities, including in the field of return.[38] The underlying logic is that of the 'overall control' over the movement of persons, from departure, thorough their travel, to arrival.[39]

Finally, Regulation 2019/1896 assigned Frontex a pivotal role in the effective management of return procedures at the EU level.[40] Frontex assists Member States 'at all stages of the return process'.[41] While return decisions are the sole responsibility of Member States, the agency plays a proactive role in coordinating and organising return operations on its own initiative, and with its own personnel.[42] The agency is further mandated to develop and operate 'an integrated return management platform and a communication infrastructure' that enables the linking of national return management systems 'for the purpose of exchanging data and information, including the automated transmission of statistical data'.[43] This may prove detrimental not only to people seeking protection outside the Schengen area but to those already within it.[44]

III. Governance Structure

Atop Frontex's administrative and management structure is its executive director, assisted by three deputy executive directors.[45] The executive director acts independently, without seeking or taking instructions from any government or any other body.[46] Among other tasks, they prepare and implement Frontex's strategic decisions; evaluate the results of the agency's activities, programmes and activities; and assess whether the agency's activities involve any serious or persistent human rights violation and, accordingly, decide whether to withdraw financing or suspend or terminate an operation.[47] The executive director is appointed by the agency's governing body, the management board, on the basis of a proposal by the Commission and having considered the European Parliament's opinion.[48] The European Parliament can provide its views and indicate a preferred candidate; when its advice is not followed by the management board, the latter should justify its decision.[49]

[38] Arts 60 and 77(3), Regulation 2019/1896. See also Frontex, Cooperation with third countries in 2019, Report to the European Parliament, the Council and the Commission, 2020, www.statewatch.org/media/1370/eu-frontex-coop-third-countries-2019.pdf.

[39] Moreno-Lax (n 8) 42.

[40] Art 48, Regulation 2019/1896.

[41] ibid, Art 10(n).

[42] ibid, Art 50.

[43] ibid, Art 48(d).

[44] FRA, Opinion 5/2018, The revised European Border and Coast Guard Regulation and its fundamental rights implications, 27 November 2018, 44.

[45] Arts 99 and 107(3), Regulation 2019/1896.

[46] ibid, Art 106.

[47] ibid, Arts 106 and 46.

[48] ibid, Art 107(2).

[49] ibid.

The executive director is accountable to the management board.[50] The latter is composed of representatives from each Member State plus two representatives of the Commission.[51] The management board takes the agency's strategic decisions; for example, it adopts decisions on the nature and terms of the deployment of liaison officers and approves working arrangements with third countries.[52] Among its various functions and activities, the management board adopts Frontex's annual activity report, work programme and budget, as well as a technical and operational strategy for the EIBM.[53] It exercises disciplinary powers over the executive director and, in exceptional circumstances, it may temporarily suspend them.[54]

A. The Agency's Staff and its Training

Since its inception, Frontex's human resources have been growing. This tendency will continue in the future, as the agency's permanent staff is meant to increase to 10,000 persons by 2027.[55] Every year, the management board adopts a decision concerning the number and the profiles of the agency's statutory staff, as well as the staff seconded from Member States.[56]

Article 54 of Regulation 2019/1896 details the four categories of operational staff that make up the permanent body. The first category includes the statutory staff of the agency, employed within teams to be deployed in the operational areas, in addition to the personnel responsible for the operation of the ETIAS Central Unit.[57] The second category includes long-term staff seconded to the agency by the Member States.[58] The third category includes the Member States' staff available to the agency for short-term employment.[59] Finally, the fourth category includes

[50] ibid, Art 106(5).

[51] Ireland, which is a EU Member State not participating in the Schengen acquis, is invited to attend meetings of the management board on a case-by-case basis, where cooperate with the agency. Since the withdraw agreement between the EU and the United Kingdom, its cooperation with Frontex is subject to special arrangements. ibid, Article 101 and recitals 128–129.

[52] Art 100, Regulation 2019/1896. The management board is supported by five Divisions, a Cabinet, Offices (Media and Public Relations; Inspection and Control; Data Protection; Accounting) and Task Forces (ETIAS and Interoperability; Permanent premises for the Frontex headquarters).

[53] ibid, Art 100. The management board is supported by five Divisions, a Cabinet, Offices (Media and Public Relations; Inspection and Control; Data Protection; Accounting) and Task Forces (ETIAS and Interoperability; Permanent premises for the Frontex headquarters).

[54] Art 100(8), Regulation 2019/1896.

[55] Regulation 2019/1896, Annex I. Note, however, that though a Mission Letter to the European Commissioner for Home Affairs the President of the European Commission urged the recruitment of 10,000 border guards by 2024. 'Mission letter' from Ursula von der Leyen to Ylva Johnsson, 10 September 2019, https://ec.europa.eu/commission/sites/beta-political/files/mission-letter-ylva-johansson_en.pdf.

[56] Art 54(4), Regulation 2019/1896. See, eg: Management Board Decision 1/2020 on adopting the profiles to be made available to the European Border and Coast Guard Standing Corps, 4 January 2020.

[57] ibid, Art 55.

[58] ibid, Art 56.

[59] ibid, Art 57.

the reserves for rapid reaction; pursuant to article 58, this consists of staff from the Member States ready to be employed in rapid interventions.

All the agency's statutory staff should receive adequate training related to their tasks and powers. Every person deployed during Frontex joint operations, including participants from the host third countries, must receive appropriate training in EU and international law.[60] This includes preparation

> on fundamental rights, access to international protection, guidelines for the purpose of identifying persons seeking protection and directing them towards the appropriate procedures, guidelines for addressing the special needs of children, including unaccompanied minors, victims of trafficking in human beings, persons in need of urgent medical assistance and other particularly vulnerable persons, and, where it is intended that they participate in sea operations, search and rescue, prior to their initial deployment.[61]

Frontex training materials acknowledge the likelihood of psychological stress, among other health risks for the agency's staff.[62] The agency is becoming more aware of risks linked to unmanaged responses to emotional stress and indirect trauma. They can decrease a person's ability to cope with adverse circumstances and in turn increase the risk of violence. Yet, the responsibility for the mental health of Frontex staff, their ability to manage stress and deal with 'poverty, agony, chaos and violence', seems decisively placed on the individual border guards.[63] This approach, aside from the agency's responsibility to safeguard the health of its employees, is likely to affect those people they regularly encounter, many of whom have experienced trauma themselves.[64]

B. Fundamental Rights Bodies

Since its establishment, Frontex has undertaken some important steps in the direction of human rights awareness. While the operative provisions of its original regulation made no reference to fundamental rights or international protection obligations, Frontex's current mandate mentions them more than two hundred times. Apart from these formalistic observations, the agency has taken some concrete action to strengthen fundamental rights protection during its activities.

[60] OPLAN (Main Part), JO Flexible Operational Activities, Albania, 2019 [On file with the author] 7.
[61] Art 62(2), Regulation 2019/1896.
[62] See: Frontex training presentation, 'Medical precautionary measures for escort officers', undated http://statewatch.org/news/2020/mar/eu-frontex-presentation-medical-precautionary-measuresdeportation-escorts.pdf.
[63] See, EASO, Europol and Frontex, Occupational health and safety, 12 August 2019, para 4.4.
[64] Jane Kilpatrick, 'Frontex launches "game-changing" recruitment drive for standing corps of border guards', March 2020, www.statewatch.org/media/documents/analyses/no-355-frontex-recruitment-standing-corps.pdf.

In 2011, two fundamental rights bodies were introduced into the agency's structure: the Consultative Forum and the Fundamental Rights Officer (FRO).[65] The former is endowed with monitoring powers, while the latter contributes to the agency's Fundamental Rights Strategy and ensures the agency complies with fundamental rights. The most recent reform of the agency's mandate reaffirmed the inclusion of the FRO – appointed by the management board – within Frontex's administrative and management structure;[66] it also reinforced the independence of the Consultative Forum by clarifying that it is not part of that structure.[67]

The Consultative Forum is composed of EU agencies, civil society and international organisations.[68] Its composition is decided by the management board, following a proposal by the FRO in consultation with the executive director, and based on a number of criteria that have been amended over the years.[69] The Consultative Forum advises the agency on the further development and implementation of its Fundamental Rights Strategy, on the functioning of its complaints mechanism, and on codes of conduct and on the common core curricula. In addition, it publishes annual reports informing the public about how the agency operates.[70] Regulation 2019/1896 provides that the Consultative Forum should have access, in a timely and effective manner, to all information related to the respect of fundamental rights in all the agency's activities – this includes conducting visits to joint operations, rapid border interventions, hotspot areas and return operations or interventions.[71] Moreover, the agency is obliged to inform the Consultative Forum of follow-up measures taken regarding its recommendations.[72]

The FRO issues recommendations and opinions on specific issues related to fundamental rights; monitors the agency's compliance with fundamental rights, including by conducting investigations and visits; and publishes annual reports. The FRO reports directly to the management board and cooperates with the Consultative Forum, also by providing it with its secretariat.[73] For many years, however, Frontex has been criticised for failing to provide adequate staff and resources to the FRO.[74] This has been formally addressed by the 2019 reform,

[65] Art 26, Regulation (EU) 1168/2011.

[66] Art 100(2)(z), Regulation 2019/1896.

[67] Art 99, Regulation 2019/1896.

[68] At the time of writing the CF is composed of 14 organisations. The full list is available at: https://frontex.europa.eu/fundamental-rights/consultative-forum/general/.

[69] Art 108(2), Regulation 2019/1896; Management Board Decision No 29/2015 on the composition of the Frontex Consultative Forum on Fundamental Rights, 9 September 2015.

[70] Art 108 (3) and (4), Regulation 2019/1896. For a detailed study of the functioning of the CF, see most notably: Leila Giannetto, 'More than Consultation: Civil Society Organisations Mainstreaming Fundamental Rights in EU Border Management Policies. The Case of Frontex and Its Consultative Forum' PhD Thesis University of Trento 2018 [On file with the author].

[71] ibid, Art 108(5).

[72] ibid, Art 108(3).

[73] ibid, Art 109(4).

[74] See, eg: Consultative Forum Annual Report 2017, 6.

which introduced the position of deputy Fundamental Rights Officer,[75] as well as a team of Fundamental Rights Monitors (FRMs) who will assist the FRO in the performance of their tasks.[76]

The FRO assigns a FRM to each operation undertaken by the agency or any other relevant activity.[77] FRMs should have access to all areas in which Frontex operational activities take place and to all documents relevant to the implementation of those activities.[78] They monitor compliance with fundamental rights and provide advice and assistance on fundamental rights in the preparation, conduct and evaluation of Frontex operational activities. They also act as forced-return monitors and contribute to the training activities on fundamental rights.[79]

These are welcome developments that evidence the increased attention to fundamental rights during Frontex activities over the years. Yet, beyond questions about how these bodies will function in practice, questions remain about their independence from the agency they are mandated to monitor and advise. The FRO and the FRMs should be independent in the performance of their duties.[80] Yet, they remain Frontex employees and, as such, cannot act with the required impartiality and independence. This seems even more relevant if one considers that the FRO oversees Frontex's internal complaints mechanism.[81]

IV. Functions

The implementation of the EIBM is a shared responsibility of Frontex and the Member States.[82] While Member States retain primary responsibility for the management of their external borders, Frontex supports Member States in the application of EIBM measures by reinforcing, assessing and coordinating their actions.[83] To that end, the agency performs various interconnected tasks.[84] Frontex's main operational role is complemented by policy-orienting, supervisory and capacity-building functions. These tasks have been enhanced by the subsequent amendment to the agency's legal framework.

[75] Art 109(6), Regulation 2019/1896.

[76] ibid, Art 110. See, also: Frontex. News Release, Frontex and FRA agree to establish Fundamental Rights Monitors, 10 June 2020, https://frontex.europa.eu/media-centre/news-release/frontex-and-fra-agree-to-establish-fundamental-rights-monitors-OBabL6.

[77] Art 110 (3), Regulation 2019/1896.

[78] ibid.

[79] Art 110 (2), Regulation 2019/1896.

[80] ibid, Arts 109(5) and 110(5).

[81] ibid, Art 111.

[82] ibid, Art 7 and Recital 12.

[83] ibid, Recital 12.

[84] ibid, Art 10.

A. Supporting Technical and Operational Activities

Frontex's principal function is to provide technical and operational support in border control activities. The agency is mandated to assist Member States in controlling and surveilling their external borders, implementing the Union's return and readmission policy, and fighting cross-border crime and terrorism. To do so, it coordinates and organises joint operations, rapid border interventions, return operations and return interventions; it cooperates with other EU agencies and third countries and may deploy its operational staff in their territories; it offers technical and operational assistance to Member States' authorities in screening, debriefing, identifying and fingerprinting people in hotspot areas, and provides initial information to those in need of international protection.

Since its establishment, Frontex's operational capacities have been steadily expanding. Frontex's operational role is reinforced by its capacity to acquire, maintain and operate its own technical equipment, which is intended to become 'the backbone of the operational deployments' in exceptional circumstances at the EU external borders.[85]

To ensure the coherence of the EIBM,[86] Frontex established a technical and operational strategy for integrated border management.[87] All Member States have a duty to comply with Frontex technical and operational strategy. Member States may still cooperate outside the scope of the agency's strategy, but only to the extent that such cooperation is compatible with the agency's activities.[88]

B. Analysing Risks and Orienting Policies

All the agency's operational activities are based on its risk analyses. Frontex gathers and analyses data on migratory patterns and trends based on a common integrated risk analysis model (CIRAM).[89] Risk analyses aim at assessing the 'vulnerabilities' of Member States to potential 'threats' at the EU's external borders and consequently detecting them or organising pre-emptive responses, including joint border control operations or interventions.[90] The knowledge Frontex produces and circulates is a policy-orienting tool. It informs EU policies and practices in the field of border control without shifting the competence over it from the national to the supranational level.[91] The Commission uses risk analyses, for example, to

[85] ibid, Recital 71.

[86] ibid, Art 5(3).

[87] ibid, Art 8.

[88] ibid, Recital 85.

[89] ibid, Art 29.

[90] See: Frontex, Common Integrated Risk Analysis Model Summary booklet, 2013, https://frontex.europa.eu/assets/CIRAM/en_CIRAM_brochure_2013.pdf.

[91] Johannes Pollak and Peter Slominski, 'Experimentalist but Not Accountable Governance? The Role of Frontex in Managing the EU's External Borders' (2009) 32 *West European Politics* 904; Neal

justify the distribution of EU funding in the border control domain;[92] to prepare the EIBM multiannual strategic policy cycle;[93] and to plan unannounced visits to inspect Member States' compliance with the SCB.[94] Frontex's risk analyses contribute to the informal expansion of European border controls. In fact, the agency regularly cooperates with authorities in third countries to promote monitoring and 'situational awareness' and further develop a 'common pre-frontier intelligence picture'.[95]

Leaving aside questions about the (more or less rigorous) method adopted to produce Frontex's risk analyses,[96] the agency's knowledge-production function is problematic because of its underlying assumptions, which obscure the predicament of irregular migrants with a security-centred language. Risk analysis, like any form of knowledge production, is not objective and neutral but co-constitutive of the reality it observes.[97] Underneath the technocratic discourse of risk analysis, there is a political function; Frontex's risk analyses are securitising tools underpinned by a hegemonic rationalisation of migration.[98] This emerges clearly from the risk indicators included in the CIRAM, which, rather than being focused on people on the move, are being determined by the capacity of a system to mitigate the 'threat' irregular migrants embody.[99]

(n 9); Satoko Horii, 'The Effect of Frontex's Risk Analysis on the European Border Controls' (2016) 17 *European Politics and Society* 242; Regine Paul, 'Harmonisation by Risk Analysis? Frontex and the Risk-Based Governance of European Border Control' (2017) 39 *Journal of European Integration* 689.

[92] Regulation (EU) No 513/2014, OJ L 150, 20 May 2014.

[93] See arts 8 and 29(2), Regulation 2019/1896.

[94] Art 7, Regulation (EU) 1053/2013, OJ L 295/27.

[95] See eg: Frontex, Cooperation with third countries in 2019, Report to the European Parliament, the Council and the Commission, 2020, 9.

[96] Some maintain that Frontex risk analysis serves a 'regulatory' function, providing the EU institutions and Member States with technical information related to the management of external borders. Jorrit J Rijpma, 'Building Borders: The Regulatory Framework for the Management of the External Borders of the European Union' (PhD Thesis, 2009). For others, risk analysis is not a rigorous scientific practice, and therefore cannot be compared to those carried out by EU regulatory agencies. Lena Karamanidou and Bernd Kasparek 'Fundamental Rights, Accountability and Transparency in European Governance of Migration: The Case of the European Border and Coast Guard Agency Frontex' (*RESPOND* Working Paper, 2020). One may retort that the analyses of both social and natural phenomena are equally falsifiable. Among the many scholars attempting to describe and predict migration patterns, see most notably: EG Ravenstein, 'The Laws of Migration' (1885) 48 *Journal of the Statistical Society of London* 167; Emmanouil Tranos, Masood Gheasi and Peter Nijkamp, 'International Migration: A Global Complex Network' (2015) 42 *Environment and Planning B: Planning and Design* 4; Douglas S Massey and others, 'Theories of International Migration: A Review and Appraisal' [1993] *Population and Development Review* 431.

[97] Saskia Stachowitsch and Julia Sachseder, 'The Gendered and Racialized Politics of Risk Analysis. The Case of Frontex' (2019) 7 *Critical Studies on Security* 107.

[98] Sarah Léonard, 'EU Border Security and Migration into the European Union: FRONTEX and Securitisation through Practices' (2010) 19 *European Security* 231; Nina Perkowski, 'Frontex and the Convergence of Humanitarianism, Human Rights and Security' (2018) 49 *Security Dialogue* 457.

[99] I acknowledge that this vocabulary is common in risk analyses; yet its indiscriminate use to describe people appears inappropriate at best.

C. Supervising and Intervening in Case of Emergency

In addition to conducting risk analyses, Frontex supervises the Member States' capability and readiness to implement EIBM measures. This supervisory function is carried out mainly through vulnerability assessments designed to identify operational weaknesses in external border management.[100] While risk analyses aim to identify migratory trends and related challenges at the external borders, vulnerability assessments are concerned with operational weaknesses in national border control systems. These assessments are based on monitoring activities carried out by Frontex liaison officers seconded to the Member States[101] and on recommendations by the executive director.[102] The Commission shares the results of the vulnerability assessments with the Schengen evaluation teams for the purposes of the Schengen evaluation mechanism as it relates to external border management.[103]

The discipline of vulnerability assessment clarifies the relationships between different levels of EU border management. Where necessary, the executive director can recommend measures to eliminate the identified weaknesses and the time limit for their implementation. If the recommended actions are not taken, the management board can take a binding decision;[104] where this decision is not implemented, the Council can trigger a complex mechanism that would lead to the direct intervention of the agency at the borders of the Member State concerned.[105] Such a situation might materialise where Member States fail to take appropriate measures according to the agency's recommendations or where insufficient external border controls put the overall functioning of the Schengen area at risk.[106] Continuing non-compliance or persistent deficiencies can eventually trigger the procedure for reinstatement of the internal borders provided by the SBC.[107]

D. Capacity Building

To prevent structural deficiencies, Frontex serves a capacity-building function. It monitors and contributes to research and innovation activities relevant to border management and trains border guards.[108] While Member States are not obliged to train their border guards following Frontex's standards,[109] those standards exercise

[100] Art 32, Regulation 2019/1896.
[101] ibid, Art 31(3).
[102] ibid, Art 32 (7) and (9).
[103] ibid, Art 33.
[104] ibid, Art 32(10).
[105] ibid, Art 42.
[106] Art 19 (1) Regulation 2016/1624.
[107] Art 29, SBC.
[108] ibid, Art 62.
[109] Art 17(4), SBC.

a growing influence on the socialisation and professionalisation of European border guards.[110]

While supporting capacity-building activities among the national border authorities of Member States, Frontex also offers its know-how to third countries, for example, training on risk analysis and return-related matters.[111] The agency is further charged with developing a common information-sharing environment, including interoperability of systems.[112] This aligns with the technical and informal externalisation of border control underpinning the EIBM.

In sum, an unconcealed hierarchical relationship between the agency and Member States is being consolidated. Besides supervising the operations of Member States, the agency adopts the technical and operational strategy for the EIBM (to which the national strategies of Member States should adhere)[113] and develops training programmes for border guards.[114] At the same time, Member States should also refrain from any activity that could jeopardise the attainment of the agency's objectives.[115]

V. The Legal Personality of Frontex

The nature and the broadening scope of Frontex's powers and functions raise questions about its legal status within the EU institutional architecture and under international law. A precise definition of Frontex's legal status is relevant to determining and attributing responsibility for potential human rights violations. Being an international legal person implies that an entity is capable of bearing rights and obligations distinct from those of its members or creators. It follows that only an organisation endowed with international legal personality may violate international obligations and consequently be held responsible for doing so. Furthermore, legal personality is directly relevant to identifying the judicial fora competent to adjudicate the agency's responsibility.

As an EU agency, Frontex was created by EU secondary legislation to perform the mandate defined in its constituent instrument. Its creation and evolution are to be assessed in light of the institutional pluralisation of the EU.[116] Agencies should be enabled to operate autonomously from their political principals, but at the same time, they should be bound by several procedural and substantive constraints.

[110] Satoko Horii, 'It Is about More than Just Training: The Effect of Frontex Border Guard Training' (2012) 31 *Refugee Survey Quarterly* 158.
[111] Frontex, Cooperation with third countries in 2019, Report to the European Parliament, the Council and the Commission, 2020, 17.
[112] Art 10 (ac), Regulation 2019/1896.
[113] ibid, Art 8(5)(6).
[114] ibid, Art 55(3).
[115] Art 7(5), Regulation 2019/1896.
[116] Berthold Rittberger and Arndt Wonka, *Agency Governance in the EU* (Abingdon, Routledge, 2013).

To this end, Frontex has been provided with legal personality. In this respect, its founding regulation evokes the laconic formulation of Article 47 TEU, assigning legal personality to the EU.[117] The agency is accordingly able to act as a subject of the legal system of each EU Member State. Yet, the mere fact that an entity has legal personality at the domestic level does not automatically imply that the same holds at the international level.[118]

A. International Legal Personality

Despite the great diversity of opinions on the attributes necessary to qualify as an international legal person, one can broadly distinguish three main approaches to international personality. The first approach bases legal personality on objective attributes implicitly derived from an analogy of the state as the primary subject of international law. These qualities can be summarised as the capacity to conclude international agreements, the capacity to establish diplomatic relations and the capacity to bring international claims.[119] In reaction to this rigid state-centric notion of legal personality, the second approach conceives legal personality depending on a single requirement: the capacity to bear rights and duties under international law.[120] A compromise between these two positions was found by the International Court of Justice (ICJ) in the famous *Reparations for Injuries* Advisory Opinion, where the Court found that '[t]he subjects of law in any legal system are not necessarily identical in their nature or in the extent of their rights, and their nature depends upon the needs of the community'.[121]

Given the very fluidity of its nature, legal personality can be conceived as existing in a continuum. The location of a given entity between the opposite poles of the spectrum of (legal) existence depends on its international legal capacities.

[117] Cf, Art 93, Regulation 2019/1896.

[118] Melanie Fink, 'Frontex Working Arrangements: Legitimacy and Human Rights Concerns Regarding "Technical Relationships"' (2012) 28 Merkourios-Utrecht Journal of International and European Law 20.

[119] Giovanni Distefano, 'Observations Éparses Sur Les Caractères de La Personnalité Juridique Internationale' (2007) 53 *Annuaire français de droit international* 105; Christian Dominicé, 'La Personnalité Juridique Dans Le Système Du Droit Des Gens' in Jerzy Makarczyk (ed), *Theory of International Law at the Threshold of the 21st Century* (Alphen aan den Rijn, Kluwer Law International, 1996) 56.

[120] This approach has different facets. One position conceives legal personality as an a posteriori concept: anyone being the addressee of an international norm is an international person. See, most notably: Hans Kelsen, *Pure Theory of Law* (Berkeley, University of California Press, 1967). Another perspective accords individual rights and duties with a fundamental role in the international legal system. See, most notably, Hersch Lauterpacht, 'The Subjects of the Law of Nations' (1947) 63 *Law Quarterly Review* 438. Others prefer to examine concrete rights and obligations and focus on participation in international law-making rather than personality. See Rosalyn Higgins, *Problems and Process: International Law and How We Use It* (Oxford, Oxford University Press, 1995); Andrew Clapham, *Human Rights Obligations of Non-State Actors* (Oxford, Oxford University Press, 2006).

[121] ICJ, *Reparation for Injuries Suffered in the Service of the United Nations*, Advisory Opinion of 11 April 1949, ICJ Reports 237, 178.

In *Reparation for Injuries*, the ICJ alluded to at least two: the right to conclude treaties and bring international claims.[122] These are not rigorous legal requirements, but indicators of legal personality: 'to the extent that proposed subjects score on any of these indicators, they can be deemed subjects of international law'.[123]

When it comes to international institutions, it is widely agreed that the common denominator of these features is the independence of the organisation from its Member States.[124] In this context, independence is understood as the distinction between the organisation and Member States in terms of powers and functions. International organisations deserve international legal personality by virtue of their distinctiveness from Member States (or, in the words of Jan Klabbers, their 'organisationhood').[125] Legal personality is also a means to maintaining such distinctiveness. In this sense, independence is both a postulate and an effect of international organisations' legal personality.

B. Autonomy and (In)Dependence

Frontex is a body of the EU; nonetheless, it has a separate legal personality and enjoys the most extensive legal capacity accorded to legal persons under the laws of each Member State.[126] It has the capacity to be a party to legal proceedings[127] and enjoys the same privileges and immunities as the EU.[128] Moreover, it is endowed with specific functions[129] and permanent organs;[130] it has an autonomous budget[131] and maintains relations with other EU agencies and institutions, with international organisations[132] and with third countries.[133] Finally, Frontex is independent in implementing its technical and operational mandate.[134] The presence of these attributes may be seen as an indicator of international legal personality. Accordingly, some observers have associated Frontex with an international organisation.[135]

[122] ibid, 179–81.
[123] Jan Klabbers, *An Introduction to International Institutional Law* (Cambridge, Cambridge University Press, 2009) 40.
[124] Henry G Schermers and Niels M Blokker, *International Institutional Law* Sixth Revised Edition (Leiden, Brill Nijhoff, 2018); Niels Blokker, 'International Organizations and Their Members' [2004] *International Organizations Law Review* 139.
[125] Klabbers (n 123).
[126] Art 93(2), Regulation 2019/1896.
[127] ibid.
[128] ibid, Art 96.
[129] ibid, Art 8.
[130] Art 99, Regulation 2019/1896.
[131] ibid, Arts 115 and 116.
[132] ibid, Arts 68 and 69.
[133] ibid, Arts 71 and 73.
[134] ibid.
[135] Izabella Majcher, 'Human Rights Violations During EU Border Surveillance and Return Operations: Frontex's Shared Responsibility or Complicity?' [2015] *Silesian Journal of Legal Studies* 45, 51.

However, for Frontex to qualify as an international legal person, separate from the EU, it should be independent. The independence of an international organisation is often used as a synonym for, or an implication of, its autonomy.[136] There are one, none and one hundred thousand ideas of autonomy and independence in different disciplines. For the present purposes, autonomy and independence are understood as related but distinct concepts. They are related because they both stem from the idea of freedom. However, independence is here understood as freedom from dependence on other subjects; it signals institutional and political freedom – whereas autonomy corresponds to the ability to freely self-regulate and self-organise. An agent can thus be autonomous without necessarily being independent.

Autonomy may signal independence, but it does not *per se* constitute sufficient evidence of an independent legal person. Frontex is autonomous in the performance of its technical and operational tasks; it has a governance structure analogous to that of an international organisation, with its own organs, separate from that of the EU and its Member States; it is self-organised when it comes to its own resources; it is able, to a certain extent, to entertain relations with other legal persons. Yet even though the adjective 'independent' is profusely employed in Frontex's founding regulation, the agency is functionally dependent on the EU. Indeed, the agency depends on the political will of its parent organisation and cannot lead a separate international life.

Regulation 2019/1896 clarifies the terms of Frontex's relationship of subsidiarity with the EU, which can be inferred from the important normative powers that EU institutions exercise over the agency. The development of policy and legislation on external border control, including the development of an EIBM strategy, is a competence of the EU's institutions.[137] Along the same line, EU institutions exercise some significant procedural and substantial constraints over the agency's action. This emerges, for instance, from the discipline of vulnerability assessments and crisis prevention.[138] Moreover, when the agency concludes working arrangements with third countries, which might be qualified as international agreements,[139] it does so under the umbrella of the EU's international legal personality. This is corroborated by the requirement that it drafts working arrangements based on a model drawn up by the Commission, which should give its approval before their adoption.[140]

[136] See: Jean d'Aspremont, 'The Multifaceted Concept of the Autonomy of International Organizations and International Legal Discourse' in Richard Collins and Nigel D White (eds), *International Organizations and the Idea of Autonomy* (Abingdon, Routledge, 2011), who suggests that institutional and political independence are two separate dimensions of the autonomy of international organisations.

[137] ibid, Art 8(4).

[138] Arts 32 to 42, Regulation 2019/1896.

[139] See extensively: Fink (n 118).

[140] Art 76, Regulation 2019/1896.

Ultimately, Frontex's international capacities depend on the normative powers that the EU exercises by virtue of its competence to develop a common policy on border management. The agency is thus conceived as the executive arm of the Union regarding the implementation of the EIBM. This is not to obscure the interdependence between the agency and the EU. For instance, the Frontex risk analyses and expertise are essential when urgent measures are to be taken by the EU. This interdependence might be explained by the technocratic logic on which the agency rests. Frontex is a response to the need for politically neutral and efficient operational decisions that legitimate the choices of the EU concerning its border policies. Frontex's significant technical and operational independence hints at the presence of a separate legal subject, not only at the domestic level – as expressly recognised in its founding regulation – but also at the supranational level. The rationale is that an entity with control over its activities should be regarded as a discrete legal person. This is essential to enabling EU agencies to perform their mandates – and to protect EU institutions from liability resulting from the activity of those agencies.[141]

In sum, while the agency should be regarded as a legal person under national and EU law, it does not enjoy a discrete legal personality under international law. Frontex's international legal capacities derive from those of the EU, upon which the agency functionally depends. This justifies the application to Frontex of the primary rules concerning the human rights obligations of its parent organisation, as well as the secondary rules governing the attribution of responsibility for their violation.

VI. Joint Operations

Frontex's primary function consists of operational activities aimed at promoting, coordinating and developing the EIBM. The agency organises and coordinates joint operations, pilot projects or rapid border interventions to support one or more Member States in managing their external borders.

Joint operations assist Member States in border control and return activities, which can occur within the Schengen area or in the territory of third states. Rapid border interventions are triggered by situations at the borders of a Member State requiring immediate action.[142] While rapid border interventions run for limited periods, many standard joint operations have become permanent activities of the agency. Both types of operation are mainly carried out through the deployment of Frontex's standing corps (including statutory Frontex staff and officers seconded

[141] For a similar reasoning applied to UN subsidiary bodies, see 'Question of juridical personality and legal capacity in relation to United Nations agencies, programmes and funds' (UN Juridical Yearbook, 26 July 1994) 479.

[142] Art 39, Regulation 2019/1896.

from Member States) and technical equipment. The term 'host Member State' generally refers to a country receiving this assistance, while those contributing operational resources are commonly referred to as 'participating Member States'.[143]

Every joint operation is based on the agency's risk analysis and vulnerability assessments,[144] and should be implemented in accordance with relevant international, EU and national law.[145] Standard joint operations and rapid border interventions are generally carried out at the request of the host Member State. Yet, rapid border interventions can be triggered by a decision of the Council; this occurs based on a Commission's proposal, when border control has been rendered so ineffective as to put the functioning of the Schengen area at risk. The situation can be triggered by a Member State's non-compliance with Frontex's recommendations – and its management board's binding decision concerning a vulnerability assessment – or by disproportionate challenges at a Member State's external borders.[146]

A. Operational Plans and their Implementation

Every joint operation should be implemented in accordance with relevant international, EU and national law.[147] More specifically, Frontex's joint operations are implemented under an operational plan.[148] Each operational plan is drawn up by the agency, under the responsibility of its executive director,[149] and should be read in light of the multiannual strategic policy cycle for the EIBM.[150]

The executive director and the Member State hosting a joint operation should agree upon the plan in consultation with other participating Member States.[151] Where a joint operation is carried out in the territory of a third country, the operational plan should be agreed to by the agency and the third country concerned, but also by the Member State or states bordering that country.[152] Operational plans bind Frontex, the host and participating Member States.[153] All the team members deployed in joint operations act under the instructions of the host Member State.

[143] ibid, Art 2 (21) and (22).
[144] ibid, Art 39(3).
[145] Arts 36(2), 48(1), 82(2)(3), Regulation 2019/1896.
[146] ibid, Art 42(1).
[147] ibid, Arts 36(2), 48(1), 82(2)(3).
[148] ibid, Art 38.
[149] The operational plans are generally drafted by operational managers and then approved by the executive director. See Handbook to the OPLAN of Joint Air Border Operations, undated; Handbook to the OPLAN of Joint Land Border Operations, undated; Handbook to the OPLAN of Joint Maritime Operations, 30 January 2017 [On file with the author].
[150] Art 9, Regulation 2019/1896.
[151] ibid, Art 38(1).
[152] ibid, Art 74(3).
[153] ibid, Art 38(3).

However, these instructions should be given following the specific operational plan previously designed by the agency's executive director.[154]

The operational plan covers all aspects 'considered necessary for carrying out the joint operation', including the precise temporal and geographical scope of the deployment, its modus operandi and objectives, the composition, tasks and powers of deployed teams, their technical equipment, command and control provisions, incident reporting procedures and instructions on fundamental rights safeguards.[155] Frontex's operational plans are not available to the public. While it is possible to request access to these documents, access is generally partial, when granted.

The implementation of Frontex's operational plans is described very scarcely in the agency's legal framework. The most relevant information about its role in joint operations is inferred from the Handbooks to the operational plans. An operational manager is responsible for the overall administration of every operation, from drafting the operational plan to its evaluation. The concrete implementation of the operational plan is assigned to a coordinating officer.[156] The coordinating officer monitors the correct execution of the operational plan, including the protection of fundamental rights, and reports back to the executive director. Last, an operational coordinator is deployed during all operational activities.

The coordination of each joint operation is ensured by an international coordination centre composed of the host state authorities, Frontex coordinating officer and representatives of border-guard authorities of the participating Member States.[157] All operational information is gathered by the Frontex situation centre, located in the agency's headquarters in Warsaw.[158]

Frontex's legal framework provides that team members perform their tasks and powers under instructions from and in the presence of the authorities of the host Member State.[159] The latter may authorise team members to act on its behalf. More specific rules on command-and-control structure for each joint operation are defined in the relevant operational plan. In general, the international coordination centre decides on the activities of deployed personnel and aerial or maritime assets. Yet, when it comes to large military equipment, the operational command remains with the contributing Member State.[160]

[154] ibid, Art 38(3).

[155] ibid.

[156] ibid, Art 4.

[157] European Commission, 'Factsheet: How does Frontex Joint Operation Triton support search and rescue operations?' (undated).

[158] Fink (n 5) 65.

[159] Arts 82(4) and 95(6), Regulation 2019/1896.

[160] See eg: OPLAN (Main Part), Joint Operation Themis, 2018, 23; OPLAN (Main Part), Joint Operation EPN Triton, 2015/SBS/05, 2015, 11; OPLAN (Main Part), Joint Operation EPN Poseidon Sea, 2015/SBS/07, 2015, 10; OPLAN (Main Part), Joint Operation EPN Hera, 2014/SBS/03, 2014, 9.

B. Joint Operations at the External Borders

The self-evident objective of joint border operations is border control, mainly consisting of border checks and border surveillance.[161] Border checks are 'carried out at border crossing points, to ensure that persons, including their means of transport and the objects in their possession, may be authorised to enter the territory of the Member States or authorised to leave it'.[162] Border surveillance is implemented between border crossing points 'in order to prevent persons from circumventing border checks'.[163]

The principal objectives of Frontex's joint operations are detecting, preventing and controlling irregular migration flows.[164] To achieve these objectives the agency provides additional personnel and equipment to Member States. Frontex improves Member States' border-checking capacities by facilitating document fraud detection,[165] supporting screening and debriefing interviews[166] and conducting fingerprinting and registration activities.[167] Frontex further supports Member States with surveillance equipment (such as night-vision devices, radar, drones and aerostats) to prevent and detect irregular entries at the land and sea borders.[168]

Concerning joint maritime operations, Frontex is mandated to provide technical and operational assistance to Member States and third countries during search-and-rescue (SAR) operations.[169] Once involved in a search-and-rescue operation, all the participating officers are placed at their disposal and act under the instructions of the Rescue Coordination Centre responsible for the concerned region.[170] Yet, as further discussed below, the trigger of Frontex SAR duties is difficult to ascertain, not least because the operational area of maritime operations has been reduced so as to limit its SAR duties.[171]

[161] Art 2(10), SBC.
[162] ibid, Art 2(11).
[163] ibid, Art 2(12).
[164] See, eg: Joint Operation EPN Hera, 2014/SBS/03, 2014, 5; Joint Operation EPN Triton, 2015/SBS/05, 2015, 5; Joint Operation EPN Poseidon Sea, 2015/SBS/07, 2025, 5 [On file with the author].
[165] In April 2020, Frontex became responsible for the management of the False and Authentic Documents Online system (FADO). Frontex, 'News Release: False and Authentic Documents Online system', https://frontex.europa.eu/media-centre/news-release/false-and-authentic-documents-online-system-fado--o2Ky1q.
[166] See: Handbook to the OPLAN of Joint Air Border Operations (n 149) 7–11; Handbook to the OPLAN of Joint Land Border Operations, undated (n 149) 6–13; Handbook to the OPLAN of Joint Maritime Operations (n 149) 6–13. Detailed information about the modalities of these activities, the use of information obtained and the possibility of having access to interpreters or cultural mediators during interviews was not accessible to the author.
[167] See: Handbook to the OPLAN of Joint Land Border Operations (n 149) 14–15; Handbook to the OPLAN of Joint Maritime Operations (n 149) 14–15.
[168] See: News Release, Frontex begins testing use of aerostat for border surveillance, 31 July 2019, https://frontex.europa.eu/media-centre/news-release/frontex-begins-testing-use-of-aerostat-for-border-surveillance-ur33N8.
[169] Arts 3(1) (b) and 36 (2)(e), Regulation 2019/1896.
[170] See eg: Joint Operation Themis, Annexes to the OPLAN 2018, 33–34.
[171] For further discussion and analysis: Violeta Moreno-Lax, 'Protection at Sea and the Denial of Asylum' in C Costello, M Foster and J McAdam (eds), *The Oxford Handbook of International Refugee Law* (Oxford, Oxford University Press, 2021).

C. Joint Return Operations

Frontex plays a pivotal role in the implementation of the EU expulsion policy. The agency organises, coordinates and finances or co-finances Member States' return operations, and, with the agreement of the Member State concerned, it can organise joint return operations on its own initiative.[172]

Frontex's regulation emphasises that the agency cannot enter into the merits of return decisions, which remain the sole responsibility of Member States.[173] Frontex is nonetheless involved in a number of pre-return and return-related activities that might have a severe impact on such a decision and its implementation. Most notably, Frontex assists Member States by collecting the information necessary for issuing return decisions, identifying irregularly staying third-country nationals and assisting in obtaining travel documents.[174] In this context, the agency enjoys extensive data-management powers. To ensure the coherence and efficiency of returns, the agency is tasked with developing and operating an integrated return-management platform for processing all information relevant to return operations.[175] This platform incorporates the existing national and EU-wide return-management systems.[176] The information collected can be shared with EU institutions and agencies,[177] and the authorities of third countries.[178]

Joint return operations are carried out by return escorts and specialists whose actions are supervised by forced-return monitors.[179] According to Article 8(6) of the Return Directive, each Member State should establish an effective forced-return monitoring system.[180] Whereas all EU Member States have some form of return monitoring in their legal frameworks, not all of them have monitoring bodies sufficiently independent from the authority responsible for returns.[181] The Fundamental Rights Agency (FRA) suggested the involvement of an international body with human rights monitoring expertise in such cases.[182] Frontex regulation allows the European Committee for the Prevention of Torture and Inhuman or Degrading Treatment or Punishment of the Council of Europe (CTP) to visit joint

[172] Art 50, Regulation 2019/1896.

[173] ibid, Art 50(1).

[174] ibid, Art 48.

[175] Arts 49 and 50(2), Regulation 2019/1896.

[176] ibid, Art 49.

[177] ibid, Art 12(2).

[178] ibid, Art 73(4).

[179] ibid, Art 52. See also: Management Board, Decision No 21 12012 adopting the content and the modus operandi of the rolling operational plan for Join Return Operations, 27 September 2012.

[180] Directive (EC) 2008/115 on common standards and procedures in Member States for returning illegally staying third-country nationals [2008] OJ L 348/98.

[181] See: FRA, 'Forced return monitoring systems – 2020 update' 3 July 2020, https://fra.europa.eu/en/publication/2020/forced-return-monitoring-systems-2020-update.

[182] See: FRA, Opinion 5/2018, The revised European Border and Coast Guard Regulation and its fundamental rights implications, 21 November 2018, 36–37.

return operations.[183] Yet, visits by the CTP remain the exception to the rule of Frontex internal forced-return monitors.[184]

Besides, not all return operations are monitored, or the monitoring does not cover all return phases.[185] The effectiveness of the monitoring mechanism is further called into question by a lack of appropriate follow-up procedures to the reports of forced-return monitors.[186] If the forced-return monitors are to support human rights compliance during return operations, it is fundamental that they be systematically deployed in every return-related activity and that they be provided with appropriate follow-up competences concerning eventual complaints.[187] Complementing these internal efforts with external and independent monitoring mechanisms is also crucial for effective human rights protection during joint return operations.[188]

D. Joint Operations Hosted by Third States

The consolidation and further expansion of Frontex's legal mandate are generally presented as a functional necessity for maintaining the Union's internal security. To that end, the agency is mandated to implement a 'proactive management of migration, including the necessary measures in third countries'.[189] In line with its 'overall control' logic, Frontex ensures the persistent surveillance of people on the move by initiating operational cooperation with third countries.

The agency can conduct joint border control operations in the territory of third countries provided that its activities are carried out: (1) based on an operational plan drafted jointly by the agency and the third country concerned; (2) with the agreement of the bordering EU Member States; and (3) based on a status agreement between the EU and the third country if members of the deployed team will exercise executive powers, or where otherwise required.[190]

[183] Recital 82, Regulation 2019/1896.

[184] See: Mariana Gkliati, 'Frontex Return Operations and their Human Rights Implications' in Ibrahim Soysüren and Mihaela Nedelcu (eds), *Deportation of Foreigners: EU Instruments, Nation-State Practices and Social Actors' Involvement* (Lausanne, Peter Lang, 2020).

[185] Commission, Recommendation Establishing a Common 'Return Handbook' to be Used by Member States' Competent Authorities When Carrying Out Return-Related Tasks [2017] C(2017) 6505.43 para 8(6).

[186] The reports of forced-return monitors are submitted to Frontex's executive director, the FRO and the competent national authorities, but no specific procedure or criteria to determine the admissibility of complaints are mentioned. Art 50(5) Regulation 2019/1896.

[187] Frontex, Consultative Forum Annual Report 2019, 65–66. For detailed analysis: Mariana Gkliati, 'The EU Returns Agency: The Commissions' Ambitious Plans and Their Human Rights Implications' (2022) 24 *European Journal of Migration and Law* 545.

[188] See: Markus Jaeger, Apostolis Fotiadis, Elspeth Guild and Lora Vidović, 'Feasibility Study on the Setting up of a Robust and Independent Human Rights Monitoring Mechanism at the External Borders of the European Union' (Pro Asyl et al 2022).

[189] Recital 9, Regulation 2019/1896.

[190] Arts 73(3) and 74(3), Regulation 2019/1896.

All status agreements must be in line with the model status agreement drafted by the Commission.[191] In 2021, the Commission adopted an updated model, including the possibility of deploying team members with executive powers to any third country – and not only in neighbouring ones – in accordance with the 2019 Frontex reform.[192] Based on Frontex's previous mandate,[193] the EU has concluded status agreements with Albania, Serbia and Montenegro.[194] Similar arrangements have also been initialled with other Balkan countries.[195] In the meantime, these agreements are being re-negotiated and others have been concluded in light of Frontex's reinforced mandate, to expand its operational activities in the territories of third countries.[196] Negotiations on status agreements that would allow Frontex operations in Senegal and Mauritania are also ongoing.[197]

Regulation 2019/1896 requires that these status agreements cover all aspects necessary for operations in third-countries territory.[198] Yet, many crucial aspects of Frontex operations in third countries still need to be addressed. First, all status agreements contain a provision on the privileges and immunities of team members, granting them extensive immunities from the jurisdiction of the host third states. While Frontex and the participating Member States decide whether to waive these immunities,[199] border guards are not exempted from the

[191] ibid, Art 76.

[192] Cf: European Commission, Communication – Model status agreement as referred to in Regulation 2019/1896, COM(2021) 829, 21 December 2021; European Commission, Communication from the Commission to the European Parliament and the Council on the model status agreement as referred to in Article 54(5) of Regulation (EU) 2016/1624, COM(2016) 747 final, 22 November 2016.

[193] Art 54, Regulation (EU) 2016/1624.

[194] Status Agreement between the European Union and the Republic of Albania on actions carried out by the European Border and Coast Guard Agency in the Republic of Albania [2019] OJ L 46/3; Status Agreement between the European Union and the Republic of Serbia on actions carried out by the European Border and Coast Guard Agency in the Republic of Serbia [2020] OJ L 202; Status Agreement between the European Union and Montenegro on actions carried out by the European Border and Coast Guard Agency in Montenegro [2020] OJ L 173.

[195] See eg: Council Decision (EU) 2019/634 on the signing, on behalf of the Union, of the Status Agreement between the European Union and Bosnia and Herzegovina on actions carried out by the European Border and Coast Guard Agency in Bosnia and Herzegovina, [2019] OJ L 109.

[196] Agreement between the European Union and the Republic of Moldova on operational activities carried out by the European Border and Coast Guard Agency in the Republic of Moldova [2022] OJ L 91/4; Agreement between the European Union and the Republic of North Macedonia on operational activities carried out by the European Border and Coast Guard Agency in the Republic of North Macedonia [2023] OJ L 61; Agreement between the European Union and Montenegro on operational activities carried out by the European Border and Coast Guard Agency in Montenegro [2023] OJ L 140.

[197] Council Decision (EU) 2022/1169 of 4 July 2022 authorising the opening of negotiations on a status agreement between the European Union and the Republic of Senegal on operational activities carried out by the European Border and Coast Guard Agency in the Republic of Senegal, [2022] OJ L 181; Council Decision (EU) 2022/1168 of 4 July 2022 authorising the opening of negotiations on a status agreement between the European Union and the Islamic Republic of Mauritania on operational activities carried out by the European Border and Coast Guard Agency in the Islamic Republic of Mauritania [2022] OJ L 181.

[198] Art 73(3), Regulation 2019/1896.

[199] Art 6(4), Status Agreement between the EU and the Republic of Albania (n 194); Art 7(4), Status Agreement between the EU and the Republic of Serbia (n 194); Article 12(3) Agreement between the

jurisdiction of the respective authorities of home Member States.[200] The latter possibility seems, however, limited to team members seconded by Member States for Frontex does not have a 'home Member State'. Second, the tasks and powers of team members are vaguely enunciated as those required for border control and return operations.[201] The same provisions transfer the authority to issue instructions to team members to the host third-state authorities leading the joint operation.[202] This implies that the personnel of Frontex and its Member States will be placed at the disposal of a third country not bound by EU law nor by the European Convention on Human Rights (ECHR) in case of agreements with non-European states. This may be partially addressed by the operational plan, binding on all participating authorities, and requiring that all persons involved in such operations should comply not only with the domestic law of the host third country, but also with EU and international law, including fundamental rights.[203] Indeed, recent agreements specify that the host member state shall issue only instructions that follow the operational plan. If Frontex coordinating officer considers that those instructions do not comply with the operational plan or with applicable legal obligations, they shall immediately communicate this to the host member state authorities and to Frontex executive director, who may take appropriate measures.[204] Yet, besides the suspension or termination of Frontex activities, the consequences of a breach of these obligations remain unclear, even where a memorandum of understanding between Frontex and the host state on the respective complaints mechanisms is in place.[205] Finally, Article 73 of Frontex regulation provides that the agency should comply with Union law when cooperation with third countries occurs on their territory. This cannot, however, exclude situations of negligence or complicity in breaches of EU and international human rights law.

EU and Moldova (n 196). More recent status agreements foresee the possibility of a waiver by Frontex executive director. Art 12(2) Agreement between the EU and North Macedonia (n 196); Art 12(3), Agreement between the EU and Montenegro (n 196).

[200] Art 6(8), Status Agreement between the EU and the Republic of Albania (n 194); Art 7(8), Status Agreement between the EU and the Republic of Serbia (n 193); Art 12(3) Agreement between the EU and Montenegro (n 196). This provision is not present in the Agreements with North Macedonia and Moldova (n 196).

[201] Art 5(1), Status Agreement between the EU and Serbia (n 194); Status Agreement with Albania refers to the operational plan. See: Art 2(12), Status Agreement between the EU and Albania (n 194), Art 12(3), Agreement between the EU and Montenegro (n 196).

[202] Art 5(3), Status Agreement between the EU and Serbia (n 194); Art 4(3), Status Agreement between the EU and Albania (n 194); OPLAN (Main Part), Joint Coordination Points, Land, 2017/ORD/3, 2018 [on file with the author] 11; OPLAN (Main Part), JO Flexible Operational Activities, Albania, 2019 [on file with the author] 22.

[203] OPLAN (Main Part), JO Flexible Operational Activities, Albania, 2019 [on file with the author] 8.

[204] Eg: Art 7(4), Agreement between the EU and Moldova (n 196); Art 7(4), Agreement between the EU and Montenegro (n 196).

[205] Memorandum of Understanding on the complaints mechanisms related to actions carried out by the European Border and Coast Guard Agency in the Republic of Albania, 16 February 2022.

VII. Responding to Migrant Rights Violations

The EIBM in general, and Frontex's joint operations, in particular, incur a variety of human rights implications and risks.[206] The opacity surrounding joint operations, combined with their possible extraterritorial scope, may intensify those risks.[207] The agency's inadequate human rights compliance, exacerbated by its vague legal framework and lack of public accountability, has exposed it to severe criticism.[208] In response, over the years, Frontex has endorsed various Codes of Conduct for all border control and return operations coordinated by the agency,[209] a Fundamental Rights Strategy[210] and a Fundamental Rights Action Plan.[211] Also, since 2016, Frontex's legal mandate has included an internal accountability mechanism for human rights violations. Despite these important steps towards more accountable management of EU borders, the following pages will show that, in practice, Frontex's human rights compliance remains questionable, and its subsequent accountability is limited.

A. Reporting Incidents

All incidents occurring during Frontex's operational activities are reported via the joint operations reporting application (JORA).[212] Every deployed officer

[206] See ch 3.

[207] Anneliese Baldaccini, 'Extraterritorial Border Controls in the EU: The Role of FRONTEX in Operations at Sea' in *Extraterritorial Immigration Control: Legal Challenges* (Leiden, Martinus Nijhoff Publishers, 2010); Violeta Moreno-Lax, 'Seeking Asylum in the Mediterranean: Against a Fragmentary Reading of EU Member States' Obligations Accruing at Sea' (2011) 23 *International Journal of Refugee Law* 174; Majcher (n 135).

[208] Eg: HRW, *The EU's Dirty Hands Frontex Involvement in Ill-Treatment of Migrant Detainees in Greece*, HRW Greece, 2011; Report of the Special Rapporteur on the human rights of migrant: Banking on mobility over a generation: follow-up to the regional study on the management of the external borders of the European Union and its impact on the human rights of migrants, A/HRC/29/36, 8 May 2015; European Parliament, Report on the fact-finding investigation on Frontex concerning alleged fundamental rights violations, 14 July 2021; OLAF, Final Report, Case Mo OC/2021/0405/A1, Olaf.03(2021)21088. Among the growing literature, see most notably: Mungianu (n 8); Lisa Heschl, *Protecting the Rights of Refugees Beyond European Borders: Establishing Extraterritorial Legal Responsibilities* (Antwerp, Intersentiam 2018); Melanie Fink, 'The Action for Damages as a Fundamental Rights Remedy: Holding Frontex Liable' (2020) 21 *German Law Journal* 532.

[209] Code of Conduct applicable to all persons participating in Frontex operational activities (2017); Code of Conduct for Return Operations and Return Interventions coordinated or organised by Frontex (2018).

[210] Frontex Fundamental Rights Strategy, endorsed by the Frontex Management Board on 31 March 2011. Amended by Frontex, Management Board Decision 12/2021 adopting the Fundamental Rights Strategy, 14 February 2021.

[211] Management Board Decision 61/2021 adopting the Fundamental Rights Action Plan for the implementation of the Fundamental Rights Strategy, 9 November 2021.

[212] See: Handbook to the OPLAN of Joint Air Border Operations (n 149) 16; Handbook to the OPLAN of Joint Land Border Operations (n 149) 22; Handbook to the OPLAN of Joint Maritime Operations (n 149) 50.

can use the JORA to report a serious incident (SI) during Frontex's operations. A SI is defined as

> an event or occurrence, natural or caused by human action, which may affect, or be relevant to a particular Frontex activity, the safety and security of participants in Frontex activities, the Agency's mission and reputation, or any combination thereof. [Serious incidents] also includes situations of alleged violations of Fundamental Rights and EU acquis or international law, particularly related to international protection obligation, and of the Frontex Code of Conduct for all persons participating in Frontex activities and for Joint Return Operations coordinated by Frontex.[213]

The ordinary procedure to be followed in case of an SI starts with an initial report, including an informal summary of the preliminary information available about the occurrence. This is followed by a formal report into the JORA, with a comprehensive overview of the information available. At the same time, under the coordination of the respective operational manager and in cooperation with the host state authorities, Frontex's actors on the ground should monitor the situation. If, at a later stage, some additional information is acquired, the report should be updated accordingly. A final report summarising its outcomes closes the procedure.[214]

In situations related to human rights obligations, an extraordinary procedure takes place.[215] All participants in agency activities who witness, are involved in or have grounds to suspect the occurrence of an incident representing a possible human rights violation have an obligation to report it immediately to Frontex. They can do so using the standard serious reporting mechanism or, in case the disclosure of sensitive information on alleged violation could have negative consequences on the reporting persons, they can make use of an exceptional reporting procedure.[216] In addition, in light of new powers to use force and service weapons, special rules have been established for serious incidents that involve the use of force by Frontex standing corps officers.[217]

Crucially, these internal reporting mechanisms have not identified any human rights problem in various situations where there was consistent evidence thereof. In 2020, for instance, a joint media investigation uncovered, with videos and satellite photos, a series of migrant pushbacks conducted by the Greek authorities towards Turkiye, with Frontex's vessels and planes witnessing or participating

[213] See: Handbook to the OPLAN of Joint Air Border Operations, 24; Handbook to the OPLAN of Joint Land Border Operations (n 149) 31; Handbook to the OPLAN of Joint Maritime Operations (n 149) 35.

[214] Handbook to the OPLAN of Joint Air Border Operations (n 149) 25–26; Handbook to the OPLAN of Joint Land Border Operations (n 149) 32–33; Handbook to the OPLAN of Joint Maritime Operations (n 149) 36–37.

[215] Executive Director, Decision No 2012/87, Standard Operating Rules to ensure respect for human rights in Frontex joint operations and pilot projects, 19 July 2012 [On file with the author].

[216] Management Board Decision 17/2019 adopting the Frontex Guidelines on Whistleblowing, 18 July 2019.

[217] Management Board Decision 7/2021 establishing a supervisory mechanism to monitor the application of the provisions on the use of force by statutory staff of the European Border and Coast Guard Standing Corps, 20 January 2021.

in the operation.[218] This was not the first time the agency was involved in such unlawful manoeuvres, but it has consistently rejected any allegations.[219] Frontex emphasised that it did not have any power to investigate and must rely on Member States,[220] but after pressure from the Commission, the management board decided to create an internal subgroup to look into the suspected incidents at the Greek maritime border.[221] The agency's main concerns, however, were about legal uncertainties regarding sea surveillance operations and 'hybrid threats', rather than alleged human rights violations.[222]

In 2021, in reaction to these scandals, Frontex adopted a new Standard Operating Procedure (SOP), reinforcing the role of the FRO.[223] The 2021 SOP assigns a 'Serious Incident Handler' to every SI. The SOP applies to three categories of incidents, including those involving 'potential violations of fundamental rights or international protection obligations', 'potential violations of Codes of Conduct' and 'serious actual or potential negative implications on Frontex core tasks'. However, despite the fact that there might be considerable overlaps between these categories, the FRO is directly involved in the verification and assessment of only the first category of SI. In addition, while every participant in the agency operations is under the obligation to report any event which could be a SI, there seems to be no sanction for failure to do so.

Ultimately, Frontex's supervision of Member States' border control operations might enhance their human rights compliance. Yet, the agency's inertia and its silence about systematic human rights violations at Member States' external borders may contradict this assumption.

B. Frontex's Complaint Mechanism

Since the agency's inception, Frontex accountability problems have been pointed out by many.[224] In 2012, the European Ombudsman, on its own initiative, opened

[218] Giorgos Christides, Emmanuel Freudenthal, Steffen Lüdke und Maximilian Popp, 'Frontex Complicit in Greek Refugee Pushback Campaign –' *Der Spiegel* (23 October 2020) www.spiegel.de/international/europe/eu-border-agency-frontex-complicit-in-greek-refugee-pushback-campaign-a-4b6cba29-35a3-4d8c-a49f-a12daad450d7.

[219] Human Rights Watch, 'Croatia: Migrants Pushed Back to Bosnia and Herzegovina' (*Human Rights Watch*, 11 December 2018); Human Rights Watch, 'Human Rights Watch Letter to Frontex' (*Human Rights Watch*, 15 July 2019); Human Rights Watch, 'EU: Probe Frontex Complicity in Border Abuses' (*Human Rights Watch*, 9 November 2020). See also: CoE, Commissioner for Human Rights, Letter to Andrej Plenkovic, Prime Minister of Croatia, 20 September 2018.

[220] Frontex, 'Frontex launches internal inquiry into incidents recently reported by media' (News Release, 27 October 2020).

[221] European Commission, Extraordinary meeting of Frontex Management Board on the alleged push backs on 10 November 2020, 11 November 2020, https://ec.europa.eu/home-affairs/news/extraordinary-meeting-frontex-management-board-alleged-push-backs-10-november-2020_en.

[222] ibid.

[223] Executive Director Decision No R-ED-2021-51, Standard Operating Procedure (SOP) – Serious Incident Reporting, 19 April 2021.

[224] See, among the abundant literature, Johannes Pollak and Peter Slominski, 'Experimentalist but Not Accountable Governance? The Role of Frontex in Managing the EU's External Borders' (2009) 32

an investigation into Frontex's human rights compliance.[225] The Ombudsman found that Frontex lacked a mechanism to deal with individual incidents involving breaches of fundamental rights potentially occurring during its border control activities.[226] This implied that Frontex was not fully aware of human rights concerns during its activities; therefore, it had little possibility of correcting its performances and that affected people did not have the opportunity to have their complaints heard by the agency.[227]

According to Frontex, the agency was not competent to receive complaints against the conduct of Member States' border officers – as ultimate responsibility lies with the particular Member State on whose territory the incident occurred.[228] The disciplinary powers and reporting obligations of Frontex staff were considered sufficient by the agency.[229] In the same year, Frontex's executive director introduced the standard operating procedure to ensure respect for human rights. The decision establishing this procedure emphasised the importance of the monitoring and reporting obligations of every participant – both to fundamental rights compliance and to the executive director's own obligation to terminate any operation where fundamental rights violations are 'serious' or 'likely to persist'.[230] Nonetheless, as the Ombudsman observed, while monitoring and reporting obligations are important, they are not sufficient to ensure fundamental rights protection.[231] Furthermore, terminating an operation only where serious human rights breaches occur or are likely to endure does not seem to provide enough guarantees, especially considering the absolute nature of some of the violations potentially occurring.

Despite Frontex's initial rejection of the Ombudsman's recommendations, they led to some important changes in the agency's legal framework.[232] In particular, the agency's 2016 regulation included a specific fundamental rights complaints mechanism.[233] This mechanism turned out to be rather ineffective, however;[234]

West European Politics 904; Mariana Gkliati and Herbert Rosenfeldt, 'Accountability of the European Border and Coast Guard Agency: Recent Developments, Legal Standards and Existing Mechanisms' (RLI Working Paper 2018) Working Paper 30; Marco Stefan and Leonhard den Hertog, 'Frontex: Great Powers but No Appeals' in Merijn Chamon, Annalisa Volpato and Mariolina Eliantonio (eds), *Boards of Appeal of EU Agencies* (Oxford, Oxford University Press, 2022).

[225] See European Ombudsman, Implementation by FRONTEX of its fundamental rights obligations, Case OI/5/2012/BEH-MHZ, 6 March 2012.

[226] European Ombudsman, Case OI/5/2012/BEH-MHZ, *Decision closing own-initiative concerning Frontex*, 12 November 2013.

[227] European Ombudsman, Case OI/5/2012/BEH-MHZ, *Special Report OI/5/2012/BEH-MHZ in own-initiative inquiry concerning Frontex*, 7 November 2013.

[228] ibid, para 22.

[229] ibid, para 16.

[230] Executive Director, Decision No 2012/87 on the adoption of the Frontex Standard Operating Procedure to ensure respect of Fundamental Rights in Frontex joint operations and pilot projects, 19 July 2012.

[231] European Ombudsman, Special Report (n 227) para 23.

[232] European Parliament, Resolution on the Special report of the European Ombudsman in own-initiative inquiry concerning Frontex, OJ C 399/2, 22 November 2017.

[233] Art 72, Regulation 2016/1624; now Art 111, Regulation 2019/1896.

[234] See: Sergio Carrera and Marco Stefan, *Complaint Mechanisms in Border Management and Expulsion Operations in Europe: Effective Remedies for Victims of Human Rights Violations? CEPS Paperback,*

it lacked a clear definition of what could be considered an 'appropriate follow-up' by Frontex or by Member States. Moreover, it largely relied on the discretionary powers of internal oversight bodies, such as the executive director and the FRO, with their respective histories of mismanagement[235] or chronic understaffing.[236] In light of these shortcomings the Ombudsman opened a new inquiry on the agency's complaints mechanism and made several suggestions for improvement with a view to improving its accessibility, including in third countries and by anonymous complainants.[237]

Regulation 2019/1896 introduced some significant improvements to the legal framework. First, the FRO is now assisted by a deputy Fundamental Rights Officer and a team of FRMs overseeing Frontex's operational activities in the field.[238] Second, while under the 2016 regulation a complaint could be submitted only with regard to the actions of staff involved in the agency's operational activities, the new regulation includes possible complaints about a failure to act by Frontex's authorities or those of Member States.[239]

Despite these progresses, as discussed in further detail below, the current complaint mechanism cannot be considered to be truly effective.[240] Significantly, the complaints mechanism is still administered by internal oversight bodies, and it lacks clarity about the possibility of appealing against their decisions.[241] Moreover, the FRO is still lacking the necessary staff and resources to follow up on complaints.[242] The 2019 regulation requires the agency to develop an 'independent and effective' complaints mechanism.[243] But this noble declaration of intent (*rectius*, obligation) is contradicted by persistent shortcomings.

C. Decisions to Suspend, Terminate or not Launch Activities

Even if they are commonly extended over time, Frontex's joint operations have a limited duration. Yet, under Article 46 of Regulation 2019/1896, they should be terminated if the executive director determines that 'the conditions to conduct

26 March 2018 (Brussels, CEPS Paperbacks, 2018); Report of the Special Rapporteur on the human rights of migrants, UN Doc A/HRC/38/41, 4 May 2018, para 84.

[235] Jennifer Rankin, 'Head of EU border agency Frontex resigns amid criticisms' (*The Guardian*, 29 April 2022).

[236] See: Consultative Forum Annual Report 2015, 36; European Parliament, LIBE Committee, Final Mission Report following the LIBE Mission to the European Border and Coast Guard Agency (Frontex) in Warsaw, Poland, 24–25 February 2020, 18.

[237] European Ombudsman, Case OI/5/2020/MHZ, *Decision on the functioning of the European Border and Coast Guard Agency's (Frontex) complaints mechanism for alleged breaches of fundamental rights and the role of the Fundamental Rights Officer*, 8 June 2022.

[238] Art 110, Regulation 2019/1896.

[239] ibid, Art 111(2).

[240] See ch 3, s IV.H.iii.

[241] Cf, European Ombudsman, *Decision OI/5/2020/MHZ*, 8 June 2022.

[242] Consultative Forum Annual Report 2020, 107.

[243] Art 111(1), Regulation 2019/1896.

those activities are no longer fulfilled'. Most notably, the executive director has an obligation to withdraw the financing for any activity by the agency – or suspend, or terminate any of the agency's activities, in whole or in part – in the presence of serious or persistent human rights violations. The 2019 regulation further introduced the right of the executive director to decide not to launch any activity 'where he or she considers that there would already be serious reasons at the beginning of the activity to suspend or terminate it because it could lead to violations of fundamental rights or international protection obligations of a serious nature'.[244]

These provisions substantiate Frontex's duty to act in due diligence in the protection of human rights during its operations. The agency should not only respect the rights of individuals subjected to its power, but it should also protect them from potential violations by taking appropriate preventive measures. Evidence that a given joint operation should not have been launched, or should have been terminated or suspended, might entail the agency's human rights responsibility for failure to protect. Such evidence can emerge not only from Frontex's documents (such as incident reports or internal complaints) but also from reports of EU institutions' bodies, offices and agencies or international organisations.

After consulting the FRO and informing the Member State concerned, the executive director should take the decision to suspend, terminate or not launch activities, 'if he or she considers that there are violations of fundamental rights or international protection obligations related to the activity concerned that are of a serious nature or are likely to persist'.[245] On the one hand, the executive director *shall* suspend, terminate or not launch activities that would contribute to serious or persistent violations. On the other hand, the decision to suspend, terminate or not launch activities depends on the executive director's evaluation of the specific situation. Such decisions should be based on 'duly justified grounds'.[246] The executive director should take into account relevant information 'such as the number and substance of registered complaints that have not been resolved by a national competent authority, reports of serious incidents, reports from coordinating officers, relevant international organisations and Union institutions, bodies, offices, and agencies'.[247]

In the absence of a well-defined procedure to assess the human rights impact of a given operation, the evaluation is left to the discretion of the executive director.[248] It is therefore hardly surprising that no decision to suspend the agency's activities was taken before 2021. The repeated judicial admonishments against Hungarian asylum and return legislation,[249] and the growing pressure on the agency to stop

[244] ibid, Art 46(5).
[245] ibid, Art 46(4).
[246] ibid, Art 46(6).
[247] ibid.
[248] Frontex press office confirmed that a specific procedure is undergoing 'international consultations'. Email of 4 December 2020 [On file with the author].
[249] Case C-924/19 PPU e C-925/19 PPU, *FMS and Others*, 14 May 2020, ECLI:EU:C:2020:367; Case C-808/18, *Commission v Hungary*, 17 December 2020, ECLI:EU:C:2020:1029. See also: Judith Toth,

assisting in its implementation,[250] led Frontex to announce the suspension of all its operational activities in Hungary.[251] This decision came at a time when the agency was under severe criticism for complicit conduct in several incidents at the Greek border and for consequent mismanagement.[252]

The obligation to suspend or terminate activities entailing serious or persistent human rights violations is particularly relevant to the cooperation with third countries. Per definition, these countries are not subject to the same political oversight and judicial scrutiny as Member States. Hence, the decision to suspend or terminate an operation can be a pragmatic tool of persuasion and one of the most immediate consequences of eventual breaches. Whether the agency will use this tool more systematically in the future remains to be seen. The large margin of discretion left to the executive director is not particularly promising.

VIII. Transparency and Accountability in Frontex Activities

Frontex should conduct its work as openly as possible[253] and should maintain a regular public and transparent dialogue with civil society.[254] The most recent amendment to the agency's legal framework addressed some critical issues related to the democratic scrutiny of its activities. The agency should report to the European Parliament, the Council and the Commission to the fullest extent.[255] It should also transmit its annual activity report to the national parliaments.[256]

The increased scrutiny by these institutions of the agency's activities has not always been matched by their effective overview of the operational strategies the agency should implement. The European Parliament controls the agency's budget and should be consulted on the adoption of the multiannual strategic policy for the EIBM.[257] It also receives information about several specific aspects related to

'Hungary at the Border of Populism and Asylum' in Sergio Carrera and Marco Stefan (eds), *Fundamental Rights Challenges in Border Controls and Expulsion of Irregular Immigrants in the European Union: Complaint Mechanisms and Access to Justice* (Abingdon, Routledge, 2020).

[250] Marton Dunai, 'Hungary Keeps Deporting Migrants, EU Border Guard Turns Blind Eye – NGO' (*Reuters*, 12 January 2021) www.reuters.com/article/us-europe-migrants-hungary-frontex-idCAKBN29H1W1.

[251] Mariana Gkliati, 'The Next Phase of The European Border and Coast Guard: Responsibility for Returns and Push-Backs in Hungary and Greece' (2022) 7 *European papers* 171, 179–180. See, however: Frontex, Fact Sheet -2020 Frontex discharge, 2–3.

[252] See European Parliament, 'Recent allegations on pushbacks during Frontex operations in the Eastern Mediterranean: extracts from the presentation by Fabrice Leggeri', 1 December 2020.

[253] Art 15, TFEU.

[254] Art 11(2), TUE.

[255] Recital 116, Art 121, Regulation 2019/1896.

[256] ibid, Art 112(3).

[257] ibid, Art 8(4).

Frontex's activities, including the deployment of liaison officers to third states[258] and the general and strategic risk analyses based on which the multiannual strategic policy for the EIBM is elaborated.[259] Yet, the Parliament continues to suffer from an informational deficit regarding tailored risk analyses for operational activities.

While the new legal framework has partially remedied the informational deficit of the European Parliament, the agency remains an essentially intergovernmental body, with a management board dominated by national representatives. The agency must invite a representative from the FRA to attend its management board's meetings. By contrast, while Frontex has the faculty to invite experts from the European Parliament,[260] the provision to ask external observers to participate in the agency's activities seems merely focused on exchanging best practices among executive actors.[261]

This may be partially alleviated by the possibility that members of the European Parliament have to invite the executive director to report on the agency's activities at any moment.[262] The executive director is under an obligation to answer in writing any of their questions.[263] Significantly, the classification of relevant information does not preclude its availability to the Parliament.[264] Furthermore, the European Parliament can initiate ad hoc investigations on the agency's human rights compliance. A notable (and overdue) example of such Parliamentary investigations is the creation of a scrutiny working group to oversee all aspects of Frontex's activities.[265]

In addition to being accountable to political bodies, the agency must provide access to relevant information to civil society, most notably through the Consultative Forum.[266] The members of the Consultative Forum have the power to conduct on-the-spot visits, including in third countries, to verify compliance with fundamental rights during operational activities.[267] Yet, these prerogatives are not as effective in practice as they might seem in theory. The Consultative Forum continues to face challenges in accessing information;[268] and its delegations are often not allowed to observe border guards in the performance of their duties directly.[269]

[258] ibid, Art 76(5).
[259] ibid, Art 29.
[260] ibid, Art 104(6)–(7).
[261] ibid, Art 78.
[262] ibid, Art 106(2).
[263] Art 106(2), Regulation 2019/1896.
[264] ibid, Art 92(3).
[265] LIBE Committee Frontex Scrutiny Working Group (FSWG) Draft mandate, 29 January 2021. See ch 5, s VII.D.
[266] Art 108(5), Regulation 2019/1896.
[267] ibid.
[268] See, eg, Consultative Forum Annual Report 2017, 17; Consultative Forum Annual Report 2019, 150.
[269] Consultative Forum Annual Report 2019, 32.

Many of the agency's documents are open to the public. These documents include annual reports, reports of the Consultative Forum, work programmes and general risk analyses.[270] Operational plans and serious incident reports, however, are classified as sensitive and confidential, although it is possible to request access to these documents, subject to the conditions laid down in Regulation 1049/2001.[271] The main requirement to qualify for the right to access documents held by Frontex is EU citizenship or residency in an EU Member State.[272] As many of the people concerned by Frontex's activities are third-country nationals without residency in the EU, the right to access to documents is rather limited.[273] Frontex's regulation provides that 'any natural or legal person' can address the agency and receive an answer.[274] Yet this does not imply that the agency has a duty to disclose the information requested.

When access to information is granted, it is generally partial. Furthermore, Frontex does not assume responsibility for any information included in transmitted documents,[275] and it invokes copyright law to warn applicants against sharing them.[276] Gaining access to documents for this work has been particularly challenging. The information provided was both limited and contradictory.[277]

Frontex's refusal to release documents has been challenged before the CJEU and the European Ombudsman. In both cases, the applicants were unsuccessful; Frontex's refusal to disclose information was justified on the grounds of public interest in public security.[278] Notably, the CJEU found that Frontex enjoys 'wide discretion' in determining whether a document is covered by the public security exceptions provided in Regulation 1049/2001. Moreover, the Court specified that its review of the legality of a decision to refuse access to information is 'limited to verifying whether the procedural rules and the duty to state reasons have been complied with, whether the facts have been accurately stated and whether there has been a manifest error of assessment or a misuse of powers'.[279] By virtue of its broad discretion regarding exceptions to the right of access to documents, the agency can select the information that it considers appropriate to share with the

[270] Art 114, Regulation 2019/1896.

[271] Regulation (EC) No 1049/2001 of the European Parliament and of the Council of 30 May 2001 regarding public access to European Parliament Council and Commission documents, OJ L 145/43.

[272] ibid, Art 2.

[273] Migrants are generally third country nationals who do not have (yet) established their residency in the EU.

[274] Art 114(4), Regulation 2019/1896.

[275] See: Karamanidou and Kasparek (n 96).

[276] Exchange of letters between the author and Frontex Transparency Office, Application for access to documents, 6 February 2020 [On file with the author].

[277] For instance, in the past, Frontex disclosed a Handbook to the OPLAN of Return Operations (Fink (n 5) 36, n 88); but when asked by the present author, the agency's Transparency Office denied the existence of 'any such documents'. See Frontex Letter of 11 June 2019 [On file with the author].

[278] European Ombudsman, *Decision on the refusal by Frontex to grant access to a document concerning the vessels used in the Poseidon and Triton border control operations*, Case 1328/2017/EIS, 23 November 2017; Case T-31/18, *Izuzquiza*, 27 November 2019, ECLI:EU:T:2019:815.

[279] *Izuzquiza*, ibid para 65.

public. This epistemic power enables Frontex to direct the narrative (at least to the general public) around its human rights compliance.

The opacity surrounding Frontex's daily activities exacerbates the difficulties in allocating responsibilities for migrant rights violations among the various actors participating in the agency's joint operations.[280] These actors operate under a chain of command and control included in each operational plan. The limitations in accessing these documents imply serious difficulties in identifying who is responsible for what during Frontex's joint operations. People affected by Frontex's operations find themselves in a vulnerable situation, and 'it cannot possibly be expected from them to investigate what is undoubtedly a complex allocation of responsibility'.[281] Overall, the aura of secrecy covering Frontex's activities not only hinders the regular ex-ante democratic overview of the agency's conduct but also encumbers its ex-post judicial review.

IX. Conclusion: Frontex a Catalyst for Complexity

Frontex is the expression of the composite nature of the EIBM assemblage. Two mutually supporting logics underpinned the establishment of the agency. First, its creation responded to the need for a uniform application of border control standards across all the Schengen Member States. Second, since its inception, the agency has had a security-driven character, reacting to the security emergencies that might arise outside the external borders. As a result, the agency consolidated the link between security, border management and migration.

Along these lines, Frontex serves a preventive and reactive function at the same time. With its risk analyses, Frontex prevents future challenges at the external borders by anticipating the movements of potential irregular migrants and taking appropriate border control measures. Where Member States are unable to face these challenges, the agency can recommend the proper reaction, including deploying additional personnel and equipment. These two mutually supportive functions are reflected in the agency's operational and technical nature, increasingly bolstered by subsequent amendments to its legal framework.

The pervasive influence Frontex exercises over border management enables it to gradually erode Member States' powers in that area, without formally undermining their sovereignty. On the one hand, Frontex's technical character conceals a de-politicising tool that enables the agency to legitimise the EU border control policies it implements as purely technical – and therefore neutral and insulated from political debate. On the other hand, the agency's operational power, coupled with its informational hegemony and capacity to disseminate knowledge, place

[280] See: Majcher (n 135); Fink (n 5); Mariana Gkliati and Jane Kilpatrick, 'Crying Wolf Too Many Times: The Impact of the Emergency Narrative on Transparency in FRONTEX Joint Operations' (2022) 17 *Utrecht Law Review* 57.

[281] European Ombudsman, Case-OI/5/2012/BEH-MHZ (n 227).

Frontex in a pivotal position within the EIBM. Frontex is allowed to act more and more autonomously, while the Member States are reduced to mere 'consumers' of its technical and operational strategies.[282] This growing autonomy is problematic, not least because of the absence of independent and effective remedies for human rights violations that its activities might occasion.

Another major challenge in Frontex's activities is that they radiate within and beyond the external European borders. Frontex cooperates with third countries, training their border guards, sharing information with them and enforcing border controls in their territories. All in all, this promotes EIBM standards and lengthens the reach of EU border control far beyond the physical frontiers of the Schengen Member States.[283]

Frontex catalyses the dislocation and proliferation of borders underlying the EIBM. In doing so, it challenges the conception of the border as a technology of state-territorial power. State territorial power remains nonetheless relevant for many purposes, most notably to establish the applicability of human rights obligations. As discussed in the next part of this study, by straying onto Member States' borders, Frontex also trespasses their territorial jurisdiction. This might result in the frustration of the human rights obligations binding the EU and its Member States.

Furthermore, Frontex's enhanced legal mandate contributes to further blurring the lines of responsibility between the various actors involved in Frontex's operational activities. The interplay of multiple actors in the EIBM allows them to shift the blame for the harmful consequences of their border control activities. Whereas the implementation of the EIBM is a 'shared responsibility' of Frontex and the competent national authorities,[284] the agency's stance regarding human rights violations occurring in such a context has generally been evasive. Frontex's official position has been that the Member States are the primary (if not exclusive) agents responsible for human rights violations occurring during its activities.[285]

The next chapter will show that the agency's extensive human rights obligations contradict this assumption. Frontex is mandated not only to respect human rights but also to ensure their protection and promotion.[286] Far from serving a mere auxiliary role, Frontex plays a decisive role in defining and implementing the EIBM. In this line, Frontex should 'be fully responsible and accountable for any decision it takes and for any activity for which it is solely responsible'.[287] Yet, the complex organisational structure and the secrecy under which Frontex operates

[282] Campesi (n 14) 134–35.
[283] Art 71(4), Regulation 2019/1896.
[284] ibid, Art 7.
[285] See Frontex Fundamental Rights Strategy, 31 March 2011, para 13; Frontex, Executive Director Letter responding to Amnesty International reports: Waves of Impunity and Between life and death, 13 October 2020, https://frontex.europa.eu/assets/Images_News/2020/Frontex_responds_Amnesty_International_report.pdf.
[286] Art 10(ad), Regulation 2019/1896.
[287] ibid, Art 7(4).

makes it difficult to prove that the agency was *solely* responsible for a human rights violation.

The following analysis will try to unravel the knot of obligations and concomitant responsibilities for their potential breach by Frontex and/or the States implementing the EIBM. Accordingly, the next chapter will identify the relevant international obligations binding Frontex and the Member States in their concerted border management activities. The analysis will then proceed by tracing the jurisdictional reach of applicable international obligations and discussing the international responsibility for their breach.

3

The Protection of Migrant Rights and Administration of the European Borders

I. Introduction: Rights and Obligations in the EIBM

This chapter will examine how international and EU law both frame and respond to the challenges related to the respect and protection of migrant rights in the EIBM in general and Frontex's joint operations in particular. The following pages, rather than analysing all the rights to which migrants are entitled, will attempt to explore the situations in which migrant rights are more likely to be infringed during the EIBM activities.

Migrant rights, qua human rights, arise from a relationship between a duty-bearer and a rights-holder.[1] While human rights can be general and abstract, human rights obligations must be concrete and specific.[2] For every right, there are several correlative duties and duty-bearers that undertake its realisation. The main duty-bearers addressed by this study are the European states cooperating in the protection of their external borders and Frontex, the 'spider in the web of border guard authorities' implementing the EIBM.[3] As seen in the previous chapter, Frontex's legal personality depends on that of the EU. Consequently, Frontex must comply with its obligations under EU law and the international obligations binding the EU under international law. The objective of this chapter is therefore to elucidate the obligations binding the EU, Frontex, and the Member States when they implement the EIBM.

Because Frontex and the Member States arrange and orchestrate the integrated management of the European borders, they are assumed to be the main responsible actors in case of mismanagement resulting in a violation of migrants' rights.

[1] For further discussion, see ch 4.

[2] Henry Shue, *Basic Rights: Subsistence, Affluence, and U.S. Foreign Policy* (40th anniversary edition, Princeton, Princeton University Press, 2020); Samantha Besson, 'The Bearers of Human Rights Duties and Responsibilities for Human Rights – A Quiet (R)Evolution.' (2015) 32 *Social Philosophy and Policy* 244.

[3] Jorrit J Rijpma and Melanie Fink, 'The Management of The European Union's External Borders', in Philippe De Bruycker and Lilian Tsourdi (eds), *Research Handbook on EU Asylum and Migration Law* (Cheltenham, Edward Elgar, 2022).

Those actors are presented as duty-bearers, in so far as their obligations represent the flip side of the migrants' rights coin. The analysis will thus explore the respective rights, originating from various legal sources, that might be at stake for migrants in vulnerable situations at the borders of Europe.

An overview of the pluralistic legal framework within which Frontex and the Member States operate will lay the ground for evaluating their activities through the lens of migrants' protection. The goal is to clarify the way international and EU law uphold migrant rights and how these norms can impact the border control practices of national and supranational authorities.

Before delving into the details of this pluralistic legal framework, I will first provide a brief outline of its legal sources and their interaction (Section II). International and EU law are intertwined in many ways. With particular regard to the protection of migrants at the borders of Europe, EU law has incorporated – and occasionally transformed – international human rights and refugee law standards. I will then discuss the nature of the obligations binding the EU and its Member States. After a few reminders about the distinction between positive and negative human rights obligations, I shall highlight their significance in the context of border management (Section III). The rest of the analysis will follow the trajectory of a protection continuum, counterbalancing the continuum of coercive and surveillance practices described in the previous part of this work (Section IV). The chapter concludes by reflecting on how migrant rights stemming from different legal sources can respond to the challenges of border control measures implemented by multiple actors and technologies (Section V).

II. Sources of Obligation

Within the EIBM assemblage, many actors, mainly EU agencies such as Frontex and the Member States, interact to construe a continuum of control that may result in breaches of these actors' international obligations. The following sections will identify the sources of the international obligations binding the EU and its Member States in the context of their border control activities.

A. The International Obligations of the EU

As discussed in chapter two, Frontex does not enjoy a discrete international legal personality; instead, the agency derives its legal capacitates and duties from those of the EU, its parent organisation.[4] The following analysis is therefore devoted to the international obligations of the EU (and Frontex). To clarify

[4] Ch 2, s V.

this matter, this section will examine the EU's international legal nature and its legal consequences. I will then turn to the relationship between EU law and international human rights law, as they represent the main legal framework concerning the protection of migrant rights in Europe.

The EU's legal nature can be characterised in many ways and from various perspectives – perhaps none of them entirely persuasive, but many of them plausible.[5] Observed from the inside, the EU legal order looks like a new legal entity with unique constitutionalising features. This view is grounded in the EU's self-perception, according to which the Union constitutes 'a new legal order of international law'.[6] Considered from the outside, the EU is generally described as an international organisation, that is, a creature of international law. The EU legal order appears as a special legal regime embedded in the general system of public international law from which it enjoys 'relative autonomy'.[7] Whereas its special features distinguish the EU from any other international institution,[8] its *sui generis* character does not automatically create a separate legal order;[9] instead, it remains 'a subsystem of international law'.[10]

The EU is difficult to pigeonhole in a single legal category and has accordingly been compared to 'a unicorn amidst a coterie of strange creatures'.[11] I will not attempt to argue for a specific interpretation, nor will I seek to find a new legal category for the EU. Instead, my analysis will start from the presumptive (and generally accepted) international legal personality of the EU,[12] and focus on the EU's tangible presence in the international sphere – as a creature of the international legal system from which it originates.[13] The EU has a distinct legal

[5] Jan Klabbers, 'Straddling the Fence: The European Union and International Law' in Damian Chalmers and Anthony Arnull (eds), *The Oxford Handbook of European Union Law* (Oxford, Oxford University Press, 2015).

[6] Case 26/62, *van Gend & Loos*, 5 February 1963, ECLI:EU:C:1963:1, para 3.

[7] Alain Pellet, 'Les Fondements Juridiques Internationaux Du Droit Communautaire' (1994) 5 *Collected Courses of the Academy of European Law* 226, 245–47.

[8] ILC, Responsibility of International Organizations: Comments and Observations Received from International Organizations, UN Doc A/CN.4/582, 1 May 2007, 24. See also: Joxerramon Bengoetxea, 'The EU as (More Than) an International Organization' in Jan Klabbers and Åsa Wallendahl (eds), *Research Handbook on the Law of International Organizations* (Cheltenham, Edward Elgar, 2012).

[9] Jan Klabbers, 'Sui Generis? The European Union as an International Organization' in Dennis Patterson and Anna Södersten (eds), *A Companion to European Union Law and International Law* (Oxford, John Wiley & Sons, 2016).

[10] Bruno Simma and Dirk Pulkowski, 'Of Planets and the Universe: Self-Contained Regimes in International Law' (2006) 17 *European Journal of International Law* 483, 516.

[11] Klabbers (n 5).

[12] Art 47, TEU. See most notably: Ramses A Wessel, 'Revisiting the International Legal Status of the EU' (2000) 5 *European Foreign Affairs Review*; Jan Klabbers, 'Presumptive Personality: The European Union in International Law' in Martti Koskenniemi (ed), *International Law Aspects of the European Union* (Leiden, Martinus Nijhoff, 1998); Jan Wouters and others, 'Personality and Powers of the EU' in Jan Wouters and others (eds), *The Law of EU External Relations: Cases, Materials, and Commentary on the EU as an International Legal Actor* (Oxford, Oxford University Press, 2021).

[13] Jed Odermatt, *International Law and the European Union* (Cambridge, Cambridge University Press, 2021) 131–67.

personality and enjoys an extensive autonomy from its Member States. At the same time, the EU legal order is also closely intertwined with those of its Member States. In this sense, the Union is 'both independent from, and dependent on, its Member States'.[14] Beyond this paradox, however, the EU international presence is unquestionable. In its action on the international scene, the EU must safeguard its 'values, fundamental interests, security, independence and integrity',[15] but it must also respect international law.[16] What follows will explore the tension between these two goals and how international law binds and, at the same time, is shaped by the EU and its organs.[17]

Whereas international law is not an original European idea,[18] it is undoubtedly part of the narrative that has shaped and influenced the development of the EU.[19] Due to the derived international subjectivity of the EU, its Member States' international obligations further shape the Union as an international organisation.[20] The original EEC Treaty and the treaties that succeeded it (today, the TFEU and the TEU, together with the Euratom Treaty) are the sources of all EU legislation.[21] International law continues to regulate the life of the EU since, in the absence of any special rule of EU law, secondary rules of international law will apply, such as rules on the international responsibility of states or international organisations,[22] or rules on treaty interpretation.[23] That notwithstanding, the EU has developed an ambivalent posture towards international law.[24] This EU ambivalence oscillates between the recognition of the EU's

[14] ibid, 208. See also: Pieter Jan Kuijper and Esa Paasivirta, 'EU International Responsibility and its Attribution: From the Inside Looking Out' in Malcom Evans and Panos Koutrakos (eds), *The International Responsibility of the European Union: European and International Perspectives* (Oxford, Hart Publishing, 2013) 38.

[15] Art 21(2)(a), TFEU.

[16] ibid, Art 21(1).

[17] See extensively: Odermatt (n 13).

[18] Alexander Orakhelashvili, 'The Idea of European International Law' (2006) 17 *European Journal of International Law* 315.

[19] Anthony Pagden, *The Idea of Europe: From Antiquity to the European Union* (Cambridge, Cambridge University Press, 2002); Martti Koskenniemi, 'International Law in Europe: Between Tradition and Renewal' (2005) 16 *European Journal of International Law* 113.

[20] Katja S Ziegler, 'The Relationship between EU Law and International Law' in Dennis Patterson and Anna Södersten (eds), *A Companion to European Union Law and International Law* (Oxford, John Wiley & Sons, 2016).

[21] Treaty establishing the European Economic Community (Treaty of Rome), 298 UNTS 3, 25 March 1957; Treaty Establishing the European Atomic Energy Community, 298 UNTS 167, 25 March 1957; Consolidated versions of the Treaty on European Union and the Treaty on the Functioning of the European Union, 7 June 2016, OJ C202/1.

[22] ILC, Articles on Responsibility of International Organizations, Yearbook of the International Law Commission, 2011, vol. II, Part Two.

[23] Vienna Convention on the Law of Treaties, 155 UNTS 331, 22 May 1969.

[24] See Violeta Moreno-Lax, 'The Axiological Emancipation of a (Non-) Principle: Autonomy, International Law and the EU Legal Order' in Sacha Garben and Inge Govaere (eds), *The Interface Between EU and International Law* (Oxford, Hart Publishing, 2019); Enzo Cannizzaro, 'The Neo-Monism of the European Legal Order' in Enzo Cannizzaro, Paolo Palchetti and Ramses A Wessel (eds), *International Law as Law of the European Union* (Leiden, Brill, 2012).

rootedness in the international legal order[25] and the protection of the integrity and autonomy of the EU legal order.[26]

From the perspective of international refugee and human rights law, however, the autonomy of EU law seems rather limited. First, it is now well established that in the exercise of its powers, 'the EU is bound to observe international law in its entirety, including not only the rules and principles of general and customary international law but also the provisions of international conventions that are binding on it'.[27] The EU is bound by international refugee and human rights law as a matter of both treaty and customary international law. Second, international law is deeply entrenched in the structure of EU law, and as such, it binds the EU, its institutions, and Member States. The EU is bound, by the very Treaty by which it was established, to adopt all measures necessary to enable its Member States to fulfil their international obligations.[28] Finally, EU institutions are committed to respecting fundamental (human) rights as general principles of EU law.[29]

The interaction between EU law and international human rights law can be considered from two perspectives: a formal one that is directly reflective of the sources of obligations; or a 'substantive' one that cuts across the distinction by source.[30] The following sections are organised following the formal distinction among sources, but the analysis is developed according to the substantive interaction between them.

i. The EU Human Rights Obligations and Treaty Law

According to Article 216 of the TFEU, agreements concluded by the Union are binding upon its institutions and Member States.[31] As such, treaties entered into by the EU are an integral part of the Union legal order.[32] In addition, various legal instruments of primary and secondary EU law explicitly endorse relevant human rights and refugee law treaties, inferring their applicability to the EU and its Member States.

[25] See, eg, Case C-162/96, *Racke*, 16 June 1998, ECLI:EU:C:1998:293, para 45; Joined cases C-402/05 P and C-415/05 P, *Kadi and Al Barakaat*, 16 January 2008, ECLI:EU:C:2008:461, para 291; Case C-308/06, *Intertanko*, 3 June 2008, ECLI:EU:C:2008:312, para 51; Case C-366/10, *Air Transport Association of America (ATAA)*, 21 December 2011, ECLI:EU:C:2011:864, para 123; CJEU, *Inuit Tapiriit Kanatami*, Case T-526/10, 25 April 2013, ECLI:EU:T:2013:215, para. 112.

[26] *Opinion 2/13*, 18 December 2014, ECLI:EU:C:2014:2454, paras 170 and 174.

[27] *ATAA* (n 25) para 123; *Inuit Tapiriit Kanatami* (n 25) para 112; *Western Sahara Campaign UK*, Case C-266/16, 27 February 2018, EU:C:2018:118, para 47.

[28] See: Case T-315/01, *Kadi v Council and Commission*, 21 September 2005, ECLI:EU:T:2005:332 para 204.

[29] *Stauder*, Case 29-69, 12 November 1969, ECLI:EU:C:1969:57.

[30] See: Ziegler (n 20).

[31] Art 216(2) TFEU.

[32] Case 181/73, *Haegeman*, 30 April 1973, ECLI:EU:C:1974:41, para 5; Case 12/86, *Demirel*, 30 September 1987, ECLI:EU:C:1987:400, para 7; Case C-135/10, *Società Consortile Fonografici*, 15 March 2012, ECLI:EU:C:2012:140, para 39.

The direct effect of international law on EU law implies that 'the validity of an act of the European Union may be affected by the fact that it is incompatible with such rules of international law'.[33] Yet, the fact that international law can permeate EU law does not mean that it is self-executing. Within the framework of its jurisdiction under the treaties, the CJEU has the power to determine 'what effect the provisions of the agreement are to have in the internal legal order of the contracting parties'.[34] In order to be accorded direct effect, international treaties are subject to fulfilling three conditions: first, the EU must be bound by the treaty in question; second, the 'nature and broad logic' of a treaty must not hinder its direct applicability; and third, the relevant provision must be sufficiently clear, precise and unconditional to be directly applicable.[35]

Currently, the EU is a party to one international human rights treaty: the Convention on the Rights of Persons with Disabilities.[36] At the regional level, beyond the prolonged negotiations to accede to the ECHR, which is a legal obligation for the EU under Article 6(2) TEU, the EU has acceded to the Istanbul Convention.[37] The possibility of joining other treaties is limited, as human rights treaties have been traditionally open only to state membership, and the EU has considered itself to lack the competence to become party to such agreements.[38] This gap has been noted for decades, and after numerous setbacks, it has also become part of the political and legal agenda of the EU.[39] On the one hand, the Lisbon Treaty stipulated that the EU should accede to the ECHR – albeit with the caveat that the competences of the EU should not be affected;[40] on the other hand, Protocol No 14 to the ECHR provided for such a possibility within the ECHR legal framework.[41] However, the Draft Agreement on the Accession of the EU to the ECHR, presented by the two institutions in 2013, was subsequently held incompatible with EU law.[42] This step back postponed EU accession to the

[33] *ATAA* (n 25) para 51.

[34] Case C-149/96, *Portuguese Republic v Council*, 23 November 1999, ECLI:EU:C:1999:574, para 34; *ATAA* (n 25) para 49.

[35] *Intertanko* (n 25), paras 44–45; *ATAA* (n 25) paras 52–54.

[36] Convention on the Rights of Persons with Disabilities, 2515 UNTS 313, December 2006. The EU, however, has not ratified the Optional Protocol to the CRPD. Optional Protocol to the Convention on the Rights of Persons with Disabilities, 2518 UNTS 28313 December 2006.

[37] Council of Europe Convention on preventing and combating violence against women and domestic violence, 11 May 2011, ETS 210; Council Decision (EU) 2023/1076 [2023] OJ L143/4; Council Decision (EU) 2023/1075 OJ L [2023] 143/1.

[38] See, *mutatis mutandis*, *Opinion 2/94*, 28 March 1996, ECLI:EU:C:1996:140, paras 26–28 and 34–36.

[39] See Rick Lawson, 'Human Rights: The Best Is Yet to Come: Article I-7 and Part II Draft Convention' (2005) 1 *European Constitutional Law Review* 27; Paul Craig, 'EU Accession to the ECHR: Competence, Procedure and Substance' (2013) 36 *Fordham International Law Journal* 1114; Sionaidh Douglas-Scott, 'Autonomy and Fundamental Rights: The ECJ's Opinion 2/13 on Accession of the EU to the ECHR' [2016] *Swedish European Law Journal.*

[40] Art 6(2), TEU.

[41] Art 17, Protocol No 14 amending the control system of the Convention, CETS No 194, 13 May 2004.

[42] Draft Agreement on the Accession of the European Union to the Convention for the Protection of Human Rights and Fundamental Freedoms, CM(2013) 93 add1, 9 July 2013; *Opinion 2/13* (n 26).

ECHR to a distant future.[43] In 2019, however, the European Commission informed the Secretary-General of the Council of Europe that the EU was ready to resume the negotiations, which are still ongoing.[44]

The EU's international obligations can also originate from the functional succession of its Member States' obligations. This was famously the case for the GATT.[45] However, the CJEU subsequently adopted a narrower approach allowing for the EU succession into the obligations of Member States only where the EU 'assumed, and thus had transferred to it, all the powers previously exercised by the Member States that fall within the convention in question'.[46] This position, which has virtually ruled out EU succession into the human rights obligations of Member States, has been criticised by the scholarship.[47] The CJEU is, however, the only judicial body competent to adjudicate on the matter.

That notwithstanding, the EU's adherence to international or regional human rights treaties remains an open possibility. This could be realised through formal accession or a unilateral declaration.[48] The first scenario would require an amendment to existing human rights treaties allowing for accession by an international organisation, introducing a similar provision to that included in the CRPD. This amendment could be an additional protocol, such as Protocol No 14 to the ECHR.[49] The same concrete result could be reached through a unilateral declaration. The ICJ has held that a sufficiently specific public declaration manifesting the will to be bound may create legal obligations.[50] The EU could thus accept to be bound by international human rights treaties. Arguably, this has been the case because various legal instruments of primary and secondary EU law explicitly endorse relevant human rights and refugee law treaties.

[43] Despite the complexity of the issues raised by Opinion 2/13, the EU accession to the ECHR was kept on the agenda. See eg: CoE, Committee of Ministers, Declaration of Copenhagen, 12–13 April 2018, para 63; European Parliament, Resolution of 12 February 2019 on the implementation of the Charter of Fundamental Rights of the European Union in the EU institutional framework (2017/2089(INI)), para 29.

[44] Joint statement by the Secretary General of the Council of Europe and the European Commission's Vice President for Values and Transparency, 29 September 2020.

[45] Joined cases 21 to 24-72, *NV International Fruit Company*, 12 December 1972, ECLI:EU:C:1972:115, paras 10–15.

[46] *ATAA* (n 25) para 63, and references therein.

[47] Henry G Schermers, 'The European Communities Bound by Fundamental Human Rights' (1990) 27 *Common Market Law Review* 249; Tawhida Ahmed and Israel de Jesús Butler, 'The European Union and Human Rights: An International Law Perspective' (2006) 17 *European Journal of International Law* 771.

[48] Israel de Jesús Butler, 'The EU and International Human Rights Law', OHCHR Regional Office for Europe (2009).

[49] Art 17, Protocol No 14 Amending the Control System of the Convention, CETS No 194, 13 May 2004.

[50] ICJ, *Nuclear Tests (Australia v France; New Zealand v France)*, Judgments dated 20 December 1974, ICJ Reports 267-8, paras 43 and 46; See also: ILC, Guiding Principles applicable to unilateral declarations of States capable of creating legal obligations, with commentaries thereto, Yearbook of the International Law Commission, 2006, vol. II, Part Two.

In this respect, the EU approach regarding the Geneva Convention Relating to the Status of Refugees (Refugee Convention) and its 1967 Protocol is emblematic.[51] Since the creation of the Common European Asylum System in the 1999 Tampere Conclusions of the European Council, it was agreed that such a system should be 'based on the full and inclusive application of the Geneva Convention'.[52] Article 78 TFEU provides that the EU common policy on asylum, subsidiary protection and temporary protection must be in accordance with the Geneva Convention, its 1967 Protocol and other relevant treaties.[53] Furthermore, Article 67 TFEU requires the Union to respect fundamental rights in establishing an area of freedom, security and justice. This implies that the EU human rights obligations extend beyond the area of the common European asylum system to cover all EU measures dealing with migration management, including border control. This commitment is further reflected in instruments of secondary EU law, such as the Qualification Directive,[54] the Asylum Procedures Directive[55] and the Dublin Regulation.[56] With particular regard to the common immigration policy, the Member States in implementing the SBC are mandated to comply with 'relevant international law', including the Refugee Convention;[57] similarly, the Frontex Regulation requires the agency to act in accordance with relevant international law, including the refugee Convention and the Convention on the Rights of the Child.[58] The EU capacity to accept to be bound by international obligations derives from its international legal personality, that is, from the powers conferred on the organisation (in express or implied terms). It follows that in so far as the constitutive treaties authorise the organisation to do so, the EU can be bound by unilateral declarations.[59]

A further way in which international law penetrates EU law is through the CJEU's consistent interpretation. Where the EU is bound by an international treaty, the CJEU has a duty of harmonious interpretation of EU rules in conformity with the agreement in question.[60] In cases where the EU is not formally bound by an international treaty, but where it nevertheless implements aspects of it due to Member States' international obligations, the CJEU has generally interpreted EU law measures in conformity with the international rule they are (indirectly) implementing. So, although not formally binding on the EU, human rights and

[51] Case C-443/14 and C-444/14, *Alo and Osso*, 1 March 2016, EU:C:2016:127, para 30; Case C-720/17, *Mohammed Bilali*, 23 May 2019, ECLI:EU:C:2019:448, para 54.

[52] Council of the European Union, Presidency Conclusions, Tampere European Council 15 and 16 October 1999, para 13.

[53] See Case C-369/17, *Ahmed*, 13 September 2018, EU:C:2018:713, para 37; *Alo and Osso* (n 51) para 30; *Mohammed Bilali* (n 51) para 54.

[54] Art 21, Directive (EU) 2011/95 [2011] OJ L 337/9.

[55] Arts 9(3), 28, 35, 38, 39(4), 41, Directive (EU) 2013/32 [2013] OJ L 180/60.

[56] Recital 3, Regulation (EU) 604/2013 [2013] OJ L 180.

[57] Art 4, SBC.

[58] Art 3(1)(b), 10(1), 36(2), 48(1), 80(1), 82(3), Annex 5(3)(b), Regulation (EU) 2019/1896 [2019] OJ L 295.

[59] On this point, see the Opinion of AG Sharpston in *Parliament (C-103/12) and Commission (C-165/12) v Council*, Joined Cases C-103/12 and C-165/12, 15 May 2014, ECLI:EU:C:2014:334, paras 86 ss.

[60] Joined Cases C-335/11 and C-337/11, *HK Denmark*, 11 April 2013, ECLI:EU:C:2013:222, para 32.

refugee law treaties have played a relatively important role within EU law by means of harmonious interpretation.[61] In that respect, the ECHR has been held to bear special significance.[62] In contrast to this tradition of consistent or harmonious interpretation, the CJEU has at times also found itself not competent to interpret international treaties to which the EU is not (formally) a party, such as the Refugee Convention.[63] This position is not constant in the jurisprudence of the Court.[64] Yet, it contributes to cast some doubts on the role that the CJEU can play in giving concrete effect to international law within the EU legal system.

ii. The EU Human Rights Obligations and Customary International Law

Unlike other sources of legal obligation, such as treaties, which states must ratify or accede to be bound by their terms, customary international law may emerge without the express consent of its addressees.[65] But is the EU, as an 'international legal experiment',[66] bound by customary international law?

In the *WHO-Egypt* Advisory Opinion, the ICJ clarified that '[i]nternational organizations are subjects of international law and, as such, are bound by any obligations incumbent upon them under general rules of international law, under their constitutions or under international agreements to which they are parties'.[67] The ICJ's reference to general rules of international law appears somehow ambiguous. This vagueness is often resolved by reference to customary international law. However, this interpretation has been questioned on two different levels. First, if the Court meant to refer to customary international law, it would probably have directly done so. Second, the concept of customary international law is closely linked to the community from which it emerges and to which it applies, which is the community of states. Two interpretative pathways are thus open: one would lead to the inclusion of non-state actors, such as the EU and other international organisations, in the international community. This would require, however, an additional step in the reasoning that was not made at that time by the ICJ. The second way entails applying customary international law to

[61] See, eg, Case C-244/06, *Dynamic Medien*, 14 February 2008, ECLI:EU:C:2008:85, paras 39–40; Joined Cases C-175, 176, 178 and 179/08, *Salahadin Abdulla and Others*, 2 March 2010, ECLI:EU:C:2010:105, para 53; Case C-73/08, *Bressol*, 13 April 2010, ECLI:EU:C:2010:181, paras 85–88.

[62] *Opinion 2/94* (n 38) para 33; *Kadi* (n 25) para 283; *Opinion 2/13* (n 26) para 37.

[63] Case C-481/13, *Qurbani*, 17 July 2014, ECLI:EU:C:2014:2101, paras 22–24.

[64] Case C-181/16, 19 June 2018, *Gnandi*, EU:C:2018:465, para 53; Joined Cases C-391/16, C-77/17 and C-78/17, *M, X and X*, 19 May 2019, ECLI:EU:C:2019:403, paras 74–75.

[65] Conclusion 2, Draft Conclusions on Identification of Customary International Law, with commentaries, Yearbook of the International Law Commission, vol II, Part Two, 2018.

[66] Bruno de Witte, 'The European Union as an International Legal Experiment', in Graine de Búrca and Joseph Weiler (eds), *The Worlds of European Constitutionalism* (Cambridge, Cambridge University Press, 2011).

[67] ICJ, *Interpretation of the Agreement of 25 March 1951 Between the WHO and Egypt*, Advisory Opinion of 20 December 1980, ICJ Reports 1980, para 37.

international organisations without their consent or participation in its creation.[68] But, again, this would clash with the consent-based conception of international law-making. These two contradictory outcomes seem to suggest that the notion of general rules of international law was probably meant to refer to something different from customary international law. In this line, Jan Klabbers suggests that international organisations are bound by *ius cogens* obligations and by secondary rules of the international legal system.[69]

At first glance, this interpretation appears very narrow but congruent with the current reality. However, the assumption that international organisations do not participate in the development of the international community and, therefore, cannot be considered as its legitimate members can be challenged on various levels. First, the recognition of their international legal personality allows international organisations to act autonomously and independently in the international sphere. Furthermore, as Klabbers observed, international organisations can be conceived as places for action or as fora for discussion.[70] Both these interpretations seem to hint at their role in the community of which they are part. Along these lines, the ILC concluded that in certain cases, the practice of international organisations also contributes to the formation of rules of customary international law, and pointed at the EU as a relevant example.[71] The EU may even supplant the practice of its Member States, 'Europeanising' their interpretations, applications and contributions to custom.[72] From this angle, the EU international engagement and its independence from Member States make it part of a 'bounded political community' which is generally but not exclusively constituted by states.[73]

Along these lines, a different interpretation of the ICJ dictum in the *Egypt-WHO* case is advanced by Guglielmo Verdirame, who argues that obligations 'under

[68] Andrew Clapham, *Human Rights Obligations of Non-State Actors* (Oxford, Oxford University Press, 2006) 28.

[69] Jan Klabbers, '(I Can't Get No) Recognition: Subjects Doctrine and the Emergence of Non-State Actors' in J Petman and J Klabbers (eds), *Nordic Cosmopolitanism: Essays in International law for Martti Koskenniemi* (Leiden, Martinus Nijhoff, 2003). The notion of secondary rules of the international legal system derives from Hart's famous distinction between primary rules that define the obligations in a legal system and secondary rules that regulate those obligations. HLA Hart, *The Concept of Law (1961)* (Joseph Raz, Penelope A Bulloch and Leslie Green eds, Oxford, Oxford University Press, 2012).

[70] Jan Klabbers, 'Two Concepts of International Organization' (2005) 2 *International Organisations Law Review* 277.

[71] ILC, Conclusion 4(2), Draft Conclusions on Identification of Customary International Law, with commentaries, Yearbook of the International Law Commission, 2018, vol II, Part Two. For further discussion, see: Odermatt (n 13) 33–58.

[72] Alessandra Gianelli, 'Customary International Law in the European Union' in Enzo Cannizzaro, Paolo Palchetti and Ramses A Wessel (eds), *International Law as Law of the European Union* (Leiden, Martinus Nijhoff, 2011).

[73] Christina Binder and Jane A Hofbauer, 'Applicability of Customary International Law to the European Union as a Sui Generis International Organization: An International Law Perspective' in Andreas Th Müller, Fernando Lusa Bordin and Francisco Pascual-Vives (eds), *The European Union and Customary International Law* (Cambridge, Cambridge University Press 2022); Jan Klabbers, 'The Sources of International Organizations Law' in Samantha Besson and Jean d'Aspremont (eds), *The Oxford Handbook on Sources of International Law* (Oxford, Oxford University Press, 2017).

general rules of international law' flow automatically from the legal personality of international organisations.[74] A second reading of the Court's opinion seems thus possible: '[i]nternational organizations are subjects of international law and, *as such*, are bound by any obligations incumbent upon them under general rules of international law'.[75] Subjecting international organisations to general rules of international law follows the approach adopted with respect to newly independent states; by virtue of their statehood and the ensuing legal personality, they were considered bound at least by general custom.[76] The very fact of being recognised as subject to international law implies subjection to the general rules of that legal system.[77]

The view that international organisations are bound by general international law by virtue of their international legal personality is, however, still subject to criticism and debate.[78] For example, it has been observed that the question about the sources of international law should be distinguished from that of international subjectivity as the capacity to bear rights and duties, for an entity's capacity to bear obligations, does not imply the existence of those obligations for that entity in the first place: it is a necessary, but not a sufficient condition for those duties to arise.[79] Moreover, the International Law Commission (ILC) held that most obligations incumbent on international organisations 'are likely to arise from the rules of the organization'.[80] This does not, however, exclude that international organisations are also bound by general rules of international law. A further, and perhaps more important, question that remains to be solved concerns the meaning of the expression 'general rules of international law' and the difference between general custom and general principles of law.[81] In this respect, Christian Tomuschat proposed the category of 'deductive customary law' comprising some general principles of

[74] Guglielmo Verdirame, *The UN and Human Rights: Who Guards the Guardians?* (Cambridge, Cambridge University Press, 2011) 71.

[75] *Interpretation of the Agreement of 25 March 1951 Between the WHO and Egypt* (n 67) para 37, emphasis added.

[76] For further discussion and references, see Fernando Lusa Bordin, *The Analogy between States and International Organizations* (Cambridge, Cambridge University Press, 2018) 80–81.

[77] Olivier de Schutter, 'Human Rights and the Rise of International Organisations: The Logic of Sliding Scales in the Law International Responsibility' in J Wouters and others (eds), *Accountability for Human Rights Violations by International Organizations* (Antwerp, Intersentia, 2011); Eyal Benvenisti, *The Law of Global Governance* (Leiden, Brill, 2014) 119.

[78] See eg August Reinisch, 'General Reflections on International Organizations Adapting to a Rapidly Changing World' in *Proceedings of the Annual Meeting* (American Society of International Law 2015) 285; Klabbers (n 73).

[79] Samantha Besson, 'The Sources of International Human Rights Law: How General is General International Law?' in Samantha Besson and Jean d'Aspremont (eds), *The Oxford Handbook on Sources of International Law* (Oxford, Oxford University Press, 2017).

[80] ILC, Articles on Responsibility of International Organizations, with commentaries, Yearbook of the International Law Commission, vol II, Part Two, 2011, Commentary to Article 10, para 4.

[81] On this question literature is abundant. See, most notably: Giuseppe Sperduti, *La fonte suprema dell'ordinamento internazionale* (Milan, Giuffrè, 1946); Prosper Weil, 'Towards Relative Normativity in International Law' (1983) 77 *American Journal of International Law* 413; Bruno Simma and Philip Alston, 'Sources of Human Rights Law: Custom, Jus Cogens, and General Principles, The' (1988) 12 *Australian Yearbook of International Law* 82.

international law, refined by practice, which are essential for the constitutional foundations of the international community.[82] But, again, significant divergences and uncertainties persist about which international law rules bind international organisations.[83]

All in all, one may be tempted to conclude that the applicability of customary law to international organisations raises more questions than answers. Nevertheless, the indeterminacy surrounding the applicability of customary international law to international organisations is delimited by two basic caveats.[84] First, international organisations can be bound by customary internal rules arising from their well-established practice. For the present purposes, this practice results from the EU's manifold legal and non-legal commitments to respect and promote human rights. A practice confirmed in the jurisprudence of the CJEU, which recognised on various occasions the EU's duty to comply with rules of customary international law.[85] Second, the applicability of *jus cogens* norms to international organisations, including the EU albeit its special features, is unquestionably regarded as reflecting the current state of international law.[86]

Ultimately, it can be cautiously concluded that both customary international law and *jus cogens* represent legal obligations binding the EU. This is relevant for our purposes, namely with regard to the principle of *non-refoulement*, which has been recognised as a norm of customary international law if not *jus cogens*.[87] As further detailed below, many other customary international law norms are

[82] Christian Tomuschat, 'Obligations Arising for States without or against Their Will' (1993) 241 *Collected Courses of the Hague Academy of International Law* 195, 293–304; Christian Tomuschat, 'International Law: Ensuring the Survival of Mankind on the Eve of a New Century General Course on Public International Law' (1999) 281 *Collected Courses of the Hague Academy of International Law* 9. Cf: Robert Kolb, 'Selected Problems in the Theory of Customary International Law' (2003) 50 *Netherlands International Law Review* 119; Stefan Talmon, 'Determining Customary International Law: The ICJ's Methodology between Induction, Deduction and Assertion' (2015) 26 *European Journal of International Law* 417.

[83] See generally Kristina Daugirdas, 'How and Why International Law Binds International Organizations' (2016) 57 *Harvard International Law Journal* 325.

[84] See Vincent Chetail, 'The International Organization for Migration and the Duty to Protect Migrants: Revisiting the Law of International Organizations' in J Klabbers (ed), *Cambridge Companion to International Organizations Law* (Cambridge, Cambridge University Press, 2022).

[85] Case C-286/90, *Poulsen*, 24 November 1992, ECLI:EU:C:1992:453, para 9; Case T-115/94, *Opel Austria*, 15 July 1998, ECLI:EU: T:1998:166, para 90; *Racke* (n 25) paras 45–46; Case C-266/16, *Western Sahara Campaign UK*, 27 February 2018, ECLI:EU:C:2018:118, para 47.

[86] See: Arts 26, 41 and 42, ARIO.

[87] See eg, IAmCommHR, *The Haitian Centre for Human Rights et al v United States*, Case No 10.675, 13 March 1997, para 167; IAmCtHR, *Rights and Guarantees of Children in the Context of Migration and/or in Need of International Protection*, Advisory Opinion OC-21/14, 19 August 2014, para 211; IAmCtHR, *The institution of asylum, and its recognition as a human right under the Inter-American System of Protection*, Advisory Opinion OC- 25/18, (Ser A) No 25, 30 May 2018, para 179; For doctrinal acknowledgements, see most notably: Jean Allain, 'The Jus Cogens Nature of Non-refoulement' (2001) 13 *International Journal of Refugee Law* 533; Elihu Lauterpacht and Daniel Bethlehem, 'The Scope and Content of the Principle of Non-Refoulement: Opinion' in Erika Feller, Volker Türk and Frances Nicholson (eds), *Refugee Protection in International Law* (Cambridge, Cambridge University Press, 2003); Aoife Duffy, 'Expulsion to Face Torture? Non-Refoulement in International Law' (2008) 20 *International Journal of Refugee Law* 373; Seline Trevisanut, 'The Principle of Non-Refoulement and

relevant for protecting migrants, including the prohibition of collective expulsion, the right to leave, and the principle of non-discrimination.[88]

Having determined that both customary international law and *jus cogens* norms are binding upon the EU, it is now necessary to look at their judicial application. As in many domestic legal systems, the CJEU's approach is to apply customary international law directly.[89] However, in *ATAA*, the Court restricted the possibility of individual complaints based on customary international law, introducing a set of restrictive criteria according to which:[90] first, the rule relied upon should be capable of calling into question the competence of the EU to adopt the disputed act; second, the act in question should be capable of affecting individual rights or obligations under EU law; and third, as 'a principle of customary international law does not have the same degree of precision as a provision of an international agreement', the EU institutions should have made 'manifest errors of assessment' in applying customary international law.[91] This limits the application of customary international law within the EU legal system but does not imply that other international bodies could, in case they were competent to do so, decide on the application of customary international law to the EU in a less restrictive way.

iii. Soft Law and the EU Human Right Obligations: Exploring Boundaries

As a doctrinal creation, soft law is not a definite and uncontested category of norms. Article 38(1) of the Statute of the ICJ does not include any reference to

the De-Territorialization of Border Control at Sea International Law and Practice' [2014] *Leiden Journal of International Law* 661; Walter Kälin, Martina Caroni and Lukas Heim, 'Article 33, Para. 1 (Prohibition of Expulsion or Return ("Refoulement")/Défense d'expulsion et de Refoulement)' in Andreas Zimmermann, Jonas Dörschner and Felix Machts (eds), *The 1951 Convention Relating to the Status of Refugees and Its 1967 Protocol: A Commentary* (Oxford, Oxford University Press, 2011) 1343–46; Cathryn Costello and Michelle Foster, 'Non-Refoulement as Custom and Jus Cogens? Putting the Prohibition to the Test' in *Netherlands Yearbook of International Law* (The Hague, T.M.C. Asser Press, 2016); Violeta Moreno-Lax, *Accessing Asylum in Europe: Extraterritorial Border Controls and Refugee Rights under EU Law* (Oxford, Oxford University Press, 2017) 247–336; Vincent Chetail, *International Migration Law* (Oxford, Oxford University Press, 2019) 119–24; Guy S Goodwin-Gill and Jane McAdam, *The Refugee in International Law* 300–306 (Oxford, Oxford University Press, 2021). Contra: Kay Hailbronner, 'Non-Refoulement and "Humanitarian" Refugees: Customary International Law or Wishful Legal Thinking?', in David A Martin (ed) *The New Asylum Seekers: Refugee Law in the 1980s* (Dordrecht, Springer, 1988); Jean-Yves Carlier, 'Droit d'asile et Des Réfugiés : De La Protection Aux Droits' (2008) 332 *Collected Courses of the Hague Academy of International Law* 123–30; James C Hathaway, *The Rights of Refugees under International Law* (Cambridge, Cambridge University Press, 2021) 435–64.

[88] For a complete analysis, see Chetail (n 87) 76–157.

[89] *Opel Austria* (n 85), para 90; *Racke* (n 25) paras 45–46. For further discussion, see Andreas Th Müller, 'The Direct Effect of Customary International Law: The "Treaty Analogy" and Its Limits' in Andreas Th Müller, Fernando Lusa Bordin and Francisco Pascual-Vives (eds), *The European Union and Customary International Law* (Cambridge, Cambridge University Press, 2022).

[90] *ATAA* (n 25), para 107.

[91] ibid, para 110.

soft law as a possible source of international law. Some would say that soft law is a misleading concept, as it implies that law can come in varying degrees of bindingness, thus blurring the distinction between law and politics instead of clarifying legal norms.[92] Furthermore, soft law is generally drafted in closed negotiations and so lacks democratic scrutiny. Most importantly, the non-binding nature of soft law implies that its violations cannot give rise to legal responsibility. At best, the breach of a soft law rule could trigger forms of 'soft responsibility' such as administrative or political accountability, resulting in 'soft sanctions' such as disciplinary measures.

All these shortcomings, however, do not necessarily imply the inconsequentiality of soft law.[93] Soft law may support the formation of binding legal norms, as in the case of customary law, and it may inform the interpretation of those norms. For the present purposes, a relevant example of such an evolution is the European Charter on Fundamental Rights (CFR), signed as a non-binding document and transformed into a binding legal instrument with the entry into force of the Lisbon Treaty.[94]

Soft law may also perform an independent normative function as an alternative to hard law. In fact, '[n]onbinding norms and informal social norms can be effective and offer a flexible and efficient way to order responses to common problems. They are not law, and they do not need to be in order to influence conduct in the desired manner'.[95] Most recently, the EU participated in the negotiation of the Global Compact on Safe and Orderly Migration and the Global Compact on Refugees.[96] The EU, as a regional group, has been granted standing status in order to participate in the negotiations and the conclusion of the Global Compacts, and the Commission took the lead in the drafting process.[97] Notwithstanding the contradictory stances of EU Member States,[98] the Global Compacts provide a reference framework to critically assess EU migration policies in light of the non-binding commitments of UN Member States.[99]

[92] Jan Klabbers, 'The Undesirability of Soft Law' (1998) 67 *Nordic Journal of International Law* 381; Jean d'Aspremont, 'Softness in International Law: A Self-Serving Quest for New Legal Materials' (2008) 19 *European Journal of International Law* 1075.

[93] Among the vast literature, see: Christine Chinkin, 'The Challenge of Soft Law: Development and Change in International Law' (1989) 38 *The International and Comparative Law Quarterly* 850; Kenneth W Abbott and Duncan Snidal, 'Hard and Soft Law in International Governance' (2000) 54 *International Organization* 421; with particular regard to the impact of soft law on international migration law, see most notably: Chetail (n 87) 281–300.

[94] Fabien Terpan, 'Soft Law in the European Union – The Changing Nature of EU Law' (2015) 21 *European Law Journal* 68.

[95] Dinah Shelton, 'Normative Hierarchy in International Law' (2006) 100 *The American Journal of International Law* 291.

[96] Global Compact for Safe, Orderly and Regular Migration, UN doc A/RES/73/195, 19 December 2018; Global Compact on Refugees, UN doc A/RES/73/151, 17 December 2018.

[97] See Tamás Molnár, 'The EU Shaping the Global Compact for Safe, Orderly and Regular Migration: The Glass Half Full or Half Empty?' (2020) 16 *International Journal of Law in Context* 321.

[98] Pauline Melin, 'The Global Compact for Migration: Lessons for the Unity of EU Representation' (2019) 21 *European Journal of Migration and Law* 194.

[99] Sergio Carrera and Roberto Cortinovis, 'The EU's Role in Implementing the UN Global Compact on Refugees' [2019] CEPS Policy contribution No 2018-04.

In addition the EU produces a vast number of soft law documents that play a pivotal role in designing the European approach to the management of migration. Soft law instruments generally include human rights clauses, and where those clauses are defective or absent the instruments have been strongly criticised.[100] The Global Approach to Migration and Mobility (GAMM),[101] followed by regional dialogues and less formal types of interstate cooperation, such as the New Partnership Framework with Third countries,[102] or the EU- Türkiye deal,[103] are good examples in this sense.[104]

Frontex regularly employs soft law instruments to ensure that its activities fully respect migrants' rights. As already discussed, the agency adopted a Fundamental Rights Strategy,[105] a Code of Conduct for return operations,[106] and a Code of Conduct applicable to all persons participating in Frontex operational activities.[107] The most recent version of the Fundamental Rights Strategy includes several important developments concerning the agency's human rights compliance. For instance, it covers the responsibilities of participants in Frontex's operational activities and specifies the 'proactive' role that the agency should play in ensuring respect for, protection and promotion of fundamental rights. An Action Plan complementing the Strategy further develops the operational aspects of the implementation of the EIBM and articulates specific outputs, activities and indicators of fundamental rights.

While the Codes of Conduct are usually part of the Agency's operational plans and, therefore, could be considered legally binding, Frontex's Fundamental Rights Strategy is a non-binding instrument. Its violations may be the object of an internal complaint procedure resulting in administrative or disciplinary sanctions, which, however, cannot directly entail legal responsibility or sanction. Yet, despite their lack of legal enforceability, the commitments expressed in the Strategy reflect, to a large extent, the legal obligations binding on the agency and

[100] See, eg, Report of the Special Rapporteur on the human rights of migrants: Banking on mobility over a generation: follow-up to the regional study on the management of the external borders of the European Union and its impact on the human rights of migrants, 8 May 2015, A/HRC/29/36, para 38.

[101] Commission, Communication from the Commission to the European Parliament, the Council, the European Economic and Social Committee and the Committee of the Regions, The Global Approach to Migration and Mobility, COM (2011)743, 18 November 2011.

[102] Commission, Communication from the Commission to the European Parliament, the European Council, the Council and the European Investment Bank on establishing a new Partnership Framework with third countries under the European Agenda on Migration, COM (2016) 385, 7 June 2016.

[103] European Council, EU-Turkey statement, 18 March 2016, www.consilium.europa.eu/en/press/press-releases/2016/03/18/eu-turkey-statement/.

[104] François Crépeau and Idil Atak, 'Global Migration Governance: Avoiding Commitments on Human Rights, Yet Tracing a Course for Cooperation' (2016) 34 *Netherlands Quarterly of Human Rights* 113.

[105] Art 80, Regulation 2019/1896; Frontex, Management Board Decision 12/2021 adopting the Fundamental Rights Strategy, 14 February 2021.

[106] Frontex, Code of Conduct for return operations and return interventions coordinated or organised by Frontex, 2018.

[107] Frontex, Code of Conduct applicable to all persons participating in Frontex operational activities, 2017.

its Member States under both international and EU law. For example, the Strategy restates that Frontex and the Member States must comply with relevant national, EU and international law.[108] In this sense, the legal relevance of the Strategy rests on its interpretative guidance regarding binding legal obligations.[109]

From another perspective, the Strategy and its Action Plan create the expectation that Frontex and the Member States would respect the specific commitments expressed therein. To be sure, on this matter, such an expectation cannot be equated to a legal obligation.[110] Nonetheless, a reading in line with the principle of good faith would, at any rate, require a duty to respect soft law commitments to the extent that they specify legally binding obligations.[111]

iv. Human Rights as Fundamental Rights in the EU Legal Order

Human rights permeate the EU legal order in a number of ways: they inform EU law as general principles (deduced from international human rights law and the constitutional traditions of Member States), they are foundational elements of primary EU legislation and they bind the EU in its participation in the life of the international community.

Human rights have been incorporated in the EU legal framework first as general principles of EU law, then as fundamental rights enshrined in the CFR. The 'Europeanisation' of human rights as fundamental rights substantively borrows from the international regimes of human rights law, embedding its guarantees in the EU law.[112] While the aborted draft of the European Political Community Treaty included a specific reference to the ECHR, the EU funding Treaties omitted any allusion to human rights.[113] The CJEU, however, gradually incorporated the protection of fundamental (human) rights as general principles of EU law.[114]

Fundamental rights as general principles of EU law derive from both the constitutional traditions of Member States and from their international human rights obligations.[115] Yet their incorporation into the EU legal system is not

[108] Frontex, Fundamental Rights Strategy, 4–6.

[109] Chinkin (n 93); Chetail (n 87) 288–89.

[110] Tadeusz Gruchalla-Wesierski, 'A Framework for Understanding Soft Law' (1984) 30 *McGill Law Journal* 37, 62; Chetail (n 87) 297.

[111] Institut de Droit International, Textes internationaux ayant une portée juridique dans les relations mutuelles entre leurs auteurs et textes qui en sont dépourvus, Rapporteur: Michel Virally, Session de Cambridge, 1983, 6.

[112] Moreno-Lax (n 87) 214–15; Piet Eeckhout, 'Human Rights and the Autonomy of EU Law: Pluralism or Integration?' (2013) 66 *Current Legal Problems* 169.

[113] Arts 3 and 45, Draft Treaty Embodying the Statute of the European Community, Information and Official Documents of the Constitutional Committee, October 1952–April 1953. See also: Gráinne De Búrca, 'The Road Not Taken: The European Union as a Global Human Rights Actor' (2011) 105 *American Journal of International Law* 649.

[114] Case 4/73, *Nold*, 16 November 1974, ECLI:EU:C:1974:51, para 13.

[115] See generally: Katja S Ziegler and Aristi Volou, 'Human Rights and General Principles: Beyond the EU Charter of Fundamental Rights' in Katja S Ziegler, Päivi J Neuvonen and Violeta Moreno Lax (eds), *Research Handbook on General Principles in EU Law* (Cheltenham, Edward Elgar, 2022).

automatic.[116] According to the CJEU, the only parameter to decide on the validity of EU law measures is EU law itself.[117] Thus, while incorporating the protection of human rights into the EU legal order, the Court has constantly endorsed the autonomy of EU law from both the domestic legal systems of Member States and that of public international law.[118] The CJEU has thus filtered the norms that could be considered as general principles of EU law following a 'selective approach', oscillating between the identification of minimum standards to the more abstract recognition of commonly shared notions.[119]

With regard to international human rights treaties of EU Member States, while they are not directly binding upon the EU, they are considered useful guidelines for the application of fundamental rights protection within the EU.[120] The ECHR is the most relevant of these treaties and bears 'special significance' within the EU legal framework.[121] In this line, under Article 6(3) TEU, fundamental rights, as guaranteed by the ECtHR and as they result from the constitutional traditions common to the Member States, constitute general principles of EU law.[122] The jurisprudence of the CJEU does not provide a clear interpretation of this provision. On the one hand, in some cases, the Court, while recognising its special significance, has granted the ECHR the same status as other human rights international treaties.[123] On the other hand, the Court has referred to the ECHR as forming part of the general principles of EU law.[124] This has been nuanced by Opinion 2/13, which asserted that 'as the EU has not acceded to the ECHR, the latter does not constitute a legal instrument which has been formally incorporated into the legal order of the EU'.[125] Nonetheless, the fact that the rights enshrined in the ECHR are formally recognised as general principles of EU law should not be overlooked.[126] Indeed, the wording of Article 6(3) is clear: the ECHR, through the formal intermediary of general principles, is part of the EU legal order. A parallel could be drawn with the Refugee Convention, explicitly incorporated in EU law through Article 78 TFEU. Both Article 6(3) TEU

[116] Case 11/70, *Internationale Handelsgesellschaft*, 17 December 1970, ECLI:EU:C:1970:114, para 4.
[117] ibid, paras 3–4.
[118] Moreno-Lax (n 24).
[119] Katja S Ziegler, 'Piecing the Puzzle Together Beyond Pluralism and Autonomy: Systemic Harmonization as a Paradigm for the Interaction of EU Law and International Law' (2016) 35 *Yearbook of European Law* 667.
[120] *Nold* (n 114).
[121] *Opinion 2/94* (n 38) para 33; Case C-94/00, *Roquette Frères*, 22 October 2002, ECLI:EU:C:2002:603, para 25.
[122] Consolidated versions of the Treaty on European Union, 7 June 2016, OJ C202/1.
[123] *Nold* (n 114) paras 12–13; *Kadi* (n 25) paras 283–84; *Opinion 2/13* (n 26) para 180.
[124] Case C-465/07, *Elgafaji*, 17 February 2009, ECLI:EU:C:2009:94, para 28.
[125] *Opinion 2/13* (n 26) para 179.
[126] Bruno De Witte, 'The EU and the International Legal Order: The Case of Human Rights' in Malcolm Evans and Panos Koutrakos (eds), *Beyond the Established Legal Orders. Policy Interconnections between the EU and the Rest of the World* (Oxford, Hart Publishing, 2011) 129–31.

and 78 TFEU recognise an obligation to act in accordance with an international legal instrument to which the EU is not yet a party.[127]

Beyond the judicial recognition of fundamental rights as general principles of EU law, they have also been included in several primary and secondary EU laws, thus strengthening the EU political and legal commitment to their protection.[128] The objective of the CFR was to reaffirm and strengthen the protection of fundamental rights

> as they result, in particular, from the constitutional traditions and international obligations common to the Member States, the Treaty on European Union, the Community Treaties, the [ECHR], the Social Charters … and the case law of the [CJEU] and of the [ECtHR].[129]

While a certain degree of innovation was also introduced by the Charter,[130] the objective was to consolidate already existing guarantees, making them 'more visible'.[131]

Whereas, as a matter of international law, the Charter cannot be considered *strictu sensu* a treaty, as a matter of EU law, under Article 6 TEU, it has acquired the same legal values as the EU's founding treaties. Furthermore, under Article 52(3) of the Charter, as long as it includes rights that correspond to those guaranteed by the ECHR, the meaning and scope of those rights are to be interpreted as the same as those laid down by that Convention. Union law can, however, provide more extensive protection. This provision is intended to guarantee the 'necessary consistency' between the Charter and the ECHR[132] while avoiding 'regressive constructions of fundamental rights protection below the ECHR threshold'.[133]

EU fundamental rights grant equal if not better protection than the ECHR minimum standards.[134] In order words, while the EU enjoys the autonomy not to accede to the ECHR, it does not enjoy any autonomy to offer lesser protection to the rights enshrined in that Convention.[135] Similarly, the CFR should be interpreted consistently with other relevant treaties to which EU primary law refers and to which the EU Member States are parties, including the Refugee Convention and relevant international human rights conventions.[136]

[127] Roberta Mungianu, *Frontex and Non-Refoulement: The International Responsibility of the EU* (Cambridge, Cambridge University Press, 2016) 113.

[128] Eg Arts 2, 3 and 21 TEU.

[129] Preamble, Explanations relating to the Charter of Fundamental Rights, OJ C 303, 14 December 2007.

[130] Preamble to the CFR, para 4.

[131] ibid.

[132] Explanations, Art 52, para 3.

[133] Moreno-Lax (n 87) 230.

[134] ibid 232–33.

[135] See, *mutatis mutandis*, Steve Peers, 'Taking Rights Away? Limitations and Derogations' in Steve Peers and Angela Ward (eds), *The European Union Charter of Fundamental Rights* (Oxford, Hart Publishing, 2004) 171.

[136] Art 53, CFR.

B. The International Obligations of Member States

International institutions belong 'to all members, and to none'.[137] With this paradox, Lorimer identified an existential contradiction in the life of international organisations. International organisations are created by and depend on their Member States, yet they are also independent of them.

With the increasing integration into regional and specialised international organisations, states delegate powers and functions as well as a degree of autonomy to supranational organisations to execute those functions. Yet, this delegation of powers and functions does not affect states' international obligations. It is well established that states may not relieve themselves of obligations they have assumed through existing treaties and conceal their responsibility behind the organisational veil.[138]

The Member States of the EU remain responsible for ensuring their compliance with the other international obligations they have undertaken, including the UN Charter, the Refugee Convention and human rights treaties. As a consequence, the EU's expanded competences in the field of migration management do not exclude Member States' responsibility with regard to these international treaties. In implementing the EIBM, the EU (via Frontex) and its Member States should respect the international obligations binding the latter. Furthermore, Member States remain responsible for breaches of EU law. This implies that violations of EU fundamental rights, as included in the CFR or as general principles of EU law, entail the liability of Member States under Union law.[139]

III. The Nature of the EU and the Members States' Obligations

The foregoing discussion reveals that multiple international obligations bind the EU and its Member States. These obligations imply different concrete requirements. In some situations, it might be sufficient to abstain from certain conduct to protect individuals from human rights violations. However, often this would not

[137] See: James Lorimer, *The Institutes of The Law of Nations*, vol II (Oxford, Blackwood and sons, 1883). See also, Niels Blokker, 'International Organizations and Their Members. "International Organizations Belong to All Members and to None" – Variations on a Theme' (2004) 1 *International Organizations Law Review* 139.

[138] See Art 60, Articles on Responsibility of States for Internationally Wrongful Acts, 2001, *Yearbook of the International Law Commission*, 2001, vol II, Part Two. With regard to EU Member States compliance to the ECHR, see also: ECtHR, *Bosphorus Hava Yolları Turizm ve Ticaret Anonim Şirketi v Ireland*, Appl No 45036/98, 30 June 2005, para 154; ECtHR, *Capital Bank Ad v Bulgaria*, Appl No 49429/99, 24 November 2005, para 111; ECtHR, *Waite and Kennedy v Germany*, Appl No 26083/94, 18 February 1999, para 67.

[139] See extensively: Melanie Fink, *Frontex and Human Rights: Responsibility in'multi-Actor Situations' under the ECHR and EU Public Liability Law* (Oxford, Oxford University Press, 2018) 180–316.

be enough.[140] A case in point is the duty of *non-refoulement*. Not only do states have the negative obligation to refrain from sending people to places where they might be at risk of serious human rights violations, but they also must prevent such violations by taking preventive actions.[141] Before delving into the discussion of the specific international obligations binding the EU and its Member States, the following will draw some conceptual distinctions between their positive and negative nature.

A. Due Diligence and Positive Obligations

While implementing the EIBM, the EU and its Member States are bound by positive and negative obligations. The EU and Frontex are under an obligation to ensure that fundamental rights are respected during the implementation of the EIBM generally,[142] and during Frontex operations more specifically.[143] Accordingly, the agency should be held accountable whenever its officers' actions or failure to act cause a human rights violation.[144] Member States have a duty to ensure that third parties whose action they are in a position to affect, such as the EU and its agency Frontex, do not breach their human rights obligations. This duty derives from the due diligence duty binding all states joining an international organisation whose membership might lead them to breach their human rights obligations.[145] Crucially, as a due diligence duty, this positive obligation is independent of any separate human rights obligation of the organisation.

The concept of due diligence, as developed under general international law, is closely related to the doctrine of positive human rights obligations.[146] The expression 'due diligence' is generally employed to designate a standard of conduct. Due diligence duties are obligations of means, as opposed to those of result.[147] The due

[140] Dinah Shelton and Ariel Gould, 'Positive and Negative Obligations' in Dinah Shelton (ed), *The Oxford Handbook of International Human Rights Law* (Oxford, Oxford University Press, 2013).

[141] Vincent Chetail, 'Are Refugee Rights Human Rights? An Unorthodox Questioning of the Relations between Refugee Law and Human Rights Law' in R Rubio-Marin (ed), *Human Rights and Immigration, Collected Courses of the Academy of European Law* (Oxford, Oxford University Press, 2014).

[142] Art 3, Regulation 2019/1896.

[143] ibid, Arts 38(l), 73(3) and 80.

[144] ibid, Arts 98 and 111(2).

[145] *Waite and Kennedy* (n 138) para 67.

[146] On due diligence in general international law see, most notably: Riccardo Pisillo Mazzeschi, *'Due Diligence' e Responsabilità Internazionale Degli Stati* (Milan, Giuffrè, 1989); Samantha Besson, 'La Due Diligence En Droit International' [2020] *Recueil des cours de l'Académie du droit international de La Haye* 409; Maria Monnheimer, *Due Diligence Obligations in International Human Rights Law* (Cambridge, Cambridge University Press, 2021), Alice Olliono, *Due Diligence Obligations in International Law* (Cambridge , Cambridge University Press, 2022).

[147] See Jean Combacau, 'Obligations de résultat et obligations de comportement: quelques questions et pas de réponse' in *Mélanges offerts à Paul Reuter : le droit international : unité et diversité* (Paris, Pedone, 1981); PM Dupuy, 'Reviewing the Difficulties of Codification: On Ago's Classification of Obligations of Means and Obligations of Result in Relation to State Responsibility' (1999) 10 *European Journal of International Law* 371.

diligence standard is inherent in a number of conventional and customary rules in various fields of international law.[148] Human rights law is no exception. Here, the due diligence standard helps to establish whether states have lived up to their positive obligations.[149]

The key feature of positive human rights obligations is that they require state authorities to take the necessary protective and preventive measures to safeguard the rights of individuals and to punish, investigate, or redress the harm caused.[150] International human rights tribunals and monitoring bodies have long deemed both acts and omissions to be sources of human rights violations.[151] The duty to respect and ensure human rights, like the duty to prevent their violation, not only prohibits states from breaching their international obligations, but also obliges them to take reasonable and appropriate measures to avoid the commission of human rights violations by third parties – whether private individuals,[152] states or international organisations,[153] armed opposition groups or corporations.[154] What is deemed reasonable and appropriate depends on the specific right at stake and the specific positive obligations of the duty holder – it also depends on the specific context underpinning the risks of violation and the capacities and opportunity to take action.[155] The due diligence standard emerging from general international law has contributed to conceptualising and making states' human rights obligations more concrete.[156] In sum, the standard of due diligence functions as the benchmark of positive obligations.

[148] See generally: Heike Krieger, Anne Peters and Leonhard Kreuzer (eds), *Due Diligence in the International Legal Order* (Oxford, Oxford University Press, 2020).

[149] Riccardo Pisillo Mazzeschi, 'Responsabilite de l'Etat pour violation des obligations positives relatives aux droits de l'homme' 333 (2008) *Collected Courses of the Hague Academy of International Law.*

[150] Among the abundant literature, see: Alistair R Mowbray, *The Development of Positive Obligations Under the European Convention on Human Rights by the European Court of Human Rights* (Oxford, Hart Publishing, 2004); Laurens Lavrysen, *Human Rights in a Positive State: Rethinking the Relationship Between Positive and Negative Obligations Under the European Convention on Human Rights* (Antwerp, Intersentia, 2016); Vladislava Stoyanova, *Positive Obligations under the European Convention on Human Rights: Within and Beyond Boundaries* (Oxford, Oxford University Press, 2023).

[151] See, eg, CESCR, General Comment No 3: The Nature of States Parties' Obligations, 14 December 1990, UN Doc E/1991/23, 14 December 1990, para 1; HRC, General Comment No 31: The Nature of the General Legal Obligation Imposed on States Parties to the Covenant, UN Doc CCPR/C/21/Rev.1/Add.13, 26 May 2004, paras 6 and 8; IACtHR, *Velasquez-Rodriguez*, (Ser C) No 4, 29 July 1988; ECtHR, *Case 'relating to certain aspects of the laws on the use of languages in education in Belgium' v Belgium*, 23 July 1968, para 7. For a detailed discussion, see Shelton and Gould (n 140).

[152] Thomas Gammeltoft-Hansen, *Access to Asylum: International Refugee Law and the Globalisation of Migration Control* (Cambridge, Cambridge University Press, 2011) 225–26.

[153] Cedric Ryngaert and Holly Buchanan, 'Member State Responsibility for the Acts of International Organizations' (2011) 7 *Utrecht Law Review* 131.

[154] Carla Ferstman, 'Human Rights Due Diligence Policies Applied to Extraterritorial Cooperation to Prevent "Irregular" Migration: European Union and United Kingdom Support to Libya' (2020) 21 *German Law Journal* 459.

[155] ibid.

[156] Christine Chinkin, 'Addressing Violence against Women in the Commonwealth within States' Obligations under International Law' (2014) 40 *Commonwealth Law Bulletin* 471, 579. See, however: Vladislava Stoyanova, 'Due Diligence versus Positive Obligations' in J Niemi, L Peroni and V Stoyanova (eds), *International Law and Violence Against Women: Europe and the Istanbul Convention* (Abingdon, Routledge, 2020).

B. Mitigating Risks, Ensuring Rights: Meeting Positive Obligations in the EIBM

Positive obligations extend virtually to all human rights when there is a foreseeable risk of violation, and the state or international organisation in question has the reasonable capacity to prevent or mitigate this risk. Hence, when participating in Frontex joint operations, Member States are bound to take positive and preventive measures to ensure that the principle of *non-refoulement* and, more generally, the human rights of migrants are respected and protected. Likewise, Frontex is under an obligation to ensure that human rights are guaranteed during its operations.[157] The agency's Fundamental Rights Strategy underscores its positive obligations throughout all Frontex activities.[158]

More specifically, Frontex has an obligation not to launch any activity that could lead to serious fundamental rights violations.[159] When activities entailing serious or persistent fundamental rights violations are already taking place, the agency should withdraw its financing or suspend or terminate them.[160] Accordingly, the FRO developed the 'Fundamental Rights Due Diligence Procedure' through which it provides advice to the Executive Director before they take decisions on launching a new activity or decisions to suspend, withdraw or terminate an ongoing activity.[161] Yet the requirements and the timeline of this procedure remain unclear.[162] Despite a rather vague formulation, those obligations require the agency to conduct a scrupulous fundamental rights impact assessment before funding any activity or deploying its personnel to a Member State; they also require it to constantly monitor the activities to which the agency contributes.

This logic is analogously applied to Frontex cooperation with third countries. While the first status agreements signed with third countries lacked an explicit provision in this sense,[163] the upgraded model status agreement and the most recent status agreements signed with third countries include an obligation not to launch an activity in case of fundamental rights concerns, albeit diluted with the executive director's discretion.[164]

[157] Art 80, Regulation 2019/1896.

[158] Fundamental Rights Strategy, 2021, 6 and 12.

[159] Art 46(5), Regulation 2019/1896.

[160] ibid, Art 46(4).

[161] Management Board Decision 61/2021 Adopting the Fundamental Rights Action Plan, 9 November 2021.

[162] European Ombudsman, Case OI/4/2021/MHZ, *Decision on how the European Border and Coast Guard Agency (Frontex) complies with its fundamental rights obligations and ensures accountability in relation to its enhanced responsibilities*, 17 January 2022, paras 16–25.

[163] Art 5, Status Agreement between the European Union and the Republic of Albania on actions carried out by the European Border and Coast Guard Agency in the Republic of Albania [2019] OJ L 46/3.

[164] Art 3(2), Model status agreement as referred to in Regulation (EU) 2019/1896 of the European Parliament and of the Council of 13 November 2019 on the European Border and Coast Guard and repealing Regulations (EU) No 1052/2013 and (EU) 2016/1624, COM(2021) 829, 21 December 2021;

At any rate, in *Front Polisario*, the CJEU ruled that the EU has a duty to assess carefully and impartially the impact that an agreement with third countries might have on fundamental rights.[165] Along this line, Frontex's Fundamental Rights Strategy demands it to 'identify any potential fundamental rights challenge while cooperating with non-EU countries'.[166] This should be realised through a 'due diligence assessment of fundamental rights risks and the impacts of such cooperation *prior* to entering into any formal cooperation'.[167] A fortiori, where fundamental rights concerns emerge from this assessment, cooperation should not occur.

In addition to an obligation to monitor their activities, Frontex and the Member States also have positive duties during the implementation of their joint operations. For example, along with elements necessary for carrying out a given operation, the operational plans should include concrete guidance concerning respect for fundamental rights. The training of officers deployed during Frontex joint operations should consider the human rights sensitivities of those operations, especially in the screening and debriefing phases. All participants in Frontex operational activities are required to be 'proactive in the identification of and assistance to persons in need of international protection' and persons in vulnerable situations.[168] In this context, the availability of adequate means, such as the presence of medical personnel or interpreters or cultural experts during Frontex's activities, is essential to implement positive and preventive obligations.[169]

Beyond assuring their respect and protection, Frontex should promote fundamental rights.[170] The agency's FRO should enhance fundamental rights awareness among Frontex staff, also through training and monitoring activities.[171] Yet, absent any data on the impact of these activities on the people affected, it remains unclear whether and how they concretely improved the work of border guards.[172]

Art 3(2), Agreement between the European Union and the Republic of Moldova on operational activities carried out by the European Border and Coast Guard Agency in the Republic of Moldova [2022] OJ L 91/4.

[165] Case T-512/12, *Front Polisario v Council*, 10 December 2015 ECLI:EU:T:2015:953, paras 225 and 228.

[166] Frontex Fundamental Rights Strategy, 2021, 14.

[167] ibid.

[168] Management Board Decision 12/2021 adopting the Fundamental Rights Strategy, 14 February 2021, 7.

[169] See eg, Consultative Forum Annual Report 2019, 117; FRO's Observations to return operations conducted in the 1nd Semester of 2020 (1 January–30 June 2020), 9 December 2020, 3.

[170] ibid, Arts 10(ad) and 110(1).

[171] Fundamental Rights Strategy, 2021, 16.

[172] See Management Board Decision 61/2021 adopting the Fundamental Rights Action Plan for the implementation of the Fundamental Rights Strategy, 9 November 2021. See also: Satoko Horii, 'It Is about More than Just Training: The Effect of Frontex Border Guard Training' (2012) 31 *Refugee Survey Quarterly* 158.

In addition, positive obligations entail a duty to respond to a human rights violation. While this duty binds Member States to investigate, prosecute, and punish any alleged violation occurring during a joint operation, Frontex should also monitor its activities and provide an effective and independent complaint mechanism culminating in adequate redress to the victims. As further detailed below, the agency's legal framework still appears inadequate in this respect. As a consequence, Member States could be held responsible for failure to act with due diligence. This is because Frontex's complaint mechanism does not offer protection that could be considered equivalent to what the ECHR provides.[173]

Ultimately, where the Member States contributing to Frontex's joint operations have the required level of knowledge and the capacity to prevent human rights violations, the state authorities' failure to take preventive measures and supervise their implementation could engage the Member States' responsibility for breach of their positive duties.[174]

IV. The Protection of Migrant Rights in the Implementation of the EIBM

The following sections will examine the substantive international obligations binding the EU and its Member States in the context of their border control activities. The most relevant human rights at stake during EU border control measures will be analysed through the lenses of EU and international human rights law. The main point of reference for the sections that follow will be universal human rights treaties and the ECHR, which binds all Schengen Member States and will (hopefully in a not-too-distant future) become a binding source of legal obligations also for the EU and its agency Frontex.

A. The Prohibition of *Refoulement*

The principle of *non-refoulement* is commonly regarded as the cornerstone of both international refugee and human rights law. It has its roots in multiple sources at various normative levels and binds both the EU and its Member States as a matter of customary and treaty law. It has further been embedded in EU primary law, with which secondary law governing the EIBM should comply.

Defining the prohibition of *non-refoulement* might seem redundant. Still, the 'cardinal principle of refugee protection',[175] has been interpreted and applied in many different ways.[176] According to one conservative view, the prohibition of

[173] *Bosphorus* (n 138) para 155.
[174] See ch 5, s IV.E.
[175] Lauterpacht and Bethlehem (n 87).
[176] See note 87 above.

refoulement applies to any refugee already within the asylum country's territory.[177] In another more cogent interpretation, it applies to asylum seekers threatened with persecution as soon as they come under the jurisdiction of a state party.[178] From a broader perspective, deriving from human rights law, the prohibition of *refoulement* involves a duty not to return anyone to a place where she would be at risk of serious human rights violations.[179]

The development of international human rights law expanded the scope of the application of the prohibition of *refoulement*, whereby the principle grew beyond the boundaries of international refugee law. Today, not only the prohibition of *non-refoulement* is included in several universal and regional legal instruments,[180] but most human rights treaties, including the ECHR,[181] have been interpreted as entailing an implicit prohibition of *refoulement*.[182]

The duty of *non-refoulement* derived from the prohibition of torture or other ill-treatment does not permit any limitation, whereas, under Art 33(2) of the Refugee Convention, it applies to cases where the risk of persecution would not equate to torture or ill-treatment but would nonetheless allow for derogations based on national security or public safety. Nevertheless, the permeation of human rights law into EU law has reinforced the protection against *refoulement*. It requires Member States to implement such derogations only where this is not contrary to their international obligations, including the absolute prohibition of torture or other inhuman or degrading treatment or punishment.[183] Importantly, the absolute nature of this duty, derived from the prohibition of torture or ill-treatment, prevents any restriction or derogation to its application, including in times of emergency.[184]

Despite its considerable acknowledgements, human rights courts and treaty bodies have remained remarkably elusive about the theoretical foundation of the

[177] Kay Hailbronner, 'Comments on the Right to Leave, Return and Remain', in Vera Gowlland-Debbas (ed), *The Problem of Refugees in the Light of Contemporary International Law Issues* (Leiden, Martinus Nijhoff, 1996).

[178] Hathaway (n 87) 340–55.

[179] Costello and Foster (n 87). See also: Lauterpacht and Bethlehem (n 87); Goodwin-Gill and McAdam (n 87).

[180] Art 3, Convention against Torture and Other Cruel, Inhuman or Degrading Treatment or Punishment, 1465 UNTS 85, 10 December 1984; Art 16, International Convention for the Protection of All Persons from Enforced Disappearance, 2716 UNTS 3, 20 December 2006; Art 19, Charter of Fundamental Rights of the European Union, OJ C 364/01, 18 December 2000.

[181] The first case in which the (now defunct) European Commission of Human Rights was held in 1961 and was confirmed by subsequent case law, until the ECtHR definitely endorsed this *non-refoulement* jurisprudence in its leading case *Soering*. See: ECommHR, *P v Belgium*, Appl No 984/61, 29 May 1961; ECtHR, *Soering v The United Kingdom*, Appl No 14038/88, 7 July 1989.

[182] HRC, General Comment No 20: Article 7 (Prohibition of Torture, or Other Cruel, Inhuman or Degrading Treatment or Punishment), 10 March 1992, para 9; CRC, General Comment No 6: Treatment of Unaccompanied and Separated Children Outside their Country of Origin, UN Doc CRC/GC/2005/6, 1 September 2005, paras 27–28; ACommHR, *John K Modise v Botswana*, Comm No 97/93, 2000, para 91; IACommHR, *The Haitian Centre for Human Rights* (n 87) para 167.

[183] Joined Cases C-391/16, C-77/17, *M, X and X*, 14 May 2019, Opinion AG Whatelet, paras 57–58.

[184] Vincent Chetail, 'Crisis Without Borders: What Does International Law Say About Border Closure in the Context of Covid-19?' (2020) 2 *Frontiers in Political Science*.

principle of *non-refoulement*.[185] Many uncertainties still surround the 'cornerstone of international refugee law'.[186] Persistent debates concern the nature of the threat (persecution, serious human rights violations such as torture, inhuman or degrading treatment or punishment), the beneficiaries of the prohibition of *refoulement* and the (ir)relevance of their conduct, the legal nature of the duty of *non-refoulement* (a rule, a principle or a mechanism[187]), as well as its extraterritorial application.[188] In the following pages, the duty of *non-refoulement* is understood as prohibiting return to sufficiently real and serious human rights violations.[189] For the sake of accuracy, this prohibition equally applies to anyone claiming to be within the ambit of the definition regardless of whether they formally requested asylum, their refugee status was revoked, or not yet established.

The EU and its Member States are bound by the *non-refoulement* duty as a norm of customary international law, deriving from Article 33 of the Refugee Convention and the customary rule prohibiting torture and cruel, inhuman or degrading treatment or punishment.[190] The case law of the CJEU does not specifically deal with the reception of the prohibition of *refoulement* in EU law as a norm of customary international law. Yet, as the Court has repeatedly affirmed, customary international law is part of the EU legal order,[191] and the duty of *non-refoulement* is conceivably part of it.[192]

In the realm of EU law, the prohibition of *refoulement* arises from the international obligations of the EU and its Member States. Those international obligations were incorporated in the TEU and the CFR and further reflected in the case law of the CJEU and various instruments of secondary EU law.[193] It follows that where EU law would require a Member State to breach its *non-refoulement* duty arising from the Refugee Convention or other relevant treaties, that legal measure

[185] Kathryn Greenman, 'A Castle Built on Sand? Article 3 ECHR and the Source of Risk in Non-Refoulement Obligations in International Law' (2015) 27 *International Journal of Refugee Law* 264, 278.

[186] UNHCR, 'Advisory Opinion on the Extraterritorial Application of Non-Refoulement Obligations under the 1951 Convention relating to the Status of Refugees and its 1967 Protocol', 26 January 2007; Cornelis Wolfram Wouters, *International Legal Standards for the Protection from Refoulement* (Antwerp, Intersentia, 2009) 23.

[187] Hathaway (n 87) 438.

[188] Thomas Gammeltoft-Hansen, *Access to Asylum: International Refugee Law and the Globalisation of Migration Control* (Cambridge, Cambridge University Press, 2011)44; Maarten den Heijer, *Europe and Extraterritorial Asylum* (Oxford, Hart Publishing, 2012)120–141; Moreno-Lax (n 87)247–336; Lisa Heschl, *Protecting the Rights of Refugees Beyond European Borders: Establishing Extraterritorial Legal Responsibilities* (Antwerp, Intersentia, 2018)80–93.

[189] Costello and Foster (n 87).

[190] See Lauterpacht and Bethlehem (n 87) 153; Mungianu (n 127) 103.

[191] See above, section II.A.ii.a.

[192] The vast majority of scholars favour the view that the duty of *non-refoulement* has crystallised as a norm of customary international law, notwithstanding some persistent debate on this question. Lauterpacht and Bethlehem (n 87); Kälin, Caroni and Heim (n 87) 1343–46; Costello and Foster (n 87). Cf Hathaway (n 87) 437–59.

[193] Art 21, Directive 2011/95; Arts 9(3), 28, 35, 38, 39(4), 41, Directive 2013/32; Art 4, SBC; *Ahmed* (n 53) para 37; *Alo and Osso* (n 51) para 30; *Mohammed Bilali* (n 51) para 54.

would not only breach international law but would also be invalid as a matter of EU primary law.[194]

Beyond Article 4, which reproduces *verbatim* Article 3 ECHR, the CFR includes a specific provision regarding the duty of *non-refoulement*. This fundamental principle is enshrined in Article 19(2) of the CFR, according to which '[n]o one may be removed, expelled or extradited to a State where there is a serious risk that he or she would be subjected to death penalty, torture or other inhuman or degrading treatment or punishment'. As the Explanations confirm, this provision incorporates the relevant case law from the ECtHR.[195] In line with Article 52(3) of the CFR, the prohibition of *refoulement* included in the Charter and that jurisprudentially developed from Article 3 ECHR should have the same meaning and scope.[196] Besides, the scope of application of the prohibition of *refoulement* as included in the CFR extends as far as EU law applies.[197]

The CJEU explicitly endorsed the Strasbourg Court jurisprudence,[198] but it somehow distorted the substance of the *non-refoulement* protection offered by the ECHR in interpreting the Dublin Regulation.[199] The CJEU held that compliance with fundamental rights by Member States should be presumed, for the Dublin Regulation is a system based on mutual trust. Even if this presumption can be rebutted, this may be the case only in exceptional circumstances. The ECtHR has subsequently made clear that the source of risk – which can stem from systemic flows in the national asylum system or other factual circumstances – is immaterial for the application of the prohibition of *refoulement*.[200] What is relevant is the effect of the removal rather than its cause.[201] States are therefore not exempted 'from carrying out a thorough and individualised examination of the situation of the person concerned and from suspending enforcement of the removal order, should the risk of inhuman or degrading treatment be established'.[202]

The SBC and the Frontex regulation encompass explicit obligations of *non-refoulement*.[203] The same obligations are EU also included in other secondary law instruments that form part of the EIBM legal framework.[204] The SBC sets out

[194] *M, X and X* (n 64) paras 72–74.

[195] Explanations relating to the Charter of Fundamental Rights, OJ C 303, 14 December 2007, Art 19.

[196] Moreno-Lax (n 87) 283–85.

[197] See Ch 4, s 3.

[198] Joined Cases C-411/10 and C-493/10, *N.S. and M.E.*, 21 December 2011, ECLI:EU:C:2011:865, paras 88–90.

[199] ibid, paras 79–83.

[200] ECtHR, *Tarakhel v Switzerland*, Appl No 29217/12, 4 November 2014.

[201] See Hemme Battjes and Evelien Brouwer, 'The Dublin Regulation and Mutual Trust: Judicial Coherence in EU Asylum Law?' (2015) 8 *Review of European Administrative Law* 183; Cathryn Costello, *The Human Rights of Migrants and Refugees in European Law* (Oxford, Oxford University Press, 2015) 182.

[202] *Tarakhel* (n 200) para 104.

[203] Recital 36, Arts 3 and 4, SBC; Recitals 84 and 103, Arts 36, 48(1), 50(3), 71(2), 72(3), 73(2), 80, 86(4), Regulation 2019/1896.

[204] See: Recital 4, Arts 3(2) and 5(e), Regulation (EU) 2019/1155 [2019] OJ L 198/88; Art 41, Regulation (EU) 2017/2226 [2017] OJ L 327/20; Art 2, 20(3) and 22, Regulation (EU) 1052/2013 [2013]

the criteria for admission in the Schengen area.[205] By way of derogation, non-nationals who do not fulfil entry conditions may be authorised to enter a Member State's territory in view of that state's international obligations.[206] Any refusal of entry should be without prejudice to the application of special provisions concerning the right of asylum and international protection.[207] In practice, however, when issuing a refusal-of-entry decision, Member States are required to issue an alert to the Schengen Information System on one of two grounds: national decisions based on a threat to public policy, public security or national security; or those based on entry bans under the Return Directive.[208] Since 2018, the vague and disproportional scope of application of the first ground has been expanded. It now encompasses not only minor crimes and those where there are 'serious grounds for believing that third-country nationals committed a serious criminal offence',[209] but also cases in which they circumvented or attempted to circumvent EU or national immigration laws.[210] The wide margin of appreciation left to state authorities in this context should be reconciled with the prohibition of *non-refoulement*, as well as with the principle of non-penalisation of irregular entry included in Article 31 of the Refugee Convention. Under international law, the principle of *non-refoulement* does not merely proscribe states from expelling people to a place where they would risk serious human rights violations; in such circumstances, it also implies a prohibition from refusing entry to their territory.[211]

Yet the practices of refusal of entry and non-admission practices, coupled with new externalization techniques, are on the rise in Europe.[212] A growing number of Member States have erected legal and physical barriers on their external borders to obstruct access to their territory. In Greece, maritime pushbacks and border violence are enduring – if not normalised – practices.[213] Simultaneously, the practice of abandoning people at sea in inflatable life rafts, while weaponising rescue material, pursues the same objective.[214] In several Member States, emergency measures have legalised *refoulement* policies and impeded the exercise of the right

OJL 295/11; Preamble and Art 4, Regulation (EU) 656/2014 [2014] OJ L 189/93; Arts 2, 5 and 9, Directive (EC) [2008] OJ L 348/98.

[205] Art 6(1), SBC.

[206] ibid, Art 6(5).

[207] ibid, Art 14(1).

[208] Art 24(1), Regulation (EU) 2018/1861 [2018] OJ L312/14.

[209] ibid, Art 24(2)(b).

[210] ibid, Art 24(3)(c).

[211] Goodwin-Gill and McAdam (n 87) 296–298.

[212] See CoE, Parliamentary Assembly, *Pushback policies and practice in Council of Europe Member States*, Resolution 2299 (2019); FRA, *Fundamental Rights Issues at Land Borders* (2020) 18–25. See also: Iris Goldner Lang and Boldizsár Nagy, 'External Border Control Techniques in the EU as a Challenge to the Principle of Non-Refoulement' (2021) 17 *European Constitutional Law Review* 442.

[213] Lena Karamandidou and Bernd Kasparek, 'From Exception to Extra-Legal Normality: Pushbacks and Racist State Violence against People Crossing the Greek-Turkish Land Border' (2022) 11 *State Crime Journal* 12.

[214] Niamh Keady-Tabbal and Itamar Mann, 'Weaponizing Rescue: Law and the Materiality of Migration Management in the Aegean' (2023) 36 *Leiden Journal of International Law* 61.

to seek and enjoy asylum.[215] The most prominent example is that of Hungary, where, based on new legislative developments, asylum seekers approaching the Hungarian border are denied entry and are directed to designated Hungarian embassies to claim asylum.[216] Similarly, along the EU border with Belarus, several Member States have suspended their *non-refoulement* obligations and restricted the right to asylum as well as access to border zones for lawyers and humanitarian actors. Meanwhile, an increasing number of reports indicate systematic pushbacks occurring in many other EU Member States.[217] Yet, at the time of writing, Hungary was the only Member State referred by the Commission to the CJEU, which found its legislation incompatible with EU law.[218] In contrast, while it has been striking a balance between states' interest in controlling migratory movements and the respect for human rights, the ECtHR has emphasised the need to ensure a minimal level of protection of migrants against *refoulement* practices within and beyond the Schengen area.[219]

At the same time, EU migration policies have focused predominantly on securing external borders and furthering cooperation with third countries also through Frontex engagement. The Member States' *non-refoulement* obligation impacts their cooperation with Frontex. Frontex's action can be effectively influenced by its Member States that bear a positive obligation to ensure that the agency does not breach the prohibition of *refoulement*.[220] Conversely, when assisting Member States in their border control practices, Frontex is required to comply with 'the relevant Union and international law, including the principle of *non-refoulement*'.[221] In performing its tasks, the agency should guarantee the protection of fundamental rights, especially the principle of *non-refoulement*.[222] Frontex Fundamental Rights Strategy further explains that:

> Disembarking, forcing people to enter, conducting them to or handing them over to the authorities of a country where inter alia, there is a serious risk of being subjected to the death penalty, torture, persecution or other inhuman or degrading treatment

[215] Report of the Special Rapporteur on the human rights of migrants, Felipe González Morales, 'Human rights violations at international borders: trends, prevention and accountability', UN Doc A/HRC/50/31, 22 April 2022, paras 27–39.

[216] Lang and Nagy (n 210) 458–59.

[217] Anja Radjenovic, Briefing: Pushbacks at the EU's external borders, European Parliament, 2022, www.europarl.europa.eu/RegData/etudes/BRIE/2022/738191/EPRS_BRI(2022)738191_EN.pdf.

[218] Case C-808/18, *Commission v Hungary*, 17 December 2020, ECLI:EU:C:2020:1029; Case C-821/19, *Commission v Hungary*, 16 November 2021, ECLI:EU:C:2021:930. See also: Maciej Grześkowiak, 'The "Guardian of the Treaties" Is No More? The European Commission and the 2021 Humanitarian Crisis on Poland–Belarus Border' (2023) 42 *Refugee Survey Quarterly* 81.

[219] Eg ECtHR, *M.A. v Lithuania*, Appl No 59793/17, 11 December 2018; ECtHR, *M.K. and others v Poland*, Appl No 40503/17, 42902/17 and 43643/17, 23 July 2020; ECtHR, *M.H. and Others v Croatia*, Appl Nos 15670/18 and 43115/18, 18 November 2021. See also: Francesco Gatta, 'Migration and Rule of (Human Rights) Law in the EU: A "Constitutional" Crisis' (2022) Forum Transregionale Studien Working Paper.

[220] See *mutatis mutandis*: *Waite and Kennedy* (n 138) para 67.

[221] Art 36(4), Regulation 2019/1896.

[222] ibid, Art 80.

> or punishment, or where life or freedom would be threatened on account of race, religion, nationality, sexual orientation, membership of a particular social group or political opinion, or from which there is a serious risk of expulsion, removal or extradition to another country in contravention of the principle of non-*refoulement*, is prohibited.[223]

Whereas the agency organises or coordinates return operations, which entail an inherent risk of *refoulement*, return decisions remain the sole responsibility of the Member States.[224] Still, Frontex should monitor the respect for fundamental rights, including the duty of *non-refoulement*, at all stages of the return process, from pre-departure to the handing over the returnees to third countries' authorities.[225] Frontex is engaged in 'post-return' activities and is currently developing Joint Reintegration Services offering assistance after voluntary or forced return.[226] The Fundamental Rights Strategy, in cases of return activities involving children, proposes the establishment of post-return monitoring to assess whether a return operation to a specific country was in line with international law, namely the principle of *non-refoulement*.[227] This could be a significant development if implemented and incorporated into the agency's legal framework.

However, this might obscure the consequence of observing the *non-refoulement* duty in all pre-departure activities. Significantly, Frontex's Guide for Joint Return Activities includes no mention of the principle of *non-refoulement* in relation to pre-return and pre-departure activities.[228] In this respect, 'Frontex assumes that all return decisions which are executed via [its joint return operations] are in compliance with fundamental rights, including the *non-refoulement* duty, and other provisions of EU, international and national law'.[229] Yet, as further discussed below, despite the primary responsibility of Member States, Frontex remains responsible as a facilitator in cases violating the prohibition of *refoulement*.

For the moment, it seems sufficient to point out that the agency should pay as much attention to Member States' capabilities to control their sections of the external borders of the EU as it does to their fundamental rights compliance.[230] Similarly, Frontex should ensure respect for fundamental rights, particularly the prohibition of *refoulement*, when it cooperates with third states.[231] Frontex's Fundamental Rights Strategy clarifies that the agency will undertake 'a due diligence assessment of fundamental rights risks and the impacts' of any formal

[223] Frontex Fundamental Rights Strategy, 2021, 8.
[224] Art 50(1), Regulation 2019/1896.
[225] ibid, Art 50(5).
[226] Frontex Programming Document 2020–2022.
[227] Frontex, Fundamental Rights Strategy, 2021, 9.
[228] See Frontex, Guide for Joint Return Operations by Air coordinated by Frontex, 12 May 2016, 19–32.
[229] ibid, 10.
[230] See Art 32, Regulation 2019/1896.
[231] ibid, Art 73.

cooperation with third countries.[232] Furthermore, any exchange of personal data with third countries should 'strictly uphold the principle of *non-refoulement*'.[233]

To summarise the preceding discussion, the principle of *non-refoulement* has developed from the cornerstone of international protection of refugees to a human right protecting migrants at the universal and regional level. Both Frontex and the Member States have an obligation to respect this fundamental principle as a matter of international and EU law. By the same token, Frontex and the Member States have a positive duty to avert any violation of the prohibition *refoulement* caused by their cooperation. At a moment when states are increasingly endorsing migration deterrence laws and policies, which explicitly or implicitly legitimise *refoulement* practices,[234] Frontex (and the EU's) positive duty to monitor Member States' compliance with their fundamental rights obligations is crucial.[235] Nonetheless, this duty depends on a wanting legal framework and a focus on effective migration management rather than fundamental rights.

B. The Prohibition of Torture or Inhuman and Degrading Treatment

Torture, inhuman and degrading treatment and punishment are the archetypical forms of harm from which the absolute prohibition of *refoulement* in major human rights instruments originates. Yet, the right to personal integrity, as a self-standing norm expressed in the prohibition of torture or other forms of ill-treatment, is relevant for protecting self-standing migrants' rights. Not only is it non-derogable in times of war and emergency; but it is also ensured without any restriction whatsoever in various regional and universal treaties.[236]

The widespread human suffering caused by the detention conditions imposed on migrants and asylum seekers is widely agreed to amount to inhuman and degrading treatment under human rights law. On multiple occasions, the ECtHR condemned the appalling conditions in which migrants in vulnerable situations were left in Greek and Italian detention centres. Perhaps the strongest evidence of these violations emerged after the case of *MSS v Greece*.[237] Greek detention facilities held migrants in deplorable sanitary conditions, in overcrowded cells,

[232] Frontex Fundamental Rights Strategy, 2021, 14.

[233] ibid, 12.

[234] Report of the Special Rapporteur on the human rights of migrants, Felipe González Morales, 'Human rights violations at international borders: trends, prevention and accountability', UN Doc A/HRC/50/31, 22 April 2022, paras 27–56.

[235] Art 80, Regulation 2019/1896. See also: *Pushed beyond the limits*, Recommendation by the Council of Europe Commissioner for Human Rights, April 2022.

[236] See eg: Art 5, UDHR; Art 3, common to all four Geneva Conventions 1949; Art 3 and 15(2) ECHR; Art 7 and 4(2), ICCPR; Art 5(2) and 27(2), ACHR; Art 5, ACHPR.

[237] ECtHR, *M.S.S. v Belgium and Greece*, Appl No 30696/09, 21 January 2011.

and with little or no access to legal or medical services.[238] Access to asylum procedures was minimal, and where an asylum application was refused, detention could be extended *ad infinitum*. In *Khlaifia and Others v Italy*, the Second Section of the ECtHR found similar violations in Italy's detention centres.[239] That decision was, however, partially reversed by the Grand Chamber.[240] The Court recalled the absolute character of the prohibition of torture and other forms of ill-treatment – a value of civilisation underlying the very essence of the Convention – which must be respected even in times of public emergency.[241] These statements would suggest the judges' unwillingness to erode the protection offered by Article 3. Yet the contextual approach adopted later in the decision disproves this expectation. In evaluating the applicants' situation, the context of the humanitarian emergency confronting the Italian authorities had to be taken into due consideration, leading the ECtHR to exclude a violation of Article 3.[242]

In a string of cases concerning the detention conditions in Greece, the ECtHR has confirmed the contextual approach developed in *Khlaifia*.[243] The Court reiterated the relevance of the difficulties experienced by Greece in relation to the massive influx of migrants and considered the short period of time in which the applicants were held in detention (30 days) to find that conditions at the centres had not reached a level of severity in inhuman or degrading treatment at the relevant time.[244] This approach was criticised as part of a more general strategy adopted by the Court to react to state pressure aimed at achieving a more restrictive interpretation of absolute human rights.[245]

As already mentioned, within the EU legal framework, Article 4 of the CFR encompasses the prohibition of torture and inhuman or degrading treatment. This provision reproduces *verbatim* the ECHR; thus, by virtue of Article 52(3) of the Charter, it has the same meaning and scope as the ECHR.[246] As an EU agency, Frontex, in all its activities, should respect the prohibition of torture and inhuman or degrading treatment or punishment,[247] especially with regard to return operations and the use of coercive measures.[248] Subject to the agreement of the

[238] See CoE, *Report to the Greek Government on the Visit to Greece Carried Out by the European Committee for the Prevention of Torture and Inhuman or Degrading Treatment or Punishment (CPT) from 4 to 16 April 2013*, Report No CPT/Inf (2014) 26, 16 October 2014.

[239] ECtHR, *Khlaifia and Others v Italy* (Second Section), Appl No 16483/12, 1 September 2015, para 136.

[240] ECtHR, *Khlaifia and Others v Italy* (Grand Chamber) Appl No 16483/12, 15 December 2016.

[241] ibid, para 158.

[242] ibid, paras 178–86.

[243] ECtHR, *J.R. et autres c Grèce*, Appl No 22696/16, 25 Janvier 2018; ECtHR, *O.S.A. and others* 39065/16, 21 June 2019; ECtHR, *E.K. v Greece*, Appl No 73700/13, 14 January 2021.

[244] *J.R. et autres* (n 243) paras 183–84. *O.S.A. and others v Greece* (n 243) para 80; ECtHR, *Kaak and others v Greece*, Appl No 34215/16, 3 October 2019, para 65.

[245] See extensively: Anuscheh Farahat, 'Human Rights and the Political: Assessing the Allegation of Human Rights Overreach in Migration Matters' (2022) 40 *Netherlands Quarterly of Human Rights* 180.

[246] Explanations relating to the Charter of Fundamental Rights, OJ C 303, 14 December 2007.

[247] Arts 2 and 6, TEU; Recital 103, Regulation 2019/1896.

[248] Frontex, Guide for Joint Return Operations by Air coordinated by Frontex, 12 May 2016, 15.

Member State concerned, the agency should allow the European Committee for the Prevention of Torture and Inhuman or Degrading Treatment or Punishment of the Council of Europe to conduct visits where it carries out return operations.[249]

Human rights violations occurring in situations like those of *MSS* and *Khlaifia* are frequently facilitated by Frontex. Beginning in 2010, for example, Frontex assisted Greek authorities in their border control activities and were arguably aware of conditions in Greek migrant detention centres.[250] Yet they continued to transfer apprehended irregular migrants to these facilities, potentially exposing them to ill-treatment and other serious violations of their fundamental rights.[251] Whether assisting Member States in prohibited practices could entail the agency's responsibility under EU or international law is a question yet to be determined.

The so-called 'hotspot approach' can exacerbate the human rights challenges of these situations, enhancing the role of EU agencies that remain largely unaccountable. First announced by the European Commission in its 2015 European Agenda on Migration,[252] the 'hotspot approach to migration' consists of a common core of EU agencies (namely, the European Asylum Support Office, Frontex, Eurojust and Europol) that should intervene, rapidly and effectively, at the external borders under specific and disproportionate migratory pressure.[253] 'Hotspots' are reception centres aimed at identifying, assisting and processing newly arrived migrants, generally disembarking after search-and-rescue operations.

As suggested in a 2014 feasibility study,[254] and later confirmed by Regulation 2019/1896, Frontex was to become the *primus inter pares* among the EU agencies cooperating in 'hotspot areas'.[255] Arguably, the agency's significant influence in hotspot areas evidences a focus on border control rather than on the protection needs of the people involved. Ultimately, the hotspot approach has led to transforming the reception system in 'frontline' Member States 'into a tool for preventing the secondary movement of asylum seekers and keeping them under close police surveillance'.[256]

At the time of writing, reception facilities in Greece and Italy remain severely overcrowded. Their lack of adequate medical, psychological, and social support

[249] Recital 82, Regulation 2019/1896.

[250] See eg: HRW, *The EU's Dirty Hands Frontex Involvement in Ill-Treatment of Migrant Detainees in Greece*, 2011.

[251] Ioannis Kalpouzos and Itamar Mann, 'Banal Crimes against Humanity: The Case of Asylum Seekers in Greece' (2015) 16 *Melbourne Journal of International Law* 1.

[252] Commission, A European Agenda on Migration, COM(2015) 240, 13 May 2015, 6.

[253] Commission, Managing the Refugee Crisis: State of Play of the Implementation of the Priority Actions under the European Agenda on Migration, COM (2015) 510 final, 14 October 2015.

[254] Unisys, Final Report for European Commission, DG Home, Study on the feasibility of the creation of a European System of Border Guards to control the external borders of the Union (16 June 2014).

[255] Art 40(1), Regulation 2019/1896.

[256] Maarten Den Heijer, Jorrit Rijpma and Thomas Spijkerboer, 'Coercion, Prohibition, and Great Expectations: The Continuing Failure of the Common European Asylum System' (2016) 53 *Common Market Law Review* 607.

services, lack of security and inadequate hygiene facilities make reception conditions hardly compatible with Article 3 ECHR. In light of these realities, the Court recalled that the difficulties deriving from the increased migratory pressure, in particular in hotspot areas at the EU external borders, do not exonerate Member States from their absolute obligations under Article 3 ECHR.[257]

This timid disavowal of the contextual approach developed in *Kalafia* is a crucial jurisprudential improvement. Nonetheless, with the 2020 Migration and Asylum Pact, the EU and its Member States seem to look in another direction. The Pact envisions a substantial tightening of border procedures by creating a new screening mechanism, to be implemented at or in proximity to the external borders. During the screening process, people would not be considered authorised to enter the Member States' territory, irrespective of protection needs.[258] While this proposal should not affect existing procedures nor abridge the exercise of individual rights,[259] the standards of treatment included in the reception conditions directive would not apply, and migrants' potential vulnerabilities will be assessed only 'where relevant'.[260]

C. The Right to Life

The right to life has been described as a 'supreme right',[261] 'which constitute the irreducible core of human rights'.[262] This 'foundational and universally recognized right',[263] permeates the structure and process of general international law.[264] And yet, human life is still vulnerable to governmental abuse, private violence or natural disasters. The lives of migrants, especially those who find themselves in an irregular situation before the laws of destination countries, are often endangered by one or a combination of these factors.

Migrants' deaths typically occur when people seek to cross borders while trying to evade immigration controls.[265] The death toll of irregular border crossers raises serious questions concerning state responsibility, the foreseeability of these

[257] ECtHR, *J.A. and others v Italy*, Appl No 21329/18, 30 March 2023, para 65; ECtHR, *A.D. v Greece*, Appl No 55363/19, 4 April 2023, para 30.

[258] Art 4(1), Proposal for a Regulation of the European Parliament and of the Council introducing a screening of third country nationals at the external borders and amending Regulations (EC) No 767/2008, (EU) 2017/2226, (EU) 2018/1240 and (EU) 2019/817, COM/2020/612 final.

[259] ibid, Explanatory Memorandum, 7.

[260] ibid, Art 9(2).

[261] HRC, General Comment No 36: Art 6 Right to Life, CCPR/C/GC/36, 30 October 2018, para 2.

[262] ICJ, *Legality of the Threat or Use of Nuclear Weapons*, Advisory opinion of 8 July 1996, ICJ Reports 66, Dissenting opinion of Judge Weeramantry, 506.

[263] Report by the Special Rapporteur on extrajudicial, summary or arbitrary executions, UN Doc A/HRC/41/36 4 October 2019, para 26.

[264] Christian Tomuschat, 'The Right to Life' in Christian Tomuschat, Evelyne Lagrange and Stefan Oeter (eds), *The Right to Life – Legal and Political Foundations* (Leiden, Brill, 2010).

[265] A reliable, but geographically limited dataset is the Deaths at the Borders Database developed by Human Costs of Border Control project, www.borderdeaths.org/.

deaths, and state obligations during border control efforts that directly or indirectly result in migrants' deaths.[266] Interceptions at sea, the forced removal of irregular migrants by Member States (individually or collectively under the coordination of Frontex), by their very nature, involve a degree of coercion and human rights risk. In all its activities involving the use of force, Frontex is required to comply with the principles of necessity and proportionality, to observe its duty of precaution, and to 'fully respect and aim to preserve human life and human dignity'.[267] In practice, however, incidents involving shooting at migrant boats during maritime operations are not uncommon.[268]

International human rights law imposes on all EU Member States a duty to respect, protect and ensure the right to life of every individual within their jurisdiction.[269] On the one hand, states are bound by the negative obligation to respect, and therefore not arbitrarily interfere with, the right to life of any individual subject to their jurisdiction; on the other hand, states are also under the positive obligation to protect and ensure such right, exercising due diligence to protect the lives of individuals against deprivations that are not directly attributable to a state.[270]

The ECtHR has developed its own stance with regard to positive obligations and the protection of the right to life. In broad terms, the ECtHR has highlighted three criteria to determine whether a state has failed to safeguard the right to life.[271] First, it must be established whether the authorities knew or ought to have known of the existence of a real and immediate risk to the life of an identified individual;[272] second, it must be ascertained whether the authorities took all reasonable measures to avoid that risk, bearing in mind that the duty to take those measures is an obligation of means and not of result;[273] and third, if that risk materialised, it must be established whether the state's reaction was adequate, particularly with regard to its duty to investigate alleged violations and redress victims.[274]

[266] Thomas Spijkerboer, 'The Human Costs of Border Control' (2007) 9 *European Journal of Migration and Law* 127; Thomas Spijkerboer, 'Moving Migrants, States, and Rights Human Rights and Border Deaths' (2013) 7 *The Law & Ethics of Human Rights* 213.

[267] Annex V, Regulation 2019/1896.

[268] Sangeetha Iengar, 'Europe's Borderlands: The New Shooting Range for Power Politics' (BorderCriminologies, 5 March 2020), https://blogs.law.ox.ac.uk/research-subject-groups/centre-criminology/centreborder-criminologie s/blog/2020/03/europes.

[269] General Comment No 36 (n 261), para 7; ECtHR, *Alhowais v Hungary*, Appl No 59435/17, 2 February 2023, para 108.

[270] Vladislava Stoyanova, 'Fault, Knowledge and Risk within the Framework of Positive Obligations under the European Convention on Human Rights' [2020] *Leiden Journal of International Law* 1.

[271] Spijkerboer, 'The Human Costs of Border Control' (n 266).

[272] ECtHR, *Osman v United Kingdom*, Appl No 23452/94, 28 October 1998, para 116.

[273] ECtHR, *Kurt v Austria*, Appl No 62903/15, 15 June 2021, paras 158–60; ECtHR, *Safi and Others v Greece*, Appl No 5418/15, 7 July 2022, para 157; *Alhowais* (n 269) para 132.

[274] ECtHR, *Nachova and Others v Bulgaria*, Appl No 43577/98 43579/98, 6 July 2005, para 110; ECtHR, *Ciechońska v Poland*, Appl No 19776/04, 14 June 2011, paras 66–67.

'Border deaths' are generally – yet not always – an indirect and accidental consequence of certain policy choices and result from a series of different factors.[275] While Article 2 ECHR cannot be interpreted as guaranteeing an absolute level of security to everyone everywhere within state jurisdiction, it also enshrines one of the basic values of democratic societies. In the context of 'border deaths', this means not only observing the prohibition of arbitrary deprivation of life but also fulfilling their positive duty to protect the lives of those individuals at their borders, including by taking proactive and coordinated measures and ensuring an adequate response where lives have been lost in circumstances potentially engaging the responsibility of public authorities.

While border controls are not always the exclusive or even the main cause of migrant deaths, arguably, those fatalities give rise to three discrete positive obligations: first, the obligation to prevent or minimise the number of fatalities, also by assessing and amending European border control policies;[276] second, the obligation to effectively investigate migrant fatalities at the borders, with the meaningful participation victims' next of kin;[277] and third, identify the victims, inform their relatives and dispose of remains in a dignified and respectful manner.[278]

Undeniably, European states and the EU, and more specifically Frontex, possess the required knowledge about the risks migrants undertake to reach their borders.[279] The European Commission has often recognised the need to reduce dangerous journeys by creating safe and legal alternatives.[280] In addition, the EU and its Member States have the resources to take preventive measures that could save lives that otherwise would be lost, especially at their maritime borders. Frontex provides aerial surveillance through its joint operations and its multipurpose aerial surveillance assets deployed to the external maritime borders.[281] The information gathered is analysed by Frontex officers and passed to Member States and other EU agencies for SAR or other law enforcement purposes. In addition, through risk analyses, Frontex gains crucial knowledge regarding migrants' journeys. However, this knowledge is reportedly used to predict and consequently hinder migratory

[275] Paolo Cuttitta and Tamara Last (eds), *Border Deaths: Causes, Dynamics and Consequences of Migration-Related Mortality* (Amsterdam, Amsterdam University Press, 2019).

[276] ECtHR, *Furdík v Slovakia*, Appl No 42994/05, 2 December 2008; *Alhowais* (n 269) para 115.

[277] *M.H. and others* (n 219) paras 160–64; *Safi* (n 273) para 116.

[278] Global Compact for Safely, Orderly and Regular Migration, objective 8. See also: Mytilini Declaration for the Dignified Treatment of all Missing and Deceased Persons and their Families as a Consequence of Migrant Journeys, 11 May 2018.

[279] Over the years, the number of reports and investigations on the mass casualties of refugees and migrants during their journey has grown so much that it is impossible to include them all in a footnote. Among them, see in particular: Report of the Special Rapporteur on Extrajudicial, Summary or Arbitrary Executions, Unlawful Death of Refugees and Migrants, UN Doc A/72/335, 15 August 2017.

[280] See eg: European Council, The Stockholm Programme – an open and secure Europe serving and protecting the citizen, doc 17024/09, 10–11 December 2009, 59; European Agenda on Migration (n 236); Commission, Communication from the Commission to the European Parliament, the European Council and the Council, Progress report on the Implementation of the European Agenda on Migration, COM(2019) 481 final, 19 October 2019.

[281] Consultative Forum, Tenth Annual Report (2022), Annex III.

movements, rather than being used better to organise SAR operations or reception facilities.[282] Further, Frontex and the Member States define the means to prevent and respond to border fatalities. While Frontex's instruments to react to human rights violations remain largely inefficient,[283] the Member States dispose of appropriate means to conduct effective investigations, identify the deceased, inform the next of kin about their fate, and give the dead a dignified burial.[284] As Spijkerboer has aptly put it: 'the least we can do is to notice, to register, and to take account of the human costs – to others – of protecting our European project'.[285]

i. A Right to be Rescued at Sea?

Arrivals of irregular migrants on unseaworthy boats are not an emergency but a structural predicament of migration management policies. A central effect of these policies has been the synchronous increase in border deaths at sea.[286] The scaling down of the Italian SAR operation Mare Nostrum despite its foreseeable deadly consequences led to a massive loss of lives.[287] Importantly, contrary to Mare Nostrum, the subsequent Frontex joint operations Triton and Themis were primarily focused on border surveillance, with increasingly reduced SAR capacities.[288] Overall, this withdrawal policy from state-led SAR missions shifted the burden of extremely dangerous operations to private vessels that were ill-fitted and legally obstructed from conducting life-saving operations.[289]

This policy shift, read through the lens of positive obligations, could amount to a violation of migrants' right to life. The EU and its Member States knew the risks of reducing SAR operations; they could have adopted preventive measures to avoid their materialisation, but no adequate response was taken. SAR operations were increasingly reduced, and NGOs rescue activities were hindered, their vessels seized,[290] and refused access to Italian ports.[291]

282 Judith Sunderland and Lorenzo Pezzani, *Airborne Complicity* (HRW/Border Forensic, 8 December 2022).

283 See Ch 2, s VII.

284 Report of the Special Rapporteur on Extrajudicial, Summary or Arbitrary Executions, Unlawful Death of Refugees and Migrants, UN Doc A/72/335, 15 August 2017, paras 65–78.

285 Spijkerboer, 'Moving Migrants, States, and Rights Human Rights and Border Deaths' (n 266).

286 See Lisa-Marie Komp, *Border Deaths at Sea under the Right to Life in the European Convention on Human Rights* (Abingdon, Routledge, 2022), 9–15.

287 See Forensic Oceanography, *Death by Rescue*, April 2016, https://deathbyrescue.org/report/narrative/.

288 Sergio Carrera and Leonard Den Hertog, 'Whose Mare? Rule of law challenges in the field of European border surveillance in the Mediterranean', CEPS paper No 79, January 2015; Sergio Carrera and Roberto Cortinovis, 'Search and Rescue, Disembarkation and Relocation Arrangements in the Mediterranean: Sailing Away from Responsibility?' CEPS Paper No 2019-10, June 2019.

289 See generally: Itamar Mann, 'The Right to Perform Rescue at Sea: Jurisprudence and Drowning' (2020) 21 *German Law Journal* 598.

290 Eg, Italy, Corte di Cassazione, Sentenza No 56138/18, 13 December 2018.

291 Silvia Aru, '"Battleship at the Port of Europe": Italy's Closed-Port Policy and Its Legitimizing Narratives' (2023) 104 *Political Geography* 102902.

In this context, the right to life at sea is intertwined with the duty to assist those in peril on vessels in distress, as set out by Article 98 of the United Nations Convention on the Law of the Sea (UNCLOS).[292] The same duty is also included in the Convention for the Safety of Life at Sea (SOLAS Convention),[293] the Search and Rescue Convention (SAR Convention),[294] and the International Convention on Salvage.[295] Its reiteration in treaty and domestic law, as well as its affirmation in state practice (even if not always consistently), reveals the customary law nature of the duty to assist persons in distress at sea.[296]

The EU and its Member States are parties to the UNCLOS, but the EU has not made any declaration regarding the duty to render assistance governed by Article 98 of that instrument.[297] The implementation of UNCLOS is carried out both by the EU and its Member States within their respective competences. Yet, by virtue of the duty of sincere cooperation,[298] they should act uniformly, maintaining the unity of the EU.[299] Furthermore, contrary to its Member States, the EU has not acceded to the SAR or the SOLAS conventions.[300] Arguably, however, the duty to assist people in distress at sea binds the EU as a norm of customary international law. A further argument could be made that such obligation derives from widely recognised general principles of law, namely elementary considerations of humanity; as such, it would bind the EU and its Member States.[301]

[292] UN Convention on the Law of the Sea, 10 December 1982, 1833 UNTS 3. Most of the provisions included in the Convention are widely recognised as part of customary international law. See: Convention on the Law of the Sea, Report on its 24th Session, UN Doc SPLOS/277, 14 July 2014, para 14.

[293] Chapter 5, Regulation 33(1), International Convention for the Safety of Life at Sea, 1184 UNTS 3, 1 November 1974.

[294] Convention on Maritime Search and Rescue, 1405 UNTS 97, 27 April 1979.

[295] Art 10, International Convention on Salvage, 1953 UNTS 193, 28 April 1989. See also: Art 11, Brussels Convention for the Unification of Certain Rules with Respect to Assistance and Salvage at Sea (Brussels, 23 September 1910).

[296] See: Richard Barnes, 'Refugee Law at Sea' (2004) 53 *International & Comparative Law Quarterly* 47; Seline Trevisanut, 'Search and Rescue Operations in the Mediterranean: Factor of Cooperation or Conflict' (2010) 25 *International Journal of Marine and Coastal Law* 523; Efthymios Papastavridis, *The Interception of Vessels on the High Seas* (Oxford, Hart Publishing, 2013).

[297] The ratification status of the UNCLOS is available at: https://treaties.un.org/Pages/ViewDetailsIII.aspx?src=TREATY&mtdsg_no=XXI-6&chapter=21&Temp=mtdsg3&clang=_en#EndDec. See also: Council Decision 98/392/EC, of 23 March 1998, concerning the conclusion by the European Community of the United Nations Convention of 10 December 1982 on the Law of the Sea and the Agreement of 28 July 1994 relating to the implementation of Part XI thereof, 23 June 1998, OJ L 179/1.

[298] Art 4(3), TEU.

[299] Esa Paasivirta, 'The European Union and the United Nations Convention on the Law of the Sea' (2015) 38 *Fordham International Law Journal* 1045, 1050.

[300] IMO, Comprehensive information on the status of multilateral Conventions and instruments in respect of which the International Maritime Organization or its Secretary-General performs depositary or other functions, 16 December 2019.

[301] International Tribunal for the Law of the Sea, M/V Saiga (No 2) (Saint Vincent and Grenadines v Guinea), 1 July 1999, ITLOS Report 1999 10, para 155. For a detailed discussion, see: Irini Papanicolopulu, *International Law and the Protection of People at Sea* (Oxford, Oxford University Press, 2018) 163–65.

The concrete application of this fundamental maritime obligation suffers from several problems. First, while the SAR Convention, in compliance with Article 98(2) of the UNCLOS, aims to create an international system for coordinating rescue operations that guarantee their efficiency and safety, agreements with neighbouring states to regulate and coordinate SAR operations and services have proven difficult.[302] States should also ensure that SAR operations occur to disembark rescued persons at a 'place of safety'.[303] However, determining such a place of safety has been subject to divergent interpretations and practices.[304] Denying access to ports may affect the right to life, the protection against inhumane treatment and *refoulement* for those on board.[305]

Human rights and search and rescue obligations are intertwined and should be read in conjunction.[306] Indeed, the International Maritime Organisation's Guidelines on the Treatment of Persons Rescued at Sea define a place of safety as a 'place where the survivors' safety of life is no longer threatened and where their basic human needs (such as food, shelter and medical needs) can be met' and further require that 'delivery to a place of safety should take into account the particular circumstances of the case'.[307] The Guidelines also highlight that the 'need to avoid disembarkation in territories where the lives and freedoms of those alleging a well-founded fear of persecution would be threatened is a consideration in the case of asylum-seekers and refugees recovered at sea'.[308]

The External Sea Borders Regulation includes provisions related to disembarkation that apply to the operations at sea coordinated by Frontex,[309] which generally does not disembark rescued people in third countries.[310] Yet, it is worth

[302] Lisa-Marie Komp, 'The Duty to Assist Persons in Distress: An Alternative Source of Protection against the Return of Migrants and Asylum Seekers to the High Seas?' in Violeta Moreno-Lax and Efthymios Papastavridis (eds), *'Boat Refugees' and Migrants at Sea: A Comprehensive Approach: Integrating Maritime Security with Human Rights* (Leiden, Brill, 2016).

[303] Annex, Chapter 1, Art 1.3.2, SAR Convention; Chapter V, Regulation 33, SOLAS Convention.

[304] See Martina Tazzioli and Nicholas De Genova, 'Kidnapping Migrants as a Tactic of Border Enforcement' (2020) 38 *Environment and Planning D: Society and Space* 867.

[305] For further analysis, see: Eugenio Cusumano and Kristof Gombeer, 'In Deep Waters: The Legal, Humanitarian and Political Implications of Closing Italian Ports to Migrant Rescuers' 25 [2018] *Mediterranean Politics* 245.

[306] Violeta Moreno-Lax, 'Seeking Asylum in the Mediterranean: Against a Fragmentary Reading of EU Member States' Obligations Accruing at Sea' (2011) 23 *International Journal of Refugee Law* 174, 199. See also: Andreas Fischer-Lescano, Tillmann Löhr and Timo Tohidipur, 'Border Controls at Sea: Requirements under International Human Rights and Refugee Law' (2009) 21 *International Journal of Refugee Law* 256.

[307] IMO, Resolution MSC 167(78), Guidelines on the Treatment of Persons Rescued at Sea, 20 May 2004, paras 6.12 and 6.15.

[308] ibid, para 6.17. See also: UNHCR, Background Note on the Protection of Asylum-Seekers and Refugees Rescued at Sea,18 March 2002, para 31.

[309] Regulation (EU) No 656/2014 [2014] OJ L 189.

[310] For instance, the agency's operational plans in the South Mediterranean Sea and annual reports on sea surveillance explicitly state that rescued migrants should be disembarked in Italy rather than in a third country. Frontex, Annual report on the implementation of Regulation (EU) 656/2014, 2017, 6; when disembarkation in third countries was envisaged (in case of JO Poseidon Rapid Intervention 2015-16/ EPN Poseidon Sea 2016, JO EPN Indalo 2016 and JO EPN Hera 2016), Frontex required the

specifying that the scope of application of the External Sea Borders Regulation is limited to border surveillance operations carried out by the Member States during Frontex joint operations at sea.[311] Notwithstanding the Commission's proposal to establish a 'common European approach to SAR',[312] search and rescue and disembarkation activities pertain to Member States, while Frontex is supposed to play a merely coordinative role.[313] In this line, Frontex has recalled that it does not have a specific mandate to save lives at sea.[314] Despite the agency's humanitarian narrative,[315] its role has always been reactive rather than proactive in protecting lives at sea.[316] This approach, limiting Frontex's mandate, might conflict with the agency's legal framework and with a good-faith interpretation of it.

Two important questions remain to be answered. The first concerns an important lacuna of the current legal framework, which lacks a commonly accepted definition of what constitutes 'distress'.[317] The master of an intercepting ship is given the discretion to decide whether a vessel is in need of rescue and/or if it is merely unseaworthy.[318] Despite the restrictive interpretations given to the term distress, the wording of the maritime Conventions implies that the central purpose of the duty to render assistance at sea is to prevent the loss of human life. This duty denotes an obligation of conduct, rather than one of result. States are under a due diligence obligation to take appropriate rules and measures to avoid loss of lives at sea, but also to exercise a certain vigilance over their effective implementation. Conversely, the master of a ship may fulfil her duty to assist if they exercise the

host Member State to provide a 'general assessment' of the situation in the concerned third country. See: Frontex, Annual report on the implementation of Regulation (EU) 656/2014, 2016, 10. However, Frontex's new mission Themis no longer mentions Italy as the unique place of disembarkation but stipulates that migrants should be taken to the nearest port. Ministero dell'Interno, 'Al via Themis, la nuova operazione navale di Frontex', 13 February 2018. Available at : www.interno.gov.it/it/notizie/themis-nuova-operazione-navale-frontex.

311 See Recital 4, Regulation 656/2014.

312 European Commission, Communication from the Commission to the European Parliament, the Council, the European Economic and Social Committee and the Committee of the Regions, on a New Pact on Migration and Asylum, COM(2020) 609 final, 23 September 2020, para 4.3. See also: Commission Recommendation on cooperation among Member States concerning operations carried out by vessels owned or operated by private entities for the purpose of search and rescue activities, C(2020) 6468, 23 September 2020.

313 See Juan Santos Vara and Soledad R Sánchez-Tabernero, 'In Deep Water: Towards a Greater Commitment for Human Rights in Sea Operations Coordinated by Frontex?' (2016) 18 *European Journal of Migration and Law* 65.

314 See Frontex, Executive Director Letter responding to Amnesty International reports: Waves of Impunity and Between life and death, 13 October 2020. https://frontex.europa.eu/assets/Images_News/2020/Frontex_responds_Amnesty_International_report.pdf.

315 See eg: Frontex News Release, 'Frontex expands its Joint Operation Triton', 2015. https://frontex.europa.eu/media-centre/news-release/frontex-expands-its-joint-operation-triton-udpbHP.

316 For an analysis of the evolution of Frontex sea operations and their curtailment, see: Moreno-Lax (n 87) 188–97.

317 Cf Chapter 1 (13), SAR Convention; Art 9(1)(e), Regulation 656/2014.

318 Thomas Gammeltoft-Hansen, 'The Perfect Storm: Sovereignty Games and the Law and Politics of Boat Migration' in Violeta Moreno-Lax and Efthymios Papastavridis (eds), *'Boat Refugees' and Migrants at Sea: A Comprehensive Approach: Integrating Maritime Security with Human Rights* (Leiden, Brill, 2016) 67.

required level of diligence in assisting people in distress, 'in so far as he can do so without serious danger to the ship, the crew or the passengers'.[319]

The second issue concerns the identification of the beneficiary of the obligation to render assistance: is it a purely interstate obligation, or does it entail a right to be rescued for people in distress at sea?[320] The law of the sea aims to allocate rights and obligations among states in different maritime zones. The individual is accorded relatively little relevance in this legal framework. However, the proliferation of maritime activities has led to the protection of the human element at sea, namely the application of human rights at sea.[321] The right to life under human rights law serves the same purpose as the customary law duty to assist people in distress at sea: to prevent loss of lives where states can reasonably be expected to do so. These obligations, therefore, should be read jointly in the context of the protection of human life at sea. This does not mean importing 'distinct types of obligations into the law of the sea *de novo*',[322] rather it cautiously suggests a holistic approach to international obligations in the maritime environment.[323]

The last issue concerns the scope of application of the duty to rescue beyond SAR zones. The relevant provisions use the generic term 'at sea', which does not allow for geographical restrictions.[324] Hence, whenever a vessel has 'reason to believe' a ship is in distress, it is under an obligation to assist that ship regardless of its geographical location by alerting the nearest Rescue Coordination Centre and remaining at its disposal.[325] Yet, does this imply an obligation to intervene?

ii. Killing by Omission

The ECtHR has provided some jurisprudential guidance to the application of human rights at sea. The ECHR has been applied in several situations beyond the territory of contracting states in situations concerning interceptions at sea.[326] However, as Trevisanut observes, while human rights law applies to situations

[319] Art 98(1), UNCLOS.

[320] Cf, Seline Trevisanut, 'Is There a Right to Be Rescued at Sea?: A Constructive Overview' [2014] *Questions of International Law* 3; Efthymios Papastavridis, 'Is There a Right to Be Rescued at Sea? A Skeptical View' [2014] *Questions of International Law* 17. For a different perspective, see Jean-François Durieux, 'The Duty to Rescue Refugees' (2016) 28 *International Journal of Refugee Law* 637.

[321] Trevisanut (n 317) 7; Tullio Treves, 'Human Rights and the Law of the Sea' (2010) 28 *Berkeley Journal of International Law* 1; Papanicolopulu (n 296). See also: Human Rights at Sea, Geneva Declaration on Human Rights at Sea, first draft 5 April 2019, https://gdhras.com/.

[322] Papastavridis (n 320) 21.

[323] See extensively: Aphrodite Papachristodoulou, 'The Recognition of a Right to Be Rescued at Sea in International Law' (2022) 35 *Leiden Journal of International Law* 337.

[324] See generally: Violeta Moreno-Lax, 'Protection at Sea and the Denial of Asylum' in Cathryn Costello, Michelle Foster and Jane McAdam (eds), *The Oxford Handbook of International Refugee Law* (Oxford, Oxford University Press, 2021).

[325] See Art 9 (2)(a), Regulation 656/2014.

[326] See most notably: ECtHR, *Xhavara and Others v Italy and Albania*, Appl No 39473/98, 11 January 2001; ECtHR, *Medvedyev and Others v France*, Appl no 3394/03, 29 March 2010; ECtHR, *Hirsi Jamaa and Others v Italy*, Appl No 27765/09, 23 February 2012.

involving interception or SAR operations, the non-performance of such services is a quite different matter.[327] It is a platitude to affirm that an omission can be as effective, or as deadly, as an act. Under the law of international responsibility, states and international organisations can be held responsible for their internationally wrongful conduct, which encompass acts as well as omissions.[328] However, operationalising this principle is not straightforward when it comes to omissions substantiating the obligations that were breached and attributing the conduct to the relevant actor can be problematic, especially in the maritime environment.[329]

Two situations can be distinguished: one concerning distress situations occurring within the SAR zone of a state – where jurisdiction can be established based on the SAR agreement – and the other concerning those occurring beyond it. With regard to the former situation, a coastal state in its SAR zone has positive obligations, which extend 'to the provision of emergency services where it has been brought to the notice of the authorities that the life or health of an individual is at risk on account of injuries sustained as a result of an accident'.[330] States are under a concrete due diligence obligation to take preventive measures to avoid loss of lives in their SAR zone. With regard to situations of distress occurring beyond states' SAR zones, however, it is unclear whether there is a legal obligation to intervene.[331] Arguably, under certain conditions, a distress call can establish a jurisdictional link between the receiving state and the individuals in peril at sea, for their fate depends on the conduct of the state's authorities.

This is the line of argument followed by the majority of the HRC in the *A.S., D.I., O.I. and G.G.* case.[332] I will further detail the circumstances of this case and their legal implications for the scope of human rights obligations in the next chapter. Here, I shall however stress its relevance in relation to the content of SAR duties. The communication regarded a shipwreck in the Mediterranean Sea, resulting in the death of over 200 migrants. The vessel transporting them was beyond Italy's SAR zone and within the Maltese one. Yet, in the HRC's view, the distress call received by the Italian authorities, the proximity of an Italian ship and Italy's relevant legal obligations under the international law of the sea established a 'special relationship of dependency' between the individuals on the vessel and the state.[333] The Italian authorities had the power and the capacity to intervene

[327] Trevisanut (n 320) 12.

[328] For further discussion, see ch 5, s IV.C.

[329] This is even more true where international organisations are involved. On the notion of 'omission' in relation to the responsibility of international organisations, see extensively: Jan Klabbers, 'Reflections on Role Responsibility: The Responsibility of International Organizations for Failing to Act' (2017) 28 *European Journal of International Law* 1133.

[330] *Furdík* (n 276) para 1.

[331] See, eg, CoE, Parliamentary Assembly, *Lives lost in the Mediterranean Sea: Who is responsible?* Resolution 1872 (2012).

[332] HRC, *A.S., D.I., O.I. and G.D. v Italy*, Comm No 3042/2017, UN Doc CCPR/C/130/D/3042/2017, 27 January 2021.

[333] ibid, para 7.8.

promptly to avoid the foreseeable deaths of the persons on the vessel. But they did not; rather, they kept passing the responsibility to the Maltese MRCC. Italy was thus found responsible both for its negligent acts and omissions, which endangered the victims' lives and resulted in their death and for having failed to conduct a prompt investigation of allegations relating to a violation of the right to life.[334]

The members of the Committee were anything but in agreement about these findings. For the present purposes, it is worth recalling the dissenting opinion of Yuval Shany, Christof Heynes and Photini Pazartzis, according to which the mere fact of the ship's contacting Italian authorities was not sufficient to establish jurisdiction.[335] Admittedly, the views of the majority compound the existence of Italy's jurisdiction and its substantive obligations. In this respect, the specificity of due diligence obligations merits some attention. Due diligence obligations generally apply under two cumulative conditions: (1) the duty-bearer had foreseen, or ought to have reasonably foreseen, the risk of harm; and (2) the duty-bearer had a sensible capacity to intervene to avoid or minimise the harmful outcome.[336] As opposed to the effective control over the right-owner – necessary to establish jurisdiction – due diligence obligations are qualified by the duty-bearer's control over the cause of harm.[337] It is, therefore, necessary to ascertain independently the existence of jurisdiction – that is, some form of state control or power over the right-holder and not merely the existence of a causal relationship between the duty-bearer and the source of harm. Conflating the two forms of control risks diluting the relational specificity of human rights and their correlative duties.[338] In practice, and in the jurisprudence of various human rights bodies, however, the difference between these two expressions of control is not so straightforward.

On one hand, the 'special relationship of dependency' between Italy and the victims of the shipwreck triggered the state's jurisdiction.[339] The people on the vessel in distress were dependent upon the action of the alerted authorities. This factual and legal control or power to affect those individuals substantiated the existence of Italy's jurisdiction. On the other hand, the SAR Convention establishes that any state's 'search and rescue unit receiving information of a distress incident shall initially take immediate action if in the position to assist'.[340] This is a due diligence obligation, requiring a state to make its best efforts within the available means. The Italian authorities were capable of intervening, and the risks of failing to do so were predictable. This sensible capacity to intervene and the predictability of the harm that occurred qualify the SAR diligence obligation.

[334] ibid, paras 8.2 and 8.7.
[335] Dissenting opinions of Yuval Shany, Christof Heynes, Photini Pazartzis, para 3.
[336] ICJ Reports 43, para 43; ILA Study Group on Due Diligence in International Law Second Report July 2016.
[337] Samantha Besson, 'ESIL Reflection – Due Diligence and Extraterritorial Human Rights Obligations – Mind the Gap!' European Society of International Law, 28 April 2020.
[338] ibid.
[339] For further discussion on the issue of jurisdiction see Ch 4, s IV.B.iii.
[340] SAR Convention, Annex 4.3.

Whereas the Mediterranean Sea remains among the deadliest migration routes in the world, SAR activities are often delayed or inadequate.[341] These delays and failures are primarily caused by uncertainties regarding the responsible MRCC authority and the designated safe port for disembarkation, particularly where SAR zones overlap. A more coordinated EU approach to SAR and migrants' protection at sea was put forward in the Pact on Migration and Asylum. Nonetheless, the Pact primarily focuses on effective migration management and preventing irregular arrivals, rather than prioritising the protection of migrants at sea and addressing the structural factors that drive them to embark on dangerous journeys.[342]

At the same time, the ECtHR seemed to suggest – somehow alluding to Member States' positions – that people in distress at sea bear a degree of responsibility for having exposed themselves to unjustified danger.[343] While this assumption seems morally questionable, from a legal perspective, states SAR obligations are universal and benefit *anyone* in distress at sea.[344] Furthermore, when a distress situation occurs within the SAR zone of a state and its authorities intervene, their engagement in SAR operations cannot legitimise *refoulement* practices,[345] nor absolve them from their positive obligations, namely to ensure that the life of people at sea is protected in a sufficient and adequate manner.[346] In this context, the ECtHR recalled that public authorities' duty to safeguard the right to life 'involves the setting up of an appropriate regulatory framework for rescuing persons in distress and ensuring the effective functioning of such a framework'.[347] This implies that states not only have an obligation to assist migrants in distress at sea, but they must do so with appropriate legal and practical means.

D. Freedom of Movement and the Right to Leave to Seek Asylum

The right to freedom of movement emerges in international law in three main manifestations. First, it involves the right to move freely within the territory of one's country and to choose one's place of residence there.[348] Second, it encompasses the right to leave any country including one's own; in other words, it

[341] OHCHR, *"Lethal Disregard": Search and rescue and the protection of migrants in the central Mediterranean Sea*, May 2021.

[342] Violeta-Moreno-Lax, 'A New Common European Approach to Search and Rescue? Entrenching Proactive Containment' (Odysseus Blog, 3 February 2021) https://eumigrationlawblog.eu/a-new-common-european-approach-to-search-and-rescue-entrenching-proactive-containment/.

[343] *Safi* (n 273) para 165.

[344] See extensively Violeta Moreno-Lax, 'The Interdiction of Asylum Seekers at Sea: Law and (mal) practice in Europe and Australia' (2017) Kaldor Centre Policy Brief 4.

[345] *Hirsi Jamaa* (n 326) paras 134–38.

[346] *Safi* (n 273) para 148.

[347] *Alhowais* (n 269) para 118.

[348] Art 12(1), ICCPR; Art 13(1), UDHR; Art 2(1), Protocol No 4 to the ECHR.

embraces the right to cross an international border.[349] Third, it extends to the right to enter or return to one's own country.[350] In the EU, whereas every citizen of the Union has the right to move and reside freely within the Member States' territory, third-country nationals 'may be granted' such rights in accordance with the TFEU.[351]

The related rights to leave, reside and return are interdependent: the denial of any of these rights contradicts the affirmation of the other.[352] Among the manifestations of freedom of movement, the right to leave involves a twofold obligation, not to impede departure and to facilitate it by issuing travel documents (at least to nationals).[353] It has been argued, however, that the right to leave is not a full right but only an imperfect claim towards a particular country of destination.[354] In fact, the right to leave and the right to return are mainly addressed to countries of origin,[355] while there is no analogous right to enter other countries.[356] Concretely, the right to leave largely depends on the will of destination states, which are traditionally assumed to retain exclusive control over the admission of foreigners into their territory.[357] The right to leave was thus considered just 'half a right',[358] for without a state allowing entry, it becomes an empty promise. In this sense, 'the normative asymmetry between entry and exit is the product of contemporary international law',[359] which has endorsed and restated the right to emigrate while overlooking that the corresponding right to immigrate remains a matter primarily regulated by domestic law.[360] No *de lege ferenda* approach that seeks to surmount the deficiencies of the current legal framework can deny this normative asymmetry. At this stage of its development, international law does not recognise a general right to freedom of movement.

[349] Art 12 (2), ICCPR; Art 13 (2), UDHR; Art 2(2), Protocol No 4 to the ECHR.

[350] Art 12 (4), ICCPR; Art 13 (2), UDHR; Art 3, Protocol No 4 to the ECHR.

[351] Art 45, CFR.

[352] Rosalyn Higgins, 'The Right in International Law of an Individual to Enter, Stay in and Leave a Country' (1973) 49 *International Affairs (Royal Institute of International Affairs)* 341, 342.

[353] HRC, General Comment No 27, Freedom of Movement, UN Doc CCPR/C/21/Rev.1/Add.9, 2 November 1999, paras 9–10.

[354] Chetail (n 87) 91; Goodwin-Gill and McAdam (n 87) 382.

[355] For a historical account see: Andrew Wolman, 'The Role of Departure States in Combating Irregular Emigration in International Law: An Historical Perspective' (2019) 20 *International Journal of Refugee Law* 1.

[356] For further discussion, see: Chetail (n 87) 91.

[357] ECtHR, *Abdulaziz, Cabales and Balkandali v the UK*, Appl Nos 9214/80 9473/81 9474/81, 28 May 1985. For an historical reconstruction see: Jane McAdam, 'An Intellectual History of Freedom of Movement in International Law: The Right to Leave as a Personal Liberty' (2011) 12 *Melbourne Journal of International Law* 27.

[358] Satvinder S Juss, 'Free Movement and the World Order' (2004) 16 *International Journal of Refugee Law* 289, 293.

[359] Chetail (n 87) 91–92.

[360] This asymmetry has been questioned legally and philosophically. Among the copious literature on the topic, see: Joseph H Carens, 'Aliens and Citizens: The Case for Open Borders' (1987) 49 *The Review of Politics* 251; Satvinder Juss, *International Migration and Global Justice* (Farnham, Ashgate, 2006); Catherine Wihtol de Wenden, *Le Droit d'Emigrer* (Paris, CNRS Editions, 2013); Oberman Kieran, 'Immigration as a Human Right' in Sarah Fine and Lea Ypi (eds), *Migration in Political Theory:*

Still, states' sovereignty over their borders does not imply absolute discretion but must comply with the prohibition of *refoulement* and other human rights obligations. On the one hand, albeit it may not be squarely equated to a legal right of entry and stay, the prohibition of *refoulement* circumscribes state discretion over their borders.[361] On the other hand, the right to seek and enjoy asylum is now increasingly recognised not only as a right of states but also of individuals – to the extent that they have the right to seek protection elsewhere.[362] Article 18 of the CFR explicitly recognises this right. Accordingly, the right to asylum should be understood to entail a positive obligation on the EU and its Member States to ensure that it can be effectively exercised and relied upon by its beneficiaries.[363]

The right to leave complements the prohibition of *refoulement* as a precondition for the right to seek and enjoy asylum. In this sense, one can refer to the 'right to leave to seek asylum'.[364] The conceptual link between the right to leave and the right to seek and enjoy asylum is created by the prohibition of *refoulement*. The notions of *non-refoulement* and asylum are two faces of the same coin. While the former implies the prohibition to remove anyone to a place where she would be exposed to serious harm, the latter entails admission to the territory of a state where the individual will be granted protection from that harm.[365] A gap, however, continues to persist between *non-refoulement* and asylum. The latter always implies a prohibition of *refoulement*; but the opposite is not true: *non-refoulement* does not involve an obligation to grant asylum.[366] At a bare minimum, however, it entails an obligation to grant individuals seeking international protection access to the territory and adequate procedures to determine if these persons should be granted protection.[367] Thus, within the narrow perimeter of the prohibition

The Ethics of Movement and Membership (Oxford, Oxford University Press, 2016); Justin Desautels-Stein, *The Right to Exclude: A Critical Race Approach to Sovereignty, Borders, and International Law* (Oxford, Oxford University Press, 2023).

[361] Goodwin-Gill and McAdams (n 87) 241–349.

[362] See Maria-Teresa Gil-Bazo, 'The Charter of Fundamental Rights of the European Union and the Right to Be Granted Asylum in the Union's Law' (2008) 27 *Refugee Survey Quarterly* 33; William Thomas Worster, 'The Contemporary International Law Status of the Right to Receive Asylum' (2014) 26 *International Journal of Refugee Law* 477; Madalina Moraru, 'The EU Fundamental Right to Asylum: In Search of Its Legal Meaning and Effects' in Maribel González Pascual and Sara Iglesias Sánchez (eds), *Fundamental Rights in the EU Area of Freedom, Security and Justice* (Cambridge, Cambridge University Press, 2021).

[363] Case C-72-22 PPU, *M.A. v Valstybės*, 30 June 2022, ECLI:EU:C:2022:505, paras 60–61.

[364] This argument was put forward by Goodwin-Gill and McAdam (n 87) 431–432 and further developed by Moreno-Lax with the notion of the 'right to flee'. See extensively: Violeta Moreno-Lax, 'Theorising the (Intersectional) Right to Flee in the ECHR: A Composite Entitlement to Leave to Escape Irreversible Harm' in Başak Çalı, Ledi Bianku and Iulia Motoc (eds), *The European Convention on Human Rights and Migration* (Oxford, Oxford University Press, 2021).

[365] Alice Edwards, 'Human Rights, Refugees, and The Right "To Enjoy" Asylum' (2005) 17 *International Journal of Refugee Law* 293.

[366] CLC Mubanga-Chipoya, Final Report, The Right of Everyone to Leave any Country, including His Own, and to Return to His Country, UN doc E/C.4/Sub.2/1988/35, June 1988, 482; Guy Goodwin-Gill, *The Refugee in International Law* (Oxford, Clarendon, 1996) 202.

[367] In this sense: HRC, *A.B. and B.D. v Poland*, Comm No 3017/2017, UN Doc CCPR/C/135/D/3017/2017, 3 February 2023, para 9.5; ECtHR, *A.B. and Others v Poland*, Appl No 42907/17, 30 June 2022, para 38;

of *refoulement*, a right to enter to seek asylum exists and does not allow for any restriction.

The notion of the right to leave to seek asylum is an aspect of the right to leave capable of imposing a correlative duty not only on the state of origin but also on states of destination.[368] In this sense, 'the nearest correlative duty may be not to frustrate the exercise of that right in such a way as to leave individuals exposed to persecution or other violations of their human rights'.[369] Practices of remote containment, maritime interdiction, visa restriction and other procedural hurdles may breach this obligation, for they indiscriminately prevent migrants from reaching the borders of a state where they could seek protection. Besides, imposing barriers on individuals seeking to leave a country where they would face persecution or irremediable harm is difficult to reconcile with the principle of good faith that should permeate the implementation of any international obligation.[370] Ultimately, anchoring the right to leave to the prohibition of *refoulement* and the effective exercise of the right to seek asylum suggests the existence of the corresponding obligations to allow departure from transit or departure countries and grant access to appropriate asylum procedures in destination states.[371]

Along these lines, during their collective activities, Frontex and Member States' authorities should 'fully respect fundamental rights, including access to asylum procedures'.[372] The right to seek asylum must be 'effectively respected in all circumstances, regardless of where the persons are detected or apprehended or whether they express a [wish] to seek asylum'.[373] In this respect, timely identification and referral to the competent national authorities are essential. Frontex's Code of Conduct, binding in all its operational activities, includes the obligation of referral to national authorities competent for receiving asylum requests.[374] Yet, the Consultative Forum has regularly identified a number of shortcomings, including inconsistencies in data reporting and deficiencies in referral mechanisms.[375]

ECtHR, *Amuur v France*, Appl No 19776/ 92, 25 June 1996, para 43; Tribunale di Roma, Prima Sezione Civile, RG 5615/2016, 28 November 2019. See also: Gregor Noll, *Negotiating Asylum: The EU Acquis, Extraterritorial Protection and the Common Market of Deflection* (Leiden, Martinus Nijhoff, 2000).

[368] Nora Markard, 'The Right to Leave by Sea: Legal Limits on EU Migration Control by Third Countries' (2016) 27 *European Journal of International Law* 591, 595.

[369] Goodwin-Gill and McAdam (n 87) 431.

[370] See Guy S Goodwin-Gill, 'The Right to Leave, the Right to Return and the Question of a Right to Remain' in V Gowlland-Debbas (ed), *The Problem of Refugees in the Light of Contemporary International Law Issues* (Amsterdam, Kluwer Academic, 1995) 95–106.

[371] Under EU law, a similar approach was taken by Advocate General Paolo Mengozzi in the case of *X and X*. See: *X and X v Etat Belgium*, Opinion of the AG Paolo Mengozzi, Case C-638/16 PPU, 7 February 2017, ECLI:EU:C:2017:93. For similar acknowledgements, see: Guy S Goodwin-Gill, 'The Right to Seek Asylum: Interception at Sea and the Principle of Non-Refoulement' (2011) 23 *International Journal of Refugee Law* 443; Markard (n 368); Moreno-Lax (n 364).

[372] Art 43(4), Regulation 2019/1896.

[373] Frontex Fundamental Rights Strategy (2021), 5.

[374] Art 5, Code of Conduct applicable to all persons participating in Frontex operational activities, 2017.

[375] Eg: Consultative Forum Annual Report 2015, 28; Consultative Forum Annual Report 2016, 35; Consultative Forum Annual Report 2019, 118. See also European Ombudsman, Case 1452/2022/MHZ,

Most recently, the agency's Fundamental Rights Strategy further specified that all participants in Frontex operational activities are required to be 'proactive in the identification of and assistance to persons in need of international protection' and persons in vulnerable situations.[376]

From a different angle, the right to leave entails not only a negative obligation – that is, not to impede departures – but also a positive one.[377] This positive duty consists of providing the necessary conditions for the effective exercise of the right to leave, notably by issuing travel documents.[378] As a general rule, the positive obligation to provide adequate travel documents rests on the country of origin.[379] This cannot however exclude that, absent any alternative – for example, in the exceptional circumstances in which refugees find themselves – a positive obligation to issue travel documents could rest with the receiving country, provided a jurisdictional link is established with the latter.[380] People who are unable to receive any protection from their government against irreparable harm – and, *a fortiori*, any adequate travel document – should be enabled to exercise their right to leave to escape that harm.[381] This possibility could be opened by a reading of the right to leave in light of the principle of *non-refoulement*.

Frontex's joint operations on the territory of third countries raise serious questions about its respect for the right to leave, the prohibition of *refoulement* and the right to seek asylum. Joint operations hosted by third countries support those countries in implementing border control measures.[382] These measures mainly concern the entry of third-country nationals into the territory of the state hosting the operation, to prevent their transit and exit to the EU.[383] In fact, the principal objective of operational cooperation in the territory of third countries is to 'protect external borders and the effective management of the Union's migration policy'.[384] Put differently, instead of focusing on irregular entries, joint operations in third countries are directed at preventing exits. This may result not only in the violation

How the European Border and Coast Guard Agency (Frontex) handled a complaint concerning the rights of migrants in 'debriefing' interviews, 21 September 2022.

376 Management Board Decision 12/2021 adopting the Fundamental Rights Strategy, 14 February 2021, 7.

377 Colin Harvey and Robert P Barnidge, 'Human Rights, Free Movement, and the Right to Leave in International Law' (2007) 19 *International Journal of Refugee Law* 1.

378 HRC, General Comment No 27 (n 353) para 9.

379 HRC, *Varela Nunez v Uruguay* Comm No 108/1981, UN Doc CCPR/C/OP/2, 22 July 1983, paras 2.6 and 9.2; HRC, *Samuel Lichtensztejn v Uruguay*, Comm No 77/1980, UN Doc CCPR/C/OP/2, 31 March 1983, para 8.3.

380 See Vladislava Stoyanova, 'The Right to Leave Any Country and the Interplay between Jurisdiction and Proportionality in Human Rights Law' (2020) 32 *International Journal of Refugee Law* 403.

381 On the question whether states are under an obligation to process asylum requests in embassies or consulates, see: Gregor Noll, 'Seeking Asylum at Embassies: A Right to Entry under International Law?' (2005) 17 *International Journal of Refugee Law* 542; Kate Ogg, 'Protection Closer to Home? A Legal Case for Claiming Asylum at Embassies and Consulates' (2014) 33 *Refugee Survey Quarterly* 81.

382 See Art 2 (10–12), SBC.

383 See, eg, Operational Plan (Annexes), Joint Coordination Points, Land, LBS/03, 2017; Operational Plan (Annexes), Joint Coordination Points, Land, 2018/LBS/03, 2018 [on file with the author].

384 Recital 87, Regulation 2019/1896.

of the right to leave, but also in the circumvention of the prohibition of *refoulement*. A similar result may be obtained by sharing information regarding the position of migrant vessels in distress in the Central Mediterranean with the Libyan authorities, when it is reasonably foreseeable that, if intercepted, the people on board would suffer serious human rights violations upon disembarkation in Libya.[385]

The EU and its Member States' cooperation with third states, such as Türkiye or Libya, further challenges the prohibition of *refoulement* in connection with the right to leave and to seek asylum. This cooperation aims to indirectly hinder migrants from leaving third countries and reaching Europe to seek protection. Moreover, it has numerous dangerous side effects, such as exposing migrants to ill-treatment and arbitrary detention in third countries, which, if not intended as deterrence measures, are at least willingly accepted by European actors.

While human rights law appears to confine the opposability of the right to leave to departure states, containment measures largely serve the interest of destination states. One could argue that even though states of origin are the main addresses of the right to leave, the same right could in certain situations, such as those of people in need of international protection, be opposable to states of destination. Yet, the jurisdictional requirement in situations where no physical contact with the people concerned is established remains difficult to fulfil. An alternative that would recognise the role of destination states in violating the right to leave would rely on their indirect responsibility. But again, as further detailed below, the regime of indirect responsibility under international law is not free from complications.[386]

The ostensible effort by the EU and its Member States to design measures that both keep people at a distance and shield them from any direct responsibility raises serious doubts over their bona fide compliance with the prohibition of *refoulement*. International and EU migration law are part of the problem. On the one hand, the EIBM frames the arrangement of a continuum of control that extends to third countries without direct contact with the people involved. In this sense, EU migration law and policy facilitate the violation of the right to leave to seek asylum. On the other hand, international law offers no clear solutions to this problem. On the contrary, in many ways, contemporary international law not only denies the right to immigrate but also structures and bolsters impediments to the effective exercise of the right to leave and seek and enjoy asylum.

E. The Right to Family Reunification and the Protection of Migrant Children

Beyond the prohibition of *non-refoulement*, a second ground for admission is based on the right to family life as codified in an array of international and regional

[385] Consultative Forum (n 281), 27.
[386] See Ch 5, s IV.B.ii.

human rights conventions. The UDHR provides that the family 'is entitled to protection by society and the State'.[387] The same principle is enshrined in many universal and regional human rights treaties.[388] In Europe, the right to private and family life is mainly protected by Article 8 of the ECHR, reproduced in Article 7 of the CFR.

The HCR has clarified that though the ICCPR does not recognise the right to enter or reside in the territory of a state party, 'in certain circumstances an alien may enjoy the protection of the Covenant even in relation to entry or residence, for example, when considerations of non-discrimination, prohibition of inhuman treatment and respect for family life arise'.[389] In the same vein, under Article 19(6) of the Revised European Social Charter, Member States must 'facilitate as far as possible the reunion of the family of a foreign worker permitted to establish himself in the territory'.[390] This obligation must include 'at least the worker's spouse and unmarried children, as long as the latter are considered to be minors by the receiving State and are dependent on the migrant worker'.[391]

The circumstances under which the right to family reunification may arise have been broadly considered in the case law of human rights monitoring bodies.[392] Most importantly, the ECtHR has developed a comprehensive jurisprudence concerning the protection of the family unit in the context of the right to respect for family life under Article 8 of the Convention. The Court recognised that where the family cannot reasonably be expected to relocate to the country of origin or elsewhere, Article 8 places contracting states under a positive obligation to admit family members.[393] Even though state authorities exercise a certain margin of appreciation in assessing such an obstacle, they should evaluate each case considering the applicants' individual situation.[394] As family reunification

[387] Art 16(3), UDHR.

[388] Art 23(1) and 17, ICCPR; Art 10(1), ICESCR; Art 44(1), ICRMW; Art 17(1), ACHR; Art 15(1), Protocol of San Salvador; Art 18(1), ACHPR; Arts 18(1) and 25, African Charter on the Rights and Welfare of the Child, 1 July 1990; Art 33(2), ArCHR; Art 8(1) Covenant on the Rights of the Child in Islam, OIC/9-IGGE/HRI/2004/Rep Final, June 2005; Art 13, Arts 7 and 33, CFR; Art 8, ECHR.

[389] HRC, General Comment No 15: The Position of Aliens under the Covenant, UN Doc HRI/GEN/1/Rev1, 1986, para 5.

[390] CoE, European Social Charter (revised), ETS No163, 3 May 1996.

[391] CoE, Parliamentary Assembly, *Recommendation 1686 (2004), Human mobility and the right to family reunion*, Doc 10581, 17 June 2005, para 9.

[392] Among the copious literature see: Vladislava Stoyanova, 'Populism, Exceptionality, and the Right to Family Life of Migrants under the European Convention on Human Rights' (2017) 10 *European Journal of Legal Studies* 83; Elspeth Guild, 'EU Citizens, Foreign Family Members and European Union Law' (2019) 21 *European Journal of Migration and Law* 358; Wouter Vandenhole, Gamze Erdem Türkelli and Sara Lembrechts, 'Family Reunification' in *Children's Rights: A Commentary on the Convention on the Rights of the Child and its Protocols* (Cheltenham, Edward Elgar, 2019); Frances Nicholson, 'The Right to Family Reunification' in Cathryn Costello, Michelle Foster and Jane McAdam (eds), *The Oxford Handbook of International Refugee Law* (Oxford, Oxford University Press, 2021).

[393] *Abdulaziz, Cabales and Balkandali* (n 357) paras 67–68; ECtHR, *Ahmut v the Netherlands*, Appl Nos 73/1995/579/665, 26 October 1996, paras 69–73.

[394] See eg: ECtHR, *Gül v Switzerland*, Appl No 23218/94, 19 February 1996, para 38 and dissenting opinion of Judge Martens approved by Judge Russo; ECtHR, *Şen v Pays-Bas*, Appl No 31465/96, 21 December 2001, para 37; ECtHR, *Tuquabo-Tekle v The Netherlands*, Appl No 60665/00, 19 October 2004,

is not an absolute obligation, state authorities must strike a balance between the interests of the state and those of the individuals concerned.[395] The focus of the ECtHR has mainly been on the individual's circumstances, which results in treating the right to family reunification as an exception to the general rule of a state's right to exclude migrants.[396] In any event, the decision must be proportional to its legitimate aim. More specifically, in cases involving children, the Court emphasised that national authorities must give precedence to the best interests of the child in the review of the proportionality of the interference with family life.[397] In addition, the decision to allow a foreigner to enter the country based on the right to family reunion should not infringe on the principle of non-discrimination enshrined in Article 14 ECHR.[398]

What constitutes a family encompasses a wide range of human relations. The jurisprudence of the ECtHR has individuated two main categories of relationships: relationships between children and their parents; and partnerships between adults.[399] In general, the existence of family life depends on 'the existence of close, continuing, and practical ties'.[400] Compared to human rights law, EU law embraces a narrower definition of family for the purposes of family reunification. Directive 2003/86 on the right to family reunification recognises such right for the spouse of a third-country national lawfully residing in a Member State and for minor, unmarried children, including adopted children, of the non-national and of the spouse.[401] With regard to refugees and asylum seekers, the Qualification Directive includes a similar definition of family members, but it also specifies that it refers to relationships that already 'existed in the country of origin'.[402] Lastly, the Citizenship Directive provides a right to enter and reside in the EU for third-country nationals who are family members of EU citizens.[403]

In implementing Directive 2003/86/EC, Member States should comply with Article 8 ECHR, 'without discrimination on the basis of sex, race, colour, ethnic or social origin, genetic characteristics, language, religion or beliefs, political or

paras 56–61; ECtHR, *Omoregie and Others v Norway*, Appl No 265/07, 31 July 2008, para 59; ECtHR, *Berisha v Switzerland*, Appl No 948/12, 20 January 2014, para 56.

[395] See eg: *Tuquabo-Tekle v The Netherlands* (n 394) para 91.

[396] See extensively: Marie-Bénédicte Dembour, *When Humans Become Migrants: Study of the European Court of Human Rights with an Inter-American Counterpoint* (Oxford, Oxford University Press, 2015) ch 4.

[397] ECtHR, *Mugenzi c France*, Appl No 52701/09, 10 July 2014, para 39.

[398] ECtHR, *Biao v Denmark*, Appl No 38590/10, 24 May 2016, paras 93-94.

[399] ECtHR, *Onur v United Kingdom*, Appl No 27319/07, 17 February 2009, para 43.

[400] Costello (n 201) 164.

[401] Art 4(1), Directive (EC) 2003/86 on the Right to Family Reunification, [2003] OJ L 251/13.

[402] Art 2 (j), Directive (EU) 2011/95. See also: Case C-374/22, XXX, 23 November 2023, ECLI: EU: C: 2023: 902.

[403] Art 5, Directive (EC) 2004/38 on the right of citizens of the Union and their family members to move and reside freely within the territory of the Member States [2004] L 158/ 77. For a complete analysis of the interaction between the protection of family life under EU law and the ECHR, see: Sergio Carrera, Elspeth Guild and Katharina Eisele, *No Move without Free Movement: The EU-Swiss Controversy over Quotas for Free Movement of Persons* (Bruxelles, CEPS, 2015).

other opinions, membership of a national minority, fortune, birth, disabilities, age or sexual orientation'.[404] Still, the narrow definition included in EU law may result in the violation of the international obligation to facilitate family reunification and the principle of non-discrimination.[405] Family reunification under Directive 2003/86 can be denied on the grounds of public policy, public security or public health. Additional grounds for refusal include the end of the relationship and marriages of convenience.[406] However, the CJEU clarified that the conditions therein must be construed narrowly.[407]

Under international law, there seems to be an emerging consensus around the customary nature of the right to family reunification for nuclear families,[408] or at least minor children.[409] In this sense, the CRC protects the best interest of the child[410] and mandates states not to separate children from their parents, except when this separation is in their best interest.[411] This is not to say that the child's best interest displaces every other consideration. However, there seems to be growing support for the idea that children's best interests can only be overridden by other rights-based considerations, as opposed to the state's general interest in immigration control.[412] In this regard, it should be noted that the right of the child to family life has a broader scope in the CRC than in general human rights law (applicable to adults). Therefore, it is hard to argue that family reunification is not in the best interests of the child.[413]

At the EU level, the protection of migrant children is fragmented into various legal instruments largely designed for adults. Most notably, migrant children's rights are unsystematically scattered across different EU legal instruments, depending on whether the children are seeking asylum, have been trafficked or are subject to return procedures. This implies inconsistencies and gaps, not least because children may simultaneously fall within the scope of different legal

[404] Preamble, recitals 2 and 5, Directive (EC) 2003/86.

[405] See Sonia Morano Foadi and Karin de Vries, 'The Equality Clauses in the EU Directives on Non-Discrimination and Migration/Asylum' in Sonia Morano-Foadi and Micaela Malena (eds), *Integration for Third-Country Nationals in the European Union* (Cheltenham, Edward Elgar, 2012).

[406] Directive 2003/86, Art 16.

[407] Case C-540/03, *European Parliament v Council*, 27 June 2006, ECLI:EU:C:2006:429, para 60; CJEU, *Chakroun*, Case C-578/08, 4 March 2010, EU:C:2010:117, para 43.

[408] See: Guy S Goodwin-Gill, *International Law and the Movement of Persons Between the States* (Oxford, Oxford University Press, 1978) 197; Sonja Starr and Lea Brilmayer, 'Family Separation as a Violation of International Law' (2003) 21 *Berkeley Journal of International Law* 213.

[409] Chetail (n 87) 126–27.

[410] Art 9, CRC.

[411] ibid, Art 3(1).

[412] See: CRC, General Comment No 6, Treatment of unaccompanied and separated children outside their country of origin, UN Doc CRC/GC/2005/6, 1 September 2005, para 86; UNHCR, Guidelines on Determining the Best Interests of the Child, May 2008, para 76; ECtHR, *Neulinger and Shuruk v Switzerland* (Grande Chambre), Appl No 41615/07, 6 July 2010.

[413] Ciara M Smyth, 'Family Life and the Best Interests of the Child in the Field of Migration' in Maribel González Pascual and Sara Iglesias Sánchez (eds), *Fundamental Rights in the EU Area of Freedom, Security and Justice* (Cambridge, Cambridge University Press, 2021).

frameworks. The case law of the CJEU reflects the ambiguity of this sensitive area of law and policy.[414] For example, the best interest of migrant children, as protected by the CRC and particularly those who are unaccompanied, seems not sufficiently protected in EU return procedures. The current Return Directive does not include any specific protection regarding unaccompanied migrant children.[415] Its proposed recast seems to perpetuate this gap and at the same time expand the grounds for detention, which could increase the risk of arbitrary detention of migrant children.[416] Yet, the ECtHR enhanced the best interest of the child originally proclaimed by the CRC.[417] Albeit inconsistently, the Strasbourg Court developed a sophisticated jurisprudence on migrant children arbitrary detention and ill-treatment at the borders, including against invasive age assessment procedures,[418] lack of age-appropriate detention facilities or effective guardianship.[419]

The enhanced powers of Frontex in return procedures may have an impact on the protection of migrant children. Namely, the VEGA Children Handbooks to Frontex joint air, land and sea operations provide border guards with essential indications on how to effectively apply the principle of the best interests of the child and on how to deal and communicate with children.[420] Furthermore, improving child-sensitive training and forced-return monitoring mechanisms is likely to increase the alignment of national standards to those set in the agency's regulation.[421] In this context, Frontex 'makes available forced-return monitors with specific expertise in child protection for any return operation involving children'.[422] Yet, the number of national return operations with forced-return monitors present is limited.[423] Frontex's new legal framework might somewhat improve this situation, as it gives the FRO the power to appoint fundamental rights monitors as forced-return monitors.[424]

[414] ibid.

[415] Directive 2008/115/EC of the European Parliament and of the Council on common standards and procedures in Member States for returning illegally staying third-country nationals [2008] OJ L 348.

[416] Article 18, Proposal for a Directive of the European Parliament and of the Council on common standards and procedures in Member States for returning illegally staying third-country nationals (recast), 19 September 2018, COM(2018) 634 final. Cf: Ciara Smyth, 'Towards a Complete Prohibition on the Immigration Detention of Children' (2019) 19 *Human Rights Law Review* 1.

[417] Ciara M Smyth, 'The Jurisprudence of the European Court of Human Rights Relevant to Child Migrants' in Jacqueline Bhabha, Kanics Jyothi and Daniel Senovilla Hernández (eds), *Research Handbook on Child Migration* (Cheltenham, Edward Elgar, 2018).

[418] ECtHR, *Yazgül Yılmaz c. Turquie*, Appl No 36369/06, 1 February 2011.

[419] ECtHR, *Sh.D. et autres c. Grèce, Autriche, Croatie, Hongrie, Macédoine du Nord, Serbie et Slovénie*, Appl No 14165/16, 13 June 2021.

[420] VEGA Handbook: Children at airports, 2015; VEGA Handbook: Children at land borders, 2021; VEGA Handbook: Children at sea borders, 2021.

[421] See Arts 51 and 62, Regulation 2019/1896.

[422] Art 51(4), Regulation 2019/1896.

[423] For example, in 2019, Frontex's forced-return monitors were present in 55 per cent of national return operations. Frontex, Evaluation Report, Return Operations, 17 December 2019, 8.

[424] Art 109(2)(c), Regulation 2019/1896. However, this power has been concretely obstructed over the years. Consultative Forum Annual Report 2021, 15–16.

More generally, the agency's Fundamental Rights Strategy underlines that the best interests of the child should be central to any decision affecting children.[425] To do so, in all their activities, Member States and Frontex should implement specific measures to ensure that children's rights are respected, especially regarding unaccompanied children or those separated from their families. That includes not only taking the best interests of the child into primary consideration, but also respecting the right of the child to be heard in all procedures.[426]

F. The Right to Privacy and Protection of Personal Data

The right to privacy is included in several human rights treaties of universal and regional scope, as well as in specific conventions.[427] While the ECHR does not include a specific provision on the right to data protection, it has been derived from the right to private and family life under Article 8. These two rights can be conceptually linked through the notion of informational self-determination, which implies control over one's personal information.[428] In the EU legal order, the right to privacy and the protection of personal data are enshrined in Articles 7 and 8 of the CFR. While the former reflects Article 8 of the ECHR, the latter is a provision specific to the CFR, which is unique in recognising the right to data protection as separate from the right to privacy.[429] It grounds the right to data protection in the principles of consent; in the principle of specific, explicit and legitimate purpose of data collection; and in the right to access to data and rectification. The CJEU has interpreted the current legal framework as also including the right to delete data, or the right to be forgotten.[430]

In the past, the importance of data protection has been often overlooked in border control and migration policy.[431] Yet, the challenges that link information technologies and data protection are far from negligible in a field in continuous and rapid development.[432] The increased use of centralised databases, the

[425] Fundamental Rights Strategy, 2021, 5.

[426] ibid.

[427] Art 12, UDHR; Art 17, ICCPR; Art 16, CRC; Art 14, ICRMW; Art 22, CRPD; ACHR; Art 16(8), ArCHR; Art 8, ECHR; CoE, Convention for the Protection of Individuals with regard to Automatic Processing of Personal Data, ETS 108, 28 January 1981; CoE, Modernised Convention for the Protection of Individuals with Regard to the Processing of Personal Data, 18 May 2018.

[428] See generally: Herke Kranenborg, 'Article 8 – Protection of Personal Data' in Steve Peers and others (eds), *The EU Charter of Fundamental Rights: A Commentary* (Oxford, Hart Publishing, 2021).

[429] See also Objective 1, GCM.

[430] Case C-131/12, *Google v Spain*, 13 May 2014, ECLI:EU:C:2014:317.

[431] See however: Evelien Brouwer, *Digital Borders and Real Rights: Effective Remedies for Third-Country Nationals in the Schengen Information System* (Leiden, Brill, 2008).

[432] Among the burgeoning literature, see: Izabella Majcher, 'The Schengen-Wide Entry Ban: How Are Non-Citizens' Personal Data Protected?' (2020) 48 *Journal of Ethnic and Migration Studies* 1944; Niovi Vavoula, 'Artificial Intelligence (AI) at Schengen Borders: Automated Processing, Algorithmic Profiling and Facial Recognition in the Era of Techno-Solutionism' (2021) 23 *European Journal of Migration and Law* 457; Ana Beduschi, 'International Migration Management in the Age of Artificial Intelligence' (2021) 9 *Migration Studies* 576.

application of biometric data matching, and the enhanced interoperability of these systems have enabled the ever-closer tracking of individuals' movements. The EU and its Member States are investing in technological applications, ranging from centralised databases to drones or remotely piloted aircraft, to deploy the most effective technological means against security threats allegedly coming from outside.[433]

Migration technology enables and buttresses the process of externalising border surveillance and border control, and this entails several risks. First and foremost is the risk of profiling, with consequent serious discriminatory effects.[434] Border authorities can use legal technologies that apply machine-learning algorithms to implement predictive analysis and generate risk profiles for visas, residence permits or asylum applications (for instance by assessing the probability of criminal offences or welfare dependency). Furthermore, the multifunctional and automated use of the data in immigration databases is in tension with the purpose limitation principle.[435] According to this principle – one of the central tenets of EU data-protection law – data may be collected exclusively for previously defined and specific purposes and may only be used for such purposes.[436] Another challenge for the right to privacy and data protection – and perhaps other fundamental rights – is represented by the extension of border surveillance technologies. Within a process of continuous externalisation, the surveillance of specific areas beyond the EU borders, rather than serving life-saving purposes, can result in dissuading migrants' vessels from using safer routes and pushing them toward more dangerous journeys.[437]

The creation of the EU 'smart borders' together with the enhanced mandate of Frontex have had a significant impact on data protection, access to asylum and safeguarding of life at sea. Most notably, the 2016 Smart Borders Package introduced some important amendments to the SBC.[438] It introduced the obligation to conduct

[433] Luisa Marin and Kamila Krajčíková, 'Deploying Drones in Policing Southern European Borders: Constraints and Challenges for Data Protection and Human Rights' in Aleš Završnik (ed), *Drones and Unmanned Aerial Systems* (Cham, Springer, 2016).

[434] Report of the Special Rapporteur on contemporary forms of racism, racial discrimination, xenophobia and related intolerance, Racial discrimination and emerging digital technologies: a human rights analysis, UN Doc A/HRC/44/57, 18 June 2020; E Tendayi Achiume, 'Digital Racial Borders' (2021) 115 *American Journal of International Law* 333.

[435] Evelien Brouwer, 'Legal Boundaries and the Use of Migration Technology' in Huub Dijstelbloem and Albert Meijer (eds), *Migration and the New Technological Borders of Europe* (London, Palgrave Macmillan, 2011).

[436] Nikolaus Forgó, Stefanie Hänold and Benjamin Schütze, 'The Principle of Purpose Limitation and Big Data' in M Corrales, M Fenwick, N Forgó (eds), *New Technology, Big Data and the Law* (Singapore, Springer, 2017); N Ghani, S Hamid and I Udzir, 'Big Data and Data Protection-Issues with Purpose Limitation Principle' (2016) 8 *Int J Adv Soft Comput Appl* 116.

[437] Marin and Krajčíková, (n 433).

[438] Philip Hanke and Daniela Vitiello, 'High-Tech Migration Control in the EU and Beyond: The Legal Challenges of "Enhanced Interoperability"' in Elena Carpanelli and Nicole Lazzerini (eds), *Use and Misuse of New Technologies: Contemporary Challenges in International and European Law* (Cham, Springer, 2019).

systematic identity checks against relevant law enforcement databases on all persons (including EU citizens) crossing the EU borders.[439] Furthermore, automated border controls were operationalised through self-service and e-gates systems.[440]

The subsequent amendments to Frontex legal framework followed the expansion of the EU digital borders. Accordingly, the agency is now entrusted with the mandate to develop 'a common information-sharing environment, including interoperability of systems'.[441] To this end, EUROSUR provides a common framework for the exchange of information and cooperation between Frontex and Member States' border surveillance authorities, as well as with third countries via bilateral cooperation.[442] Besides, data exchanges are being expanded among various entities, including Europol and CSDP missions.[443]

These developments may, in turn, lead to several challenges. First, the large-scale data sharing supporting the EU 'smart borders' may impact not only the right to privacy and the protection of personal data of migrants and other border-crossers but can also have severe repercussions on other fundamental rights, such as the right to leave and the right to asylum.[444] Second, automation may disproportionately impact the rights of certain categories of border crossers, most notably undocumented migrants and asylum seekers, but also EU citizens with multiple nationalities.[445] Third, the interoperability of the various databases makes data easier to access but also to unlawfully share. The EU data protection framework regulates the transmission of data to third countries and international organisations and establishes specific safeguards.[446] Notably, the legal instrument establishing each EU database in the field of border and visas generally prohibits the transmission of data to third countries and international organisations. Yet, as an exception to this general rule, data sharing is allowed when it aims to identify a third-country national for the purpose of return.[447] This can expose the people concerned, especially if there are asylum seekers, to particular risks, such as retaliation measures in their country of origin.[448] In addition, the sharing of personal

[439] Art 1, Regulation (EU) 2017/458, [2017] OJ L 74/1.

[440] Art 1, Regulation (EU) 2017/2225, [2017] OJ L 327/1.

[441] Art 10(ac), Regulation 2019/1896. Frontex Fundamental Rights Strategy partially tackled this development by recalling that the use of new technological solutions should not only 'improve EIBM practice' but also 'ensure the Agency's compliance with fundamental rights'. See Fundamental Rights Strategy, 2021, 12.

[442] Arts 18 and 76, Regulation 2019/1896.

[443] EDPS, 'Exchange of personal data between Frontex and Europol' Hearing at the LIBE Committee (European Parliament, 8 November 2022); Frontex International Cooperation strategy, 2021–2023, 17.

[444] See for instance, the European Data Protection Supervisor's Opinion 02/2016, *EDPS' recommendations on the proposed European Border and Coast Guard Regulation*, 18 March 2016.

[445] Hanke and Vitiello (n 438).

[446] Art 46, Regulation (EU) 2016/679 [2016] OJ L 119.

[447] See eg: Art 41, Regulation (EU) 2017/2226 [2017] OJ L 327/20, 9 December 2017; Art 65, Regulation (EU) 2018/1240 [2018] OJ L 236/119, September 2018; Art 31(2), Regulation (EU) 2021/1134 [2021] OJ L 248.

[448] FRA, Fundamental rights and the interoperability of EU information systems: borders and security, July 2017, 27.

data between authorities that adhere to different data protection frameworks may entail risks regarding the different applicable standards and the accuracy of the information shared.[449] Finally, the increased number of authorities having access to the relevant databases further creates difficulty attributing responsibility where incorrect data management occurs.

The increasing digitalisation of border control operations can interfere with the fundamental rights of the person concerned. The EU legislator, however, has thus far deemed these interferences justified, as they are aimed at maintaining internal security and effectively managing the Union's borders.[450] While the objective of impeding irregular entry and residence is generally deemed an overriding reason to limit fundamental rights in the public interest, the necessity and proportionality of data processing operations, and their potential implications, in achieving this objective are far from obvious. Automated border control systems should be designed in a way that 'fully respects human dignity', in particular in cases involving persons in vulnerable situations.[451] Yet, this might be more easily said than (algorithmically) done.

G. The Protection against Arbitrary Detention

The right to liberty and security protects all individuals from unlawful or arbitrary arrest and detention. This rule, whose customary nature is well-established in international law,[452] is ubiquitous in human rights law.[453] The prohibition against arbitrary detention applies to all deprivations of liberty, including the detention of migrants at the border or within the territory of a state.[454] This does not imply the absolute character of the right to personal liberty. Therefore, the detention of irregular migrants for immigration control purposes has not been considered *ipso facto* illegal. Generally, to be considered legitimate under human rights law, a detention measure should: respect the principle of legal certainty,[455] be necessary and proportionate to its aim[456] and respect the right to an effective remedy following the minimum standards of due process.[457]

Along these lines, Article 5(1)(f) of the ECHR explicitly permits detention in two situations: to prevent unauthorised entry to the country, and pending

[449] Teresa Quintel, 'Interoperable Data Exchanges Within Different Data Protection Regimes: The Case of Europol and the European Border and Coast Guard Agency' (2020) 26 *European Public Law* 205.

[450] Recital 40, Regulation (EU) 2019/817 [2019] OJ L 135.

[451] Art 8(c), Regulation 2017/2225.

[452] Chetail (n 87) 133–38.

[453] See Art 9, ICCPR; Art 16, ICRMW; Art 37 (d), CRC; Art 5, ECHR; Art 6, CFR; Art 7, ACHR; Art 6, ACHPR; Art 20, ArCHR.

[454] See General Comment No 35: The Right of Liberty and Security of Person, CCPR/C/GC/35, 16 December 2014, para 9.

[455] See eg: ECtHR, *Amuur v France*, Appl No 19776/92, 25 June 1996, para 50.

[456] See eg: *J.R. et autres* (n 243) para 111.

[457] See eg: *Khlaifia* (n 240) paras 130–31.

deportation or extradition. Detention of migrants on other grounds, such as crime prevention or public health, is not admissible under the Convention. The grounds for any deprivation of liberty must be in accordance with and provided for by the law clearly and exhaustively.[458] The ECtHR has constantly recognised that detention measures aimed to prevent unauthorised entry or with a view to deportation do not require a necessity test under the ECHR.[459] But it has also acknowledged that

> [the] detention of an individual is such a serious measure that … it will be arbitrary unless it is justified as a last resort where other less severe measures have been considered and found to be insufficient to safeguard the individual or public interest which might require that the person concerned be detained.[460]

In addition, it is worth recalling here that Article 31 of the Refugee Convention mandates states not to impose penalties on asylum seekers on account of their illegal entry or presence.[461]

The applicability of Article 5 ECHR has been examined concerning stays in airport transit zones and reception centres for the identification and registration of migrants. In these contexts, the ECtHR determined whether a certain measure amounts to deprivation of liberty according to several factors, including the applicant's individual situation and their choices, the applicable legal regime of the respective country and its purpose, the duration of the confinement and the nature and degree of the actual restrictions imposed on the applicants.[462] The vulnerable situation of the applicant should be taken into consideration too. In particular, migrant children should not be subject to detention, which may only be applied as a last resort and for the shortest time possible.[463] Unaccompanied children should be identified as such and placed in adequate accommodations as soon as possible.[464]

In practice, however, states increasingly are employing immigration detention as both a means of deterrence and the prodromal stage of return procedures. The persistent tension between states' migration control prerogatives and the

[458] ECtHR, *H.L. v United Kingdom*, Appl No 45508/99, 5 October 2005, para 114.

[459] ECtHR, *Chahal v the United Kingdom*, preliminary objections, Appl No 22414/93, 15 November 1996, para 112; ECtHR, *Čonka v Belgium*, Appl No 51564/99, 5 February 2002, para 38; ECtHR, *Saadi v the United Kingdom*, Appl No 13229/03, 29 January 2008, paras 64–65.

[460] ECtHR, *Rusu v Austria*, Appl No 34082/02, 2 October 2008, para 58.

[461] Guy S Goodwin-Gill, 'Article 31 of the 1951 Convention Relating to the Status of Refugees: Non-Penalization, Detention and Protection' [2001] *Refugee Protection in International Law: UNHCR's Global Consultations on International Protection* 185.

[462] ECtHR, *Ilias and Ahmed v Hungary*, Appl No 47287/15, 21 November 2019, para 217.

[463] Art 37(b), CRC; ECtHR, *SH.D et autres c Grèce, Autriche, Croatie, Hongrie, Macédoine du Nord, Serbie et Slovénie*, Appl No14165/16, 13 June 2019, para 69. Note, however, that there seems to be an acceleration towards the complete prohibition of children's immigration detention. See: Joint General Comment No 4 (2017) of the CMW and No 23 of the CRC on State obligations regarding the human rights of children in the context of international migration in countries of origin, transit, destination and return, 16 November 2017; CoE, Parliamentary Assembly, Unaccompanied children in Europe: issues of arrival, stay and return, Resolution 1810 (2011), 15 April 2011, para 5.9. See generally: Smyth (n 414).

[464] Ibid, paras 5.3 and 5.9.

subjective right to liberty has often been moderated by EU law, which encompasses detailed provisions curtailing states' discretion regarding the detention of asylum seekers and irregular migrants.[465] With regard to the first category of persons, Article 8(2) of the Reception Conditions Directive provides that Member States may detain an asylum seeker only '[w]hen it proves necessary and on the basis of an individual assessment of each case', provided that 'other less coercive alternative measures cannot be applied effectively' and on grounds laid down in national law.[466] The provision introduces to EU law the necessity test, which is remarkably absent from the ECHR and the jurisprudence of its Court. This guarantee is somewhat weakened, however, by the vagueness of the various grounds for detention that it exhaustively enumerates.[467] As to the second category of persons, under Article 15 of the Return Directive, third-country nationals subject to return procedures can be detained in order to prepare and carry out the return, unless 'other sufficient but less coercive measures can be applied effectively in a specific case'.[468] EU law thus requires that the detention of migrants is a proportionate and necessary measure. Those requirements have been bolstered by judicial interactions, resulting in the expansion of judicial review powers of domestic courts.[469]

At the border, Member States may provide accelerated procedures for deciding on an application for international protection at border crossings or transit zones.[470] If the procedure exceeds four weeks, the applicant has the right to enter the territory of Member States until the application is processed.[471] Border procedures should now be coupled with the 'hotspot approach'.[472] The hotspot approach aims 'to better coordinate EU agencies' and national authorities' efforts at the external borders of the EU, on initial reception, identification, registration and fingerprinting of asylum-seekers and migrants'.[473] In the meantime, they should remain in 'hotspot areas' currently established across Italy and Greece.[474] Although labelled 'restriction of liberty' for a few days, prohibitions to leave the hotspot premises should be considered de facto detention.[475] Living conditions in those facilities have been criticised for the security conditions and the prolonged detention of

[465] Justine N Stefanelli and Elspeth Guild, 'The Right to Liberty in the Field of Migration, Asylum and Borders' in Maribel González Pascual and Sara Iglesias Sánchez (eds), *Fundamental Rights in the EU Area of Freedom, Security and Justice* (Cambridge, Cambridge University Press, 2021).

[466] Directive 2013/33/EU [2013] OJ L180/96 (Reception Conditions Directive).

[467] Art 8(3), Directive 2013/33/EU.

[468] Art 15, Directive 2008/115/EC.

[469] Galina Cornelisse and Madalina Moraru, 'Judicial Interactions on the European Return Directive: Shifting Borders and the Constitutionalisation of Irregular Migration Governance' (2022) 2022 7 *European Papers – A Journal on Law and Integration* 127, 138–43.

[470] Art 43, Directive 2013/32.

[471] Art 43(2).

[472] A European Agenda on Migration (n 252).

[473] European Parliament, Hotspots at EU external borders: State of play, June 2018.

[474] ibid.

[475] *J.R. et autres* (n 243) paras 83–84; *J.A. and Others* (n 257) para 98.

refugees and migrants,[476] where children are often held in the same facilities as adults.[477] Moreover, as noted by the Special Rapporteur on the human rights of migrants, as migrants detained in hotspots do not receive detention orders, challenging detention decisions is almost impossible.[478]

The New Pact on Migration and Asylum could normalise this situation. If adopted, the envisaged mechanism for the management of external borders explicitly endorses protracted confinement in border areas, resulting in the transformation of EU borders into 'anomalous zones' where certain legal rules are locally suspended.[479] While the Commission acknowledged the need to improve reception conditions at the EU external borders, abolishing containment policies is not a priority.[480] On the contrary, the newly introduced Pact and the proposed regulations widen the scope for increased stays at the borders, thereby increasing the potential of de facto detention.[481]

Beyond the physical frontiers of the EU, with the externalisation of migration control, the detention of migrants and asylum seekers has been equally outsourced to third countries and private actors. Reflecting the logic of concentric circles underlying the EIBM, externalised detention can be seen as an interlocking chain of diffusion processes whereby coercive measures are exported from the centre to the periphery.[482] On the one hand, this phenomenon implies a sort of 'internal externalisation' within European countries. In fact, EU migration law and policy force EU border states to serve as gatekeepers for Europe, thereby bolstering their detention practices. On the other hand, this leads to the proper externalisation and outsourcing of detention beyond the EU external borders, as EU border countries, EU agencies and international organisations together push detention practices outward to third countries. As a result, migrants are increasingly at risk of being detained in countries where the rule of law is fragile, and their most fundamental human rights are often ignored and routinely breached. The most worrying example is Libyan detention centres, where, notoriously, thousands of migrants are deprived of food, sunlight and water, and many become victims of sexual exploitation and assault, forced labour or torture.[483]

[476] OHCHR, Report of the Special Rapporteur on the human rights of migrants on his mission to Greece, UN Doc A/HRC/35/25/Add.2, 24 April 2017; ASGI, *Report sull'hotspot di Lampedusa*, August 2022.

[477] Amnesty International Report 2017/2018, The State of the World's Human Rights, 2018, 178.

[478] Report of the Special Rapporteur on the human rights of migrants (n 467) para 51.

[479] Giuseppe Campesi, 'The EU Pact on Migration and Asylum and the Dangerous Multiplication of 'Anomalous Zones' For Migration Management' in Sergio Carrera and Andrew Geddes (eds), *The EU Pact on Migration and Asylum in Light of the United Nations Global Compact on Refugees* (Florence, EUI, 2021).

[480] European Commission, 'Communication from the Commission on a New Pact on Migration and Asylum', COM(2020) 609 final, 3.

[481] Galina Cornelisse and Marcelle Reneman, 'Border Procedures in the European Union: How the Pact Ignored the Compacts' (2022) 11 *Laws* 38.

[482] Michael Flynn and Cecilia Cannon, 'Detention at the Borders of Europe' (*Global Detention Project*, 17 November 2010).

[483] See eg, OHCHR, *'Detained and dehumanised' Report on human rights abuses against migrants in Libya*, 13 December 2016; CMW, Concluding Observations on the Initial Report of Libya, UN Doc

H. Procedural Guarantees

Besides the prohibition of arbitrary detention and the procedural guarantees accompanying it, international and EU law also provide specific due process guarantees governing the situations of migrants at the borders. These procedural guarantees encompass a range of protections, including the prohibition of collective expulsions, as well as the right to a fair trial and to an effective remedy.

i. The Prohibition of Collective Expulsion

Collective expulsions are prohibited in an absolute manner by all major human rights treaties.[484] Most notably, the EU Member States are prohibited from conducting collective expulsions under Article 4 of Protocol No 4 to the ECHR (hereafter Protocol 4)[485] and Article 19(1) of the CFR.[486] Beyond its inclusion in treaty law, this absolute prohibition has arguably attained the status of customary international law, and therefore, it is binding on the EU and its Member States irrespective of their formal ratification of relevant treaties.[487] Significantly, the ECHR understanding of the concept of collective expulsion is transposable to EU law. Article 4 of Protocol 4 corresponds to Article 19(1) of the CFR, hence, pursuant to Article 52(3) of the CFR, the meaning and scope of the prohibition of collective expulsion under the CFR is the same as under the ECHR.

Under EU law, Member States issuing a return decision should do so 'in writing and give reasons in fact and in law as well as information about available legal remedies'.[488] However, in the case of irregular migrants without any legal title to stay on the territory, Member States can employ accelerated return procedures and standard forms instead of an individual return decision.[489] These simplified return practices are commonly used in the context of measures preventing admission and refusals at the border.[490] This, in turn, intensifies the risk of collective expulsions.[491]

CMW/C/LBY/CO/1, 8 May 2019; Human Rights Council, Report of the Independent Fact-Finding Mission on Libya, A/HRC/52/83, 3 March 2023, paras 40–53.

[484] Art 22(1), ICRMW; Art 22(9), ACHR; Art 12(5), ACHPR; Art 26(2), ArCHR; Art 4, Protocol No. 4 to the ECHR; Art 19, CFR. See also: CERD, General Recommendation No 30: Discrimination Against Non-Citizens, 1 October 2004, para 26; HRC, General Comment No 15 (n 389), para 10; Art 9, Draft Articles on the Expulsion of Aliens, *Yearbook of the International Law Commission*, 2014, vol. II, Part Two; GCM, objectives 8 and 21.

[485] Protocol No 4 to the Convention for the Protection of Human Rights and Fundamental Freedoms, Securing Certain Rights and Freedoms Other than Those Already Included in the Convention and in the First Protocol Thereto, ETS No 046, 16 September 1963. As of August 2023, all the states of the Schengen Area, except for Greece, Switzerland and the UK, were parties to Protocol 4.

[486] Art 19(1), CFR.

[487] Chetail (n 87) 124–32.

[488] Art 12(1), Directive 2008/115/EC.

[489] Art 12(3), Directive 2008/115/EC.

[490] See: European Commission, *State of the Union 2018: Stronger EU rules on return*, 12 September 2019.

[491] See extensively: Izabella Majcher, *The European Union Returns Directive and Its Compatibility with International Human Rights Law* (Leiden, Brill, 2020) 147–55.

With the enhanced return capacities of Frontex, its joint return operations may also imply some risk of collective expulsion. Despite many improvements having been achieved in human rights protection within the agency's legal framework, its amended regulation is still lacking an explicit reference to the prohibition of collective expulsion. A mention is included in The Appendix List of potential fundamental rights violations during operations, which should be consulted by applicants lodging a complaint to Frontex.[492] However, no preventive measure seems to be foreseen in the agency's legal or policy documents. This contrasts with the agency's positive obligation to ensure respect for fundamental rights. Furthermore, Frontex's multifaceted and broad assistance in joint return operations may arguably incentivise states to fill all the empty seats in a return flight. In this situation, the risk of assisting the implementation of return decisions taken without appropriate consideration of the individual circumstances of every person involved, deprived of adequate information, as well as medical, legal and linguistic assistance,[493] cannot be excluded.[494]

The prohibition of collective expulsion extends to every foreigner, irrespective of her lawful presence on the territory of a state.[495] It refers to any measure compelling a group of non-nationals to leave a country without a reasonable and objective examination of the situation of each individual concerned.[496] Hence, according to the ECtHR, the number of people subject to a similar expulsion measure is irrelevant.[497] The decisive element, which renders the expulsion contrary to Article 4 of Protocol 4, is therefore a procedural criterion, whereby the individuals concerned are no more considered as such, *uti singuli*, but as part of an impersonal whole. The ECtHR in *Čonka* explained that the background of the expulsion decision should be considered when determining whether the measure constitutes a collective expulsion.[498] In cases of collective expulsion, the common denominator has generally been the lack of an individual procedure.[499]

The Grand Chamber in *Khlaifia* explained however that Article 4 of Protocol 4

> does not guarantee the right to an individual interview in all circumstances; the requirements of this provision may be satisfied where each alien has a genuine and effective

[492] Potential applicants can find the list, which at the time of writing is available only in English, on the agency's website, in the section devoted to its fundamental rights complaint, https://frontex.europa.eu/fundamental-rights/complaints-mechanism/.

[493] See FRO Observations to return operations conducted in the 1st Semester of 2020, 9 December 2020, 3.

[494] For further discussion, see: Majcher (n 491) 576–621.

[495] CoE, Explanatory Report to Protocol No 4, ETS No 46, 16 October 1963, para 34.

[496] ECommHR, *Becker v Denmark*, Appl No 7011/75, 3 October 1975.

[497] ECtHR, *Andric v Sweden*, Appl No 45917/99, 23 February 1999, para 1.

[498] *Čonka* (n 459) para 59. See: Jacob D Howley, 'Unlocking the Fortress: Protocol No. 11 and the Birth of Collective Expulsion Jurisprudence in the Council of Europe System Note' (2006) 21 *Georgetown Immigration Law Journal* 111.

[499] *Čonka* (n 459) paras 60–63; *Hirsi Jamaa* (n 326) para 185; ECtHR, *Georgia v Russia (I)*, Appl No 13255/07, 3 July 2014; ECtHR, *Sharifi and Others v Italy and Greece*, Appl No 16643/09, 21 October 2014, paras 214–25.

possibility of submitting arguments against his or her expulsion, and where those arguments are examined appropriately by the authorities of the respondent State.[500]

This decision, departing as it did from the initial ruling of the Second Section, is problematic as it establishes an exception to a fundamental rights guarantee based on a vague and malleable standard. Nonetheless, the Grand Chamber also clarified that the domestic classification of 'refusal of entry with removal' instead of 'expulsion', has no bearing on whether Article 4 of Protocol 4 is applicable.[501] As the jurisprudence of the ECtHR shows, a refusal of entry, be it enforced on the territory of a contracting state or beyond, may also amount to collective expulsion.[502] In *J.A. and Others v Italy*, the Court clarified that migrants should have the possibility of appealing against their 'refusal of entry' decisions.[503] The practice of making people sign an information sheet (of which they received no copy and did not fully understand) during their identification procedures in the Lampedusa hotspot was insufficient.

The Grand Chamber overturned another momentous decision resulting in severe jurisprudential implications. The case of *N.D. and N.T.* concerned the 'hot return' policy in the Spanish enclave of Ceuta and Melilla. The Court's Third Section recognised that in the absence of any examination of the individual situation of the applicants, the refusals of entry to a group of Malian and Ivorian citizens amounted to a collective expulsion.[504] Three years later, the Grand Chamber confirmed that absent a reasonable and objective examination of the particular case of each individual of a group, an expulsion should be characterised as 'collective'.[505] Nevertheless, the Court further reasoned that, in the fulfilment of their duty to control their borders, states can require asylum seekers to submit their protection claims at the existing border-crossing points. Therefore they may refuse entry to their territory to those individuals, including asylum seekers, who do not comply with such requirements and attempt to enter the territory irregularly.[506] The fact that one of these border-crossing points was accessible to the applicants was sufficient for the Court to find that Spain provided 'genuine and effective access to procedures for legal entry into Spain',[507] despite the applicants' submission about the impossibility of claiming asylum there.[508] This impossibility was questioned by the Court.

[500] *Khlaifia* (n 240) para 248.
[501] *Khlaifia* (n 240) paras 243–44.
[502] *Hirsi Jamaa* (n 326) paras 50, 160 and 172–73.
[503] *J.A. and Others* (n 257) para 106.
[504] ECtHR, *N.D. and N.T. v Spain*, (Third Section) Appl Nos 8675/15 and 8697/15, 3 October 2017, para 107.
[505] ECtHR, *N.D. and N.T. v Spain*, (Grand Chamber) Appl Nos 8675/15 and 8697/15, 13 February 2020, paras 193 and 195.
[506] ibid, para 210.
[507] ibid, para 229.
[508] ibid, paras 218–20.

Most importantly, the Grand Chamber insisted that even if the applicants could prove a lack of access to an asylum procedure at the border, that circumstance resulted from the border control activities of the Moroccan authorities and was therefore unrelated to any Spanish responsibility.[509] This insistence came despite the notorious border control cooperation between the two states. In light of these observations, the Court considered that the lack of individual removal decisions resulted from the applicants' irregular entry, which justified their expulsion.[510]

Beyond the fact that by ignoring the border cooperation between states the Court risks disregarding the circumvention of the Conventions' obligations, *N.D. and N.H.* set a dangerous precedent. Its detrimental effects were only partially addressed in ECtHR's subsequent jurisprudence.[511] In *M.H. and Others*, for instance, the applicants were required to prove that they had 'cogent reasons'[512] for irregular entry 'on account of objective facts of which the respondent State was responsible'.[513] Given the asymmetrical documentation possibilities in expulsion cases, prima facie evidence furnished by the applicant in support of their claim is sufficient to shift the burden of proof to the government.[514] Yet, return decisions taken exclusively based on irregular entry are at variance with the non-penalisation principle expressed by Article 31 of the Refugee Convention.

The Court has reiterated that the effectiveness of the ECHR requires states whose borders coincide, at least partly, with external borders of the Schengen Area to make available 'genuine and effective access to means of legal entry', including asylum procedures.[515] Nonetheless, it also restated that the collective nature of an expulsion may be excluded where the lack of an individualised procedure 'can be attributed to the applicant's own conduct', including unauthorised entry, acts of violence or uncooperative behaviour creating a 'disruptive situation'.[516] At the same time, even where there was no violent or uncooperative behaviour on the part of migrants, their irregular entry was considered sufficient to justify the lack of individual removal decision.[517] While it remains unclear whether these are cumulative requirements, unauthorised entry remains the predicament of most asylum seekers.

The prohibition of collective expulsion concerns a fundamental procedural guarantee, whose enjoyment seems to be subordinated by the Court to the legal entry and behaviour of the individuals concerned – that is, to the states' discretion. This conditional protection from collective expulsion has no place in

[509] ibid, paras 58 and 219.
[510] ibid, para 231.
[511] *M.K. and Others* (n 219); *M.H. and others* (n 219); ECtHR, *Shahzad v Hungary*, Appl No 12625/17, 8 July 2021; ECtHR, *A.A. and Others v North Macedonia*, Appl No 55798/16 et al, 5 April 2022.
[512] *M.H. and Others* (n 219) para 295.
[513] ibid, para 294.
[514] ibid, para 300.
[515] *Shahzad* (n 511) para 62.
[516] *Shahzad* (n 511) para 59; *M.K. and Others* (n 219) para 203; *M.H. and Others* (n 219) para 294.
[517] Cf *Shahzad* (n 511) para 59; *A.A. and Others* (n 511) para 114.

human rights law and contradicts the Court's previous jurisprudence. The drafting history of Protocol No 4 reveals that, for the purposes of Article 4, the Committee of Experts explicitly chose to make no distinction between different categories of non-nationals.[518] The aliens to whom the prohibition of collective expulsion refers are all aliens, irrespective of their migration status.[519]

ii. The Right to a Fair Trial

Article 14 of the ICCPR and 6 ECHR guarantee everyone's right to a fair and public hearing by a competent, independent and impartial tribunal established by law. These requirements form the core of the due process of law. Yet, the procedural guarantees offered by human rights law to migrants at the borders have a limited scope, both *ratione materiae* and *ratione personae*. First, the due process rights included in these provisions do not apply to administrative (immigration) proceedings; second, they are not extended to the protection of irregular migrants.[520] Only foreigners 'lawfully (resident) in the territory of a state' are granted the right to an expulsion decision in 'accordance with the law'.[521] In this line, the ECtHR has clarified that the right to a fair trial under Article 6 ECHR does not apply to entry, stay or expulsion procedures, for it is applicable only in determining civil rights and obligations or criminal charges.[522]

In EU law, however, the right to a fair trial is recognised to everyone. Article 47 of the CFR recognises the right to an effective remedy and a fair trial, without distinction based on the person's legal presence in the territory of Member States. This general provision includes the right to a fair and public hearing before an independent and impartial tribunal established by law, the right to legal assistance and representation[523] and the right to legal aid in cases of minimal resources.[524] Third-country nationals should have access to legal assistance during both asylum[525] and return procedures.[526] Furthermore, the right to good administration enshrined in Article 41 CFR entails the right to have access to the file and to be heard before any measure which would adversely affect an individual is taken, linguistic communication rights, as well as the obligation of public authorities to give reasons for decisions within a reasonable time.[527]

[518] Explanatory Report (n 492), para 34.
[519] *Hirsi Jamaa* (n 326) para 174.
[520] Jaya Ramji-Nogales, 'Undocumented Migrants and the Failures of Universal Individualism' [2014] *Vanderbilt Journal of Transnational Law* 699.
[521] Art 13, ICCPR; HCR, *Everett v Spain*, Comm 961/2000, UN Doc A/59/40, 9 July 2004.
[522] ECtHR, *Maaouia v France*, Appl No 39652/98, 5 October 2000, para 40. See also: HRC, General Comment No 32: The Right to Equality Before Courts and Tribunals and to a Fair Trial, UN Doc CCPR/C/GC/32, 23 August 2007, para 17. For a critique, see Chetail (n 87) 140–41.
[523] Art 47(2), CFR.
[524] Art 47(3), CFR.
[525] Arts 20–23, Directive 2013/32/EU.
[526] Art 13(4), Directive 2008/115/EC.
[527] Art 41, CFR; Art 12(1) and (2), Directive 2008/115/EC. See also: Case C-277/11, *M.M.*, 22 November 2012, ECLI:EU:C:2012:744, para 83.

Nevertheless, the extent of the protection offered to irregular migrants based on the right to be heard in procedures potentially conducive to a removal varies, depending on whether the individual concerned is applying for international protection.[528] It is well documented that in asylum and immigration proceedings, documentary evidence is commonly lacking; this is a result of the applicants fleeing their countries in urgency and with limited opportunity to take or obtain supporting documentation.[529] Through a hearing, the individual can explain personally and without interference the reasons that led her to leave her country of origin and why she is unable or unwilling to return there. Yet, more and more Member States have limited the number of hearings in immigration status determination proceedings before issuing administrative decisions that could negatively impact individual rights based on the rationale of migrants abusing their rights and governmental efforts to reduce irregular migration.[530] The CJEU has recognised a right to be heard concerning the examination of applications for subsidiary protection, even where the same right was already exercised in the context of asylum proceedings.[531] The same logic does not apply to removal decisions concerning irregular migrants.[532] According to the CJEU, national authorities deciding whether a person's presence in the EU is lawful and – at the same time – deciding whether to return her need not necessarily hear the person concerned by the return decision. This is because the individual already had the opportunity to present her point of view and justify why she should not be returned to the hearing related to her legal stay.[533]

iii. The Right to an Effective Remedy

Beyond the controversies surrounding undocumented migrants' entitlement to a right to a fair trial, under human rights law, the right to an effective remedy is the

[528] Francesca Ippolito, 'Conceptualising a Migrant's Rights-Based EuroMed Cooperation: Political, Legal and Judicial Rationale' in Francesca Ippolito and Seline Trevisanut (eds), *Migration in the Mediterranean: Mechanisms of International Cooperation* (Cambridge, Cambridge University Press, 2016) 40.

[529] See UNHCR, Credibility Assessment Handbook, 2013.

[530] Madalina Moraru, 'The European Court of Justice Shaping the Right to Be Heard for Asylum Seekers, Returnees, and Visa Applicants: An Exercise in Judicial Diplomacy Special Issue: Adjudicating Migrants' Rights: What Are European Courts Saying?' (2021) 13 *European Journal of Legal Studies* 21.

[531] *M.M.* (n 527) paras 87–90.

[532] Case C-166/13, *Mukarubega*, ECLI:EU:C:2014:2336, 4 November 2014; Case C-249/13, *Boudjlida*, 11 December 2014, ECLI:EU:C:2014:2431.

[533] For further analysis see: Francesca Ippolito, 'Migration and Asylum Cases before the Court of Justice of the European Union: Putting the EU Charter of Fundamental Rights to Test?' (2015) 17 *European Journal of Migration and Law* 1; Evangelia (Lilian) Tsourdi, 'Of Legislative Waves and Case Law: Effective Judicial Protection, Right to an Effective Remedy and Proceduralisation in the EU Asylum Policy' (2019) 12 *Review of European Administrative Law* 143; Valeria Ilareva, 'The Right to be Heard: The Underestimated Condition for Effective Returns and Human Rights Consideration' in Madalina Moraru, Galina Cornelisse and Philippe de Bruycker (eds), *Law and Judicial Dialogue on the Return of Irregular Migration from the European Union* (Oxford, Hart Publishing, 2020).

firmer basis for the procedural guarantees offered to them.[534] The requirements in Article 13 ECHR for such guarantees are less stringent than those of Article 6 ECHR. The essence of a remedy for the purposes of Article 13 involves the possibility of having access to an effective procedure.[535] While the right to an effective remedy does not necessarily entail the review of judicial authority in the strict sense,[536] the effectiveness of the remedy depends on the powers and guarantees of the competent authority, which should be competent to take binding decisions and grant appropriate relief to the victims.[537] Concerning personal interviews, taking a somehow different approach than the CJEU,[538] the ECtHR observed that while the efficiency of the national decision-making process is important, this consideration should not be privileged at the expense of the effective protection of essential procedural guarantees aimed at protecting individuals against *refoulement*.[539]

Under EU law, the right to an effective remedy is indispensable for ensuring the rule of law within the Union.[540] It is generally recognised as a general principle of EU law, and as such, is considered a fundamental right of individuals resulting from the common constitutional traditions of the Member States.[541] This general principle, codified in Article 47 of the CFR, again seems to offer higher protection than that offered by Article 13 of the ECHR, as it explicitly refers to 'a tribunal', that is, a judicial authority. The CJEU has interpreted this notion broadly, referring to the status of 'court or tribunal' as a self-standing concept in EU law.[542] What constitutes a court or tribunal depends on various factors: whether the body is established by law; whether it is permanent; whether its jurisdiction is compulsory; whether its procedures are *inter partes*; whether it applies rules of law; and finally, whether it is impartial and independent.[543]

The CJEU has confirmed that Member States must provide appropriate legal remedies for fundamental rights violations occurring within the scope of application of EU law, including entry decisions taken by border officials.[544] After a refusal-of-entry decision is issued under the SBC, an applicant can appeal such a decision in accordance with national law.[545] The appeal does not have a suspensive effect, and no precise indication is provided as to a required effective remedy or

[534] Chetail (n 87) 141.
[535] See eg: *Čonka* (n 459) para 79.
[536] ibid, para 67.
[537] *Chahal* (n 459) paras 145 and 154; *Čonka* (n 459) para 70.
[538] See above S IV.I.i.
[539] ECtHR, *I.M. c France*, Appl No 9152/09, 2 February 2012, para 147.
[540] Art 2 TEU; Case C-294-83, *Les Verts*, 23 April 1986, ECLI:EU:C:1986:166, para 23.
[541] Herwig CH Hofmann, 'Article 47 – Right to an Effective Remedy' in Steve Peers and others (eds), *The EU Charter of Fundamental Rights: A Commentary* (Oxford, Hart Publishing, 2021).
[542] CJEU, Information note on references from national courts for a preliminary ruling, 2009/C 297/01, 5 December 2009, para 9.
[543] See: Laurent Pech, 'Article 47 – Right to an Effective Remedy' in Steve Peers and others (eds), *The EU Charter of Fundamental Rights: A Commentary* (Oxford, Hart Publishing, 2021).
[544] Case C-23/12, *Zakaria*, 17 January 2013, ECLI:EU:C:2013:24.
[545] Art 14(3), Regulation (EC) 562/2006.

fair trial guarantees. According to the CJEU, the appeal must be lodged before a court or an administrative body that provides the same guarantees as a court of law.[546] This extends to the possibility of challenging the conduct of border guards when issuing an entry decision, including when the conduct is not directly related or relevant to the adoption of such a decision.[547]

The fundamental right to good administration is pivotal for realising the right to effective remedy in administrative procedures, and more specifically in the context of border surveillance and border control measures. As already discussed, this provision entails the right of every individual to have her affairs handled impartially, fairly, and within a reasonable time, as well as the right to damages. Being entrusted with the mandate to inquiry cases of maladministration involving EU institutions, bodies, offices, and agencies,[548] the European Ombudsman can play an important role in the monitoring and potential reform of the EIBM strategy.[549] This emerged most notably regarding Frontex's complaints mechanism.[550]

Since the agency's inception, Frontex's human rights accountability has been denounced widely.[551] As discussed above, the subsequent amendments to the agency's legal framework progressively introduced an improved consideration for fundamental rights in Frontex's activities.[552] The establishment of a complaints mechanism in the 2016 regulation and its subsequent 2019 amendment follows this gradual fundamental rights awareness within the agency's mandate.

Nevertheless, the complaints mechanism included in the agency's current legal framework is still not living up to its promises. First, the procedure largely depends on the discretionary power of internal monitoring bodies. The FRO is entrusted with assessing individual complaints. In the performance of her tasks, the FRO is assisted by a deputy fundamental rights officer,[553] and by FRMs.[554] This is a fundamental improvement in view of the chronic lack of resources and staff from which the FRO suffered.[555] Yet all these figures remain formally the agency's employees,

[546] *Zakaria* (n 544) para 37.
[547] ibid, para 40.
[548] Note however, that only EU citizens or any natural or legal person registered or residing in the EU has the right to lodge a complaint before the EU Ombudsman. Art 22, TFEU; Art 43, CFR.
[549] See Sergio Carrera and Marco Stefan, *Complaint Mechanisms in Border Management and Expulsion Operations in Europe: Effective Remedies for Victims of Human Rights Violations? CEPS Paperback, 26 March 2018* (Brussels, CEPS Paperbacks, 2018); Nikos Vogiatzis, 'Frontex: Human Rights Obligations and the Role of the European Ombudsman' in Athina Karatzogianni, Dennis Nguyen and Elisa Serafinelli (eds), *The Digital Transformation of the Public Sphere* (London, Palgrave Macmillan, 2016).
[550] See Ch 2, s VII.B.
[551] Eg: CoE, Parliamentary Assembly, *Frontex: Human Rights Responsibilities*, Resolution 1932 (2013), 25 April 2013; European Ombudsman, Case OI/4/2021/MHZ, *How the European Border and Coast Guard Agency (Frontex) complies with its fundamental rights obligations and ensures accountability in relation to its enhanced responsibilities*, 17 January 2022; Elspeth Guild (ed), *Monitoring Border Violence in the EU: Frontex in Focus* (Abingdon, Taylor & Francis, 2023).
[552] Ch 2.
[553] Art 109(6), Regulation 2019/1896.
[554] ibid, Art 110.
[555] See ch 2, s III.B.

appointed by the management board, and it remains to be seen whether anything will change in practice.[556] In this respect, the Ombudsman has recognised the independence of the FRO regarding the complaints mechanism, albeit not with regard to the SIRs for fundamental rights issues.[557] This appears to be motivated by the introduction of special rules to guarantee the independence of the FRO.[558] However, the decision disregards the fact that those rules only concern the limited internal independence of the FRO, which remains fundamentally embedded in the administrative structure of the agency.[559] All in all, the numerous affirmations regarding their autonomy and independence seem mere declarations of intent.[560] This deficiency becomes even more striking when one considers that the ultimate power to take a decision regarding the violation of a fundamental right occurring during Frontex activities is entrusted to the agency's executive director, who can decide to suspend or terminate an operation.[561]

Second, and related, the effectiveness of a decision not to launch or suspend or terminate an activity or operational plan is not as evident as it would seem from Frontex's policy and legal documents. In particular, the suspension or termination occurs only where the executive director considers that fundamental rights violations are of a 'serious nature or are likely to persist'.[562] Given the absolute character of some of the human rights that could be infringed during Frontex activities, such as the prohibition of *refoulement* or of torture or ill-treatment, their suspension or termination does not seem to offer an appropriate relief to potential and actual victims.

Third, the FRO reviews the admissibility of every individual complaint. Once considered admissible by the FRO, these complaints are subjected to the scrutiny of the competent national authorities or the executive director, depending on whether the alleged complaint concerns the conduct of an officer seconded from a Member State or from the agency. The FRO recommends appropriate follow-up measures 'including disciplinary measures, referral for the initiation of civil or criminal justice proceedings as necessary, and other measures in accordance with national law'.[563] While the independence of a procedure concerning Frontex's staff is undoubtedly compromised by the direct involvement of the agency's executive director, not every Member State has in place human rights institutions or bodies to ensure an appropriate follow-up. Where those institutions exist, the

[556] Consultative Forum, Annual Report, 2020, 107.

[557] European Ombudsman, Case OI/5/2020/MHZ, *Decision on the functioning of the European Border and Coast Guard Agency's (Frontex) complaints mechanism for alleged breaches of fundamental rights and the role of the Fundamental Rights Officer*, 10 November 2020.

[558] Management Board Decision 6/2021 adopting special rules to guarantee the independence of the Fundamental Rights Office, 20 January 2021.

[559] ibid, Art 1.

[560] ibid, Arts 111(1), 109(4)–(6), 110(5).

[561] ibid, Art 46.

[562] ibid, Art 46(4).

[563] ibid, Art 111 (4) and (7).

extent to which they are involved in the assessment of the complaints is particularly unclear.[564]

A last problematic area is that of the relationship between Frontex's internal complaint mechanism and judicial remedies. Complaints can be submitted irrespective of the resort to other remedies.[565] However, no detailed rule is established. There is no set timeframe for the processing of the complaints and their eventual appeals, nor is it specified whether it is possible to lodge a complaint before the CJEU.[566] If a complaint is inadmissible or unfounded, the agency is under an obligation to provide for an 'appropriate procedure'.[567] Yet, it is not clear what this expression concretely entails, as there seems to be no possibility of appealing a decision taken by the FRO before a different decision-making body. Ultimately, despite the increased attention paid to fundamental rights, the current complaint mechanism falls short of the two basic requirements of an effective remedy: to impartially identify responsibilities and to provide appropriate relief to the victims.[568]

The procedural and practical hurdles highlighted above are amplified by the multiplicity of actors cooperating in Frontex joint operations, and, more broadly, in the EIBM. It is nearly impossible for an individual to identify the responsible actor and its respective obligations. For instance, the civil or military actors cooperating in EU maritime borders surveillance are not subjected to the same fundamental rights standard or monitoring procedures.[569] This situation becomes even more intricate with regard to Frontex joint operations implemented in cooperation with third countries' authorities, which Frontex can now coordinate alongside Member States and where its officers enjoy extensive immunities.[570]

I. Non-Discrimination and Human Dignity

The common denominator of all the human rights norms protecting migrants in general, and those at the borders more specifically, is the principle of non-discrimination.[571] This principle is fundamentally connected to the idea of equality and human dignity traditionally – yet not uncontroversially[572] – underlying

[564] For a comprehensive overview of national human rights bodies involved in supervising border control activities within the EU Member States, see: Carrera and Stefan (n 549).

[565] Article 5(5), Agency's Rules on the Complaints Mechanism https://frontex.europa.eu/assets/Key_Documents/Complaints/Annex_1_-_Frontexs_rules_on_the_complaints_mechanism.pdf.

[566] Art 111(6), Regulation 2019/1896.

[567] ibid, Art 111(5).

[568] European Ombudsman, Case OI/5/2020/MHZ (n 550).

[569] Carrera and Stefan (n 549) 26–27.

[570] Art 73, Regulation 2019/1896.

[571] Vincent Chetail, 'The Human Rights of Migrants in General International Law: From Minimum Standards to Fundamental Rights' (2013) 28 *Georgetown Immigration Law Journal* 225, 244.

[572] See for instance: Herbert Spiegelberg, 'Human Dignity: A Challenge to Contemporary Philosophy' (1971) 9 *World Futures: Journal of General Evolution* 39; Steven Pinker, 'The Stupidity of Dignity' (2008) 28

international human rights law.[573] These notions, commonly proclaimed as self-evident, are authoritatively recognised as legal rights in all major human rights treaties and international jurisprudence.[574] The general idea of human dignity has two corollaries: first, human rights do not depend on the authority of a given institution; second, they belong to all human beings, without distinction.[575]

i. *The Principle of Non-Discrimination*

The principle of non-discrimination, widely acknowledged as a norm of customary international law,[576] applies generally and independently of an individual's migration status.[577] Furthermore, the principle of non-discrimination places upon public authorities who would make distinctions in the recognition of certain rights the burden of proving that an individual's nationality is a relevant basis for differentiation, that the distinction aims to pursue a reasonable objective, and that the discriminatory measures taken or envisaged are necessary and proportional to the end to be achieved.[578]

Border control measures employed to address irregular migration shall not be discriminatory 'in purpose or effect including by subjecting migrants to profiling on the basis of prohibited grounds, and regardless of whether or not they have been smuggled or trafficked'.[579] Based on the non-discrimination and non-penalisation

The New Republic 28; Jeremy Waldron, 'Is Dignity the Foundation of Human Rights?' in Rowan Cruft, S Matthew Liao and Massimo Renzo (eds), *Philosophical Foundations of Human Rights* (Oxford, Oxford University Press, 2015).

[573] For historical, philosophical and legal accounts of human dignity in international law, among the abundant literature on the topic, see most notably: Oscar Schachter, 'Human Dignity as a Normative Concept' (1983) 77 *The American Journal of International Law* 848; Michael Rosen, *Dignity: Its History and Meaning* (Cambridge, Harvard University Press, 2012); Pablo Gilabert, *Human Dignity and Human Rights* (Oxford, Oxford University Press, 2018); Ginevra Le Moli, *Human Dignity in International Law* (Cambridge, Cambridge University Press, 2021).

[574] Preamble and Art 1(3), Charter of the United Nations, 892 UNTS 119, TS 993, 26 June 1945; Arts 1, 2, 7, UDHR; ICCPR, Art 26; Art 2(2), ICESCR; Arts 1 and 5, ICRPD; Arts 1 and 7, ICRMW; Art 24, ACHR; Art 11, ArCHR; Art 28, ACHRC; Art 14, ECHR; Arts 2 and 3, TEU; Arts 1, 20 and 21 CFR. See also: Christopher McCrudden, 'Human Dignity and Judicial Interpretation of Human Rights' (2008) 19 *European Journal of International Law* 655; Veronika Fikfak and Lora Izvorova, 'Language and Persuasion: Human Dignity at the European Court of Human Rights' (2022) 22 *Human Rights Law Review* ngac018.

[575] Schachter (n 573) 583.

[576] The IACtHR went even further and affirmed the *jus cogens* nature of the principle of non-discrimination. IACtHR, *Juridical Condition and Rights of Undocumented Migrants*, Advisory Opinion OC-18/03, 17 September 2003; IACtHR, *Case of Expelled Dominicans and Haitians v Dominican Republic* (Preliminary Objections, Merits, Reparations and Costs), 28 August 2014, para 264. On racial discrimination, see ILC, Fifth report on peremptory norms of general international law (jus cogens) by Dire Tladi, Special Rapporteur, 5 August 2022.

[577] HRC, General Comment No 15 (n 389), para 2; CERD, General Recommendation No 30: Discrimination Against Non-Citizens, 1 October 2004, paras 4, 7 and 9; CEDAW, General Recommendation No 26 on Women Migrant Workers, UN Doc CEDAW/C/2009/WP.1/R, 5 December 2008, para 2.

[578] See eg, *Biao* (n 398).

[579] OHCHR, Recommended Principles and Guidelines on Human Rights at International Borders (A/69/277), September 2014, para 8.

principles included in Articles 3 and 31 of the Refugee Convention, lack of identity or travel documents should not imply an automatic negative interference with the rights of refugees. Furthermore, the prohibition of *refoulement* applies to any person without discrimination 'and regardless of the nationality or statelessness or the legal, administrative or judicial status of the person concerned under ordinary or emergency law'.[580]

The principles of equality and non-discrimination are expressed in Article 18 of the TFEU and in Articles 20 and 21 of the CFR, and included in EU secondary legislation.[581] Accordingly, all participants in Frontex activities must

> promote and respect human dignity and the fundamental rights of every individual, regardless of their sex, race, colour, ethnic or social origin, genetic features, language, religion or belief, political or any other opinion, membership of a national minority, property, birth, disability, age or sexual orientation.[582]

Nonetheless, not only are these fundamental principles challenging to pin down in practice, but in the realm of migration and border management, they also have an essential limit. Most notably, Article 21(2) prohibits discrimination based on nationality but without prejudice to any specific provisions included in the EU Treaties.[583] As control over national borders is acknowledged as a legitimate aim in treaties[584] and jurisprudence,[585] distinctions based on nationality are generally not considered discriminatory as such. The prohibition of discrimination based on nationality is generally limited to nationals of Member States.[586] Issues of entry and residence, moreover, fall outside the scope of EU non-discrimination law.[587] This reflects the ambiguities regarding discrimination based on nationality at the international level. In this respect, it has been observed that the principle of equality is considerably constrained in migration law matters.[588] By reserving the regulation of nationality primarily to state discretion and maintaining ambiguities in the extent to which states' racialised exclusion of non-nationals is prohibited, international law was crafted to serve as 'a mostly bulletproof mechanism for racialized exclusion and differentiation'.[589]

[580] CAT, General Comment No 4: Implementation of Article 3 of the Convention in the Context of Article 22, 9 February 2018, para 10.

[581] Art 7(2), SBC.

[582] Frontex Code of Conduct, Article 4; Frontex Fundamental Rights Strategy, 5.

[583] See also: Art 18, TFEU.

[584] Art 77(1)(b), TFEU.

[585] Eg *Abdulaziz, Cabales and Balkandali* (n 354) para 67; *R v Immigration Officer at Prague Airport and Another, Ex parte European Roma Rights Centre and Others* [2004] UKHL 55, House of Lords (Judicial Committee), 9 December 2004, para 11, Lord Bingham.

[586] Joined Cases C-22/08 and C-23/08, *Vatsouras*, ECLI:EU:C:2009:344, 4 June 2009, paras 51–52.

[587] Art 3(2), Council Directive 2000/43/EC [2000] OJ L 180/22; Art 3(2), Council Directive 2000/78/EC [2000] OJ L 303/16.

[588] Jean-Baptiste Farcy, 'Equality in Immigration Law: An Impossible Quest?' (2020) 20(4) *Human Rights Law Review* 725.

[589] Tendayi E Achiume, 'Racial Borders' (2022) 110 *Georgetown Law Journal* 445.

Nationality is a facially neutral instrument of racial exclusion. While a differential treatment based on nationality may be considered pursuing a legitimate aim, measures singling out a group for differential treatment based on race, colour, descent or national or ethnic origin constitute a denial of fundamental human rights in flagrant violation of international law.[590] More specifically, refusals of admission based on racial grounds have been found to constitute a special form of interference with human dignity capable of constituting degrading treatment.[591] Furthermore, the intersections between nationality and other grounds for discrimination, such as gender, class, race or ethnic origin, may have illegal discriminating effects, especially where nationality is used as a proxy for otherwise illegal grounds for discrimination.[592]

The discriminatory potential of a racialised notion of nationality becomes apparent the EU visa regulation, which establishes the countries whose nationals are subject to a visa requirement and those exempted from it.[593] This determination results from a 'case-by-case assessment of a variety of criteria relating *inter alia* to illegal immigration, public policy and security, and to the European Union's external relations'.[594] Yet, these criteria are vague, and the methodology to be followed in the assessment is not clarified, which has raised concerns regarding the necessity and proportionality of such criteria. In this vein, the EU visa regime has been criticised as serving, at best, to keep the poor out of Europe and, at worst, to sustain its prejudice.[595]

A salient example is the situation of refugees fleeing the armed conflict in Ukraine.[596] Notoriously, refugees fleeing conflicts and violence face many legal and practical hurdles to enter the EU legally. Ukrainian nationals can cross the EU borders, as they are exempt from visa requirements. This was arguably one of the reasons for activating the Temporary Protection Directive (TPD), which covers

[590] ICJ, *Legal consequences for states of the continued presence of South Africa in Namibia notwithstanding Security Council Resolution 276 (1970)*, Advisory Opinion of 21 June 1971, General List No 53, para 131.

[591] ECtHR, *East African Asians (British protected persons) v the United Kingdom*, Appl No 440370, 14 December 1973, para 207.

[592] ICJ, *Application of the International Convention on the Elimination of All Forms of Racial Discrimination (Qatar v UAE)*, ICJ General List No. 172, 2021; Cf, CERD, Decision on the admissibility of the inter-state communication *Qatar v United Arab Emirates*, UN Doc CERD/C/99/4, 2019. For further commentary see: Cathryn Costello and Michelle Foster, 'Race Discrimination Effaced at the International Court of Justice' (2021) 115 *American Journal of International Law* 339.

[593] Regulation (EC) 539/2001 [2001] OJ L 081.

[594] ibid, Recital 5.

[595] Moreno-Lax (n 87) 81–116; Thomas Spijkerboer, 'The Global Mobility Infrastructure: Reconceptualising the Externalisation of Migration Control' (2018) 20 *European Journal of Migration and Law* 452; Salvatore Fabio Nicolosi, 'Refashioning the EU Visa Policy: A New Turn of the Screw to Cooperation on Readmission and to Discrimination?' (2020) 22 *European Journal of Migration and Law* 467.For a more nuanced account see: Maarten den Heijer, 'Visas and Non-Discrimination' (2018) 20 *European Journal of Migration and Law* 470.

[596] Cathryn Costello and Michelle Foster, '(Some) Refugees Welcome: When Is Differentiating between Refugees Unlawful Discrimination?' (2022) 22 *International Journal of Discrimination and the Law* 244.

Ukrainian nationals, as well as refugees, stateless persons, and nationals of other third countries who can prove their valid permanent residence in Ukraine.[597] Non-beneficiaries of the TPD, mostly from Africa, the Middle East and Asia, on the contrary, were subject to discriminatory treatment at the border,[598] while on the Belarusian side of the same EU external border, Syrian and Afghan refugees were stranded in freezing temperatures, or violently pushed back to Belarus.[599]

In this regard, Article 3 of the Refugee Convention prohibits discrimination among refugees based on race, religion or country of origin, without jurisdictional limits nor conditions based on state concerns such as mass influx or public order.[600] This provision is however limited to the application of the Refugee Convention and, in many respects, it has been superseded by human rights law.[601] Yet, in relation to discrimination based on nationality among refugees, the broad notion of country of origin might open new venues to challenge policies creating social and racialised hierarchies among refugees.

With regard to discrimination between refugees and other foreigners, it has been compellingly argued that a differentiated visa requirements can be in breach of Article 7(1) in conjunction with Article 3 of the Refugee Convention.[602] By approaching visa requirements as a 'treatment accorded to aliens generally', differential admissions that frustrate access to protection can constitute discrimination either directly, on grounds of country of origin, or indirectly on grounds of race or religion. More generally, even if one were to consider distinctions based on nationality justified, the lack of proportionality between the state interest and the refugee rights, hints at the potential discriminatory effect of the EU migration policy.[603]

That notwithstanding, people caught in the meshes of the EIBM are not only kept outside the territory of the Member States, but also outside the scope of application of the law constraining their discretion. The ever-expanding externalisation of EU border controls has resulted in the discriminatory denial of access to global mobility.[604] The use of database-led migration management coupled with new border surveillance technologies buttresses the discriminatory potential of the border control practices enforced by Frontex and the Member States. The

[597] Directive 2001/55/EC [2001] OJ L 212.

[598] Rachael Reilly and Michael Flynn, *Double Standards: Has Europe's Response to Refugees Changed?* (Global Detention Project, 2 March 2022).

[599] Lorenzo Tondo, 'Embraced or pushed back: on the Polish border, sadly, not all refugees are welcome' (*The Guardian*, 4 March 2022).

[600] For a detailed discussion, see: Costello and Foster (n 594) 258–61.

[601] Vincent Chetail, 'Moving Towards an Integrated Approach of Refugee Law and Human Rights Law' in C Costello, M Foster and J McAdam (eds), *The Oxford Handbook of International Refugee Law* (Oxford, Oxford University Press, 2021) 218.

[602] Maja Grundler, '"Treatment Accorded to Aliens Generally": Article 7(1) of the 1951 Refugee Convention as a Basis for Visa-Free Access to States Parties' Territory? An Examination of the Prohibition of Nationality Discrimination in the Refugee Convention' (2021) 33 *International Journal of Refugee Law* 469.

[603] Spijkerboer (n 595).

[604] ibid.

EIBM 'surveillant assemblage'[605] enables the externalisation of EU border controls in a selective way, imposing stronger controls on certain regions, disproportionally affecting certain social, ethnic and racialised groups.[606] The ensuing lack of human rights jurisdiction may result in a differentiation of rights, where the right to life of refugees fleeing conflict areas receive a lesser degree of protection than that of the passengers on a flight from Geneva to London.[607] In this vein, the legal meaning of 'foreignness' seems to coincide with 'a discriminatory status, where the discretionary nature of the power exercised by the political authorities prevails over the inherent dignity of the person that the principle of equality embodies'.[608]

ii. The Principle of Human Dignity

Every person at the border of a state has the right 'to be treated with respect for his or her human dignity rather than automatically considered to be a criminal or guilty of fraud'.[609] The general obligation to carry out immigration control measures in compliance with the right to human dignity has been reiterated in a substantial number of legal instruments and jurisprudence.[610]

Border guards, in the performance of their duties, must fully respect human dignity, in particular in cases involving persons in vulnerable situations.[611] Similarly, members of Frontex's officers are mandated to 'fully respect fundamental rights, including access to asylum procedures and human dignity, and … pay particular attention to vulnerable persons'.[612] By the same token, automated border controls performed through self-service and e-gates systems should be designed in a way that 'fully respects human dignity, in particular in cases involving vulnerable persons'.[613]

Human dignity is directly related to respect for the principle of *non-refoulement*, the prohibition of inhuman or degrading treatment[614] and the right to life.[615] Regulation 2019/1896 includes a provision directly related to the duty of precaution

[605] Kevin D Haggerty and Richard V Ericson, 'The Surveillant Assemblage' (2000) 51 *The British Journal of Sociology* 605. See also ch 1, s VI.

[606] See Report of the Special Rapporteur on contemporary forms of racism, racial discrimination, xenophobia and related intolerance, UN Doc A/75/50289, 10 November 2020, paras 43–47.

[607] Thomas Spijkerboer, 'Wasted Lives. Borders and the Right to Life of People Crossing Them' (2017) 86 *Nordic Journal of International Law* 1.

[608] François Crépeau and Ranabir Samaddar, 'Recognizing the Dignity of Migrants' (2011) 37 *Refugee Watch – A South Asian Journal on Forced Migration* 55.

[609] CoE, Commissioner for Human Rights, Recommendation concerning the rights of aliens wishing to enter a Council of Europe Member State and the enforcement of expulsion orders, CommDH(2001)19, 19 September 2001, para 1.

[610] Art 7(1), SBC; Art 8(4), Directive 2008/115; *Zakaria* (n 544) para 40.

[611] Art 7, SBC.

[612] Art 43(4), Regulation 2019/1896.

[613] Art 8(c), Regulation 2017/2225.

[614] See eg: *Ibrahim*, Joined Cases C-297/17, C-318/17, C-319/17 and C-438/17, 19 March 2019, ECLI:EU:C:2019:219, para 87; Case C-163/17, *Jawo*, 19 March 2019, ECLI:EU:C:2019:218, para 78.

[615] *X and X v Etat Belgium*, Opinion of the Advocate General Paolo Mengozzi, Case C-638/16 PPU, 7 February 2017, ECLI:EU:C:2017:93, para 137.

of Frontex personnel, who should 'fully respect and aim to preserve human life and human dignity'.[616] Not clarified, however, is whether this rule implies a positive duty to protect the lives of migrants at the EU external borders, and, more specifically, to save their lives at sea. This positive duty seems to be confirmed by Article 1 of the CFR, which states that human dignity must be respected and protected. Along these lines, Frontex's Fundamental Rights Strategy specifies that Frontex and all EU Member States are bound by positive obligations to prevent fundamental rights violations and promote their protection.[617]

Other aspects of border enforcement activities that directly impact the human dignity of migrants are immigration detention, return operations, and the ensuing procedural guarantees. First, immigration detention should be performed 'with humanity and with respect for the inherent dignity of the human person',[618] as well as in compliance with the EU Reception Directive.[619] Second, return operations of undocumented migrants entailing coercive measures must be used only as a last resort and must be strictly necessary and proportionate to the resistance of the returnees.[620] Yet, immigration detention and physical restraint are still pervasive deterrence and preventive measures.[621] Where migrant rights have been infringed, the right to human dignity imposes on states the duty to ensure that migrants have appropriate access to a legal remedy.[622] Facilitating access to justice by migrants, without fear of detention or deportation, would, on the one hand, legitimise migration policies compatible with human rights and, on the other hand, contribute to fighting fantasies and stereotypes around migration.[623]

The right to human dignity emerges as the common denominator for all these norms from its relationship with other rights. Human dignity is not only a fundamental human right; it is a fundamental principle serving a structural and normative function within the international legal order.

As such, the principle of human dignity underlies one of the most basic and contested guarantees for the non-citizen: her 'right to have rights'.[624] With this formula – used and abused by international lawyers – Hannah Arendt famously

[616] Annex V, Regulation 2019/1896.

[617] See Fundamental Rights Strategy, 2021, Preamble 7, 9, 10, 12, 13, 16.

[618] Art 10 ICCPR.

[619] Recital 18 and Art 10, Directive 2013/33; See also: Joined Cases C-473/13 and C-514/13, *Bero and Regierungspräsidium Kassel*, EU:C:2014:2095, 17 July 2014, paras 24–32.

[620] Art 80, Regulation 2019/1896; Art 8, Directive 2008/115; Art 7, Frontex Code of Conduct for Return Operations and Return Interventions Coordinated or Organised by Frontex; Case C-554/13, *Z. Zh and O.*, ECLI:EU:C:2015:377, 11 June 2015, para 47.

[621] See Frontex, FRO's Observations to return operations conducted in the 1st Semester of 2020 (1 January–30 June 2020), 9 December 2020, 5.

[622] *Zakaria* (n 544) para 40.

[623] Special Rapporteur on the human rights of migrant, Banking on mobility over a generation: follow-up to the regional study on the management of the external borders of the European Union and its impact on the human rights of migrants, A/HRC/29/36, 8 May 2015, 113.

[624] Hannah Arendt famously formulated this expression in her 1949 essay 'The Rights of Man: What Are They?' (1949) 3 *Modern Review* 24.

invoked the acknowledgement of the right of every human being to 'belong to some kind of organized community'.[625] To be clear, Arendt was sceptical about any metaphysical foundation of human rights and insisted, more or less explicitly, that 'the right to have rights' cannot be conceived of as something inherent in human nature or the dignity of every human being.[626] On the contrary, for Arendt, the 'right to have rights' is a right to belong to a community and, therefore to humanity. Even so, the right to have rights is the principal guarantee for the dignity of every individual and the political and moral articulation of the (legal) right to human dignity.[627]

The significance of human dignity is that it is the only claim that can address the predicament of anyone legally 'out of place' – stateless people, refugees and other migrants in vulnerable situations.[628] Once irregular migrants acquire some legal status, they have access to the multilayered regime of human rights measures. Yet, as the previous analysis has shown, entry remains largely beyond these measures' scope.[629] In particular, the various impediments to the effective exercise of the right to leave, coupled with the restrictive interpretation of human rights' extraterritorial reach,[630] reduce the 'right to have rights' to an empty promise. When people flee from their countries to seek protection or a better life elsewhere, the 'right to have rights' can only be realised through an effective exercise of the right to leave.[631]

V. Conclusion: A Chain of Protection

This chapter has proceeded at different levels and intertwined various international and EU law areas. The argument set out thus far has traced the trajectory of international protection that started from refugee law and developed into international and EU human rights law. Within this trajectory, international and European law mesh and form a legal structure that – despite its inconsistencies and limitations – protects migrants' rights at the border.

[625] Hannah Arendt, *The Origins of Totalitarianism (1951)* (New York, Harcourt, Brace, Jovanovich, 1973) 177; Seyla Benhabib, *The Rights of Others: Aliens, Residents, and Citizens* (Cambridge, Cambridge University Press, 2004) ch 2.

[626] Hannah Arendt, *The Burden of Our Time* (London, Martin Secker and Warburg, 1951) ch 13. For a comment, see Justine Lacroix and Jean-Yves Pranchère, *Human Rights on Trial: A Genealogy of the Critique of Human Rights* (Cambridge, Cambridge University Press, 2018) 219; Stephanie Degooyer and others, *The Right to Have Rights* (New York, Verso, 2018).

[627] Arendt (n 625) ix.

[628] Benhabib (n 625) 14.

[629] See above, S IV.D.

[630] See ch 4.

[631] *Hirsi Jamaa* (n 326) concurring opinion of judge Pinto de Albuquerque; Asher Lazarus Hirsch and Nathan Bell, 'The Right to Have Rights as a Right to Enter: Addressing a Lacuna in the International Refugee Protection Regime' (2017) 18 *Human Rights Review* 417; Michael D Weinman, 'Arendt and the Legitimate Expectation for Hospitality and Membership Today' (2018) 5 *Moral Philosophy and Politics* 127.

The continuum of protection provided to people on the move by EU and international law during the implementation of the EIBM is neither uniform nor constant.[632] In a sense, this structure mirrors the assemblage of border controls evoked in chapter one. The legal assemblage of rights and obligations stemming from different legal sources can respond to the challenges of border control measures implemented by multiple actors and technologies. Yet, the heterogeneity of this legal framework also involves concrete inconsistencies and gaps. Examples of practices working within these gaps include interception measures, remote control and containment policies to prevent access to the territory and relevant obligations, protracted detention of asylum seekers and a general lack of effective remedies.

These weaknesses emerge from the constraints and limits of substantive rights and the discrepancy between international obligations and their implementation. The procedural and substantive guarantees discussed above involve both negative and positive duties for the EU and its Member States implementing the EIBM. These duties are governed to different extents by EU and international law. Different legal sources often correspond to different degrees of protection. In this sense, the EU and international rights law interfaces mirror the assemblage of logics, measures and actors involved in the EIBM.

On closer look, however, the various obligations of Frontex and the Member States appear less unrelated and more connected or interlocked. In implementing the EIBM, Frontex and the Member States are bound by different legal norms stemming from different legal regimes, which are, however, closely related. From the synergies between these norms emerges what may be called a 'chain of protection'.[633] This chain of interlocked rights and duties is best exemplified by the correlation of the right to leave and the prohibition of *refoulement* under refugee and human rights law as a condition for effectively exercising the right to asylum under EU law.

The 'chain of protection' binds Frontex (the EU) and its Member States and results from a complex network of normative and concrete relationships, each entailing rights and duties. The level of protection accorded to any given individual within this chain depends on these relationships. This chain connects the international obligations of Frontex and the Member States. In turn, this normative interconnection may result in the concurrent responsibility of the agency and the Member States in case of violation of one of their (concurrent) obligations.

On the one hand, the various sources forming this normative chain may be coherently or cumulatively applied; moreover, where situations of disparity and friction emerge, one norm can offer correction to another, or inform its progressive

[632] The notion of a 'continuum of protection' has been developed to explain the normative interaction between human rights and refugee law. See Chetail (n 141).
[633] The image of the 'protection chain' is inspired by: Alison Kesby, 'Refugee Chains' in Jessie Hohmann and Daniel Joyce (eds), *International Law's Objects* (Oxford, Oxford University Press, 2018).

interpretation.[634] On the other hand, the tension between normative commitments and differing political interests underlie policies that work within the gaps of the protection chain, eroding its effectiveness.

Unquestionably, the EU and its Member States are bound by a set of obligations towards migrants. Yet, they have implemented various policies designed to ensure that migrants cannot claim their correlative rights. In this sense, remote control and containment policies can be seen as examples of 'creative legal thinking',[635] for they seek to exploit the uncertainties created by competing legal frameworks and the possibilities new technologies open to limit, shift or circumvent their legal obligations.

The ostensible efforts by the EU and its Member States to design measures that keep people at a distance while shielding themselves from any human rights responsibilities can indirectly violate the right to leave. This, however, does not automatically guarantee an unconditional right to enter. A significant corrective to this assertion can be found in the protection against *refoulement* and in the right to seek and enjoy asylum, which require states to grant anyone seeking protection access to their territory and adequate asylum procedures. Crucially, however, as the following chapter will reveal, these claims suffer from an inherent limitation when the violation occurs beyond the ambit of the EU law or national jurisdiction.

Human rights, including refugee and migrant rights, tend to be imagined and intellectually constructed as universal.[636] They are rights for every person by virtue of our shared but individual humanity. However, this premise is difficult to reconcile with states' prerogatives over their borders, for they assume that human rights are enjoyed within bounded communities, with a sovereign right to control admissions.[637] The idiosyncratic notion of relative human rights – depending on border crossing and, therefore, on state discretion – seems out of place in our time of interconnectedness. Yet, it has been stubbornly entrenched in the realm of migration.[638] Along these lines, a distinctive conception of sovereignty dominates the populist migration discourse, tending to equate sovereignty and unfettered state discretion to exclude aliens without justification.[639]

[634] Costello captures these interactions with the term 'human rights pluralism'. See Costello (n 200) 44.

[635] Thomas Gammeltoft-Hansen, '"Creative Legal Thinking" and the Evolution of International Refugee Law (2014) 112 *Lakimies* 99.

[636] Louis Henkin, 'The Universality of the Concept of Human Rights' (1989) 506 *The Annals of the American Academy of Political and Social Science* 10. See also: Marie-Bénédicte Dembour, 'Critiques' in Daniel Moeckli, Sangeeta Shah and Sandesh Sivakumaran (eds), *International Human Rights Law* (Oxford, Oxford University Press, 2018).

[637] Interestingly, both the right to enter a country and the right to political membership appear equally weak. See: Alexander Aleinikoff and Leah Zamore, *The Arc of Protection: Toward a New International Refugee Regime* (Standford, Public Seminar Books, 2018) note 169.

[638] See in particular: Catherine Dauvergne, *Making People Illegal: What Globalization Means for Migration and Law* (Cambridge, Cambridge University Press, 2008); Marie-Benedicte Dembour and Tobias Kelly, *Are Human Rights for Migrants?: Critical Reflections on the Status of Irregular Migrants in Europe and the United States* (Abingdon, Routledge, 2011); Costello (n 201).

[639] See Stephen Macedo, 'After the Backlash: Populism and the Politics and Ethics of Migration' (2020) 4 *The Law & Ethics of Human Rights* 153.

This assumption has been challenged on historical, ethical and legal grounds.[640] Against claims of untrammelled state power to control their borders is indeed regularly asserted that migrants have rights that state discretion cannot curtail and that '[m]ost human rights are guaranteed irrespective of an individual's immigration status: they are a function of a person's status as a human being, not as a citizen of a particular state'.[641] Beyond positive law, the emergence of global migration governance signals the need for a renewed political discourse and an inclusive dialogue among relevant actors that acknowledges global interconnections and common duties towards those beyond their borders.[642]

Ultimately, while the rights of migrants – especially those in an irregular situation – are often contested,[643] not least by the states against whom they are asserted; at the very least, the presumption of an unfettered state discretion over national borders has been seriously questioned.[644] And yet, as the next chapter will show, if the national borders are kept at a distance and absent any meaningful contact with the relevant duty-bearer, migrant (human) rights remain an empty promise, for their jurisdictional limitations seem to exclude their applicability.

[640] James AR Nafziger, 'The General Admission of Aliens under International Law' (1983) 77 *The American Journal of International Law* 804; Bas Schotel, *On the Right of Exclusion: Law, Ethics and Immigration Policy* (Abingdon, Routledge, 2013); Vincent Chetail, 'Sovereignty and Migration in the Doctrine of the Law of Nations: An Intellectual History of Hospitality from Vitoria to Vattel' (2016) 27 *European Journal of International Law* 901. For a different construction of the relationship between migrants and receiving states in light of colonial and post-colonial experiences, see: Tendayi E Achiume, 'Migration as Decolonization' (2019) 71 *Stanford Law Review* 1509.

[641] UNHCR, Protection Training Manual for European Border and Entry Officials (2006) 9.

[642] The growing role of international cooperation on migration may be a signal toward that direction See: UNGA, Resolution A/RES/71/1, New York Declaration for Refugees and Migrants, 3 October 2016; Resolution A/RES/73/195 on the Global Compact for Safe, Orderly and Regular Migration, 19 December 2018.

[643] Ramji-Nogales (n 520).

[644] Chantal Thomas, 'What Does the Emerging International Law of Migration Mean for Sovereignty?' (2013) 14 *Melbourne International Law Journal* 392.

4

Jurisdiction Over the EIBM: Migrant Rights at the European Border and Beyond

I. Introduction: Jurisdiction in its Different Declinations

The previous chapters illustrated the complex network of border control activities undertaken by multiple actors pivoting around Frontex. These activities extend within and beyond the physical frontiers of Europe and may have a range of implications for the protection of migrant rights. This chapter will then investigate the scope of the human rights obligations binding the EU (as well as Frontex) and its Member States when they operate at their borders and beyond to enforce migration controls. Within the EIBM, border control measures are supposed to exist in an assemblage of coercive and surveillance practices pivoting around the integrated management of migratory movements at entry and pre-entry stages. Border controls are intended to facilitate mobility while enhancing the internal security of Member States by precluding access to Europe and preventing the departure of unauthorised migrants.[1] As discussed in the previous chapter, this poses several human rights concerns. Crucially, the applicability of the legal framework discussed thus far largely depends on the notion of jurisdiction.

Generally, borders are presumed to delineate a state's jurisdiction and, therefore, its human rights obligations. The EIBM simultaneously reduces and intensifies the significance of borders within and beyond the Schengen area. This chapter will explore the notion of jurisdiction as a tool to accommodate, shape or react to the process of European border integration. In this respect, the central issue for a human rights lawyer or a judge in Strasbourg, Luxembourg or Palermo is how jurisdiction is defined and understood under international and EU human rights law and whether it applies extraterritorially.

[1] Thomas Gammeltoft-Hansen, *Access to Asylum: International Refugee Law and the Globalisation of Migration Control* (Cambridge, Cambridge University Press, 2011); Maarten den Heijer, *Europe and Extraterritorial Asylum* (Oxford, Hart Publishing, 2012); Violeta Moreno-Lax, *Accessing Asylum in Europe: Extraterritorial Border Controls and Refugee Rights under EU Law* (Oxford, Oxford University Press, 2017).

Jurisdiction is a polysemic term that may serve different purposes across the various branches of a legal system. Jurisdiction in international law concerns the power of a state to regulate or otherwise impact people, activities and legal interests.[2] State sovereignty is reflected in and constrained by rules of jurisdiction which delimit the powers of a plurality of sovereigns.[3] In a world composed of equal sovereign states, jurisdiction serves the distributive function of allocating their coexisting spheres of action according to various criteria.[4] The principal condition for assessing jurisdiction in international law is territorial: states are entitled to enact and enforce laws in their territories. Since the triumph of the territorial state, territory and sovereignty are understood as closely related.[5] Sovereignty is established in connection to a certain territory through jurisdiction. Of course, there are exceptions to the territorial principle. For instance, by virtue of the special bond of allegiance inherent to nationality, states are entailed to exercise jurisdiction over their nationals abroad or over aliens committing offences against their nationals.[6] States also can – and sometimes must – prosecute criminals on their territory regardless of where the crimes have been committed or of the nationality of the perpetrators and the victims.[7] Even more fundamentally, the pressures of an increasingly globalised and liberalised world led some to seriously question the territorial foundation of the idea of jurisdiction.[8] That notwithstanding, the territorial principle still dominates most of the accounts of jurisdiction in contemporary international law.[9] In sum, through the doctrine of jurisdiction, international law delimits the scope of application of domestic law just as it delimits the territory of different states.[10]

[2] Among the vast literature on the topic, see: Frederick A Mann, 'The Doctrine of Jurisdiction in International Law' (1964) 111 *Collected Courses of the Hague Academy of International Law*; Michael Akehurst, 'Jurisdiction in International Law' (1972) 46 *British Yearbook of International Law* 145; Cedric Ryngaert, *Jurisdiction in International Law* (Oxford, Oxford University Press, 2015); Stephen Allen and others (eds), *The Oxford Handbook of Jurisdiction in International Law* (Oxford, Oxford University Press, 2019).

[3] PCIJ, *Nationality Decrees in Tunis and Morocco*, Advisory Opinion, 7 February 1923, PCIJ Reports, Ser B, No 4, para 41. See also: Alex Mills, 'Rethinking Jurisdiction in International Law' (2014) 84 *British Yearbook of International Law* 187, 194.

[4] Rosalyn Higgins, *Problems and Process: International Law and How We Use It* (Oxford, Oxford University Press, 1995) 56–77.

[5] Richard T Ford, 'Law's Territory (A History of Jurisdiction)' (1998) 97 *Michigan Law Review* 843, 982; see also: Anne Orford, 'Jurisdiction without Territory: From the Holy Roman Empire to the Responsibility to Protect Symposium: Territory without Boundaries – Universal Jurisdiction' (2008) *Michigan Journal of International Law* 981.

[6] Jan Klabbers, *International Law* (Cambridge, Cambridge University Press, 2020) 100–18.

[7] Frédéric Mégret, 'The "Elephant in the Room" in Debates about Universal Jurisdiction: Diasporas, Duties of Hospitality, and the Constitution of the Political' (2015) 6 *Transnational Legal Theory* 89; Devika Hovell, 'The Authority of Universal Jurisdiction' (2018) 29 *European Journal of International Law* 427.

[8] See most notably: Bhupinder S Chimni, 'The International Law of Jurisdiction: A TWAIL Perspective' [2021] *Leiden Journal of International Law* 1; Nico Krisch, 'Jurisdiction Unbound: (Extra) Territorial Regulation as Global Governance' (2022) 33 *European Journal of International Law* 481 and references therein.

[9] Ryngaert (n 2).

[10] Marko Milanović, *Extraterritorial Application of Human Rights Treaties: Law, Principles, and Policy* (Oxford, Oxford University Press, 2011) 23–26.

The concept of jurisdiction under public international law is not coterminous with its meaning under human rights law. Whereas human rights law is rooted in public international law, both regimes have distinct origins and raisons d'être, and so operate in different ways.[11] In conventional wisdom, international law is mainly concerned with horizontal inter-state relations, while human rights law deals primarily with the vertical relationship between the state and the individual or group.[12] Human rights obligations have an objective nature: they represent compliance to a normative system that is not conditioned by reciprocity or mutual interest.[13] Accordingly, while under international law, jurisdiction is conceived as a normative framework distributing the states' right to regulate a situation using their domestic law; under human rights law, the notion of jurisdiction defines the applicability of certain international obligations to a specific relationship existing between a right-holder and a duty-bearer.[14]

There have been considerable difficulties reconciling the different meanings of jurisdiction under general international and human rights law.[15] This conceptual confusion emerged, most notably, in the famous (or by now, infamous) *Banković* decision, where the ECtHR suggested that the notion of jurisdiction included in Article 1 of the ECHR reflected that of general international law.[16] The specific interpretative methods adopted by the Court have been the subject of intense debate.[17] Notably, in its earlier jurisprudence, the Court referred to the particular

[11] Bruno Simma, 'How Distinctive Are Treaties Representing Collective Interest? The Case of Human Rights Treaties' in Vera Gowlland-Debbas (ed), *Multilateral Treaty-Making: The Current Status of Challenges to and Reforms Needed in the International Legislative Process* (Dordrecht, Springer, 2000); Scott Sheeran, 'The Relationship of International Human Rights Law and General International Law: Hermeneutic Constraint, or Pushing the Boundaries?' in Scott Sheeran and Sir Nigel Rodley (eds), *Routledge Handbook of International Human Rights Law* (Abingdon, Routledge, 2013).

[12] ICJ, *Reservations to the Convention on Genocide*, Advisory Opinion, of 28 May 1951, ICJ Reports 15, 23. Rosalyn Higgins, 'Human Rights: Some Questions of Integrity' (1989) 15 *Commonwealth Law Bulletin* 598, 607.

[13] See eg: ECtHR, *Ireland v the United Kingdom*, Appl No 5310/71, 18 January 1978, para 239. See also: René Provost, 'Reciprocity in Human Rights and Humanitarian Law' (1995) 65 *British Yearbook of International Law* 383.

[14] See extensively: Samantha Besson, 'The Extraterritoriality of the European Convention on Human Rights: Why Human Rights Depend on Jurisdiction and What Jurisdiction Amounts To' (2012) 25 *Leiden Journal of International Law* 857.

[15] Among the vast literature, see most notably: Pasquale De Sena, *La nozione di giurisdizione statale nei trattati sui diritti dell'uomo* (Turin, Giappichelli, 2002); Milanović (n 10); Yuval Shany, 'Taking Universality Seriously: A Functional Approach to Extraterritoriality in International Human Rights Law' (2013) 7 *The Law & Ethics of Human Rights* 47.

[16] ECtHR, *Banković and Others v Belgium and Others*, Appl No 52207/99, 12 December 2001, paras 59–61.

[17] See most notably: Alexander Orakhelashvili, 'Restrictive Interpretation of Human Rights Treaties in the Recent Jurisprudence of the European Court of Human Rights' (2003) 14 *European Journal of International Law* 529; Rick Lawson, 'Life after Bankovic-On the Extraterritorial Application of the European Convention on Human Rights' in Menno T Kamminga and Fons Coomans (eds), *Extraterritorial Application of Human Rights Treaties* (Antwerp, Intersentia, 2004); Sarah Miller, 'Revisiting Extraterritorial Jurisdiction: A Territorial Justification for Extraterritorial Jurisdiction under the European Convention' (2009) 20 *European Journal of International Law* 1223; Besson (n 14).

nature of the ECHR as an element supporting its extraterritorial application.[18] But in *Banković*, it referred to the regional character of the Convention as a factor limiting its applicability outside the remit of the *espace juridique* of the Council of Europe.[19]

This geographical limitation reveals a long-standing debate concerning, on the one hand, the ethos of human rights universality and, on the other hand, the significance of borders in defining state powers and responsibilities under international law. In *Banković*, the ECtHR took a clear stance in this debate by interpreting state parties' obligations in line the with the mainly territorial character of the notion of jurisdiction under general international law. This reading of the ECHR might appear as an answer to European states' general critique of human rights imperialism.[20] However, looking closer at the objective nature of the ECHR obligations, the limitation of its scope of application appears as a misconstruction of the very object and purpose of the Convention itself.[21] Of course, the Convention's obligations are established only with regard to state parties to the Council of Europe. But the substantive content of such obligations is objective and non-reciprocal and, as such, applies to every legal and factual relationship between a state party and an individual subject to its power, irrespective of where this occurs.

The divergence between the notions of jurisdiction under general international and human rights law has been endorsed in the case law of other international courts and monitoring bodies.[22] While in its subsequent jurisprudence, the ECtHR took a more flexible approach,[23] it nonetheless maintained the conceptual overlap between jurisdiction under Article 1 ECHR and its ordinary meaning in international law.[24]

As this study focuses on the responsibility of the EU and its Member States for the consequences of their integrated border control practices, it will thus focus on the jurisprudence of the ECtHR and the CJEU. However, to provide the reader with

[18] See eg: ECommHR, *Cyprus v Turkey*, Appl Nos 6780/74 6 and 6950/75, 28 May 1975, para 8; ECtHR, *Loizidou v Turkey*, preliminary objections, Appl No 40/1993/435/514, 23 March 1995, para 62.

[19] *Banković* (n 16) para 80.

[20] See *R (on the application of Al-Skeini) v Secretary of State for Defence (The Redress Trust intervening)* [2007] UKHL 26 (Lord Rodger) para 78. See: Ralph Wilde, 'Compliance With Human Rights Norms Extraterritorially: "Human Rights Imperialism"?' in Marcelo Kohen and Laurence Boisson de Chazournes (eds), *International Law and the Quest for its Implementation. Le droit international et la quête de sa mise en oeuvre* (Leiden, Brill, 2010); Conall Mallory, *Human Rights Imperialists: The Extraterritorial Application of the European Convention on Human Rights* (Oxford, Hart Publishing, 2020).

[21] In this sense, see: Orakhelashvili (n 17).

[22] Eg: ICJ, *Legal Consequences of the Construction of a Wall in the Occupied Palestinian Territory*, Advisory Opinion, ICJ Rep 136, 9 July 2004, para 109; IACtHR, *The institution of asylum, and its recognition as a human right under the Inter-American System of Protection*, Advisory Opinion OC- 25/18, (Ser A) No 25, 30 May 2018, para 171.

[23] ECtHR, *Issa and Others v Turkey*, Court, Appl No 31821/96, 16 November 2004, para 68; ECtHR, *Al-Skeini and Others v the United Kingdom*, Appl No 55721/07, 7 July 2011, para 130.

[24] See eg: ECtHR, *Ukraine v Russia (Re Crimea)*, Appl Nos 20958/14 38334/18, 16 December 2020, para 344.

a broader picture of the jurisdictional remit of the protection of migrants' human rights, I shall also engage with the case law of other human rights monitoring bodies. The ECtHR and the CJEU base their decision regarding the applicability of human rights obligations on two different legal instruments. Hence, unsurprisingly, the jurisdiction question is answered differently in Strasbourg than in Luxembourg. Jurisdiction is a legal category whose operations may appear devoid of ideological substance. Yet, its ethical and concrete implications are vast, for the very existence of any human rights obligation depends on how the notion of jurisdiction is interpreted and applied.[25]

After this brief examination of the various understandings of jurisdiction under international law, this chapter will analyse the notion of (extraterritorial) jurisdiction in the case law developed by the ECtHR (Section II) and the CJEU (Section III), tracing their points of convergence and limitations. The analysis will investigate how the two Courts applied these notions in the context of border controls and migration management (Section IV). The chapter will then expose how the EU and the Member States adapted their border control practices to the evolving notion of extraterritorial jurisdiction (Section V). I will finally identify and briefly address some of the main challenges in triggering human rights obligations absent direct physical contact with potential victims (Section VI).

It will emerge that the trigger of human rights obligations in both systems lies in the relationship between duty bearers and right-holders – that is, for the present purposes, between the EU or its Member States and the people affected by their conduct. The main argument rests on the simple assumption that jurisdiction is best understood as a relationship of power. Such power can be exerted directly through states' authority and control over individuals or indirectly through the control of the geographical space where those individuals find themselves – through the normative framework that will ultimately affect them or through the exercise of state power over them.

II. Jurisdiction and the ECHR

Article 1 ECHR provides that the Contracting Parties' obligations apply to everyone *within their jurisdiction*. The meaning of the phrase 'within their jurisdiction' has been the object of a number of legal and philosophical theories. A common departure point is the general (yet rebuttable) presumption that a state exercises jurisdiction over its own territory. Like any general rule, however, this presumption is subject to exceptions – implying the exercise of jurisdiction outside a state territory. However, the appraisal of the exceptions to the general rule of territorial jurisdiction has changed over time.

[25] Bradin T Cormack, *A Power to Do Justice* (Chicago, University of Chicago Press, 2008).

The notion of extraterritorial jurisdiction in the jurisprudence of the ECtHR remains erratic and, at times, unpredictable.[26] A summary of over half a century of case law fluctuations risks selectivity and inaccuracies. Hence this section does not intend to find a path to coherence on the extraterritorial application of the ECHR. Instead, it will underline some of the key jurisprudential developments to extrapolate a common thread running through both models of extraterritorial jurisdiction and lead to a reflection on the nature of jurisdiction.

A. Extraterritorial Jurisdiction in the Jurisprudence of the ECtHR

Over the years, the ECtHR has employed various tests to determine whether the Convention applies to the extraterritorial conduct of its state parties.[27] Two main views of extraterritorial jurisdiction emerged so far in the Court's case law: one based on a spatial and the other on a personal connection to the state.[28] The first view requires effective control over foreign territory, while the second involves the exercise of power and authority over an individual abroad.

The spatial model was applied, for instance, to cases where a state lost control over part of its territory.[29] The scope of such a model extends to situations where the exercise of the state's authority is limited in part of its territory.[30] This limitation of the presumption of territorial jurisdiction was substantiated in the *Ilaşcu* decision, involving human rights violations occurring in the separatist Moldavian Republic of Transdniestria.[31] The Court found that both Moldova and Russia exercised jurisdiction in the sense of Article 1 ECHR over the contested separatist territory of Transdniestria; the former's was territorial on the basis of sovereign title, and the latter's was extraterritorial on the basis of its control over an area. However, while the Russian extraterritorial jurisdiction concerned all the ECHR obligations deriving from it, the Moldovan jurisdiction was limited to certain specific positive obligations.[32] This approach was confirmed in subsequent case law dealing, particularly with the Convention's application to Transdniestria.[33]

[26] See Conall Mallory, 'A Second Coming of Extraterritorial Jurisdiction at the European Court of Human Rights?' (2021) 82 *QIL QDI* 51.

[27] Işıl Karakaş and Hasan Bakırcı, 'Extraterritorial Application of the European Convention on Human Rights: Evolution of the Court's Jurisprudence on the Notions of Extraterritorial Jurisdiction and State Responsibility' in Anne van Aaken and Iulia Motoc (eds), *The European Convention on Human Rights and General International Law* (Oxford, Oxford University Press, 2018).

[28] These models were extensively set forth in *Al-Skeini* (n 23) paras 133–39.

[29] *Loizidou* (n 18) para 62; *Cyprus v Turkey* (n 18) para 76.

[30] See generally: Marko Milanović and Tatjana Papić, 'The Applicability of the ECHR in Contested Territories' (2018) 67 *International & Comparative Law Quarterly* 779.

[31] ECtHR, *Ilaşcu and Others v Moldova and Russia*, Appl no 48787/99, 8 July 2004.

[32] Ibid, paras 331–35.

[33] *Ilaşcu* (n 31); ECtHR, *Ivantoc and others v Moldova and Russia*, Appl No 23687/05, 15 November 2011; ECtHR, *Catan and Others v Republic of Moldova and Russia*, Appl nos 43370/04 18454/06 8252/05,

The Court developed further its spatial model of jurisdiction, positing that state jurisdiction is triggered not only by control over a territory or a wider geographical area but also by control over a place, namely a detention facility where the applicants were kept under de facto and de jure control of state authorities.[34] Arguably, this approach blurs the lines between the spatial and personal models: the smaller the area in question, the more artificial it becomes to conceive control over space instead of control over persons.

The personal model concerns a state's exercise of power and authority over an individual outside that state's territory. The UN treaty bodies and regional human rights courts have supported this model of jurisdiction,[35] and the European Commission of Human Rights took the same position in its earlier case law.[36] This approach was reversed in *Banković*, where the Court adopted a strict spatial jurisdictional model.[37] In constraining the extraterritorial potential of the ECHR, the Court affirmed that the rights and freedoms defined in the Convention could not be 'divided and tailored in accordance with the circumstances of the extraterritorial act in question'.[38] The Court was, however, soon faced with cases where such a rigid 'all or nothing approach' would lead to unacceptable consequences. In later cases, going back to its earlier jurisprudence, the Court substantially overruled the limitations to extraterritorial jurisdiction designed in *Banković*.[39]

The Court's attempts to reconcile restrictive tendencies with more progressive views came with ambiguity and a certain degree of incoherence.[40] In *Banković*, for example, the Court held that the Convention could not be 'divided and tailored', but then it did precisely that in *Ilaşcu*, limiting Moldova's responsibility to positive

19 October 2012; ECtHR, *Mozer v the Republic of Moldova and Russia*, Appl No 11138/10, 23 February 2016; ECtHR, *Sandu and Others v the Republic of Moldova and Russia*, Appl Nos 21034/05 and 7 others, 17 July 2018.

[34] ECtHR, *Al-Saadoon and Mufdhi v The United Kingdom*, admissibility, Appl No 6198/08, 2 March 2010, para 88.

[35] HRC, *Delia Saldias de Lopez Burgos v Uruguay*, Comm No 52/1979, UN Doc CCPR/C/13/D/52, 29 July 1981, para 12.3; HRC, *Lilian Celiberti de Casariego v Uruguay*, Comm No 56/1979, UN Doc CCPR/C/13/D/56, 29 July 1981, para 10.3; HRC, Article 6 Right to Life, General Comment No 36, CCPR/C/GC/36, paras 22 and 63; ACHPR, *Mohammed Abdullah Saleh Al-Asad v Republic of Djibouti*, communication 383/10, 2014; IACtHR, Advisory Opinion OC-21/14, *Rights and Guarantees of Children in the Context of Migration and/or in Need of International Protection*, OC-21/14, 19 August 2014, para 61; IACtHR, *The Environment and Human Rights*, Advisory Opinion, OC-23/17, 15 November 2017, para 81; IACtHR, *The institution of asylum, and its recognition as a human right under the Inter-American System of Protection*, OC-25/18, 30 May 2018 para 171.

[36] ECommHR, *X v the Federal Republic of Germany*, Appl No 1611/62, 25 September 1965, 158; ECommHR, *Cyprus v Turkey*, Appl Nos 6780/74 6 and 6950/75, 28 May 1975, para 8; ECommHR, *Hess v the United Kingdom*, Appl No 6231/73, 28 May 1975 p 73; ECtHR, *Stocké v Germany*, Appl No 11755/85, 12 October 1989, para 166; ECommHR, *Illich Sanchez Ramirez v France*, Appl No 28780/95, 24 June 1996, 155.

[37] *Banković* (n 16) para 75.

[38] ibid.

[39] ECtHR, *Öcalan v Turkey*, Appl No 46221/99, 12 March 2003, para 93; ECtHR, *Öcalan v Turkey*, Appl No 46221/99, 12 May 2005, para 91; ECtHR, *Ukraine and the Netherlands v Russia*, Appl No 8019/16, 43800/14 and 28525/20, 25 January 2023, para 571.

[40] Mallory (n 26).

human rights obligations.[41] While *Banković* suggested that instantaneous acts could not trigger jurisdiction, the Court later found that the fire-power from helicopters or across UN buffer zones could establish the jurisdictional link.[42] In its subsequent jurisprudence, the Court seems to have, yet again, reversed this position distinguishing two situations: those implying a form of prolonged control and those where the extraterritorial conduct was instantaneous. For instance, in *Medvedyev*, a case involving the interception on the high seas and transfer to France of a Cambodian vessel allegedly carrying narcotics, the Court considered that the applicants were under France's jurisdiction since France exercised complete and exclusive control over the ship and its crew continuously and uninterruptedly.[43]

In its seminal *Al-Skeini* judgment, the Court attempted to introduce some coherence in its previous jurisprudence.[44] It explained the exercise of extraterritorial jurisdiction as based on effective control over an area abroad and on authority and control over individuals.[45] The Court started its reasoning by retaining the idea of the exceptionality of extraterritorial jurisdiction established in *Banković*. However, when outlining its two main strands of jurisprudence regarding the notion of jurisdiction, the Court explicitly rejected the *espace juridique* doctrine adopted in *Banković*.[46] One would have expected the Court to continue by applying a far-reaching spatial notion of jurisdiction to the case. Rather, the ECtHR posited that exercising certain public powers in the territory of another state in accordance with custom, treaty or other agreement implies jurisdiction.[47] Accordingly, the Court found that in the circumstance of the case, the UK exercised 'some of the public powers normally to be exercised by a sovereign government' and therefore deemed that British soldiers exercised authority and control over the individuals killed during security operations in Iraq.[48] The Court arrived at this conclusion in applying the personal model, even if it is not entirely obvious why the exercise of public powers should not be relevant in the context of the spatial model. The ECtHR gave no further explanation for such a choice.[49] Nonetheless, if read in the light of its subsequent case law, it seems that the Court started to merge the two fundamental elements of effective control over a particular area and authority and control over individuals to establish jurisdiction.[50]

[41] *Ilaşcu* (n 31).

[42] ECtHR, *Pad and others v Turkey*, Appl no 60167/00, 28 June 2007, para 54.

[43] ECtHR, *Medvedyev and Others v France*, Appl no 3394/03, 29 March 2010, paras 62–67.

[44] *Al-Skeini* (n 23).

[45] ibid, paras 138–39.

[46] *Banković* (n 16) para 80.

[47] *Al-Skeini* (n 23) para 136.

[48] ibid, paras 149–50.

[49] Milanović explains this choice with the necessity to avoid a 'cause and effect' notion of jurisdiction. See Marko Milanović, 'Al-Skeini and Al-Jedda in Strasbourg' (2012) 23 *European Journal of International Law* 121, 130–31.

[50] Cf: ECtHR, *Hassan v the United Kingdom*, Appl No 29750/09, 16 September 2014, para 75; Judge Pinto de Albuquerque's Partly Dissenting Opinion in *Georgia v Russia (II)*, Appl No 38263/08, 21 January 2021.

Al-Skeini swiftly emerged as the framework for future clarity on the Convention's extraterritorial application. Yet, novel extraterritorial situations emerged, which sat uncomfortably with the *Al-Skeini* criteria.[51] A critical area of uncertainty lies in instantaneous acts in areas not controlled by the relevant state. While the Court did not explicitly exclude the applicability of the Convention in cases of extraterritorial assassinations,[52] in *Georgia v Russia (II)*, the Grand Chamber took a more restrictive approach.[53] It recognised that the use of kinetic force may be sufficient to create a jurisdictional nexus, but it added that these situations involve 'an element of proximity'.[54] Therefore, Russian bombing and artillery shelling during the active phase of the hostilities did not meet either the spatial or the personal model requirements.[55]

The ECtHR seems to have privileged a flexible and casuistic approach to new questions of extraterritorial jurisdiction. An approach which partly rests on the set of criteria established in *Al-Skeini*, but at times resorts to the 'special features' of each case to explain the lack of a consistent interpretation of jurisdiction.[56] The circumstances giving rise to the jurisdictional link with the states cannot be defined in abstracto, but always depend on the 'special features' of each case.[57] While this pragmatic approach could help corroborate principled reasoning,[58] for the moment, it is problematic to define – let alone foresee – which features count as special.[59]

Over the years, the uncertainties of the casuistic approach embraced by the ECtHR in matters of extraterritorial jurisdiction have been a source of concern and interest for legal practitioners and academics. To bridge these discrepancies, Judge Bonello famously proposed a 'functional' test for establishing jurisdiction. By virtue of their participation in the Convention, every state serves some 'basic minimum functions', and their jurisdiction is entailed whenever the observance or the breach of any of these functions is within their authority and control.[60] To overcome case-by-case improvisations, Judge Bonello advocates a principled reading of jurisdiction, anchored in the universality of human rights, where any distinction between territorial and extraterritorial is unwarranted.

[51] ECtHR, *Jaloud v the Netherlands*, Appl No 47708/08, 20 November 2014.

[52] ECtHR, *Makuchyan and Minasyan v Azerbaijan and Hungary*, Appl No 17247/13, 26 May 2020, paras 52 and 120.

[53] ECtHR, *Georgia v Russia (II)*, Appl No 38263/08, 21 January 2021.

[54] ibid, para 132.

[55] ibid, paras 136–38.

[56] See eg, ECtHR, *Güzelyurtlu and Others v Cyprus and Turkey*, Appl No 36925/07, 29 January 2019, para 192; ECtHR, *Romeo Castaño v Belgium*, Appl no 8351/17, 9 July 2019, para 42; *Makuchyan and Minasyan* (n 52) para 51; *Georgia v Russia (II)* (n 53) para 82.

[57] *Güzelyurtlu and Others* (n 56) para 190.

[58] Mariagiulia Giuffré, 'Extraterritorial Jurisdiction: A Dialogue between International Human Rights Bodies' (2021) 82 *QIL QDI* 62.

[59] Marko Milanović and Tatjana Papić, 'Makuchyan and Minasyan v. Azerbaijan and Hungary' (2021) 115 *American Journal of International Law* 294.

[60] Concurring Opinion of Judge Bonello in *Al-Skeini* (n 23) paras 10–11.

Many UN treaty bodies have endorsed (in variations) a functional approach to jurisdiction.[61] The HRC, for example, in its General Comment 36, explained that the scope of state jurisdiction extends to the situation where individuals' right to life is affected by state activities 'in a direct and reasonably foreseeable manner' whether within or outside the country's territory.[62] The Committee on the Elimination of Discrimination Against Women (CEDAW) took a similar position in its General Recommendation No 32.[63] The Committee on the Right of the Child (CRC), the views of two Special Rapporteurs,[64] relied on the claimants' nationality and the state's capability and power to fulfil its human rights obligations towards them.[65] The common denominator of these functional approaches relies on the state's ability to impact the situation of the individuals affected by its power. Put differently, the scope of states' human rights obligations depends on their capacity to fulfil them.

Against this background, compared to UN monitoring bodies, the ECtHR appears to follow a rather restrictive understanding of extraterritorial jurisdiction, conceived as exceptional and dependent on effective control over territory or authority over people. Whilst a functional understanding of extraterritorial jurisdiction allows human rights obligations to follow the actual exercise of governmental power across borders rather than physical frontiers.[66] Legal and philosophical difficulties remain, however. The functional approach might obscure the distinction between human rights and their feasibility, and in so doing, it may result in an essentially limitless extraterritorial jurisdiction.[67]

B. Jurisdiction as a Relationship of Power

Compelling as it may be, the functional approach has been criticised for its too broad notion of jurisdiction that would lead to untenable practical outcomes,[68]

[61] See generally: Yuval Shany, 'The Extraterritorial Application of International Human Rights Law' (2020) 409 *Collected Courses of the Hague Academy of International Law*.

[62] HRC, General Comment No 36 (n 35), para 63. See also: HRC, *A.S., D.I., O.I. and G.D. v Italy*, Comm No 3042/2017, UN Doc CCPR/C/130/D/3042/2017, 27 January 2021.

[63] CEDAW, General recommendation No 32 on the gender-related dimensions of refugee status, asylum, nationality and statelessness of women, UN Doc CEDAW/C/GC/32, 5 November 2014, para 22.

[64] Special Rapporteur on the promotion and protection of human rights while countering terrorism and Special Rapporteur on extrajudicial, summary or arbitrary executions, 'Extra-territorial jurisdiction of States over children and their guardians in camps, prisons, or elsewhere in the northern Syrian Arab Republic: Legal Analysis' (2020), para 2.

[65] CRC, *L.H., L.H., D.A, C.D. and A.F v France*, Communications No 79/2019 and No 109/2019, UN Doc CRC/C/85/D/79/2019–CRC/C/85/D/109/2019, 2 November 2020.

[66] Shany (n 61).

[67] Marko Milanovic, 'The Murder of Jamal Khashoggi: Immunities, Inviolability and the Human Right to Life' (2020) 20 *Human Rights Law Review* 21; Alessandra Spadaro, 'Repatriation of Family Members of Foreign Fighters: Individual Right of State Prerogative?' (2021) 70 *International & Comparative Law Quarterly* 251, 262.

[68] Milanović (n 10) 56.

as well as theoretical complications.[69] The functional model fails to distinguish between the universality of human rights and the human rights obligations of specific duty-bearers. Along these lines, Samantha Besson argues that the 'very question of the concrete feasibility of duties only arises once jurisdiction has been established and the abstract rights recognized'.[70] In other words, if the existence of human rights depends on jurisdiction, their respect cannot logically precede the concept of jurisdiction. Without jurisdiction, the object of any violations would be something that (legally) is not a human right, to begin with.

The interpretation of jurisdiction proposed here rests on the core intuition of the functional model: the universality of human rights. However, it also recognises that jurisdiction as a threshold criterion for the applicability of human rights obligations. The legal argument – by no means original but often overlooked – relies on the specific nature of human rights obligations. The philosophical foundation of the argument is a pluralistic interpretation of universal human rights and a reflection of their relationship with state power.

A caveat is in order before delving into this twofold argument. In the models described above, the term *power* is used interchangeably with authority, (effective) control or influence.

This creates confusion regarding the very nature and the required intensity of the power underlying the exercise of jurisdiction. This confusion originates most probably in the very notion of power itself. Power is a contested and elusive concept. Classic articulations of power include the one offered by Thomas Hobbes, according to which power consists of the present means to obtain some future apparent good.[71] Along these lines, Bertrand Russell described it as 'the production of intended effects'.[72] Yet, what counts to define power? Is it the *capacity* to produce such effects or the interests that this capacity serves?[73] Max Weber, for example, defined power as the capacity to force one's own will on the behaviour of others;[74] to the contrary, Hannah Arendt understood it as the human ability 'not just to act but to act in concert'.[75] Power, in this sense, is a collective effect of communicative action. Judith Butler further notes that power 'is neither possessed nor not possessed by a subject',[76] for those exercising and those subjected to it are

[69] Besson (n 14) 868.

[70] ibid. See also, from a different angle, Shany (n 15) 68.

[71] Thomas Hobbes, *Leviathan: With Selected Variants from the Latin Edition of 1668* (Edwin Curley ed, Notations edition, Indianapolis, Hackett Publishing Company, 1994).

[72] Bertrand Russell, *Power a New Social Analysis* (London, George Allen & Unwin, 1938).

[73] A single footnote cannot even start grasping the full complexity of the discussion on this topic. For the present purposes I have drawn on the works of Max Weber, Hannah Arendt, Michel Foucault and Steven Lukes. For a selected collection of these authors' reflections on the concept of power, see: Steven Lukes (ed), *Power: A Radical View* (New York, New York University Press, 1986).

[74] Max Weber, 'Domination by Economic Power and by Authority' in Steven Lukes (ed), *Power: A Radical View* (New York, New York University Press, 1986).

[75] Hannah Arendt, 'Communicative Power' in Steven Lukes (ed), *Power: A Radical View* (New York, New York University Press, 1986). See also: Jurgen Habermas, 'Hannah Arendt's Communications Concept of Power' (1977) 44 *Social Research* 3.

[76] Judith Butler, 'Bodies and Power Revisited' (2004) *Feminism and the Final Foucault* 183.

simultaneously supported by power and in a struggle against it. Power is apparently not an inherent feature of any subject which is invested or which resists it; but the ambiguity between subjects and power is a feature of power itself, conceived as a strategy.[77] Paraphrasing Locke's famous definition, power is the ability to make or to receive any change or to resist it.[78]

Power moves and impacts persons and things. Power relations, however, are not purely causal in a deterministic sense. Drawing on Marx, Michel Foucault has observed the heterogenous nature of power. According to the philosopher, if we want to analyse power 'we must speak of powers and try to localize them in their historical and geographical specificity'.[79] Power is at once productive, diffuse and various in its forms.[80] It can be non-linear, dispositional and latent. In this vein, power is an ability or a potential that may or may not be expressed.[81] As such, power is difficult to observe.

Using power interchangeably with control, authority or influence, the ECtHR conflates the potential for its manifestation.[82] What is suggested here is that authority and control over a given space or individuals is one of the ways in which power becomes observable. On the one hand, control is the effective exercise of physical power directly over persons or indirectly over territories. On the other hand, authority is an imposition of reasons for action;[83] as such, it implies the ability to prescribe certain conduct or, more generally, to give normative guidance. The former results in the de facto exercise of power, and the latter corresponds to its de iure manifestation. Control and authority represent the effective and normative dimensions of power. Conversely, influence means impacting or affecting a situation. Whereas power is an ability, influence is an occurrence that may or may not result from exercising power.[84] In this sense, influence can be a sufficient but not necessary condition for power. The crucial point here is that power, unlike influence, best describes the ability to determine the material and legal course of events.

[77] ibid.

[78] 'Power … is twofold, viz as be able to make, or able to receive, any change'. John Locke, *An Essay Concerning Human Understanding* (Ghent, Tegg and Company, 1838). See also, Steven Lukes, 'Power and the Battle for Hearts and Minds' (2005) 33 *Millennium* 477.

[79] Michel Foucault, 'The Meshes of Power' in Jeremy W Crampton and Stuart Elden (eds), *Space, Knowledge and Power: Foucault and Geography* (Farnham, Ashgate, 2007).

[80] For an important psychoanalytical study of the social operation of power and its ambivalence, see: Judith Butler, *The Psychic Life of Power: Theories in Subjection* (Redwood City, Stanford University Press, 1997).

[81] Peter Morriss, *Power: A Philosophical Analysis* (Manchester, Manchester University Press, 2002); Lukes (n 78); Stefano Guzzini, 'Power and Cause' (2017) 20 *Journal of International Relations and Development* 737.

[82] For a similar observation, leading to different conclusions, see: Lea Raible, *Human Rights Unbound: A Theory of Extraterritoriality* (Oxford, Oxford University Press, 2020).

[83] Joseph Raz, *The Authority of Law: Essays on Law and Morality* (Oxford, Oxford University Press, 1979); Leslie Green, 'Legal Obligation and Authority' in Edward N Zalta (ed), *The Stanford Encyclopedia of Philosophy* (Metaphysics Research Lab, Stanford University, 2012).

[84] For a clear differentiation of the two concepts, see: Morriss (n 81) 29–32.

Finally, while authority and control in this context should always be linked to the exercise of public powers, this should not be equated with their legitimate exercise. It is now generally accepted that for the purposes of establishing jurisdiction it is irrelevant whether a state has a legal title to exercise its power over a territory or an individual.[85] What matters is a sufficiently close connection between the state and individuals. At the same time, the mere capacity to impact an individual or a situation cannot be regarded as decisive or sufficient conditions for jurisdiction. Doing so would turn on its head the principle of 'ought implies can',[86] with serious drawbacks for the concrete protection of human rights.[87] Put differently, state power should be effective and not merely claimed for jurisdiction to arise.[88]

The specific power relation that triggers jurisdiction can be established in two main ways. First, state power is presumed – based on sovereign title – in relation to state territory, and therefore over the people present therein.[89] However, this presumption is not absolute, particularly when a state is prevented from exercising control and authority over its territory.[90] This is the logical consequence of conceiving jurisdiction as a relation of power, where control and authority over territory are indicators of such a relation.[91] Second, jurisdiction can be established through evidence of state power in its legal or factual manifestations or a combination of both. Ultimately, jurisdiction can be described as effective and normative power exercised by a state over a situation, wherever that power impacts individuals who have the legitimate expectation that the state will respect their human rights. This expectation arises from the legal and factual relation established between the state and the individuals.[92] What makes power effective and normative is the ability to determine a change in the material or legal position of individuals. Factual and normative elements may coalesce, as they reveal the ability to determine the material and legal course of events. Through this prism, jurisdiction is composite and relational.[93] Establishing jurisdiction, therefore, requires considering the entire constellation of power present within the relationship between public institutions and individuals.

[85] ICJ, *Legal Consequences for States of the Continued Presence of South Africa in Namibia* (Advisory Opinion), ICJ Reports 1971, 21 June 1971, para 118. See also: ECommHR, *Stocké v Germany*, Appl No 11755/85, 12 October 1989, para 167; *Loizidou* (n 18) para 62.

[86] Aravind Ganesh, *Rightful Relations with Distant Strangers: Kant, the EU, and the Wider World* (Oxford, Hart Publishing, 2021) 169–75.

[87] Spadaro (n 67) 260–63; Raible (n 82) 42–73.

[88] Besson (n 14) 872; Violeta Moreno-Lax, 'The Architecture of Functional Jurisdiction: Unpacking Contactless Control – On Public Powers, S.S. and Others v. Italy, and the "Operational Model"' (2020) 21 *German Law Journal* 385, 397.

[89] ECtHR, *Assanidze v Georgia*, Appl no 71503/01, 8 April 2004, para 139; *Al-Skeini* (n 23) para 131.

[90] *Ilaşcu* (n 31) para 312.

[91] See Besson (n 14).

[92] Shany (n 61).

[93] This reading of jurisdiction is closer albeit not entirely congruent to Moreno-Lax, who describes it as the expression of state power through legislative, executive and/or adjudicative activities. Moreno-Lax (n 88) 403.

Underpinning this relational understanding of jurisdiction is the tension between the idea that human rights exist prior to any legal system and the need for their legal recognition. This tension is illustrated in the famous paradox of the 'right to have rights' elaborated by Hannah Arendt.[94] The inherent, inalienable humanity of the individual is protected by political (and therefore legal) citizenship rights. Yet not all individuals are entitled to such protections: 'The alien is the gap between the human and the citizen'.[95] This paradox is affected by human rights' individualism and a consequent denial of plurality.[96] The right to have rights, or the recognition of the humanity of every individual, should be guaranteed, according to Arendt, by humanity itself in the plural relations of unique individuals.[97] In other words, human rights find their philosophical underpinning in their relationality. Along these lines, Emmanuel Levinas argued that 'everything begins with the right of the other and with my unending responsibility'.[98] Human rights are thus grounded in a relation of responsibility – in my infinite responsibility for the other. Arguably, the objective legal nature of human rights obligations discussed above mirrors this philosophical approach to human rights. In this respect, Simone Weil, one of the most uncompromising and complex critics of the language of rights, observed that the notion of (human) rights is subordinate and relative to that of obligation. The effective exercise of a right does not spring from the individual who possesses it, but from those under a particular obligation towards that individual.[99]

To translate these philosophical reflections into legal parlance, human rights arise from an objective obligation that is not subordinated to reciprocal interest.[100] Human rights are understood here as founded in a relationship between individuals and public institutions – a relationship marked by the power of the latter to change the (legal and factual) situation of the former.

This interpretation would allow for a qualified but capacious application of the ECHR, which would not apply to everyone unconditionally but to everyone who has a specific relation with a contracting state.[101] This was probably the logic that led the Court to reverse its view according to which the Convention's rights can be

[94] Hannah Arendt, *The Origins of Totalitarianism* (New York, Harcourt, Brace, Jovanovich, 1973). For more comments on the works of Hannah Arendt and her contribution and constructive critique of human rights, see: Seyla Benhabib, *The Rights of Others: Aliens, Residents, and Citizens* (Cambridge, Cambridge University Press, 2004); Stephanie Degooyer and others, *The Right to Have Rights* (New York, Verso, 2018).

[95] Costas Douzinas, *Human Rights and Empire: The Political Philosophy of Cosmopolitanism* (Abingdon, Routledge, 2007) 99.

[96] 'From the beginning, the paradox involved in the declaration of inalienable human rights was that it reckoned with an 'abstract' human being who seemed to exist nowhere'. Arendt (n 94) 291.

[97] ibid 298.

[98] Emmanuel Levinas, *Nine Talmudic Readings* (Annette Aronowicz tr, Bloomington, Indiana University Press, 1990) 20.

[99] Simone Weil, *L'enracinement* (Paris, Gallimard, 1949) 2.

[100] Orakhelashvili (n 17).

[101] Cf, Besson (n 14) 859.

'divided and tailored'.[102] Yet, it is not the ECHR abstract rights that are divided and tailored: human rights are universal and indivisible. Instead, the concrete duties of contracting states can be tailored to be consistent with the specific circumstances of each case, irrespective of whether it takes place within or beyond their borders.[103] It therefore becomes clear that this is not a question of creating new legal rights where there were none, or of human rights imperialism – it is a question of applying the legal obligations embodied in a Convention ratified by contracting states and from which human rights derive.

III. The Applicability of the EU Charter of Fundamental Rights

One of the hallmarks of the EU CFR is that its application is not conditioned upon any territorial connection. Instead, Article 51(1) CFR links the application of EU fundamental rights to the addressees of the Charter's obligations, that is, to all EU organs and Member States. In accordance with their respective powers and respecting the limits of the Union's competences, they should 'respect the rights, observe the principles and promote the application' of the Charter.[104]

From this provision, it emerges that, contrary to many human rights treaties, the CFR includes a jurisdictional clause that is functionally defined. The Charter's applicability is not related to the territory of the EU (as the combination of the territories of its Member States) nor it is inferred from notions of authority and control over persons. The logic is that of the principle of conferral, which is reflected in the language of competence and distribution of powers, irrespective of the place where such powers are exercised. In this line, Moreno-Lax and Costello have defined the scope of applicability of EU fundamental rights in relation to the scope of EU law as an autonomous paradigm.[105] The two scholars suggest that the CFR set the principle of effectiveness of EU law as an autonomous requirement for its applicability, which is to be understood independently from the notion of jurisdiction in international human rights law.

This section builds on Moreno-Lax and Costello's argument and brings in further aspects that substantiate the claim that the protection of the fundamental rights endorsed by the Charter is based on a jurisdictional model that goes beyond the doctrines developed within the international human rights regime while accommodating the specificities of the EU legal system. This, however, does not

[102] Cf *Al-Skeini* (n 23) para 137 and *Banković* (n 16) para 75.
[103] Besson (n 14) 879.
[104] Art 51(1), CFR.
[105] Violeta Moreno-Lax and Cathryn Costello, 'The Extraterritorial Application of the EU Charter of Fundamental Rights: From Territoriality to Facticity, the Effectiveness Model' in Steve Peers and others (eds), *The EU Charter of Fundamental Rights* (Oxford, Hart Publishing, 2014) 1679.

imply an autonomous notion of human rights jurisdiction within the EU system of fundamental rights protection. The broad understanding of jurisdiction proposed above in relation to the ECHR would remain adequate in the case of the CFR.

The exercise of the EU's normative power implies the application of the Charter, with no further requirements to be met. The mere presence of an EU competence to legislate suffices to give rise to the application of the Charter, irrespective of the place where it is exercised. This argument is further supported by the absence of any textual indication that a distinction should be made (in terms of human rights obligations) between the internal and external competences of the EU.[106]

The following analysis is limited to considering the scope of the application of the fundamental rights included in the Charter and does not include a separate analysis of fundamental rights as general principles. This is because, in general, the Charter is a preferred reference in fundamental rights adjudication.[107]

A. The Scope of Application of the Charter of Fundamental Rights

The scope of application of the Charter is regulated by its Article 51. Pursuant to its terms, the Charter applies EU institutions, bodies, offices and agencies and to the Member States only when they are implementing EU law. The Charter is always applicable to the EU and its organs, as their action is premised on an EU competence. Furthermore, the EU organs remain bound by the Charter also when they act outside the EU legal framework.[108] Conversely, the extent of the Charter's applicability to Member States is less clear. In particular, the exact meaning of the verb 'implementing' has been the object of some controversy.[109] In this respect, the Explanations to the Charter offer some guidance in clarifying that the EU fundamental rights apply whenever Member States act within the scope of EU law.[110] Member States are therefore bound by the Charter whenever

[106] Arts 2, 3(5) and 21, TUE.

[107] Koen Lenaerts, J Gutiérrez-Fons and Catherine Barnard, 'The Role of General Principles of EU Law' in Eleanor Spaventa, Anthony Arnull and Michael Dougan (eds), *A Constitutional Order of States? Essays in EU Law in Honour of Alan Dashwood* (Oxford, Bloomsbury, 2011); Vivian Kube, *EU Human Rights, International Investment Law and Participation: Operationalizing the EU Foreign Policy Objective to Global Human Rights Protection* (Cham, Springer, 2019) 11–86.

[108] Joined Cases C-8/15 P to C-10/15 P, *Ledra Advertising*, 20 September 2016, ECLI:EU:C:2016:701, para 67.

[109] Deirdre Curtin and Ronald van Ooik, 'The Sting Is Always in the Tail. The Personal Scope of Application of the EU Charter of Fundamental Rights' (2001) *Maastricht Journal of European and Comparative Law* 102; Koen Lenaerts, 'Exploring the Limits of the EU Charter of Fundamental Rights' (2012) 8 *European Constitutional Law Review* 375; Nicole Lazzerini, *La carta dei diritti fondamentali dell'Unione Europea. I limiti di applicazione* (Milan, Franco Angeli, 2018).

[110] Explanations relating to the Charter of Fundamental Rights, OJ C 303/17, 14 December 2007; See also: Case 5/88, *Wachauf*, 13 July 1989, ECLI:EU:C:1989:321, para 19; Case C-260/89, *ERT*, 18 June 1991, ECLI:EU:C:1991:254, para 42; Case C-309/96, *Annibaldi*, 18 December 1997, ECLI:EU:C:1997:631, paras 13–14 (referred to by the Explanations).

they fulfil an obligation imposed by EU law.[111] In its seminal judgment *Åkerberg Fransson*, the CJEU upheld a wide interpretation of the Charter's application,[112] finding that the coincidence of domestic (administrative and criminal) measures punishing tax evasion (an interest of the EU, that is loss of revenue to its budget) implied that the Member State was implementing EU law, and therefore the Charter was applicable.[113] Accordingly, even a partial connection to EU law was deemed sufficient to trigger the application of the Charter.[114] The Court emphasised that a situation cannot be governed by EU law without fundamental rights being applicable for the applicability of Union law entails that of the Charter.[115] Hence, the application of the CFR therefore depends on the scope of application of EU law.

That notwithstanding, the precise remit of EU law and the requirements necessary to establish a link between a national measure and EU law remains uncertain.[116] In *Siragusa*, the Court posited that EU fundamental rights, including the EU Charter, are not applicable to situations tangentially touched upon by EU law.[117] Rather, the application of EU fundamental rights requires a certain degree of connection with EU law, which is determined in relation to whether EU law imposes an obligation on the Member State concerned.[118]

Article 6(1) TEU establishes that the CFR 'shall not extend in any way the competences of the Union as defined in the Treaties', and in the same line, Article 51(2) CFR clarifies once again that the Charter does not modify the competences and powers of the Union through an expansive interpretation of the scope of application of EU law. These rules express a preoccupation with competence creep and undue interference with the national sovereignty of Member States.[119] However, the CJEU frequently emphasises the importance of a coordinated separation of tasks between the Union and its Member States regarding fundamental rights protection. In this line, the Court has recognised the relevance of national fundamental rights when EU rules grant some

[111] Lenaerts (n 109) 378.

[112] Case C-617/10, *Åkerberg Fransson*, 26 February 2013, EU:C:2013:105. For further discussion see most notably: Daniel Sarmiento, 'Who's Afraid of the Charter? The Court of Justice, National Courts and the New Framework of Fundamental Rights Protection in Europe' (2013) 50 *Common Market Law Review* 1267; Cristina Izquierdo Sans, 'The Conformation of Fundamental Rights by the Court of Justice of the European Union', in Mercedes Pérez Manzano, Juan Antonio Lascuraín Sánchez and Marina Mínguez Rosique (eds), *Multilevel Protection of the Principle of Legality in Criminal Law* (Cham, Springer, 2018).

[113] *Åkerberg Fransson* (n 112) para 27.

[114] ibid, para 24.

[115] ibid, para 21.

[116] For further discussion and references, see: Eleanor Spaventa, 'The Interpretation of Article 51 of the EU Charter of Fundamental Rights: The Dilemma of Stricter or Broader Application of the Charter to National Measures' Project Report (European Parliament 2016).

[117] Case C-206/13, *Siragusa*, 6 March 2014, ECLI:EU:C:2014:126, para 24.

[118] ibid, paras 25–26. See also, Case C-87/12, *Ymeraga and Others*, 8 May 2013, ECLI:EU:C:2013:291, para 41.

[119] Sarmiento (n 112).

discretion to Member States, but it has also imposed a rule of strict primacy once a domain is governed by EU law.[120]

Crucially, within the limits of the EU competences, once it has been determined that EU law applies to a given situation, so does the Charter. There is no separation between the scope of application of EU law and the remit of EU fundamental rights protection; the two are generally understood as coextensive. In the word of Lenaerts, 'the Charter is the "shadow" of EU law. Just as an object defines the contours of its shadow, the scope of EU law determines that of the Charter'.[121] In sum, the scope *ratione materiae* of the Charter covers every situation where the EU is exercising its normative power directly, through its organs or indirectly, through one of its Member States implementing EU law.

Having identified the material scope of the Charter, it is now time to define the subjects to which it applies, either as the addressees of its obligations or as the beneficiaries of its protection. As to the first aspect, following Article 51(1), the addressees of the Charter's obligations are the EU and its organs, as well as Member States when they act within the scope of EU law. Understood in this sense, the scope *ratione personae* of the Charter is determined by reference to its scope *ratione materiae*. With regard to the second aspect of the personal scope of the CFR, people impacted by EU law are entitled to rights that emanate from multiple legal sources, enforced through a variety of mechanisms, the Charter being one among them. The personal scope of the Charter has extended to EU citizens and (some) third-country nationals a number of rights,[122] in so far as they fall within the remit of an EU competence.[123]

Territorial limitations appear equally unwarranted. In this respect, the EU treaties offer some indications as to the geographical scope of EU law. According to Article 52 TEU, the Treaties apply to all EU Member States. Paragraph 2 of the same provision refers to Article 355 of the TFEU, which in turn contains a non-exhaustive list of derogations from the principle of full application of EU law throughout Member States' territories.[124] It resonates with the so-called colonial clauses of

[120] *Åkerberg Fransson* (n 112) para 29; Case C-399/11, *Melloni*, 26 February 2013, ECLI:EU:C:2013:107, para 60; *F*, C-168/13 PPU, 30 May 2013, EU:C:2013:358, paras 52–55; Case C-42/17, *MAS, MB (Taricco II)*, 5 December 2017, ECLI:EU:C:2017:936, para 47.

[121] Speech by Koen Lenaerts, *The ECHR and the CJEU: Creating Synergies in the Field of Fundamental Rights Protection*, Solemn hearing for the opening of the Judicial Year, 26 January 2018.

[122] For a critical account of how European immigration law separates people into different types of foreigners, see most notably: Karin de Vries, 'The Non-National as "The Other": What Role for Non-Discrimination Law?' in Moritz Jesse (ed), *European Societies, Migration, and the Law: The 'Others' amongst 'Us'* (Cambridge, Cambridge University Press, 2020).

[123] Eva Kassoti, 'The Extraterritorial Applicability of the EU Charter of Fundamental Rights: Some Reflections in the Aftermath of the Front Polisario Saga' (2020) 12 *European Journal of Legal Studies* 117.

[124] Dimitry Kochenov, 'Article 355 TFEU' in Manuel Kellerbauer, Marcus Klamert and Jonathan Tomkin (eds), *The EU Treaties and the Charter of Fundamental Rights: A Commentary* (Oxford, Oxford University Press, 2019).

Article 56 of the ECHR and Article 40 of the 1951 Refugee Convention.[125] At first glance, these provisions seem to indicate a territorially confined application of EU law.[126] However, Article 52 TEU simply refers to Member States without any explicit reference to their territories. Arguably, even if a presumption that EU law applies within the combined territories of the EU Member States can be established, nothing seems to imply that such a presumption cannot be reversed.[127] Contrary to some international human rights treaties, the CFR is silent as to its scope *ratione loci*. Furthermore, there has been little jurisprudential guidance as to the extraterritorial application of the CFR so far. This silence has led Moreno-Lax and Costello to observe that 'EU fundamental rights obligations simply track all EU activities, as well as Member State action when implementing EU law'.[128] This interpretation is not only supported by the text of Article 51 CFR, exclusively devoted to the material scope of the Charter, but also by Article 52(3) CFR, which provides that EU law can provide 'more extensive protection' than the ECHR. In this line, the two scholars advocate an innovative understanding of the CRF's applicability, as rooted in the principle of effectiveness and disconnected from that of territoriality.[129]

In several cases, the CJEU determined the scope of EU law based on the principle of effectiveness of EU law, irrespective of its geographical application.[130] Further, it seems that the CJEU implicitly confirmed the extraterritorial scope of application of the CFR in cases dealing with the right to privacy and data protection. Namely, in *Schrems* and *Digital Rights Ireland*, the CJEU upheld that the protection of the right to privacy and data protection, included in Articles 7 and 8 CFR, would be rendered ineffective if the correlative obligations of the Member States stopped at the external borders of the EU.[131] With specific regard to actions

[125] Moreno-Lax (n 1) 294; Lucy Mayblin, 'Colonialism, Decolonisation, and the Right to Be Human: Britain and the 1951 Geneva Convention on the Status of Refugees' (2014) 27 *Journal of Historical Sociology* 423; Maria-Teresa Gil Bazo, 'Article 40' in Andreas Zimmermann, Jonas Dörschner and Felix Machts (eds), *The 1951 Convention Relating to the Status of Refugees and Its 1967 Protocol: A Commentary* (Oxford, Oxford University Press, 2011); Louise Moor and AW Brian Simpson, 'Ghosts of Colonialism in the European Convention on Human Rights' (2006) 76 *The British Year Book of International Law* 121.

[126] See in this sense: Case T-212, *Commune de Champagne and Others v Council and Commission*, 3 July 2007, ECLI:EU:T:2007:194, paras 89–90; Joined Cases T-108/07 and T-354/08, *Spira*, 11 July 2013, ECLI:EU:T:2013:367, para 123.

[127] From a different perspective, Joanne Scott distinguishes the concept of 'territorial extension' from that of 'extraterritorial legislation' in breach of international law. In the former conception, the trigger for the application of EU law remains a territorial connection (mainly access to the EU market), while the latter conception refers to measures that impose obligations on persons irrespective of a territorial connection. Joanne Scott, 'Extraterritoriality and Territorial Extension in EU Law' (2014) 62 *The American Journal of Comparative Law* 87.

[128] Moreno-Lax and Costello (n 105) 1658.

[129] Moreno-Lax (n 1) 289–96.

[130] See eg: Case C-214-94, *Ingrid Boukhalfa v Bundesrepublik Deutschland*, 30 April 1996, ECLI:EU:C:1996:174, para 14; Case C- 177-95, *Ebony Maritime*, 27 February 1997, ECLI:EU:C:1997:89, paras 17 ss; Case C-366/10, *ATAA*, 21 December 2011, ECLI:EU:C:2011:864.

[131] Joined cases C-293/12 and C-594/12, *Digital Rights Ireland*, 8 April 2014, ECLI:EU:C:2015:650, para 68; Case C-362/14, *Schrems*, 6 October 2015, ECLI:EU:C:2014:238, para 58.

related to fundamental rights violations that occurred as a consequence of EU action, territorial considerations are immaterial in determining the applicability of the Charter.[132] In neither *Mugraby* nor *Zaoui*, for instance, did the CJEU question the assertion that the alleged fundamental rights violations occurred extraterritorially.[133] In addition, in *Front Polisario I*, the General Court explicitly affirmed a duty of care on the part of EU institutions in the context of the Union's external policies.[134]

Even though it has been overturned by the Grand Chamber for lack of legal standing,[135] the *Front Polisario I* decision remains remarkable for leaving the door open to the extraterritorial application of the EU human rights obligations. The General Court partially annulled the Council's decision to conclude a trade agreement with Morocco that would have impacted the fundamental rights of the inhabitants of the Moroccan-controlled territories of Western Sahara.[136] The Court's reasoning departed from the affirmation that EU institutions 'enjoy a wide discretion'[137] in the conduct of external economic relations, and therefore the review of the Court was limited to 'a manifest error of assessment' of the institution in question.[138] Consequently, the Court found such a manifest error in the Council's failure to fulfil a specific positive obligation. Namely, to ensure, through an impact assessment, that the export to the EU of products originating in 'disputed territory' ('occupied territory' would perhaps be more precise[139]) was consistent with the fundamental rights of the population of that territory.[140] In this sense, the EU discretionary power turns into a positive obligation.

This same logic did not apply in the *X and X* case, where the state discretion as to the issuance of a humanitarian visa was not interpreted as implying a positive duty to protect individuals against inhuman or degrading treatment, or *refoulement*.[141]

[132] Kube (n 107) 29 et ss.

[133] Case C-581/11, *Mugraby*, 12 July 2012, ECLI:EU:C:2012:466; Case C-288/03, *Zaoui*, 14 October 2004, ECLI:EU:C:2004:633. As both applications failed – the first on the merits and the second as an exclusive causality link was missing – it has been pointed out that it might be speculative to base an argument on an unreasoned point. However, at least these cases indicate that there is no obvious hindrance to such action. See: Lorand Bartels, 'The EU's Human Rights Obligations in Relation to Policies with Extraterritorial Effects' (2014) 25 *European Journal of International Law* 1071; Enzo Cannizzaro, 'The EU's Human Rights Obligations in Relation to Policies with Extraterritorial Effects: A Reply to Lorand Bartels' (2014) 25 *European Journal of International Law* 1093.

[134] Case T-512/12, *Front Polisario v Council*, 10 December 2015, ECLI:EU:T:2015:953.

[135] The decision of the General Court has been overturned by the Grand Chamber according to which Front Polisario did not fulfil the direct and individual concern criteria required by Article 263(4) TFEU. Case C-104/16 P, *Front Polisario v Council*, 21 December 2016, ECLI:EU:C:2016:973. See, however, Case T-279/19, *Front Polisario v Council*, 29 September 2021, ECLI:EU:T:2021:639, para 218 and Joined Cases T-344/19 and T-356/19, *Front Polisario v Council*, 29 September 2021, ECLI:EU:T:2021:640, para 251 where the General Court as certained the legal standing of Front Polisario.

[136] *Front Polisario v Council* (n 134) para 247.

[137] ibid, para 164.

[138] ibid, paras 224–25.

[139] For a thorough critique of the Court decision from the point of view of the law of occupation, see Cedric Ryngaert and Rutger Fransen, 'EU Extraterritorial Obligations with Respect to Trade with Occupied Territories: Reflections after the Case of Front Polisario before EU Courts' [2018] 2 *Europe and the World: A Law Review* 1.

[140] *Front Polisario v Council* (n 134) para 241.

[141] Case C-638/16 PPU, *X and X*, 7 March 2017, ECLI:EU:C:2017:173, para 51.

In contrast to the Advocate General's opinion,[142] the Court concluded that, as the delivery of a humanitarian visa exceeds the temporary duration established by the EU Visa Code, it did not fall within the scope of EU law and hence was not within the scope of the Charter.[143] Despite its questionable results,[144] this decision confirmed the CJEU approach to the applicability of the Charter. The applicability of EU fundamental rights obligations depends on the remit of EU law and its relevance to a particular situation. In this regard, the most recent amendment to Frontex's regulation explicitly foresees the applicability of the Charter in situations where the agency operates extraterritorially.[145]

To conclude, the scope of application of EU fundamental rights transcends traditional territorial limitations and follows the constitutional structure of the Union's legal order. It follows that the Charter applies to the EU and its organs, and whenever Member States adopt measures in order to comply with the obligations imposed by the EU normative framework.[146]

B. The Applicability of EU Fundamental Rights: A Relationship of Power?

In the exercise of the powers conferred upon it,[147] the EU can affect individuals' fundamental rights, which deserve adequate protection. Potential violations of fundamental rights can occur within, as well as beyond, the borders of EU Member States. Violations can be caused by the EU or its organs, as well as by Member States implementing EU law.[148] What follows will demonstrate that the applicability of EU fundamental rights is based on the exercise of an EU competence, that is, the exercise of the EU normative power.

[142] Opinion of Advocate General Paolo Mengozzi, *X and X v Etat Belgium*, Case C-638/16 PPU, 7 February 2017, ECLI:EU:C:2017:93.

[143] For a thorough analysis, see most notably: Violeta Moreno-Lax, 'Asylum Visas as an Obligation under EU Law: Case PPU C-638/16 X, X v État belge' Part I and Part II (*EU Immigration and Asylum Law and Policy*, 16 and 21 September 2017). See also: Evelien Brouwer, *The European Court of Justice on Humanitarian Visas: Legal Integrity vs. Political Opportunism?* (Brussels, CEPS commentary, 2017); Jorrit J Rijpma, 'External Migration and Asylum Management: Accountability for Executive Action Outside EU-Territory' (2017) 2 *European Papers* 571; Giulia Raimondo, 'Visti umanitari: il caso X e X contro Belgio, C-638/16 PPU' 4 (2017) *I Quaderni di SIDIBlog*; Sílvia Morgades-Gil, 'Humanitarian Visas and EU Law: Do States Have Limits to Their Discretionary Power to Issue Humanitarian Visas?' (2017) 2 *European Papers* 1005.

[144] See s IV.B.iv below.

[145] Art 71, Regulation 2019/1896.

[146] Lenaerts (n 109) 382.

[147] *Opinion 2/94*, 28 March 1996, ECLI:EU:C:1996:140, para 23.

[148] This issue is deeply intertwined with the question of attribution, given the EU multi-level implementation system. For a comprehensive analysis, see: Andrés Delgado Casteleiro, *The International Responsibility of the European Union: From Competence to Normative Control* (Cambridge, Cambridge University Press, 2016) in particular 42–53.

As discussed above, the general idea of power is difficult to conceptualise as it can be non-linear, dispositional or latent. With regard to the EU, international relations scholars have argued that the EU normative power consists of its international influence. The different norms and policies that the EU pursues are part of a process redefining 'what can be "normal" in international relations'.[149] The notion of normative power is here understood, in a narrower sense, as the ability to change a situation through legal rules. As 'fundamental rights as guaranteed in the Union do not have any effect other than in the context of the powers determined by the Treaties',[150] the exercise of the EU normative power depends on its competence to directly or indirectly govern a particular situation through legal rules.

Moreno-Lax and Costello aptly observe that as an international organisation, the EU does not have territory of its own, and it seems difficult to provide evidence of its effective control over persons or territories.[151] The two scholars suggest that the Charter's field of application should thus be interpreted autonomously from international human rights law and 'similar extraneous constraints'. At systemic and substantive level, however, EU fundamental rights, including the Charter, are rooted in international human rights law.[152] Understanding EU fundamental rights jurisdiction as a relation of normative power has the potential to reconcile the specificities of the EU constitutional framework with the principle of indivisibility and universality of human rights. This is not an attempt to reconcile the irreconcilable. True, the Charter is not a treaty under international law, and the language of traditional international human rights treaties is difficult to apply to situations involving a non-state entity such as the EU. What is proposed here is to engage EU law with international human rights law, rather than discarding the latter as an unnecessary constraint. This approach is driven by the need to find a common language that could support and mutually reinforce the effective protection of human rights within and beyond the EU.

Of course, this reading of the scope of the CFR should be adapted to the peculiarities of the EU, a non-state entity whose international legal personality is limited and functional in nature. Therefore, the CFR applicability cannot be determined by the direct control over a territory or over the persons finding themselves within such territory. The only possible manner of substantiating the applicability of EU fundamental rights is through evidence of the EU normative power. Whenever the institutions, bodies, offices and agencies of the Union exercise their powers, and whenever Member States act within the scope of EU law, EU fundamental rights apply.[153]

[149] Ian Manners, 'Normative Power Europe: A Contradiction in Terms?' (2002) 40 *JCMS: Journal of Common Market Studies* 235, 253. For a different perspective: Sandra Lavenex, 'The Power of Functionalist Extension: How EU Rules Travel' (2014) 21 *Journal of European Public Policy* 885.

[150] Explanations relating to the Charter of Fundamental Rights, OJ C 303/17, 14 December 2007, Art 51.

[151] Moreno-Lax and Costello (n 105) 1679–80.

[152] CFR, Preamble; Art 6(1), TEU.

[153] The CJEU interpreted the scope of implementation of EU law in broad terms including when Member States (1) implement their EU law obligations, (2) when they enact provisions of primary

IV. Jurisdiction and the European Integrated Border Management

The border is the geographical threshold between interior and exterior. It defines the perimeter of territorial jurisdiction and the physical space over which a state's sovereignty is exercised, in particular, the sovereign right to admit or exclude outsiders. Yet underneath this ostensibly linear notion lies the more complex structure of border controls extending beyond the geographical frontier of a state. Those extraterritorial border controls entail serious consequences for the applicability of human rights obligations, where people are beyond the state territory.

In this respect, Hailbronner famously held that it is

> very doubtful whether the principle of *non-refoulement* implies … a general duty of States to organize their entry and immigration, visa and transport legislation in such a way that potential political refugees may use their right to seek and enjoy asylum effectively. A legal duty of receiving States arises only when and in so far as a potential refugee, claiming a danger of political persecution, has come within the scope of territorial jurisdiction of a State.[154]

Applied to the EIBM system, this stance implies that while migration control practices can operate extraterritorially, protection obligations arise only when their beneficiaries present themselves at the physical borders of the EU.[155]

This position is contested in theory and practice. As will be discussed below, the human rights obligations of the EU and its Member States do not stop at their external borders. All forms of border governance – as manifestations of state power – are within states' jurisdiction, with a strong presumption of the states' effective control at its borders.[156] The ECtHR has confirmed this orientation with particular regard to the prohibition of *refoulement*. Accordingly, the extraterritorial applicability of human rights guarantees, including the prohibition of *refoulement*, has been recognised in many ways in the legal instruments governing the EIBM system.[157] The scope of these obligations extends so far as Member States exercise their power over a given situation within or beyond their borders.[158]

The ECtHR jurisprudence of extraterritorial jurisdiction in cases of border controls is based, however, on the ambiguous connection between the manifestation of state (de iure) public powers and the exercise of physical (de facto) control

or secondary EU law or (3) when they derogate from EU legal requirements. See Explanations to the Charter of Fundamental Rights [2007] OJ C303/02, 32 (and references therein).

[154] Kay Hailbronner, 'Comments On: The Right to Leave, the Right to Return and the Question of a Right to Remain' in Vera Gowlland-Debbas (ed), *The Problem of Refugees in the Light of Contemporary International Law Issues* (Leiden, Martinus Nijhoff, 1996).

[155] Moreno-Lax (n 1) 247.

[156] IACHR, *The Human Rights Situation of Refugees and Migrant Families and Unaccompanied Children in the United States of America*, OAS/Ser.L/V/II. 155 Doc 16, 24 July 2015, para 39.

[157] See eg: Art 71(3), Regulation 2019/1896.

[158] For a similar reading, see Moreno-Lax (n 88).

over migrants attempting to reach the European borders. This ambiguity emerged in the leading case *Hirsi Jamaa* and persists in subsequent jurisprudence. *Hirsi Jamaa* is of particular relevance in the way it dealt explicitly with an extraterritorial migration control measure and placed it within the ambit of human rights protection. An opposite result was reached by the CJEU, which in the *X and X* case, declared the request for a humanitarian visa as being a matter of national law, instead of an application of EU law.[159] Thereby, it excluded the application of the CFR, including the protection against *refoulement*.

State practice, however, has evolved in line with the progressive development of human rights law in the context of extraterritorial jurisdiction.[160] New deterrence practices are less clearly extraterritorial, and they are delegated much more to third countries or private actors. This allows Member States, and the EU, to keep up appearances while escaping their international obligations, as it is more difficult to establish jurisdiction over delegated border control practices. The move to this model of cooperative deterrence has gained traction in many parts of the world. This chapter is concerned with the European context, however, and with the diffusion of border control practices inherent in the EIBM project as implemented by Frontex.

It might be argued that international law is part of the problem, as it reproduces the fundamental inequality that structures the externalisation and outsourcing of border controls, creating a system of regional containment.[161] Yet, as will be suggested below, this dysfunction rests on the problematic assumption that where there is no direct physical contact there is no jurisdiction, and therefore no responsibility.

A. At the Border

The starting point of this enquiry is the physical borders of the EU Member States. What is the scope of States' obligations in these spaces where traditional border control practices are performed? The answer to this question has been a contested issue, particularly in the first decades after the adoption of the Refugee Convention. Article 33 of the Refugee Convention prohibits the return to 'the

[159] *X and X* (n 141).

[160] Thomas Gammeltoft-Hansen and James C Hathaway, 'Non-Refoulement in a World of Cooperative Deterrence' (2014) 53 *Columbia Journal of Transnational Law* 235; Thomas Gammeltoft-Hansen and Nikolas F Tan, 'The End of the Deterrence Paradigm? Future Directions for Global Refugee Policy' (2017) 5 *Journal on Migration and Human Security* 28; Thomas Gammeltoft-Hansen, 'International Cooperation on Migration Control: Towards a Research Agenda for Refugee Law' (2018) 20 *European Journal of Migration and Law* 373; Annick Pijnenburg, 'Containment Instead of Refoulement: Shifting State Responsibility in the Age of Cooperative Migration Control?' (2020) 20 *Human Rights Law Review* 306.

[161] E Tendayi Achiume, 'Governing Xenophobia' (2018) 51 *Vanderbilt Journal of Transnational Law* 333; Loren B Landau, 'Crisis and Containment: Risks of Enhanced Global Migration Governance' in *Global Shifts Colloquium* (Perry World House University of Pennsylvania, 2018); BS Chimni, 'Aid, Relief, and Containment: The First Asylum Country and Beyond' (2002) 40 *International Migration* 75.

frontiers of territories' in which refugees' lives or freedom would be in danger.[162] On this point, commentators have emphasised that the drafters of the Refugee Convention were unwilling to include a provision on admission, as during the drafting process, the Dutch and Swiss delegates stressed that the prohibition of *refoulement* applied only to people who had entered the territory.[163] Hence, refugees who managed to elude border guards were protected by the provision, and those who did not had to face their 'hard luck'.[164]

Eventually, however, a different interpretation prevailed, one that did see rejection at the border as prohibited by Article 33 of the Refugee Convention.[165] According to the 1967 UN General Assembly Resolution on Territorial Asylum, asylum seekers should not 'be subjected to measures such as rejection at the frontier or, if he has already entered the territory in which he seeks asylum, expulsion or compulsory return to any State where he may be subjected to persecution'.[166] The prohibition of *refoulement* requires states to refrain from returning refugees 'in any manner whatsoever' to the risk of being persecuted. The specific conduct that brings about this risk is immaterial for what matters are its consequences.[167] As already discussed, the duty of *non-refoulement* is not coterminous with a right to admission. However, it forbids states form exposing individuals to a real risk of persecution. Therefore, in practice, states are required to provisionally admit anyone who claims that if rejected at the frontier they would be exposed to that risk to determine whether their claim is well-founded.[168] This interpretation has been brought forward in numerous conclusions of the UNHCR's Executive Committee,[169] and endorsed by the International Law Commission.[170] The ECtHR stressed that the 'prohibition of *refoulement* includes the protection of asylum-seekers in cases of both non-admission and rejection at the border'.[171]

[162] Convention relating to the Status of Refugees, 189 UNTS 150, 28 July 1951.

[163] UN Conference of Plenipotentiaries on the Status of Refugees and Stateless Persons, *Conference of Plenipotentiaries on the Status of Refugees and Stateless Persons: Summary Record of the Sixteenth Meeting*, 23 November 1951, A/CONF.2/SR.16.

[164] Nehemiah Robinson, 'Convention Relating to the Status of Refugees. Its History, Contents and Interpretation' (Institute of Jewish Affairs, 1953).

[165] Elihu Lauterpacht and Daniel Bethlehem, 'The Scope and Content of the Principle of Non-Refoulement: Opinion' in Erika Feller, Volker Türk and Frances Nicholson (eds), *Refugee Protection in International Law* (Cambridge, Cambridge University Press, 2003); Guy S Goodwin-Gill and Jane McAdam, *The Refugee in International Law* 4th edn (Oxford, Oxford University Press, 2021) 241–65.

[166] Note, however, that the resolution included an exception for situations of mass influx. UNGA, Declaration on Territorial Asylum, Resolution A/RES/2312(XXII), 14 December 1967, Art 3 paras 1–2.

[167] James C Hathaway, *The Rights of Refugees under International Law* (Cambridge, Cambridge University Press, 2021) 357–59.

[168] Goodwin-Gill and McAdam (n 165) 254–56.

[169] See eg: Executive Committee, *Non-Refoulement*, Conclusion No 6 (XXVIII), 12 October 1977, para c; *Protection of Asylum-Seekers in Situations of Large-Scale Influx*, Conclusion No 22 (XXXII), 21 October 1981, II.A.2(2); Conclusion *on International Protection*, No 99 (LV) 8 October 2004, para 1; Conclusion *on International Protection*, No 108 (LIX), 10 October 2008, preamble.

[170] ILC, Draft articles on the expulsion of aliens, with commentaries, 2014, commentary to Article 2, para 5 and commentary to Article 6, para 7.

[171] ECtHR, *N.D. and N.T. v Spain*, Appl Nos 8675/15 and 8697/15, 13 February 2020, para 178.

Today, in accordance with the EU Return Directive, EU Member States must respect the duty of *non-refoulement* with regard to people who are refused entry at the border or are apprehended or intercepted in connection with their irregular border crossing.[172] Furthermore, under Article 3(1) of the EU Asylum Procedures Directive, applications for international protection in the EU can be lodged 'in the territory, including at the border, in the territorial waters or in the transit zones of the Member States'.[173]

Reactions to this development were not long in coming. States sought to avoid the application of human rights law in redefining their borders. For instance, in the *Amuur* case, the French government held that it did not exercise jurisdiction in international or transit zones, therefore it was not responsible for the arbitrary detention of four Somali asylum seekers in the international zone of Paris-Orly Airport.[174] The ECtHR, however, rejected this argument and held that 'despite its name, the international zone does not have extraterritorial status' and that the applicants' detention in the international zone of Paris-Orly Airport made them subject to French law.[175] In a different context, the ECtHR also clarified that states cannot unilaterally modify their borders in order to address the needs of a specific situation.[176] Put differently, states are prevented from moving their borders inwards with the aim of preventing asylum claims.

The notion of jurisdiction played a significant role in these developments. A person presenting herself at the border is under the jurisdiction of that state, as state authorities control that area and can exercise the same control over the person. It follows that the human rights guarantees the state owes to every individual under its jurisdiction apply.[177]

B. Beyond the Border

While the applicability of the Refugee Convention and human rights law at the frontier is today undisputed,[178] the same is not true on the high seas or in the territory of third countries. Two cases are unavoidable references at this point of the analysis.[179] The first is *Sale v Haitian Centers Council*, where the US Supreme Court interpreted both the Refugee Convention and the domestic legislation

[172] Art 4 (4)(b), Directive 2008/115/EC [2008] OJ L 348.
[173] Directive 2013/32/EU [2013] OJ L 180/60.
[174] ECtHR, *Amuur v France*, Appl No 19776/92, 25 June 1996.
[175] ibid, para 52. For further commentary see: Galina Cornelisse, 'Detenion of Foreigners' in Elspeth Guild and Paul Minderhoud (eds), *The First Decade of EU Migration and Asylum Law* (Leiden, Brill, 2011).
[176] *N.D. and N.T. v Spain* (n 171) para 106.
[177] See Goodwin-Gill and McAdam (n 165) 253.
[178] See ECtHR, *M.A. v Lithuania*, Appl no 59793/17, 11 December 2018.
[179] Much ink has been spilled on both cases, which here are cursorily considered. For further references see below, footnotes 187 and 194.

implementing it as inoperative in the context of maritime interdiction on the high seas.[180] The second is the *Prague Airport* case concerning the question of pre-border controls in third countries, where the House of Lords observed that nothing in the Refugee Convention requires a state to abstain from controlling immigration outside its borders.[181] However, even if the House of Lords rejected extraterritorial application of the *non-refoulement* duty to the United Kingdom's pre-entry controls at Prague airport,[182] it did find the procedure unlawfully discriminatory.[183]

Despite the bad precedent set by these cases with regard to *non-refoulement*, the jurisprudence of international human rights bodies took a different position. The interdiction policy challenged in the *Sale* case was condemned four years later by the Inter-American Commission of Human Rights, which affirmed the extraterritorial application of the principle of *non-refoulement*.[184] In Europe, the ECtHR took a strong position regarding maritime interceptions in its leading case *Hirsi Jamaa v Italy*.[185]

i. *State Power During Border Control Operations: The EIBM and the ECHR*

The *Hirsi Jamaa* case represents a momentous step forward in the development of the ECtHR jurisprudence on extraterritorial jurisdiction. In analysing the ECHR jurisdiction, the Court had the occasion to clarify the extraterritorial reach of the principle of *non-refoulment*.[186] The case concerned the maritime interception of three migrant vessels on the high seas and their subsequent pushback to Libyan shores, where the intercepted migrants were subject to serious human rights violations.

While maritime interceptions have become a common instrument of migration deterrence, states normally take heed of refugee protection, especially the prohibition of *refoulement*. State practice offers few instances of governments officially endorsing interception policies and summary returns of refugees, regardless of any consideration for international protection and absent any kind of procedural guarantee. The US interdiction of Haitian migrants was one such rare example;[187]

[180] *Sale v Haitian Centres Council*, 113 US Supreme Court 2549, 125 L (92-344), 509 US 155, 21 June 1993.

[181] House of Lords (Judicial Committee), *R v Immigration Officer at Prague Airport and Another, Ex parte European Roma Rights Centre and Others*, [2004] UKHL 55, 9 December 2004, para 64.

[182] ibid, paras 18 and 30 (*per* Lord Bingham of Cornhill) and 67 (*per* Lord Hope of Craighead).

[183] ibid, para 97 (*per* Lord Hope of Craighead).

[184] IAmCommHR, *The Haitian Centre for Human Rights et al v United States, Case No 10.675, 13 March 1997*, para 157.

[185] ECtHR, *Hirsi Jamaa and Others v Italy*, Appl No 27765/09, 23 February 2012.

[186] See ch 3, s IV.A.

[187] Harold Hongju Koh, 'The Human Face of the Haitian Interdiction Program' (1992) 33 *Vanderbilt Journal of International Law* 483; Louis Henkin, 'Notes from the President' (1993) 1 *ASIL Newsletter*; Harold Hongju Koh, 'Reflections on Refoulement and Haitian Centers Council' (1994) 35 *Harvard*

the Italian campaign of pushbacks to Libya in 2009 – from which the *Hirsi Jamaa* case arose – was another.[188]

In the early 2000s, Italy and Libya started cooperating in the field of migration control.[189] In 2008, the two countries concluded the by now (in)famous Treaty of Friendship, Partnership and Cooperation, providing for mutual assistance to control irregular migration in the Mediterranean.[190] The agreement included the establishment of joint patrols and exchanges of intelligence.[191] Between May and November 2009, a total of nine operations were carried out, returning over 800 persons to Libya.[192] The *Hirsi Jamaa* case concerned one such operation. Hirsi Jamaa and the 23 other applicants, all Somali or Eritrean nationals, were part of a group of some 200 individuals who left the coasts of Libya on three boats bound for Italy. Once on the high seas, they were intercepted by the Italian authorities, transferred to Italian military vessels, and summarily returned to Tripoli.[193]

In deciding this case, the ECtHR made a number of observations of general significance for European migration control policies.[194] The first, regarding jurisdiction, proved to be particularly controversial. The Italian government submitted that the interception could not be labelled as a 'maritime police operation', as it took place in the context of the rescue of people in distress on the high seas, an obligation imposed by the United Nations Convention on the Law of the Sea. This, according to the government, compromised the establishment of a jurisdictional link under the ECHR.[195] The ECtHR, however, rejected this contention and confirmed that the assessment of states' human rights obligations remains unaffected by their concomitant international obligations.[196]

International Law Journal 1; Guy S Goodwin-Gill, 'The Haitian Refoulment Case, A Comment' (1994) 6 *International Journal of Refugee Law* 103; Stephen H Legomsky, 'The USA and the Caribbean Interdiction Program' (2006) 18 *International Journal of Refugee Law* 677.

[188] Maarten Den Heijer, 'Reflections on Refoulement and Collective Expulsion in the Hirsi Case' (2013) 25 *International Journal of Refugee Law* 265.

[189] Alessia Di Pascale, 'Migration Control at Sea: The Italian Case' in Bernard Ryan and Valsamis Mitsilegas (eds), *Extraterritorial Immigration Control* (Leiden, Brill, 2010); Mariagiulia Giuffré, 'State Responsibility Beyond Borders: What Legal Basis for Italy's Push-Backs to Libya?' (2012) 24 *International Journal of Refugee Law* 692.

[190] Trattato di amicizia, partenariato e cooperazione tra la Repubblica italiana e la Grande Giamahiria Araba Libica Popolare Socialista, 30 August 2008.

[191] ibid, Art 19. Such cooperation had to be partially financed by Italy and partly by the EU.

[192] Submission by the Office of the United Nations High Commissioner for Refugees in the Case of *Hirsi and Others v Italy* (Appl no 27765/09) www.refworld.org/pdfid/4d92d2c22.pdf.

[193] *Hirsi Jamaa and Others v Italy* (n 185) paras 9–12.

[194] Among the rich commentaries on the *Hirsi* case, see in particular: Violeta Moreno-Lax, 'Hirsi Jamaa and Others v Italy or the Strasbourg Court versus Extraterritorial Migration Control?' (2012) 12 *Human Rights Law Review* 574; Mariagiulia Giuffré, 'Watered-down Rights on the High Seas: Hirsi Jamaa and Others V Italy (2012)' (2012) 61 *International & Comparative Law Quarterly* 728; Den Heijer (n 188).

[195] *Hirsi Jamaa* (n 185) para 65–66. See also: Art 98, United Nations Convention on the Law of the Sea, 1833 UNTS 3, 10 December 1982.

[196] *Hirsi Jamaa* (n 185) para 79.

The Court went further and clarified that, as the applicants were on board Italian ships with crews composed of Italian military personnel, they were 'under the continuous and exclusive de jure and de facto control of the Italian authorities'.[197] This might appear to confirm the personal model elaborated in *Al-Skeini* and earlier case law. Yet, the Court emphasised the specific types of control exercised by the Italian authorities. The Court rehearsed its *Banković* decision, where it recognised flag state jurisdiction as a specific situation implying extraterritorial jurisdiction as a matter of customary and treaty law.[198] However, it went on to affirm that the (de facto) physical control exercised by Italian military personnel over the rescued migrants was also sufficient to bring the situation within the ambit of the Convention. This conclusion was reached, despite the 'allegedly minimal [de facto] control' of Italian authorities.[199] The Court did not give further indications as to the required nature or intensity of state control. In particular, the relation between the exercise of de iure and de facto control remains unclear.[200] In *Al-Skeini* the Court explicitly noted that there are cases where the use of force by states' agents over individuals outside states' territories may trigger jurisdiction. The Court emphasized that '[w]hat is decisive in such cases is the exercise of *physical power and control* over the person in question'.[201] One could therefore argue that any kind of de facto control is per se sufficient to enliven a jurisdictional link. In *Hirsi Jamaa*, however, the Court was not confronted with such questions, and subsequent case law does not seem to offer further guidance.

The *N.D. and N.T.* case illustrates the Court's ambiguous approach to this matter. The case took place in the Spanish enclave of Melilla and concerns a group of Sub-Saharan migrants who tried to cross the Spanish border, consisting of three consecutive barriers. They managed to climb the three fences, but while climbing down the third, they were apprehended by the Spanish civil guard and returned to Morocco. The Spanish government contended that the events occurred outside its jurisdiction, as the applicants had not succeeded in trespassing the fences at the Melilla border crossing and therefore had not entered Spanish territory.[202] The Court, however, explained that it was unnecessary to establish where the events occurred. The de facto control of Spanish authorities over the applicants was sufficient to establish the state's extraterritorial jurisdiction.[203] At the same

[197] ibid, para 81.
[198] *Banković* (n 16) para 73.
[199] *Hirsi Jamaa* (n 185) para 79.
[200] For a different interpretation, see: Violeta Moreno-Lax, 'Hirsi Jamaa and Others v Italy or the Strasbourg Court versus Extraterritorial Migration Control?' (2012) 12 *Human Rights Law Review* 574, 581. Comparing *Hirsi* with *Medvedyev* (where the control over the vessel was merely factual but more intense) Moreno-Lax concludes that 'the higher the level of de jure authority exercised by a Contracting Party abroad, the lesser the need to prove detailed de facto control'. However, in light of the Court's subsequent jurisprudence, it is doubtful that the relation between the de iure and de facto basis for jurisdiction is precisely governed by a principle of inverse proportionality. See eg: *Jaloud* (n 51); ECtHR, *Pisari v Russia*, Appl No 42139/12, 19 October 2015.
[201] *Al-Skeini* (n 23) para 136 (emphasis added).
[202] ECtHR, *N.D. and N.T. v Spain*, Appl Nos 8675/15 and 8697/15, 3 October 2017, para 44.
[203] ibid, para 54.

time, the Court referred to *Hirsi* to clarify the concepts of de iure and de facto control. But in that case, de iure control was equated to the flag state jurisdiction as an exception to the principle of territoriality, which was irrelevant to the case at hand.[204] While the applicants were under the de facto control of the Spanish civil guard, they could also have been under Spain's de jure jurisdiction to the extent that the Spanish authorities were legitimately entitled to exercise their border control functions and the events occurred on Spanish territory. However, neither the Chamber nor the subsequent Grand Chamber's decisions addressed this question.

The Grand Chamber confirmed the Chamber's decision regarding the exercise of jurisdiction,[205] but affirmed that Spain exercised territorial jurisdiction over the Melilla border.[206] The Court concluded that

> the special nature of the context as regards migration cannot justify an area outside the law where individuals are covered by no legal system capable of affording them the enjoyment of the rights and guarantees protected by the Convention which the States have undertaken to secure to everyone within their jurisdiction.[207]

This decision does not contradict the conclusion that the exercise of state power during border control operations impacting the applicants' situation, whether at the border or beyond, suffices to enliven a jurisdictional link. Ultimately, de iure and de facto authority and control represent, respectively, the normative and factual manifestation of state power. In *Hirsi*, as in *N.D. and N.T.*, the ECtHR was satisfied that the migrants came under state jurisdiction as a result of the combined exercise of de iure and de facto control. Arguably, they are sufficient but not necessarily cumulative conditions for the jurisdictional link to be established. The Court has still not given any indication about the nature of these two expressions of state power, their required intensity or the exact relationship between them.[208]

ii. The Ambiguity of the 'Scope of EU Law': The EIBM and the CFR

Before assessing the extraterritorial reach of the CFR in the context of border control measures, it is worth emphasising a crucial difference between the functioning of the ECHR and the CFR. As shown below, the ECtHR developed a copious and complex case law regarding the Convention's extraterritorial jurisdiction in order to clarify the reach of Member States obligations. In *Hirsi Jamaa*, taking its conclusions in earlier judgments a step further, the ECtHR established that states' extraterritorial jurisdiction follows from their de jure or de facto exercise of power;

[204] *Hirsi Jamaa* (n 185) para 77.
[205] *N.D. and N.T. v Spain* (n 171).
[206] ibid, para 108.
[207] ibid, para 110.
[208] *Hirsi Jamaa* (n 185) para 81; *N.D. and N.T.* (n 171) paras 90 and 107.

it is also based on the premise that states should not be allowed to take actions outside their territories that would be intolerable inside.[209]

By contrast, when it comes to the obligations of Member States under the CFR, their geographical reach is immaterial. As discussed above, the provisions of the Charter address the EU and its Member States whenever they act within the scope of EU law.[210] Member States are bound by the CFR whenever they are implementing EU law, irrespective of whether these actions take place in or outside EU territory. Rather than the exercise of state power over a given situation, it is the scope of EU law and the principle of effectiveness that defines the reach of the CFR. The criteria for the determination of the scope of EU law remain, however, uncertain in the case law of the CJEU.[211]

This ambiguity in the context of EU migration policy emerged in the case of *X and X*, involving a highly politicised decision on humanitarian visas.[212] The case of *X and X* concerned a Syrian family who sought to flee the city of Aleppo, which was at the time of their application under ISIS occupation. All other routes of escape being closed, the family travelled to Lebanon, reaching the Belgian Consulate in Beirut. There they applied for a visa with limited territorial validity on humanitarian grounds on the basis of the EU Visa Code.[213] In contrast to regular Schengen visas, visas with limited territorial validity grant access exclusively to the territory of the issuing Member State, instead of to the entire Schengen area. Crucially, this kind of visa would have allowed the family to arrive safely in Belgium and apply for international protection. However, their application was refused. This decision was based on Article 32(1)(b) of the EU Visa Code, according to which a visa should be refused if there are reasonable doubts as to the applicant's intention to leave the territory of the Member State before its expiry. The family explicitly mentioned their intention to apply for asylum upon arrival, and the Belgian authorities interpreted this as a clear intention to overstay in the country and refused to issue the visas. Under Belgian law, there is no obligation to accept applications for international protection in diplomatic representations.[214] The Belgian authorities further held that the prohibition of *refoulement* only applies to persons already within the Belgian (territorial) jurisdiction.[215] The applicants appealed against the decision, prompting the Belgian Court of Appeal to request a preliminary ruling from the CJEU.

[209] *Al-Skeini* (n 23) Concurring opinion of Judge Bonello, para 18; *Hirsi Jamaa* (n 185) Concurring Opinion of Judge Pinto de Albuquerque.

[210] See Explanations relating to the Charter of Fundamental Rights, OJ C 303, 14 December 2007, Art 51.

[211] Spaventa (n 116).

[212] *X and X* (n 141).

[213] Art 25, Regulation (EC) No 810/2009 establishing a Community Code on Visas (Visa Code) [2009] OJ L 243/1 (as amended).

[214] However, from an international legal perspective, see: Gregor Noll, 'Seeking Asylum at Embassies: A Right to Entry under International Law?' (2005) 17 *International Journal of Refugee Law* 542; Kate Ogg, 'Protection Closer to Home? A Legal Case for Claiming Asylum at Embassies and Consulates' (2014) 33 *Refugee Survey Quarterly* 81.

[215] *X and X* (n 141) para 25.

The Belgian Court asked the Luxembourg judges to interpret various provisions of the EU Visa Code in order to determine whether an application for a visa with limited territorial validity, such as the one made by the Syrian family, falls within the scope of the EU Visa Code and, as a consequence, is within the scope of application of the CFR. The CJEU clarified that the scope of application of the EU Visa Code concerns the issuance of visas for stays on the territory of the Member States not exceeding 90 days in any 180 days.[216] Since the family's visa application was presented to apply for international protection, requiring them to stay in Belgium for more than 90 days over a period of 180, it did not fall within the scope of application of the EU Code of Visas. Hence, the situation of the Syrian family was solely regulated by national law.[217]

The Court's relatively succinct decision appears ambiguous from many points of view.[218] First, the Court derived the inapplicability of the EU Visa Code, and the CFR, as a logical inference of the applicant's undisclosed intention to seek asylum in a Member State. However, this logical syllogism fails to consider that the EU Visa Code includes the possibility of extending the period of stay beyond the required maximum of 90 days.[219] The Court could therefore have decided based on a less restrictive interpretation of the scope of the EU Visa Code, allowing the application of the CFR in situations exceeding 90 days of stay. Second, depending on the interpretation of the relationship between Articles 25 and 32 of the EU Visa Code, the applicants' intention to overstay in Belgium could constitute a ground for the refusal of their visa applications. This, however, would not automatically impede the application of the EU Visa Code and the ensuing fundamental rights guarantees.[220] The Court, however, avoided answering this question and clarified that the defining feature of the situation at issue was not the existence of an intention to overstay, 'but the fact that the purpose of the application differ[ed] from that of a short-term visa'.[221]

The Court finally observed that imposing the issuance of humanitarian visas under the Visa Code would correspond to allowing third-country nationals to apply for international protection in the Member State of their choice, and that would destabilise the Dublin system.[222] This would have constituted an unacceptable precedent for Member States, which could trigger an unmanageable number of humanitarian visa applications. Beyond the legal irrelevance of such a scenario, this hypothesis appears empirically unverified.[223] Furthermore, even if a massive

[216] Arts 1 and 2(2)(a), Regulation 810/2009.
[217] *X and X* (n 141) para 44.
[218] The following analysis has been developed in: Giulia Raimondo, 'Visti umanitari: il caso X e X contro Belgio, C-638/16 PPU' (2017) 4 I *Quaderni di SIDIBlog*, available at: www.sidiblog.org/2017/05/01/visti-umanitari-il-caso-x-e-x-contro-belgio-c%E2%80%9163816-ppu/.
[219] Art 25(1)(b), Regulation 810/2009.
[220] Cf, Opinion of the Advocate General Paolo Mengozzi (n 142) para 51.
[221] *X and X* (n 141) para 47.
[222] ibid, paras 48–49.
[223] Opinion of the Advocate General Paolo Mengozzi (n 142) para 172; Case C-403/16, *El Hassani*, 13 December 2017, ECLI:EU:C:2017:960, para 30.

increase in visa requests occurred, considerations of political or logistical opportunity must not disregard the absolute nature of the *non-refoulement* duty binding the EU and its Member States as norms of customary international law. The last passages of the ruling betray an intention to save at any cost a system that, from its inception, has suffered from structural deficiencies that Member States are still not willing to correct and overcome.[224] Absent a formalised humanitarian visa regulation at EU level, different standards are proliferating among Member States, undermining the well-functioning of the EIBM.[225] The absence of a codified procedure, however, does not exempt from giving effect to the absolute prohibition of *refoulement*.[226]

At a time when the collateral damage of border controls has become banal, the CJEU chose to sit and watch. The same orientation was taken in an equally controversial case concerning the EU-Türkiye Statement, in which the Luxembourg Court decided not to decide.[227] The case concerned a press release published on the website of the Council of the European Union, known as the EU-Türkiye Statement.[228] This press release made public the outcomes of a meeting between the members of the European Council and their Turkish counterpart. It announced that 'the EU and Turkey … decided to end the irregular migration from Turkey to the EU', and to do so, they agreed on a number of actions. These included the return of irregular migrants arriving on the Greek islands from Türkiye; the resettlement to the EU of a number of Syrian refugees from Türkiye equivalent to the number of Syrians returned from Greece to Türkiye; as well as a number of flanking measures, such as the provision of financial assistance to Türkiye, visa liberalisation for Turkish nationals in the EU and reopening of the negotiations on Turkish accession to the EU. Shortly after its publication, the legitimacy of the EU-Türkiye Statement was challenged by an action for annulment before the CJEU.[229] The application was based on the lack of an appropriate procedure for concluding a treaty, as well as on objections based on human rights and refugee law. The Court did not take a decision on the question of whether the EU-Türkiye

[224] Sandra Lavenex, '"Failing Forward" Towards Which Europe? Organized Hypocrisy in the Common European Asylum System' (2018) 56 *JCMS: Journal of Common Market Studies* 1195; Vincent Chetail, 'The Common European Asylum System: Bric-à-Brac or System?' in P De Bruycker, F Maiani and V Chetail (eds), *Reforming the Common European Asylum System: The New European Refugee Law* (Leiden, Brill, 2016).

[225] The European Parliament has repeatedly called on the EU legislature to adopt legislative measures in this regard. See most recently: European Parliament resolution of 11 December 2018 with recommendations to the Commission on Humanitarian Visas (2018/2271(INL)).

[226] See extensively: Violeta Moreno-Lax, 'Annex I: The Added Value of EU Legislation on Humanitarian Visas – Legal Aspects', in *Humanitarian Visas. European Added Value Assessment accompanying the European Parliament's legislative own-initiative report*, Rapp Lopez Aguilar (European Parliament 2018).

[227] Case T-192/16, *NF and others v European Council*, 28 February 2017, ECLI:EU:T:2017:128.

[228] EU-Turkey Statement 18 March 2016 www.consilium.europa.eu/en/press/ press-releases/2016/03/18-eu-turkey-statement/.

[229] *NF and others v European Council* (n 227).

Statement was a legally binding treaty or a political agreement,[230] nor on whether Türkiye could be considered a safe third country.[231] Either way, the EU was not a party to the EU-Türkiye Statement, hence the action was declared inadmissible by the CJEU for lack of jurisdiction.[232]

With these rulings, the CJEU decided to avoid any judicial intervention in the migration control policies of Member States. In a situation where Member States were unable to tackle the (perceived) refugee crisis and EU institutions could not agree on various reforms,[233] among them the amendments to the Visa Code,[234] the CJEU remains silent. A silence that sends a clear message to the EU institutions and Member States.[235] An exclusively juris-centric perspective could not resolve a highly contested political issue such as migration management. To support this approach, the Court resorts to formalism. Any substantive interpretation of the EU universal human rights commitments would have risked undermining the position of the Court and eroding other fields of EU law. Instead, formal requirements are used to keep the Syrian family and asylum seekers in Greece not just outside the EU but also outside the scope of EU law and its human rights guarantees. Only legislative amendments would lead to an opposite conclusion. And yet, this non-interventionist stance implies a discriminatory reading of the scope of EU law, extending only so far as it affects Europeans.[236]

[230] Enzo Cannizzaro, 'Disintegration Through Law?' (2016) 1 *European Papers* 3; Gloria Fernández Arribas, 'The EU-Turkey Statement, the Treaty-Making Process and Competent Organs. Is the Statement an International Agreement?' (2017) 2 *European Papers* 303; Mauro Gatti and others, 'The EU-Turkey Statement: Legal Nature and Compatibility with EU Institutional Law' in *Constitutionalising the External Dimensions of EU Migration Policies in Times of Crisis* (Cheltenham, Edward Elgar, 2019).

[231] Daniela Vitiello, 'Legal Narratives of the EU External Action in the Field of Migration and Asylum: From the EU-Turkey Statement to the Migration Partnership Framework and Beyond' [2020] *Securitising Asylum Flows* 130; Sergio Carrera, Leonhard den Hertog and Marco Stefan, 'The EU-Turkey Deal: Reversing Lisbonisation in EU Migration and Asylum Policies' in Sergio Carrera, Juan Santos Vara and Tineke Strik (eds), *Constitutionalising the External Dimensions of EU Migration Policies in Times of Crisis* (Cheltenham, Edward Elgar, 2019).

[232] *NF v European Council* (n 225) paras 71–72 and 74. In the appeal procedure, the Court of Justice dismissed the case as manifestly inadmissible. Joined Cases C-208/17 P to C-210/17 P, *NF and others v European Council*, 12 September 2018, ECLI:EU:C:2018:705.

[233] See among the copious literature on this topic: Bruno Nascimbene, 'Refugees, the European Union and the "Dublin System". The Reasons for a Crisis' (2016) 1 *European Papers: A Journal on Law and Integration* 101; Felix Biermann and others, 'Political (Non-)Reform in the Euro Crisis and the Refugee Crisis: A Liberal Intergovernmentalist Explanation' (2017) 26 *Journal of European Public Policy* 246; Virginie Guiraudon, 'The 2015 Refugee Crisis Was Not a Turning Point: Explaining Policy Inertia in EU Border Control' (2018) 17 *European Political Science* 151.

[234] Proposal for a Regulation of the European Parliament and of the Council on the Union Code on visas (recast) First reading, 14213/16, 14 November 2016.

[235] See Iris Goldner Lang, 'Towards "Judicial Passivism" in EU Migration and Asylum Law?' in Tamara Ćapeta, Iris Goldner Lang and Tamara Perišin, *The Changing European Union: A Critical View on the Role of Law and Courts* (Oxford, Hart Publishing, 2022).

[236] Thomas Spijkerboer, 'Bifurcation of People, Bifurcation of Law: Externalization of Migration Policy before the EU Court of Justice' (2018) 31 *Journal of Refugee Studies* 216.

iii. Setbacks and Progress in Establishing Extraterritorial Jurisdiction

A few months after the *X and X* case, the ECHR received an application regarding facts similar to those discussed above.[237] The case of *M.N. and others v Belgium* concerns a Syrian family with two young children who applied for a humanitarian visa at the Belgian consulate in Lebanon. The applicable legal framework is different, but the question the ECtHR was called to solve was similar: was the Belgian denial of a visa to the Syrian family an exercise of jurisdiction? And if so, was the denial in breach of the prohibition of torture or inhuman and degrading treatment? Once more, these questions underline some serious challenges for triggering the jurisdictional threshold under the ECHR, especially where there is no physical control over the individuals concerned.

The Court reaffirmed its traditional emphasis on the exceptional nature of extraterritorial jurisdiction. It also reasoned that instances of extraterritorial jurisdiction are 'defined and limited by the sovereign territorial rights of the other relevant States', reviving the 'all-or-nothing' approach adopted in *Bankovic.*[238] Yet, some possibilities remained open for the applicants relying on the special features of their case.[239] In this respect, the acts of diplomatic and consular agents abroad can amount to an exceptional exercise of extraterritorial jurisdiction when they exert authority and control over other people.[240] But the Court also introduced an important qualification. The actions or omissions of diplomatic or consular agents in a foreign territory may trigger jurisdiction where they exercise their authority in respect of their state's 'nationals or their property', or where they exercise 'physical power and control over certain persons'.[241] Neither of these two alternative conditions subsisted in the case at hand, as the applicants were not Belgian nationals, and the diplomatic agents had not exercised de facto control over them.[242]

A distinction between nationals and non-nationals in jurisdictional matters was drawn from the Court's case law on diplomatic agents acting abroad.[243] The exercise of consular functions, which often depends on the existence of a bond of nationality between the state and the individual, can result in a state exercising jurisdiction over its nationals abroad. Nonetheless, the obligation to secure the ECHR rights and freedoms extends not only to a state's 'own nationals and those of other High Contracting Parties but also to nationals of States not party to the Convention and to stateless persons'.[244] However, the Court circumscribed the

[237] ECtHR, *M.N. et al v Belgium*, Appl No 3599/18, 5 May 2020.
[238] ibid, para 99.
[239] ibid, para 102.
[240] Cf, ECommHR, *X v the Federal Republic of Germany*, Appl No 1611/62, 25 September 1965, para 5; *Al-Skeini* (n 23) para 134; *M.N. et al v Belgium* (n 237) para 106.
[241] *M.N. et al v Belgium* (n 237) para 106.
[242] ibid, paras 118–19.
[243] Ibid, para 106.
[244] ECommHR, *Austria v Italy*, Appl No 788/60, 11 January 1961, 19.

situations in which the conduct of a state's diplomatic agents triggers jurisdiction over aliens to a relationship of physical power and control. This, in the Court's opinion, was primarily a question of fact, requiring the exercise of de facto power or control over individuals.[245] Any form of de iure power over the applicants' situation was deemed irrelevant.

The fact that the applicants brought proceedings at a national level to secure their entry into Belgium was also found insufficient to bring them within the jurisdiction of the state. The Court had to differentiate this situation from that where special circumstances of a procedural nature were found sufficient to enliven a jurisdictional link. What turned the tide, in the Court's opinion, was the party initiating the proceedings. While the case law on 'procedural control' found the jurisdictional link in the initiative of the state authorities opening the relevant proceedings,[246] in the case at hand, the initiative was solely the applicants' who had no other connection with the state.[247] The Court concluded that their visa application was 'a unilateral choice' incapable of creating a jurisdictional link. A different conclusion

> would amount to enshrining a near-universal application of the Convention on the basis of the unilateral choices of any individual, irrespective of where in the world they find themselves, and therefore to create an unlimited obligation on the Contracting States to allow entry to an individual who might be at risk of ill-treatment contrary to the Convention outside their jurisdiction.[248]

This logic, however, seems to confuse the scope of application of treaty obligations with their conventional origin. Of course, the ECHR obligations are established only with regard to the states that previously accepted them. Nonetheless, states are not free to choose where the Convention will apply, nor to select which ECHR obligation they are bound to respect by accepting them ex-post – for instance, by initiating civil or administrative proceedings. Limiting the applicability of the ECHR to situations where contracting states consented to the creation of a jurisdictional link implies serious risks for its good faith interpretation. The limits of the scope of application of the ECHR should thus be found elsewhere, namely in the relationship between states and individuals subject to their factual, legal or administrative power.

The problems related to a clear determination of the nature and the required intensity of state power resurfaced in *H.F. and others.*[249] The case concerned the repatriation of children and their mothers detained in Syrian camps based on their presumed ISIS association. On the one hand, regarding the prohibition of torture and ill-treatment, the Court found that neither the applicants' nationality nor

[245] *M.N.et al. v Belgium* (n 237) para 113.
[246] See eg: *Güzelyurtlu and Others* (n 56) para 107; *Romeo Castaño* (n 56) paras 54–55.
[247] ibid paras 121–23.
[248] ibid, para 123.
[249] ECtHR, *HF and others v France*, Appl No 24384/19 44234/20, 14 November 2022, para 195.

France's operational capacity to repatriate them did suffice to trigger an extraterritorial jurisdictional link. It, therefore, discarded a functional interpretation. On the other hand, regarding the right to enter one's own country, the Court noted that nationality was not an autonomous basis of jurisdiction. But under certain circumstances, it could create a jurisdictional link between a state and its nationals abroad who wish to enter that state.[250] In this case, those circumstances included the real and immediate threats to the lives and physical well-being of the applicants' daughters and their children and their numerous requests for repatriation.[251] In sum, the legal link between a state and its nationals abroad, together with the factual situation of the applicants, led the Court to find the presence of a jurisdictional connection in relation to the right to enter one's own country. But the precise relationship between the legal and factual dimensions of jurisdiction remains undetermined.

The cautious approach adopted by the ECtHR with regard to extraterritorial jurisdiction over migration and border control measures may be counterbalanced by the Views of UN Treaty Bodies. In another case concerning repatriations from Syrian camps, the CRC also relied on relevant factual considerations. Yet it arrived at a different conclusion, arguing that the 'capability and power' to influence a given situation may be sufficient to trigger jurisdiction under human rights law.[252]

In the same line, the HRC, relying on its General Comment on the Right to Life, found Italy responsible for having failed to respond in a reasonable manner to the calls of distress of a sinking vessel transporting over 400 migrants in the Mediterranean Sea.[253] The Committee's communication responded to a joint complaint lodged by four survivors who lost their families in a shipwreck on 11 October 2013 in the Mediterranean Sea.[254] Their relatives were escaping Libya on a fishing vessel, which, a few hours after departure, was shot at by a boat flying a Berber flag. The vessel started to sink. Someone on board called the Italian number for emergencies at sea. The Italian authorities reassured the persons on board that they would be rescued, but nothing happened. After several calls, the Italian authorities explained that the vessel was in the Maltese SAR zone: Italy was not competent. The Italian authorities provided people on board the sinking vessel with the contact details of the Rescue Coordination Centre of Malta. According to the applicants, the Italian authorities ordered an Italian navy ship in the vicinity of the vessel in distress (the *ITS Libra*) to move further away.[255] By the time a Maltese rescue boat arrived, the vessel had already capsized. The *ITS Libra* eventually began rescue operations after an urgent request from Malta. But it was too

[250] ibid, para 212.
[251] ibid, para 213.
[252] *L.H., L.H., D.A, C.D. and A.F v France* (n 65) para 9.7.
[253] *A.S., D.I., O.I. and G.D. v Italy* (n 62).
[254] The incident occurred in the high sea, 113 km from Italy and 218 km from Malta.
[255] *A.S., D.I., O.I. and G.D. v Italy* (n 62) para 2.4.

late: as a result of the delays, more than 200 people drowned.[256] Three of the surviving individuals sought justice before the Italian courts, before taking their case to the HRC. A parallel claim brought against Malta was dismissed on procedural grounds.[257] Both communications are relevant for the present purposes.

Before the HRC, Malta and Italy continued to pass the responsibility to one another, and their respective defences revolved around the alleged lack of jurisdiction. Yet, the HRC rejected their arguments and found that both states were concurrently exercising jurisdiction over the people involved in the shipwreck. The ship in distress was in the Maltese SAR region, in that area, Malta undertook the responsibility to provide for the overall coordination of SAR operations, and it did so in relation to the shipwreck. Malta's effective control over the rescue operation was sufficient to establish a jurisdictional link.[258] The notion of effective control here seems to encompass both the legal and factual aspects of Malta's control over the rescue operation.

With regard to Italy's jurisdiction, the HRC reasoned that a 'special relationship of dependency' was established between the state and the people involved in the shipwreck.[259] This relationship comprised factual and legal elements.[260] The first was the duty to cooperate in SAR operations and save lives at sea, which binds all states. The second was the fact that Italian authorities answered the first call from the vessel and indicated to those on board that they would be rescued. Third, was the fact that the *ITS Libra* was in closer proximity of the incident, compared to any Maltese vessel. Notwithstanding that the vessel in distress was within the Maltese SAR zone, and thus also subject to the concurrent jurisdiction of Malta, the HRC concluded that Italy exercised jurisdiction over the individuals on the vessel in distress, for they were 'directly affected by the decisions taken by the Italian authorities in a manner that was reasonably foreseeable'.[261] The jurisdictional link was created by Italy's legal and factual power over the victims, who were dependent upon its decisions.

It is worth noting that no physical contact was established between the victims and the state authorities – at least not before the *ITS Libra*'s arrival, when it was already too late to save their lives. State authorities kept communicating with the people on the vessel, reassuring them – but then ordered the closer naval unit to 'keep their distance' from the incident to avoid taking

[256] The exact number of persons who died in the shipwreck has not been established, it has been estimated that over 200 people on board died, including 60 children.

[257] HRC, *A.S., D.I., O.I. and G.D. v Malta*, Comm No3043/2017, UN Doc CCPR/C/128/D/3043/2017, 27 January 2021. Three members of the HRC (Gentian Zyberi, Arif Bulan and Duncan Muhmuza) dissented, pointing out that, the specific circumstances of the case, Maltese authorities should have launched an investigation ex officio.

[258] ibid, para 6.7.

[259] *A.S., D.I., O.I. and G.D. v Italy* (n 62) para 7.8.

[260] ibid.

[261] ibid.

responsibility for the rescue operation, which was the competence of Malta.[262] Regrettably, the HRC did not further specify how these factual circumstances impacted the establishment of Italy's jurisdiction and substantive positive obligations; nor did they clarify how states' concurrent jurisdiction, and implied shared responsibility, affected the determination of appropriate measures of reparation.[263]

This crucial decision was not unanimously accepted.[264] In their dissenting opinion some members of the HRC concluded that the majority's opinion failed to distinguish 'situations in which states have the *potential* to place under their effective control individuals who are found outside their territory or areas already subject to their effective control, and situations involving the *actual* placement of individuals under effective state control'.[265] Here, power emerges in its equivocal meanings and dispositional nature. If one accepts the notion of power as the ability to change someone else's situation, then the individuals on the sinking boat were not *potentially* affected by Italy's decisions; they were dependent – de iure and de facto – on the prompt reaction of the authorities contacted, who were closest to them.

Other members expressed concerns – shared by the ECtHR[266] – regarding the potential side effects of an expansive construction of extraterritorial jurisdiction.[267] From this perspective, an expansive approach might have chilling effects on Member States, dissuading them from undertaking their SAR obligations; states might 'even try to avoid coming close to vessels in distress' to avoid such obligations. And yet this behaviour, far from being triggered by a progressive jurisprudential approach, is prevailing since the termination of operation *Mare Nostrum*,[268] in breach of states' rescue obligations.[269]

[262] See Fabrizio Gatti, 'La legge del mare: così la Marina ha lasciato affondare il barcone dei bambini', (L'Espresso, 5 June 2017) https://video.espresso.repubblica.it/tutti-i-video/la-legge-del-mare-cosi-la-marina-ha-lasciato-affondare-il-barcone-dei-bambini/10396/10497. Also cited in the victims' claim at para 5.3.

[263] *A.S., D.I., O.I. and G.D. v Italy* (n 62) Dissenting opinion of Andreas Zimmerman, para 3 and Concurring opinion of Hélène Tigroudja.

[264] Some HRC members argued that the migrants on the vessel were neither under the jurisdiction of Malta nor Italy (dissenting opinion of Andreas Zimmerman). Others argued that they were subject only to Malta's jurisdiction (dissenting opinions of Yuval Shany, Christof Heynes, Photini Pazartzis and David Moore). Other members agreed that the concurrent jurisdiction of both states required a more in-depth analysis of the aspect of shared responsibility (opinions of Hélène Tigroudja and Gentian Zyberi).

[265] ibid, Dissenting opinions of Yuval Shany, Christof Heynes, Photini Pazartzis, para 3.

[266] ECtHR, *Hanan v Germany*, Appl No 4871/16, 16 February 2021, para 135.

[267] *A.S., D.I., O.I. and G.D. v Italy* (n 62), Dissenting opinion of Andreas Zimmerman, para 4.

[268] Eugenio Cusumano, 'Migrant Rescue as Organized Hypocrisy: EU Maritime Missions Offshore Libya between Humanitarianism and Border Control Migrant Rescue as Organized Hypocrisy: EU Maritime Missions Offshore Libya between Humanitarianism and Border Control' (2018) 54 *Cooperation and Conflict* 3.

[269] See extensively: Violeta Moreno-Lax, 'Protection at Sea and the Denial of Asylum' in Cathryn Costello, Michelle Foster and Jane McAdam (eds), *The Oxford Handbook of International Refugee Law* (Oxford, Oxford University Press, 2021).

V. Extraterritorial Jurisdiction and Migration Control: Handle with Care

Over the years, the jurisprudence of the ECtHR has in many ways challenged the false premise according to which states can insulate their responsibility by shifting migration controls beyond their borders. However, given the political sensitivity of immigration decisions, the Strasbourg Court recently adopted a rather deferential attitude, even while deterrence policies continue to spread and morph into various forms of migration governance aimed at limiting or circumventing states' international obligations.

In the wake of the Haitian refugee crisis, Koh suggested that the precedent set in *Sale* – where the US Supreme Court found legal US interception-and-return practices on the high seas – would be overturned by the 'complex enforcement' process triggered by transnational public law litigation.[270] In his view, international courts would correct the US Supreme Court's interpretation of the applicable law, protecting against extraterritorial *refoulement* and fostering compliance with human rights. In many respects, Koh's speculation was confirmed. The IACtHR found that US interception practices violated the state's international obligations, including the prohibition of *refoulement*.[271] In *Hirsi*, the ECtHR elaborated a substantial interpretation of the notion of jurisdiction, which allowed the Strasbourg Court to ensure the protection of the human rights of intercepted migrants beyond states' borders. The narrative is that of progressive development emerging as the synthesis of the dialectic of transnational legal processes. This dialectical process can ultimately realise the promise of international human rights law.

Yet, dialectical processes can also be self-defeating.[272] Progressive moves towards truly universal protection of human rights could precipitate a backlash. This counter-narrative translates into delegated border controls and measures of contactless containment. In this respect, Wilde has warned us that the expansion of extraterritorial jurisdiction in relation to border control practices might have serious side effects on migrant rights.[273] One of the main reactions against the extraterritorial application of human rights in the context of migration controls is the rise of what Giuffré and Moreno-Lax have defined as policies of 'contactless control'.[274] The aim of such policies is to sever the jurisdictional link to states

[270] Harold Hongju Koh, 'The "Haiti Paradigm" in United States Human Rights Policy' (1994) 103 *The Yale Law Journal* 2391, 2406.

[271] IAmCommHR, *The Haitian Centre for Human Rights et al v United States*, Case No 10.675, 13 March 1997.

[272] See extensively: Itamar Mann, 'Dialectic of Transnationalism: Unauthorized Migration and Human Rights, 1993-2013' (2013) 54 *Harvard International Law Journal* 315.

[273] Ralph Wilde, 'The Unintended Consequences of Expanding Migrant Rights Protections' (2017) 111 *AJIL Unbound* 487. See also: Moria Paz, 'Between the Kingdom and the Desert Sun: Human Rights, Immigration, and Border Walls' (2016) 34 *Berkeley Journal of International Law* 1.

[274] Mariagiulia Giuffré and Violeta Moreno Lax, 'The Raise of Consensual Containment: From "Contactless Control" to "Contactless Responsibility" for Forced Migration Flows' in Satvinder S Juss (ed), *Research Handbook on International Refugee Law* (Cheltenham, Edward Elgar, 2019).

sponsoring containment measures in third countries, therefore eclipsing their responsibility under international human rights and refugee law. In this sense, 'precisely when they try the hardest to protect rights beyond territorial borders, courts acquire the most significant role in providing the conditions for the rights' further violation'.[275]

A. Remote Control, Cooperative Deterrence and Neocolonial Logics

Extraterritorial migration control policies are not new. Since the 1980s, destination countries in Europe, Australia and the US have implemented *non-entrée* policies to contain irregular migration flows.[276] Such an objective was operationalised through a set of procedural measures aimed at excluding migrants already present within states' territories,[277] as well as through measures impeding their arrivals, including visa requirements, carrier sanctions and pushback operations on the high seas.[278] Yet, over time, with pushbacks banned and the development of new border control technologies, the nature of these policies has morphed. While earlier strategies required a certain degree of contact with the migrant concerned, most recent initiatives involve delegating physical control over people affected by border control measures. These policies comprise the financing, equipping, and training of border control authorities in states of origin and transit, partnership agreements marked by development aid conditionality, readmission agreements and deterrence campaigns. The overarching logic of this new generation of *non-entrée* policies is to insulate destination states from their international obligations and consequent responsibility by engaging the sovereignty of other (generally transit) states.[279] These developments suggest that destination states are learning from past judicial interventions, and so are designing their policies to prevent triggering their human rights obligations. In a nutshell, while accepting the assumptions of the human rights regime, states circumvent its implementation by preventing migrants from entering their territories, eclipsing their jurisdiction over extraterritorial migration control measures. Taken together, all these measures result in a system of 'cooperative deterrence'.[280]

Cooperative deterrence policies pivot around the reciprocal commitments of participating actors. Destination states offer political, financial and technical support in exchange for preventive border control measures directly performed by third states within their territories. The compliance with international human rights law of these synallagmatic commitments is commonly taken as a self-evident

[275] Mann (n 272) 369.
[276] See Gammeltoft-Hansen and Hathaway (n 160); Gammeltoft-Hansen and Tan (n 160).
[277] For instance, accelerated asylum procedures based on the 'safe third country' or 'safe country of origin' concepts. See Arts 35 and 38, Directive 2013/32/EU [2013] OJ L 180/60.
[278] For a detailed discussion, see: Gammeltoft-Hansen and Tan (n 160).
[279] ibid.
[280] Gammeltoft-Hansen and Hathaway (n 160).

truth. Yet, despite the presumed innocuous – and sometimes even humanitarian – nature of cooperative deterrence policies, they can have a serious human rights impact.

One of the most relevant examples of these practices is the Italian/European cooperation with Libya.[281] The conditions in Libyan detention facilities, many of which are under the control of militias, are deplorable,[282] when not amounting to crimes against humanity.[283] Shortages of water and food are frequent, and overcrowding is endemic. Stark absences of supervision and regulation mean that most detainees experience physical ill-treatment and torture; forced labour and slavery are common.[284] Nevertheless, Italy and the EU persist in their cooperation with various actors in Libya.[285] While Italy has been deploying its own naval unit within Libyan waters to support and coordinate rescue operations,[286] Frontex has been directly contributing to increasing the border control capacities of the Libyan coast guard (LCG) to reduce migration flows across the Mediterranean.[287] In parallel, the agency exchanges information on situations of distress at sea in the Libyan SAR region with the relevant authorities, including the LCG.[288] Yet, the Libyan actors are often unresponsive or acting dangerously and unlawfully. Recent investigations suggest that when Frontex aircrafts fly over boats in distress, they communicate with the LCG rather than the closest naval unit.[289]

The underlying assumption is that those policies are exclusively implemented under the jurisdiction of partner states, and therefore their effects fall within the exclusive responsibility of those countries. Undeniably, the EU and its Member States are not directly performing any migration control measure themselves; they are rather requesting third countries to fulfil their commitments to control

[281] Memorandum of understanding between Italy and Libya (n 264). Memorandum of Understanding Between the Government of National Accord of the State of Libya and The Government of The Republic of Malta in the Field of Combatting Illegal Immigration, 28 May 2020.

[282] See eg: UNML and OHCHR, *'Detained and dehumanised' Report on human rights abuses against migrants in Libya*, 13 December 2016, Report of the Special Rapporteur on extrajudicial, summary or arbitrary executions, Unlawful death of refugees and migrants, UN Doc A/72/335, 15 August 2017; HRW, *No Escape from Hell: EU Policies Contribute to Abuse of Migrants in Libya*, 21 January 2019.

[283] OHCHR, *Report of the Independent Fact-Finding Mission on Libya*, A/HRC/52/83, 3 March 2023.

[284] ibid.

[285] Camera dei Deputati, 'Relazione analitica sulle missioni internazionali delle Forze armate e delle Forze di polizia, nonché sugli interventi di cooperazione allo sviluppo a sostegno dei processi di pace e di stabilizzazione' Doc XXVI No 5, July 2022; EEAS, EUBAM Libya Strategic Review 2021, 19 February 2021.

[286] Camera dei Deputati, 'La partecipazione italiana alle missioni in Libia', Dossier No 67, 30 May 2019.

[287] EEAS, Joint Pilot Project EUBAM – FRONTEX – Italy for the Libyan General Administration for Coastal Security, 2019. See also: European Ombudsman, Case 1473/2022/MHZ, How the European Border and Coast Guard Agency (FRONTEX) assesses the potential human rights risk and general impact before providing assistance to non-EU countries to develop surveillance capabilities, 5 October 2022.

[288] European Parliament recommendation to the Council, the Commission and the Vice-President of the Commission / High Representative of the Union for Foreign Affairs and Security Policy on the situation in Libya (2021/2064(INI)), 23 November 2022, AD.

[289] Lighthouse Reports, *Frontex in the Central Mediterranean*, 29 April 2021.

migration from and through their territories towards Europe in exchange for development aid and other advantages. In such circumstances, with regard to the ECHR, the jurisdictional link required by the spatial and personal models discussed above might be difficult to identify. First, the territorial model is limited when states can impose migration control measures beyond their borders without necessarily having effective control of an area within the territory of another state. Second, a narrow interpretation adopted by the ECtHR of jurisdiction – as physical power and control over persons – would lead to the inapplicability of the Convention in situations of control with no direct physical connection to the affected individuals. As destination countries do not have any physical contact with the migrants, they cannot be said to exercise any kind of jurisdiction over them, and therefore they do not bear any responsibility for the actions or omission they facilitate beyond their borders.

Cooperative deterrence policies reflect the neocolonial and neoliberal logic that is still pervading positive international law, as well as the practice of migration control, in so far as they project political and economic power beyond the territorial borders of the power-wielding state.[290] The term neocolonialism illuminates the unique form of domination that coexisted with, and resulted from, the legacy of, formal European colonialism. The state that is subject to this subtitle form of domination is, in theory, independent and has all the exterior paraphernalia of international sovereignty. But its economic and political systems are directed from outside. Neocolonialism exposes the potential regressive impact of opaque and unfettered forms of administrative assistance, aid, trade and foreign investment in relation to poverty reduction in third countries.[291] External policy interference and economic control can reduce the independence of sovereign states disguising the objectives of partner countries. At the same time, this does not deny the responsibility of third states implementing policies implying potential human rights violations. Instead, it urges us to acknowledge and contextualise instances of cooperation that often enable and encourage human rights violations leveraging lucrative arrangements.

B. From Effective Control to the Effects of Power

The backlash of the EU and its Member States against the expansion of the ECHR extraterritorial jurisdiction is a turn to indirect and informal cooperation aimed at further externalising border controls.[292] The shift from direct to orchestrated

[290] Tendayi Achiume, 'Migration as Decolonization' (2019) 71 *Stanford Law Review* 1509.

[291] This is not to say that neocolonialism should be understood merely as an economic, political or legal system. It should also be grasped as a cultural project. See, most notably, Edward W Said, *Culture and Imperialism* (New York, Vintage, 1994).

[292] Patrick Müller and Peter Slominski, 'Breaking the Legal Link but Not the Law? The Externalization of EU Migration Control through Orchestration in the Central Mediterranean' (2020) 28 *Journal of European Public Policy* 801.

involvement in externalised border controls is more cost-effective and faster than formal cooperation. Most importantly, it also allows a reversal of the practical significance of the ECHR extraterritorial jurisdiction.[293] Human rights obligations might apply extraterritorially, but they remain abstract declarations of intent when states do not have direct contact with the people who would benefit from them. This is one of the principal issues the ECtHR will face in deciding two cases concerning Italian cooperation with Libyan actors.[294]

Recent jurisprudential and doctrinal developments seem to point to different solutions. The doctrine and some of the most recent decisions of human rights monitoring bodies suggest that the lack of physical and direct control over victims of human rights violations does not *ipso facto* preclude the exercise of jurisdiction by supporting states.[295] Nevertheless, it is difficult to predict the approach of the ECtHR. In the context of interceptions at sea, the Court concluded that jurisdiction could result from 'exclusive *de jure* and *de facto* control' over intercepted migrants.[296] It also made clear that jurisdiction can also be triggered by forms of control that do not imply direct physical contact with state authorities. For example, in a case involving a maritime blockade impeding access to territorial waters, the jurisdictional link was uncontested.[297] However, in later decisions, concerning the repatriation of nationals or the issuance of humanitarian visas abroad, it also suggested that the absence of physical power and control precludes jurisdiction.[298]

Given these uncertainties, is possible to distinguish five main avenues to challenge the current cooperative deterrence policies by means of the applicable law. First, the exercise of public powers abroad by destination states can play a crucial role in determining their jurisdiction over people subject to such measures.[299] In the *Al-Skeini* decision, the ECtHR recognised the exercise of extraterritorial jurisdiction where a state, through the consent, invitation or acquiescence of another state 'exercises all or some of the public powers normally to be exercised by that state … as long as the acts in question are attributable to it rather than to the territorial State'.[300] Taking the example of the Libyan pullback policy, it could be argued, first, that measures aimed at controlling migration constitute an exercise

[293] Wilde (n 273).

[294] ECtHR, *S.S. v Italy*, (First Chamber), Appl no 21660/18, communicated to the Italian Government on 26 June 2019; ECtHR, *C.O. and A.J. v Italy*, Appl No 40396/18 (pending). For a detailed discussion of the case, see: Moreno-Lax (n 88).

[295] See: Elspeth Guild and Vladislava Stoyanova, 'The Human Right to Leave Any Country: A Right to Be Delivered' [2018] *European Yearbook on Human Rights* 373; Gammeltoft-Hansen (n 160); Giuffré and Moreno Lax (n 274). CAT, Concluding observations on the fourth and fifth periodic reports of Australia, 26 November 2014, CAT/C/AUS/CO/4-5, para 17; HRC, Concluding observations on the sixth periodic report of Australia, 9 November 2017, CCPR/C/AUS/CO/6, para 35; *A.S., D.I., O.I. and G.D. v Italy* (n 62), para 7.8; *L.H., L.H., D.A, C.D. and A.F v France* (n 65) para 9.7.

[296] *Hirsi Jamaa* (n 185).

[297] ECtHR, *Women on Waves v Portugal*, Appl No 31276/05, 3 February 2009.

[298] *M.N. et al v Belgium* (n 237) para 112; *HF and others v France* (n 249) para 186.

[299] Gammeltoft-Hansen and Hathaway (n 160).

[300] *Al-Skeini* (n 23) para 135.

of public powers, and, second, that the Italian authorities are contributing to such measures with the consent, invitation or acquiescence of the Libyan authorities. As noted by Guild and Stoyanova, however, it is questionable whether the conduct of the LCG could be exclusively attributed to Italy.[301] Yet, this last requirement does not concern the question of jurisdiction, but that of attribution of responsibility, where the rule of exclusive attribution does not necessarily preclude the determination of multiple responsibilities.[302]

A second alternative consists in linking the question of jurisdiction to that of state responsibility, applying the legal framework on the attribution of indirect responsibility, including notions such as complicity or direction and control to instances of cooperative deterrence.[303] Jackson, for example, proposes an expansive understanding of jurisdiction that may arise as a result of the complicity of an ECHR Member State in violations committed by a third state.[304] This approach relies on the leading case of *Soering*, which made clear that the engagement of Article 3 of the ECHR revolves around the 'foreseeable consequences of extradition suffered outside their jurisdiction'.[305] The same rationale is equally applicable in cases of extraterritorial complicity for 'there is no good reason to confine its application to one very specific form of complicity'.[306] Along these lines, many authors primarily rely on the complicity framework, to the effect that destination states assist other countries in performing conducts in breach of human rights law.[307] However, despite ECtHR case law not always being coherent in this respect, the concepts of attribution of responsibility and jurisdiction serve two different purposes.[308] Confusion might relate to the fact that both concepts express a relationship between an individual and a state or an institution. Yet, attribution of responsibility refers to whether the acts

[301] Guild and Stoyanova (n 295).

[302] For further detail, see ch 5.

[303] See in particular: Maarten Den Heijer, 'Shared Responsibility before the European Court of Human Rights' (2013) 60 *Netherlands International Law Review* 411; Gammeltoft-Hansen and Hathaway (n 160); Izabella Majcher, 'Human Rights Violations During EU Border Surveillance and Return Operations: Frontex's Shared Responsibility or Complicity?' [2015] *Silesian Journal of Legal Studies* 45; Annick Pijnenburg, 'From Italian Pushbacks to Libyan Pullbacks: Is Hirsi 2.0 in the Making in Strasbourg?' (2018) 20 *European Journal of Migration and Law* 396.

[304] Miles Jackson, 'Freeing Soering: The ECHR, State Complicity in Torture and Jurisdiction' (2016) 27 *European Journal of International Law* 817.

[305] ECtHR, *Soering v The United Kingdom*, Appl No 14038/88, 7 July 1989, para 86.

[306] Jackson (n 304).

[307] Gammeltoft-Hansen and Hathaway (n 160); Nora Markard, 'The Right to Leave by Sea: Legal Limits on EU Migration Control by Third Countries' (2016) 27 *European Journal of International Law* 591; Pijnenburg (n 303); Giuffré and Moreno Lax (n 274).

[308] Cf: *Loizidou* (n 18) para 62; ECtHR, *Loizidou v Turkey*, merits, Appl No 40/1993/435/514, 18 December 1995, para 56. See most recently, the confusion in *Jaloud* (n 51) paras 154–55. For a critique, see the concurring opinion of Judge Spielmann joined by Judge Raimondi paras 3–7 and the concurring opinion of Judge Motoc. See also: Aurel Sari, 'Untangling Extra-Territorial Jurisdiction from International Responsibility in Jaloud v. Netherlands: Old Problem, New Solutions' (2014) 53 *Military Law & Law of War Review* 287; Marko Milanovic, 'Jurisdiction and Responsibility: Trends in the Jurisprudence of the Strasbourg Court' in Anne van Aaken and Iulia Motoc (eds), *The ECHR and General International Law* (Oxford, Oxford University Press, 2018).

or omissions of an individual (or a group of individuals) should be regarded as the conduct of a state or an international organisation, while jurisdiction concerns the question of a state's power over the victims of human rights violations. Jurisdiction is the necessary premise for the very existence of responsibility as a violation of an international obligation.[309] Even if responsibility could be attributed to complicit states, human rights law still demands the establishment of a jurisdictional link for any human rights obligations to arise. Attribution of responsibility can function as a precondition of jurisdiction, but this does not automatically imply the exercise of jurisdiction.[310] Conversely, the determination of jurisdiction does not entail the attribution of every human rights violation occurring in that context. To be clear, jurisdiction is not a requirement for establishing indirect responsibility under the ILC's Articles on State Responsibility.[311] Yet, if the ECtHR finds that Italy did not exercise jurisdiction under Article 1 ECHR, it will declare the case inadmissible without addressing the question of attribution.

A third alternative would be to take into full account the spill-over effect of domestic policy decisions.[312] In this line, jurisdiction may result from actions taking place within a state's own territory, but leading to human rights violations beyond it, provided that there is a jurisdictional link between the state where the decision is taken and its harmful consequences.[313] This jurisdictional link consists 'in the causal chain that would make possible violations in another jurisdiction'.[314] According to the HRC, the extraterritorial human rights violation must be the 'necessary and foreseeable consequence' of state conduct and 'must be judged on the knowledge the State party had at the time'.[315] The doctrine of extraterritorial effects of domestic acts has been developed mainly with regard to transboundary environmental harm,[316] extraterritorial harmful effects of domestic economic

[309] See: *Ukraine v Russia (Re Crimea)* (n 24) paras 264 and 266.

[310] For instance, in the *Behrami* case, the question whether the conduct of the KFOR French contingent in Kosovo was attributable to France was logically prior to the issue of French jurisdiction over a part of Kosovo. *Behrami and Behrami v France and Saramati v France, Germany and Norway*, Appl Nos 71412/01, 78166/01, 2 May 2007. See also: Marko Milanovic and Tatjana Papić, 'As Bad as It Gets: The European Court of Human Rights's Behrami and Saramati Decision and General International Law' (2009) 58 *International and Comparative Law Quarterly* 267.

[311] See: Art 16, Articles on Responsibility of States for Internationally Wrongful Acts, with commentaries, Yearbook of the International Law Commission, 2001, vol II, Part Two.

[312] Sigrun Skogly, *Beyond National Borders: States' Human Rights Obligations in International Cooperation* (Antwerp, Intersentia, 2006) 155; Tilmann Altwicker, 'Transnationalizing Rights: International Human Rights Law in Cross-Border Contexts' (2018) 29 *European Journal of International Law* 581.

[313] Peter Vedel Kessing, 'Transnational Operations Carried out from a State's Own Territory: Armed Drones and the Extraterritorial Effect of International Human Rights Conventions' in Thomas Gammeltoft-Hansen and Jens Vedsted-Hansen (eds), *Human Rights and the Dark Side of Globalisation Transnational Law Enforcement and Migration Control* (Abingdon, Routledge, 2016).

[314] HRC, *Munaf v Romania*, Comm No 1539/2006, UN Doc CCPR/C/96/D/1539/2006, 21 August 2009, para 14.2.

[315] ibid; See also: HRC, *A.R.J. v Australia*, Comm No 692/1996, UN Doc CCPR/C/60/D/692/1996, 28 July 1997, para 4.1.

[316] Alan Boyle, 'Human Rights and the Environment: Where Next?' (2012) 23 *European Journal of International Law* 613.

policies,[317] and data surveillance policies.[318] But it remains comparatively less developed in international human rights law.[319] It follows that whether a jurisdictional link can be established between the EU and its Member States and human rights violations suffered by migrants as part of cooperative deterrence policies requires a case-by-case analysis.[320] In this respect, the ECtHR has so far taken a restrictive approach.[321] But considering that the applicability of the CFR depends on the scope of application of EU law, the CJEU might have a different approach.

The fourth option to establish jurisdiction over cooperative deterrence policies is based on the notion of 'decisive influence' as developed by the ECtHR in a string of cases related to human rights violations that occurred in Transdniestria under the sponsorship of Russia.[322] In such cases, the Court held that Russia exercised jurisdiction over human rights violations that occurred in the separatist regime of Transdniestria by virtue of its decisive influence in the region. The high level of dependency on Russian military, economic, financial and political support gave a strong indication of Russia's power over the separatist regime. In the context of Italian-Libyan cooperation, arguably, the LCG would not operate if it were not for Italian support.[323] A support given to prevent departures at any cost, despite well-documented – predictable and notorious – patterns of human rights violations against migrants.[324] Accordingly, the decisive influence of the EU and its Member States in the context of cooperative deterrence policies constitutes a form of oblique but effective exercise of state power that could amount to jurisdiction under Article 1

[317] Samantha Velluti, Vassilis Tzevelekos, 'Extraterritoriality of EU law and human rights after Lisbon: The case of trade and public procurement' (2018) 2 *Europe and the World: A Law Review* 10; Lorand Bartels, 'Extraterritoriality of EU Law and Human Rights after Lisbon: The Case of Trade and Public Procurement: Conclusion' (2018) 2 *Europe and the World: A Law Review* 8.

[318] See Mistale Taylor, 'The EU's Human Rights Obligations in Relation to Its Data Protection Laws with Extraterritorial Effect' (2015) 5 *International Data Privacy Law* 246. For a critical perspective on the application of the 'effects doctrine', see Marko Milanovic, 'Human Rights Treaties and Foreign Surveillance: Privacy in the Digital Age' (2015) 56 *Harvard International Law Journal* 81.

[319] Kessing (n 313); Altwicker (n 312).

[320] *Munaf v Romania* (n 315) para 14.2.

[321] *M.N. et al v Belgium* (n 237) para 112.

[322] See: *Ilaşcu* (n 31) para 392; *Ivantoc* (n 33) para 115; *Catan* (n 33) para 122; *Mozer* (n 33) para 103; *Sandu* (n 33) para 34; ECtHR, *Turturica and Casian v the Republic of Moldova and Russia*, Appl Nos 28648/06 18832/07, 30 January 2017, para 30; ECtHR, *Soyma v the Republic of Moldova, Russia and Ukraine*, Appl No1203/05, 13 November 2017, para 22; ECtHR, *Apcov v the Republic of Moldova and Russia*, Appl No 13463/07, 28 March 2017, para 23; ECtHR, *Panteleiciuc v the Republic of Moldova and Russia*, Appl No 57468/08, 2 July 2019, para 23. Pursuing this approach, see most notably, Giuffré and Moreno Lax (n 274).

[323] Guild and Stoyanova (n 295); Moreno-Lax (n 88).

[324] See eg: OHCHR, *'Detained and dehumanised' Report on human rights abuses against migrants in Libya*, 13 December 2016; Report of the Special Rapporteur on torture and other cruel, inhuman or degrading treatment or punishment, A/HRC/37/50, 26 February 2018; OHCHR, *Desperate and Dangerous: Report on the human rights situation of migrants and refugees in Libya*, 20 December 2018; HRW, *Libya's Dark Web of Collusion: Abuses against Europe-Bound Refugees and Migrants*, 2017; Amnesty International, *No Escape from Hell: EU Policies Contribute to Abuse of Migrants in Libya*, 21 January 2019; OHCHR, *Report of the Independent Fact-Finding Mission on Libya*, A/HRC/52/83, 3 March 2023.

ECHR, thus triggering the human rights obligations of contracting states, wherever this power is exercised.[325] However, some would argue that influence cannot be equated with state power, and therefore jurisdiction as it is an occurrence which may or may not result from the exercise of state power (for example through diplomatic pressure).[326] It could also be argued that Italy's power over the LCG is not comparable to that of Russia in Transdniestria. Italy's funding of the LCG did not *directly* impact the rights of migrants intercepted by the latter. Without question, the direct causal link between Italian influence and the LCG will be difficult to prove in Court.[327] However, a large amount of information available – including reports from international independent bodies – leaves this possibility open.

The last, and in my view most promising, option would be to consider all these elements together. As long as they represent a manifestation of state sovereign power, the legal and factual means that a state uses to change the situation of individuals beyond its borders reveals a jurisdictional connection. In relation to the pending case of *S.S. and Others v Italy*, concerning the Italian cooperation with the LCG, Moreno-Lax appraised jurisdiction paying specific attention to 'the entire constellation of all the relevant channels through which factual and/or legal state functions are exercised'.[328] Accordingly, the Italian implication with the operational capacity of the LCG should be considered against the background of its legal and factual context. This cooperation entails both a direct technical and material participation, as well as an indirect yet decisive influence on the overall containment policy across the Central Mediterranean. A policy that has a foreseeable impact over the human rights of migrants in distress at sea.[329]

Moreno-Lax's reading of jurisdiction is functional as it points to the functions of state sovereignty.[330] This interpretation reveals how contactless containment policies impose European prerogatives on the borders of sovereign third countries.[331] In so doing it challenges the operation of the sovereignty doctrine, according to

[325] Written Submission on behalf of the interveners, from Amnesty International and Human Rights Watch in the case of *S.S. and others v Italy*, Appl no 21660/18, 13 November 2019. For a detailed discussion, see: Moreno-Lax (n 88).

[326] See generally: Raible (n 82).

[327] For instance, in 2020, the Italian Consiglio di Stato rejected a complaint against the use of the EU Africa Fund to reinforce the Libyan authorities involved in maritime border surveillance. The judges considered that the consequences of the Italian support to the Libyan authorities would trespass administrative discretion. The decision further compounds the question of attribution with that of jurisdiction and dismisses the claim of complicity by simply referring to the lack of (territorial) jurisdiction. Consiglio di Stato, Sentenza No 4569/2020, 15 July 2020. For further discussion see: Antonio Marchesi, 'Finanziare i Rimpatri Forzati in Libia è Legittimo? Sulla Sentenza Del Consiglio Di Stato n. 4569 del 15 Luglio 2020' (2020) 14 *Diritti umani e diritto internazionale* 796.

[328] Moreno-Lax (n 88) 414.

[329] ibid 403–13.

[330] ibid 403. See also, Maria Gavouneli, *Functional Jurisdiction in the Law of the Sea* (Leiden, Brill Nijhoff, 2007).

[331] Chantal Thomas, 'What Does the Emerging International Law of Migration Mean for Sovereignty?' (2013) 14 *Melbourne Journal of International Law* 392; Achiume (n 290); E Tendayi Achiume, 'Racial Borders' (2022) 110 *Georgetown Law Journal* 445.

which every country enjoys independence from and equality with all other states. At the same time, by referring to sovereign functions one risks perpetuating some confusion. In fact, international law has been traditionally rather agnostic or at least ambiguous about what constitutes inherently sovereign functions.[332] Jurisdiction under human rights law can sometimes overlap with sovereignty, albeit they are not coextensive. Jurisdiction denotes those legal and factual means through which state power finds concrete expression. It requires a nexus between state authorities and those concerned by their decisions through factual or legal means or a combination of both. Hence, to my mind, rather than the expression of state sovereign functions, jurisdiction serves a relational function.

In the foregoing discussion, I sought to illustrate some of the uncertainties around whether destination states exercise jurisdiction over migrants intercepted or otherwise kept from leaving by transit states on their behalf. If jurisdiction is understood as direct and physical control over a territory or an individual, this eventuality is highly improbable. Nevertheless, if one accepts the notion of jurisdiction as the exercise of state power, which can impact individuals beyond their borders in multiple (legal and factual) ways, remote and cooperative deterrence policies may trigger the jurisdiction of sponsoring states. Faced with similar questions, the CJEU avoided politically charged pronouncements, yet it remains to be seen how the Strasbourg judges will rule. Amid all these legal ambiguities and expectations, what remains certain is the inadequacy of the traditional interpretation of the applicable legal framework, which cannot respond to the demands of the evolving reality of 'contactless' migration management.

C. Concurrent Jurisdiction, Positive Obligations and Due Diligence Duties

Power is an elusive concept often difficult to observe concretely, as its manifestations are multifarious. EU cooperative deterrence policies are embedded in an unequal distribution of economic, social and political power among EU Member States and countries of origin and transit. Furthermore, cooperative deterrence policies are the expression of an imbalanced power relation, which can be difficult to individuate, given that these policies generally result from opaque and undemocratic arrangements. Multiple actors cooperating and supporting deterrence policies can engage the concurrent jurisdiction of various EU Member States and transit or destination countries. They can also engage the EU and the applicability of the CFR, for instance via Frontex when it concludes problematic working arrangements with third states.

[332] Frédéric Mégret, 'Are There "Inherently Sovereign Functions" in International Law?' (2021) 115 *American Journal of International Law* 452; Samantha Besson, 'The International Public: A Farewell to Functions in International Law' (2021) 115 *American Journal of International Law* 307.

Concurrent jurisdictions – the simultaneous exercise of jurisdiction over the same situation by multiple international actors – can occur in three main circumstances.[333] The first is when territorial and extraterritorial jurisdictions of different states over individuals coincide. This is the case, for instance, during military occupation, but it also occurs under migration control measures taking place within the territory of another state.[334] Further, there can be a concurrence of extraterritorial jurisdictions of various states exercising power over people at the same time in a foreign territory. This second circumstance is mostly the result of multilateral peace operations, but it can be assimilated to joint border control operations coordinated by Frontex on the territory of third states. Finally, one could also conceive the concurrence of territorial jurisdictions of different states whose distinct control over their territory enables them to control the same group of people in transnational circumstances; this is the case in migrants' secondary movements within the Schengen area.[335]

As discussed above, jurisdiction is the necessary requirement for the application of human rights obligations. It follows that concurrent jurisdictions give rise to concurrent human rights obligations. To the extent that they correspond to different manners in which states exercise their power over the same right-holders, concurrent jurisdictions may give rise to different types of human rights obligations (positive or negative).[336] Where they arise from joint extraterritorial jurisdictions or form parallel territorial jurisdictions, concurrent human rights duties can be identical. This is the case, for instance, when migrants move from one country to another. But concurrent human rights duties can also be complementary when they are triggered by different degrees of control and authority, that is, manifestations of state power, over a given situation.[337] This situation might arise when a state is directly patrolling the territorial waters of another state, or when it is supporting the authorities of that state in SAR operations.[338] The case law of the ECtHR and the HRC does not provide much guidance as to the allocation of these duties. Nevertheless, Besson has observed that, while the intensity and degree of state power necessary for positive human rights obligations to arise extraterritorially is often difficult to establish, this cannot be automatically excluded.[339]

Some conceptual and practical hurdles can prevent the recognition of concurrent jurisdictions during the implementation of the EIBM, in particular before the

[333] See Samantha Besson, 'Concurrent Responsibilities under the European Convention on Human Rights: The Concurrence of Human Rights Jurisdictions, Duties, and Responsibilitie' in in Anne van Aaken and Iulia Motoc (eds), *The ECHR and General International Law* (Oxford, Oxford University Press, 2018).

[334] See eg: *Loizidou* (n 309); *R v Immigration Officer at Prague Airport and Another, Ex parte European Roma Rights Centre and Others* [2004] UKHL 55, House of Lords (Judicial Committee), 9 December 2004.

[335] See eg: ECtHR, *M.S.S. v Belgium and Greece*, Appl No 30696/09, 21 January 2011.

[336] Besson (n 333) 166.

[337] See eg: *Ilaşcu* (n 31); *Jaloud* (n 51); *Pisari* (n 200).

[338] *A.S., D.I., O.I. and G.D. v Italy* (n 62).

[339] Besson (n 333) 167.

ECtHR. At the theoretical level, the idea of concurrent jurisdictions is in tension with the required unicity of legitimate state power.[340] The recognition of concurrent jurisdictions of different states under the ECHR can also be exposed to some other difficulties, mostly related to procedural requirements for the admissibility of a case before the ECtHR.[341] In fact, all states whose jurisdiction is at stake should be parties to the ECHR. As the EU is not (for the time being) a party to the ECHR,[342] Member States could avoid ECtHR scrutiny by acting through the organs of the EU, most notably Frontex. Furthermore, many of the states involved in cooperative deterrence policies on behalf of destination states are not parties to the Convention either.[343]

These procedural problems notwithstanding, states are bound by an obligation to ensure that non-state actors whose action they are in a position to regulate do not breach their human rights obligations.[344] This positive duty derives from the due diligence obligation binding all states joining an international organisation whose membership might lead them to breach their human rights obligations.[345] Crucially, this due diligence obligation is independent of any separate human rights obligation of the organisation. Therefore, all EU Member States are bound by a due diligence obligation to prevent potential human rights violations that might occur in the context of their collective action.

Human rights due diligence obligations in extraterritorial contexts have been affirmed in relation to unilateral coercive measures,[346] as well as UN support for non-UN security forces.[347] Notably, the UN's Human Rights Due Diligence

[340] ibid, 163.

[341] Marina Mancini, 'Italy's New Migration Control Policy: Stemming the Flow of Migrants From Libya Without Regard for Their Human Rights' (2018) 27 *The Italian Yearbook of International Law Online* 259.

[342] Among the copious literature on the EU accession to the ECHR, see: Jed Odermatt, 'A Giant Step Backwards-Opinion 2/13 on the EU's Accession to the European Convention on Human Rights' (2014) 47 *NYU Journal of International Law & Policy* 783; Paul Gragl, 'The Reasonableness of Jealousy: Opinion 2/13 and EU Accession to the ECHR' in W Benedek, F Benoit-Rohmer, W Karl and M Nowak (eds), *European Yearbook on Human Rights* (Antwerp, Intersentia, 2015); Turkuler Isiksel, 'European Exceptionalism and the EU's Accession to the ECHR' (2016) 27 *European Journal of International Law* 565.

[343] Libya is the most obvious example in this context. However, other countries could also be mentioned such as Tunisia, Morocco, Chad, Niger and Sudan, with whom the EU, Italy and other Member States began to cooperate with the aim of strengthening their border control capacity. See Andrea Spagnolo, 'The Conclusion of Bilateral Agreements and Technical Arrangements for the Management of Migration Flows: An Overview of the Italian Practice' (2019) 28 *The Italian Yearbook of International Law Online* 209.

[344] See: HRC, *Basem Ahmed Issa Yassin et al v Canada*, Comm No 2285/2013, UN Doc CCPR/C/120/D/2285, 26 July 2017, para 3.7; See also: Maastricht Principles, principle 24.

[345] ECtHR, *Waite and Kennedy v Germany*, Appl No 26083/94, 18 February 1999, para 67.

[346] Human Rights Council, Research-Based Progress Report of the Human Rights Council Advisory Committee Containing Recommendations on Mechanisms to Assess the Negative Impact of Unilateral Coercive Measures on the Enjoyment of Human Rights and to Promote Accountability, paras 43–58, UN Doc A/HRC/28/74, 10 February 2015.

[347] UNGA, Security Council, Identical letters dated 25 February 2013 from the Secretary-General addressed to the President of the General Assembly and to the President of the Security Council, UN Doc A/67/775–S/2013/110, 5 March 2013.

Policy (HRDDP) requires an assessment of the risk that the intended recipient of support will commit grave violations of international humanitarian, human rights, or refugee law.[348] Along the same lines, the due diligence obligations of the EU and its Member States in relation to their extraterritorial migration control policies imply a duty to perform an ex-ante human rights assessment for cooperation projects beyond the borders of EU Member States.[349]

Various international and regional human rights bodies have recently expanded their understanding of jurisdiction by identifying extraterritorial due diligence obligations in relation to the extraterritorial action of third parties.[350] Along these lines, with regard to the EIBM in general and to Frontex operations more specifically, the due diligence obligations of the EU and its Member States would depend on their actual capacity to impact the human rights situation of migrants affected by their policies and practices. This position remains contested, however;[351] and needs to be tested in practice, particularly regarding the jurisdictional reach of the ECHR which has been strictly interpreted.

A further question that needs to be resolved concerns the multiplicity of potentially responsible actors, involved in the control of the EU external borders. As already noted, not only EU Member States, but also various EU bodies, most notably Frontex, and third states are involved in the control of the EU external borders. Competence over migration control is thus disaggregated and shared among a vast array of different actors, which may thus exercise concurrent human rights jurisdiction over the people involved in their activities. Of the many obstacles that those willing to search for accountability for human rights violations through litigation must surmount is unravelling the knot of attribution of responsibilities linked to the conducts of each of these actors, who might have different human rights obligations.

An additional complication concerns the invocation of responsibility for human rights violations before a court or independent body. Migrants face numerous problems in invoking their rights. This is all the truer if they have been returned or have an irregular legal status.[352] The difficulties become insurmountable in the absence of independent fora competent to adjudicate over alleged violations. This

[348] ibid, para 2.

[349] See: GLAN, ASGI and ARCI, Complaint to the European Court of Auditors Concerning the Mismanagement of EU Funds by the EU Trust Fund for Africa's 'Support to Integrated Border and Migration Management in Libya' (IBM) Programme (April 2020); European Ombudsman, Case 1473/2022/MHZ (n 287). See also: Carla Ferstman, 'Human Rights Due Diligence Policies Applied to Extraterritorial Cooperation to Prevent "Irregular" Migration: European Union and United Kingdom Support to Libya' (2020) 21 *German Law Journal* 459.

[350] See: General Comment No 36 (n 35); *A.S., D.I., O.I. and G.D. v Italy* (n 62); *Basem Ahmed Issa Yassin* (n 345); CESCR, General Comment No 24 on State obligations under the International Covenant on Economic, Social and Cultural Rights in the context of business activities, UN Doc E/c12/GC24, 10 August 2017, paras 15–16, 27–28, 30–32; *The Environment and Human Rights* (n 35) para 104.

[351] Lea Raible, 'Extraterritoriality between a Rock and Hard Place' (2021) 82 *QIL QDI* 29.

[352] Marie-Benedicte Dembour, *When Humans Become Migrants: Study of the European Court of Human Rights with an Inter-American Counterpoint* (Oxford, Oxford University Press, 2015) 506–07.

is most notably the case for alleged human rights violations occurring during Frontex activities. Far from being independent and effective, the agency's internal complaint mechanism largely depends on the discretion of internal monitoring bodies. This, together with Frontex's immunity before national courts, and the complications of legal actions before the CJEU, might preclude access to an independent judicial forum for victims of human rights violations committed by the agency's staff. The next chapter will illuminate these questions, especially regarding the allocation of responsibility during Frontex's operational activities.

VI. Conclusion: Jurisdiction and Power Relations in the European Integrated Border Management

The EIBM involves an assemblage of different actors, practices and techniques expanding border control measures beyond the borders of European states. This involves several challenges regarding the applicability of the human rights obligations binding Frontex and its Member States. All Member States have the obligation to secure the human rights of everyone within their jurisdiction.[353] The foregoing discussion has, however, shown that a strict application of the current legal framework may result in the denial of the jurisdiction – and therefore of the legal responsibility – of European states, absent any direct physical control of the individuals involved in their collective border control activities. Moreover, the multiplicity of actors involved in the implementation of the EIBM may imply the concurrent exercise of jurisdiction by different entities over the same situation.

A few observations can be drawn in relation to the exercise of jurisdiction over the EIBM in general and over Frontex joint operations more specifically. First and foremost, the authorities of Member States hosting Frontex joint operations would generally exercise jurisdiction based on the territorial model. Second, based on the personal model, whenever a state exercises direct and physical authority and control over an individual a jurisdictional link is established. This enlivens the human rights guarantees by which every state party to the ECHR is bound. This is the case, for instance, in rejection or detention at the frontier,[354] but also in maritime interdiction operations executed beyond the territorial waters of the state concerned.[355] The host state would in these cases exercise jurisdiction based on its control over a given activity and the persons involved therein. In addition, participating states can in principle exercise jurisdiction as soon as their officers seconded to a Frontex joint operation exercise their administrative or law enforcement powers. This remains an exception to the rule according to which the officers participating in joint operations should

[353] Art 1 ECHR.
[354] *M.A. v Lithuania* (n 178).
[355] *Hirsi Jamaa* (n 185).

act on behalf of the host Member State. Nevertheless, the exercise of concurrent jurisdictions should not be *a priori* excluded.

The same conclusion can also be reached with regard to return operations, where irregular migrants are deported to third states either by a single Member State or within the framework of a joint return operation coordinated by Frontex. Arguably, jurisdiction is exercised by the Member State issuing the return decision. However, human rights violations can occur during the execution of such a decision. In a context where multiple authorities cooperate, the exact determination of the responsible agent depends on the circumstances of each case. At the same time, Frontex is also under an obligation to ensure the fundamental rights of people subject to return procedures that it coordinates.[356] As the EU is not yet a party to the ECHR, the only available remedy would be before the CJEU. The applicability of the guarantees included in the CFR will therefore depend on the applicability of EU law to the case at hand, which is highly probable given that the cooperation of return operation is explicitly governed by the Frontex Regulation.

That notwithstanding, the scope of application of EU law is open to different interpretations and this has given rise to serious difficulties, as it plays a central role in triggering EU fundamental (human) rights obligations. In this respect, the *X and X* case demonstrates the malleability of the language of human rights, as well as the ambiguity of the scope of EU law and its fundamental rights guarantees, which in substance were interpreted as applicable primarily to a limited group of privileged migrants, mostly Europeans. The same case also illustrates one of the fundamental paradoxes of international and EU refugee law.[357] Only those who have succeeded in leaving their country and reaching the territory of another can benefit from international protection. Asylum is a right that is conditioned upon a discretionary decision, that is, the crossing of borders. For those whose life and freedom depend on the very possibility to flee, international protection obligations binding states towards individuals already within their territories are largely meaningless.

In a world where the unanimous state response to the rise of people on the move is the tightening and multiplication of borders, the delimitation of states' human rights obligations needs a consonant paradigm. In delineating the scope of human rights jurisdiction, the substantial exercise of state power and the vulnerable situation of the individuals involved should play a pivotal role.

When it comes to cooperation with third countries to outsource migration controls, jurisdiction can be established in various ways, even in the absence of direct contact with the migrants concerned via pre-departure measures. Jurisdiction could be determined in relation to the public powers jointly exercised

[356] Art 50 (3), Regulation 2019/1896.

[357] See Jean-Yves Carlier, 'The X. and X. case: Humanitarian visas and the genuine enjoyment of the substance of the rights, towards a middle way?' (*EU Immigration and Asylum Law and Policy* blog, 27 February 2017) https://eumigrationlawblog.eu/the-x-and-x-case-humanitarian-visas-and-the-genuine-enjoyment-of-the-substance-of-rights-towards-a-middle-way/.

by countries of destination and departure when they implement pre-border control measures. Decisions taken within the territory of EU Member States, but engaging harmful effects beyond their borders could likewise trigger their jurisdiction. Another option would be to rely on the complicit conduct of destination states together with their decisive influence over the authorities of countries of departure who, without such support, would be unable to effectively perform pre-departure controls.

The ECtHR has not yet decided on the question of jurisdiction over contactless deterrence practices. It could avoid a decision by applying the traditional notion of extraterritorial jurisdiction as direct and physical control over people or territories. Or it could take a stronger stance, using one of the above-mentioned approaches or a combination of them. The sharing of information underlying the EU migration control databases, for example, could provide the basis for an argument regarding their decisive influence on migration policy decisions, including pre-departure measures in third countries. The CJEU could also intervene in this debate. The Luxembourg Court decision would depend on its interpretation of the scope of EU law, but also on many procedural hurdles the applicants would need to overcome before reaching the Court.[358]

And yet, in recent years, European Courts seem rather reticent in applying extraterritorially the obligations they are mandated to supervise. The current resistance to establishing extraterritorial human rights obligations in the context of migration control measures should be interpreted against the xenophobic turn in many countries' migration policies and the backlash against human rights more generally. From this angle, objections to extraterritorial human rights are, at least in part, objections to the legal protection of migrant rights. The politicised nature of this issue area may induce human rights courts and monitoring bodies to dynamically engage with the question of jurisdiction to ensure the effectiveness of human rights in the face of current regressive factions; nonetheless, the general backlash against supranational institutions may also lead judiciaries to adopt a more attentive and cautious approach, shying away from disputed cases at the admissibility stage and avoiding establishing wider precedents.[359]

The EU cooperative deterrence policies are embedded in an unequal distribution of power among the EU and the Member States, and countries of origin and transit. Such power is exercised in the ambiguous form of economic, political and technical or operational support to third states in exchange for the sealing of their borders. This elusive expression of public power would pass into oblivion if read through the prism of the conventional notion of jurisdiction. In this vein, the relational approach discussed above reflects a different understanding of jurisdiction as the exercise of state power embracing its multiple manifestations. At the same time, it does not deny the responsibility of third states that cooperate

[358] See ch 5, s VII.B.
[359] See for instance, the CJEU cases of *NF v European Council*, and *X and X* discussed above.

in deterrence policies with harmful effects on the human rights of migrants. In doing so, this approach refrains from adopting a paternalistic attitude that could perpetuate accusations of human rights colonialism. Importantly, the relational approach recognises the possibility of concurrent jurisdictions. As the next chapter will show, in this respect, a further challenge for anyone seeking accountability for human rights violations that might occur during Frontex operations concerns the distribution of responsibilities among the assemblage of different authorities participating in the agency's activities.

To conclude, the regional containment of undocumented migrants is undergirded by a sovereignty discourse that justifies their exclusion from Europe as an accident of its collective self-determination. These policies are part and parcel of the 'four-tier access control model' underlying the EIBM.[360] They aim to discourage and hinder any attempt to reach Europe – mostly by economically and politically marginal persons. Human rights courts can attempt to remedy such a situation, finding new jurisprudential solutions that take into consideration the power exerted by destination states on third countries. This can ensure the legal responsibility of supporting entities without denying that of third countries. However, the inequality inherent in the power relation between countries cannot be jurisprudentially solved. Equality may entail shifting power within the relationship instead of pushing it outside or beyond it.[361]

[360] See ch 1, s III.
[361] Achiume (n 290); Achiume (n 161).

5

International Responsibility and the Implementation of the EIBM

I. Introduction: International Responsibility and the Many Hands at the European Borders

This chapter will explore the circumstances under which Frontex and the Member States may incur international responsibility for violations of migrant rights. It examines how international responsibility can be attributed to the EU (Frontex) and/or the states participating in its border control activities and how the responsibility of one of these actors relates to that of the others.

The previous parts of this work have shown that the EIBM in general, and Frontex activities in particular, disclose a variety of implications for migrant rights. The inherent human rights sensitivity of border control activities is exacerbated by the recent developments in the management of European borders, which are increasingly secured from a distance by a panoply of different actors and technologies integrated within an assemblage of containment practices. As a result, not only human rights obligations are difficult to be established because of the jurisdictional limits of the relevant legal framework; but the plurality of actors involved in potential violations also implies serious difficulties in the distribution of the concomitant responsibilities.

This multiplicity, and its legal challenges, are patent in Frontex's joint operations. Migrant rights violations occurring during Frontex's joint operations involve the personnel and equipment of the agency, EU Member States and third countries. In this intricate situation, numerous actors are involved with different de iure mandates and de facto capabilities. In cases of migrant rights violations, these actors hand responsibility off to one another, blaming each other for the harmful consequences of their collective actions at the EU's external borders. A veil of legal uncertainty often surrounds these actions: the lack of transparency coupled with the intertwining of actors and their relative competences in the management of the European borders produce a confused factual and legal jigsaw puzzle that is difficult to re-assemble in accordance with the existing legal framework.

The allocation of responsibilities in complex settings such as the EIBM is not always straightforward. This has been described as 'the problem of many hands'.[1]

[1] Dennis F Thompson, 'Moral Responsibility of Public Officials: The Problem of Many Hands' (1980) 74 *American Political Science Review* 905. In relation to Frontex, see Mariana Gkliati and Herbert Rosenfeldt, 'Accountability of the European Border and Coast Guard Agency' RLI Working Paper No 30 (2018).

Because many different actors contribute in many ways to decisions and policies of complex organisations, it is difficult even in principle to identify who is responsible and to what extent, for the outcomes of such decisions or policies. The many hands contributing to the same wrongful conduct are covered behind the veil of their collective action. In concrete terms, this signifies that the victims are deprived of any meaningful remedy. The problem of many hands may result in such a dispersion of responsibilities that ultimately no one is to blame, for no one had decisive control over the outcome of a situation.[2]

The following analysis will address the problem of many hands relating to implementing the EIBM and Frontex operations. My investigation will start by defining the term 'responsibility' instead of the more general notion of 'accountability' (Section II); this will lead to the exploration of the international responsibility of the EU and the Member States (Section III). I will then chart the rules governing the distribution of international responsibility between the EU and the states contributing to Frontex's joint operations (Section IV). I will examine the possible consequences of the EU and its Member States' international responsibility (Section V) and outline the main issues arising from the concurrent responsibilities of individuals and of states or international organisations for migrant rights violations in the context of Frontex joint operations (Section VI). I will then briefly consider where and how the rules discussed in the chapter could be implemented (Section VII). By way of conclusion, the chapter will highlight the value of other, less formal, accountability mechanisms that may prevent potential violations or offer some form of reparation to the victims (Section VIII).

II. Responsibility in All its Variety

The term responsibility has many meanings, inside and outside the legal domain, which may lead to confusion about its underlying idea. One of the main complications of any discussion about responsibility lies in the very nature of this expression.[3] Responsibility is an 'essentially contested concept',[4] which can be best clarified by making a sketch of what Wittgenstein called 'family resemblance'.[5] Just like members of a family, different concepts having no common feature can be

[2] Mark Bovens, *The Quest for Responsibility: Accountability and Citizenship in Complex Organisations* (Cambridge, Cambridge University Press, 1998) 40.

[3] James Crawford and Jeremy Watkins, 'International Responsibility' in Samantha Besson and John Tasioulas (eds), *The Philosophy of International Law* (Oxford, Oxford University Press, 2010); Andre Nollkaemper, 'Responsibility' in Jean d'Aspremont and S Singh (eds), *Fundamental Concepts for International Law* (Cheltenham, Edward Elgar, 2017).

[4] Walter Bryce Gallie, 'Essentially Contested Concepts', *Proceedings of the Aristotelian Society* (Oxford, Oxford University Press on behalf of The Aristotelian Society, 1955).

[5] Ludwig Wittgenstein, *Philosophical Investigations (1958)* 4th edn (PMS Hacker and Joachim Schulte eds, Oxford, Wiley-Blackwell, 2009) 32–33. See also: Bovens (n 2) 24.

connected through a series of overlapping similarities. The notion of responsibility can be related to the idea of answerability[6] and linked to a 'duty to deal with something', which may or may not correspond to a legal obligation. It can be connected to a legal, political, or moral duty that derives from the role or office of a certain actor.[7] Frontex FRO, for example, is responsible for handling complaints received by the agency.

Responsibility as answerability should be distinguished from responsibility as liability. The latter has a narrower legal meaning, which conveys the idea that those who violate their obligations become liable for the legal consequences of such violations. This notion of responsibility underlies the ILC's Articles on International Responsibility of States (ARS) and International Organisations (ARIO).[8] Under these rules, an international legal person who breaches its international obligations bears a duty to right its wrongs and provide remedies.[9] The common denominator is the idea of accountability for past events or conduct. The political, moral or legal implications of past events or conduct are all covered by the ample conceptual umbrella of accountability. Accountability is often used interchangeably with responsibility.[10] In what follows, however, the term responsibility has a specific and narrow legal meaning, which is only part of the broader idea of accountability.[11]

Following its traditional formulation, international responsibility is understood to be the legal principle governing the determination of legal consequences following a violation of an international obligation.[12] The idea that a violation should be undone and reparation should be provided is central to law, and international law is no exception.[13] As such, the notion of responsibility is essential to much of how we think about international law and why it matters. However, this is not to deny the significance of the broader concept of accountability, which may be

[6] Etymologically, the term responsibility originates from the Latin verb respondēre (to answer). See: Dario Mantovani, 'From "Respondere" to "Responsibility" A Roman Lawyer's Gloss on the International Law of State Responsibility' in Samantha Besson (ed), *Theories of International Responsibility Law* (Cambridge, Cambridge University Press, 2022).

[7] HLA Hart, *Punishment and Responsibility: Essays in the Philosophy of Law (1968)* 2nd edn (John Gardner ed, Oxford, Oxford University Press, 2008) 212–14.

[8] See respectively: ILC, Articles on Responsibility of States for Internationally Wrongful Acts, 2001, in UN Doc. A/56/10 (ARS); ILC, Articles on Responsibility of International Organizations, Yearbook of the International Law Commission, 2011, vol II, Part Two (ARIO).

[9] See ARS, Commentary to Article 1, para 3.

[10] See for example: Deirdre Curtin and Andre Nollkaemper, 'Conceptualising Accountability in International and European Law' (2006) 36 *Netherlands Yearbook of International Law* 3; Jan Wouters, Eva Brems, Stefaan Smis and Pierre Schmitt (eds) *Accountability for Human Rights Violations by International Organisations* (Antwerp, Intersentia, 2010).

[11] For a similar conceptualisation see: Jutta Brunnée, 'International Legal Accountability through the Lens of the Law of State Responsibility' (2005) 36 *Netherlands Yearbook of International Law* 21.

[12] PCIJ, *Factory at Chorzów*, Judgment No 8, 26 July 1927, PCIJ Reports Series A, No 9, 21; Art 1, ARS, Commentary, para 5.

[13] Art 30, ARS, Commentary, para 1.

operationalised through less formal mechanisms, sometimes having a more effective impact on the consequences of a violation and its prevention.

The ILC's ARS and ARIO are legally binding to the extent that they codify rules of customary international law. In its work on both sets of rules, the ILC discerned the rules on international responsibility from those that place states or international organisations under certain obligations, the violation of which may be a source of responsibility. In this line, Roberto Ago famously distinguished primary rules, which define international obligations and their content, and secondary rules, which determine whether an international obligation has been violated and what the consequences of the violation should be.[14] While the previous chapters have mainly dealt with the former, what follows will examine the EIBM from the perspective of the latter, thus engaging with the consequences of a violation of any previously identified international legal obligation.

International responsibility arises from any conduct qualified as internationally wrongful.[15] Internationally wrongful conduct materialises under two cumulative conditions:[16] (a) it is attributable to a state or international organisation under international law; and (b) it constitutes a breach of their international obligations. The first condition refers to the conduct of a person or group of persons which, from the point of view of international law, can be qualified as a collective entity – a state or an international organisation – that would not be able to act without the intermediation of individuals.[17] The second requirement implies that any conduct – either an action or an omission – entailing a violation of an international obligation of a state or international organisation can trigger their international responsibility. Wrongful conduct might arise from the violation of a customary rule of international law, a general principle, a treaty, or a unilateral act. International responsibility arises independently from the source of the international obligation that has been breached.[18] The character of a violation or its gravity is also irrelevant for the purposes of establishing responsibility.[19] However, certain obligations, such as those resulting from peremptory norms, may entail a specific set of consequences.[20] The two abovementioned components – the breach of an international obligation and its attribution – are the necessary and sufficient

[14] Third Report on State responsibility, by Mr Roberto Ago, Special Rapporteur, 'The internationally wrongful act of the State, source of international responsibility', Extract from the Yearbook of the International Law Commission, 1971, vol. II, para 6. For further discussion see Eric David, 'Primary and Secondary Rules' in James Crawford, Alain Pellet and Simon Olleson (eds), *The Law of International Responsibility* (Oxford, Oxford University Press, 2010).

[15] Art 1, ARS; Art 3, ARIO.

[16] Art 2, ARS; Art 4, ARIO.

[17] Luigi Condorelli and Claus Kress, 'The Rules of Attribution: General Considerations' in James Crawford, Alain Pellet and Simon Olleson (eds), *The Law of International Responsibility* (Oxford, Oxford University Press, 2010) 221.

[18] Art 12, ARS; Art 10(1), ARIO.

[19] ibid.

[20] Arts 41–42, ARS; Arts 41–42, ARIO.

conditions for responsibility to arise, provided that there is no circumstance precluding the wrongfulness of the conduct in question.[21]

III. International Responsibility for Conduct Relating to the EIBM

As already discussed, the development of a common policy on integrated border management and the border enforcement powers underlying it is a shared competence of the EU and its Member States.[22] This raises questions regarding the conditions upon which the EU and its Member States can be held responsible for their conduct within the framework of this common policy. These questions require an examination of the relationship between the EU and its Member States, a relationship marked by the independent legal personality of both subjects involved.

Following Article 47 TEU, the EU is conceived as a unique and uniform edifice, with a discrete legal personality. This assertion, however, conceals the complex institutional structure that underlies the Union. One issue that still needs to be solved is whether and to what extent individual EU institutions and other bodies may enjoy international legal personality.[23] For the present purposes, as demonstrated in chapter two, Frontex possesses a derivative legal personality under international law and a full legal personality under EU law. Consequently, the agency can trigger the international responsibility of its parent organisation, from which its personality derives; in addition, it can be held responsible for breaches of EU law obligations.[24]

The autonomy inherent to the notion of legal personality strongly suggests that Member States cannot generally be regarded as responsible for the internationally wrongful acts of an international organisation.[25] International organisations are autonomous legal subjects, for they can express a juridical will separate from that of their creators. Where Member States are not exercising their autonomy within the processes of an organisation, they are not acting as legal subjects and therefore cannot be held responsible. In this sense, '[w]ithout *volonté distincte* international organizations cannot incur *responsabilité distincte*'.[26]

[21] Chapter V, Part I, ARS and ARIO.

[22] See Arts 4(2)(j) and 77, TFEU.

[23] Niels Blokker, 'International Legal Personality of the European Communities and the European Union: Inspirations from Public International Law' [2016] 35 *Yearbook of European Law* 471.

[24] For a detailed analysis of the allocation of responsibilities among the actors participating in Frontex joint operations under EU law, see: Melanie Fink, *Frontex and Human Rights: Responsibility in 'Multi-Actor Situations' under the ECHR and EU Public Liability Law* (Oxford, Oxford University Press, 2018) 180–316.

[25] See Art 62, ARIO, Commentary, para 3.

[26] Christiane Ahlborn, 'The Rules of International Organizations and the Law of International Responsibility' (2011) 8 *International Organizations Law Review* 397, 479.

Autonomy is a functional concept. International organisations can exercise their autonomy about a specific competence that Member States confer to them but not in relation to others. This is clear when it comes to the exclusive competences of the EU, such as fisheries matters.[27] Less clear is how the organisational veil will effectively come into play in situations of shared competences, such as the EU integrated border management. The following sections will illuminate the limits of EU international responsibility as compared to that of Member States in the context of border enforcement activities.

A. EU Responsibility

It takes a wrongful act to be held responsible. When it comes to international organisations, however, questions about which sorts of international obligations are incumbent upon them and therefore, which sorts of breaches may trigger their responsibility, are far from being obvious.[28] In fact, the nature and the sources of international organisations' human rights obligations are still a matter of debate – not least because, frequently, they are not parties to human rights treaties.[29] Nevertheless, as seen in chapter three, the EU is bound by international human rights and refugee law at various levels.

More concretely, however, formal human rights and refugee law endorsements, commendable as they are, need to reflect a reality of substantial compliance with international law. Over the years, many have questioned the compatibility of EU legislation on asylum and immigration with international law, in particular with the Refugee Convention.[30] The compatibility of the CEAS with international human rights law has been challenged in various instances before the ECtHR. Still, the Court has been competent to decide only on the Member States' responsibility.[31] Any external review of the EU's human rights responsibility is precluded until its formal accession to the ECHR.

Those concerns might be mitigated by the fact that the protection of fundamental rights in the EU legal system is now firmly grounded in the CFR, which is binding on the EU, its organs and Member States.[32] The CJEU is thus competent to adjudicate the compatibility of EU law with the fundamental rights enshrined in

[27] ITLOS, *Request for an advisory opinion submitted by the Sub-Regional Fisheries Commission (SRFC)*, Case No 21, 2 April 2015, para 172.

[28] Samantha Besson, 'The Bearers of Human Rights Duties and Responsibilities for Human Rights – A Quiet (R)Evolution' (2015) 32 *Social Philosophy and Policy* 244; Jan Klabbers, *An Introduction to International Organizations Law* (Cambridge, Cambridge University Press, 2015) 325–26.

[29] See: Kristina Daugirdas, 'How and Why International Law Binds International Organizations' (2016) 57 *Harvard International Law Journal* 325.

[30] See generally: Vincent Chetail, Philippe De Bruycker and Francesco Maiani (eds), *Reforming the Common European Asylum System: The New European Refugee Law* (Leiden, Brill Nijhoff, 2016).

[31] Eg: ECtHR, *M.S.S. v Belgium and Greece*, Appl No 30696/09, 21 January 2011; ECtHR, *Sharifi et autres c Italie et Grèce*, Appl No 16643/09, 21 October 2014.

[32] Art 51, CFR.

the CFR, which reflect most rights included in regional or universal human rights treaties. The significance of the CFR and the judicial review of the CJEU in matters of fundamental rights should not be overestimated, however. Individuals must overcome many procedural hurdles to begin litigation before the Luxembourg Court;[33] from an international law perspective, the absence of an external review mechanism seems to be still one more obstacle to the effective implementation of human rights in the EU legal system.

B. EU Member States' Responsibility

Along with the responsibility of the EU itself, there is the question of whether Member States become or remain responsible for violations of human rights attributed to the international organisation. As a matter of international law, states are free to create international organisations and transfer powers to them. Yet, in light of the limited possibilities of bringing a claim against international organisations under international human rights law, the responsibility for exercising these powers in violation of human rights risks being disregarded.[34] For example, the conduct of any EU Member State can be challenged before the ECtHR. Still, when Member States violate the ECHR as a result of conduct put in place pursuant to EU law, the EU cannot be held responsible for the primary breach before that Court. The ECtHR has unfailingly declared inadmissible claims brought against international organisations, irrespective of whether they were formally directed against their Member States.[35] For the time being, EU Member States have not been found responsible for breaches of the ECHR on the exclusive base of their membership. This situation is different from that of Member States, who are held responsible for conduct performed in compliance with EU law.

It is well established that states may not relieve themselves of obligations they have assumed through existing treaties and conceal their responsibility behind the organisational veil.[36] In this vein, the ECtHR has consistently affirmed that, while states are free to transfer their powers to international organisations, absolving states from their responsibility under the ECHR in relation to the field of activity covered by such transfer of powers would be incompatible with the object and

[33] See below s VII.B.

[34] August Reinisch, 'Securing the Accountability of International Organizations' (2001) 7 *Global Governance* 131; Jan Wouters and others, *Accountability for Human Rights Violations by International Organisations* (Antwerp, Intersentia, 2010).

[35] See eg, ECtHR, *Senator Lines GmbH v Austria, Belgium, Denmark, Finland, France, Germany, Greece, Ireland, Italy, Luxembourg, the Netherlands, Portugal, Spain, Sweden and the United Kingdom*, Appl No 56672/00, 10 March 2004; ECtHR, *Segi and Gestoras Pro Amnistia and Others v Austria, Belgium, Denmark, Finland, France, Germany, Greece, Ireland, Italy, Luxembourg, the Netherlands, Portugal, Spain, Sweden and the United Kingdom*, Appl Nos 6422/02 and 9916/02, 23 May 2005; ECtHR, *Connolly c 15 États membres de l'Union européenne*, Appl No 73274/01, 9 December 2008.

[36] Art 61, ARS.

purpose of the Convention.[37] Yet, in the leading case *Bosphorus*,[38] the Court found that the conduct of states taken in compliance with their international obligations is justified as long as the relevant organisation is considered to protect fundamental rights 'in a manner which can be considered at least equivalent to that for which the Convention provides'.[39] Where an international organisation offers such equivalent protection, the Member State implementing obligations flowing from its membership of the organisation is presumed to comply with the requirements of the ECHR.

The presumption of equivalent protection rests upon two cumulative conditions. First, regarding the EU, a Member State should have no discretion regarding how it implements its obligations flowing from Union law. State discretion is exercised concerning instruments of EU primary law,[40] but also with regard to EU directives (which by their very nature entail obligations of result)[41] and even EU regulations, where states are granted a certain margin of manoeuvre in their implementation.[42] Second, the potential of EU law should be fully exploited, meaning that the CJEU must have the opportunity to assess the compatibility of contentious cases with fundamental rights.[43] Nonetheless, the presumption of equivalent protection is not absolute: even if the two conditions are satisfied, the presumption may be rebutted where the protection offered by EU law is considered 'manifestly deficient' in the specific case.[44] In such cases, the interests of international cooperation would be countered by the role of the ECHR as a 'constitutional instrument of European public order', and the situation in question would be subject to a thorough human rights examination.[45] This is particularly relevant in cases where the EU principle of mutual trust applies.[46] Most notably, the ECtHR acknowledged the importance and the legitimacy of mutual-recognition mechanisms in the area of freedom, security and justice referred to in Article 67 of the TFEU and of the mutual trust that they entail.[47] This should not imply

[37] See: ECommHR, *M & Co v Federal Republic of Germany*, Appl No 13258/87, 9 February 1990, para 145; ECtHR, *Waite and Kennedy v Germany*, Appl No 26083/94, 18 February 1999, para 67; ECtHR, *Matthews v the United Kingdom*, Appl No 24833/94 18 February 1999, para 34; ECtHR, *Capital Bank Ad v Bulgaria*, Appl No 49429/99, 24 November 2005, para 111.

[38] ECtHR, *Bosphorus Hava Yolları Turizm ve Ticaret Anonim Şirketi v Ireland*, Appl No 45036/98, 30 June 2005, para 154. For detailed commentaries see: Sionaidh Douglas-Scott, 'Bosphorus Hava Yollari Turizm Ve Ticaret Anonim Sirketi v. Ireland' (2006) 43 *Common Market Law Review* 243; Cathryn Costello, 'The Bosphorus Ruling of the European Court of Human Rights: Fundamental Rights and Blurred Boundaries in Europe' (2006) 6 *Human Rights Law Review* 87.

[39] *Bosphorus* (n 38), para 155.

[40] Eg, *Matthews* (n 37).

[41] Eg, *Cantoni v France*, Appl No 17862/91, 15 November 1996.

[42] Eg *M.S.S.* (n 31).

[43] See ECtHR, *Avotiņš v Latvia*, Appl No 17502/07, 23 May 2016, para 105; ECtHR, *Bivolaru and Moldovan v France*, Appl nos 40324/16 and 12623/17, 25 March 2021, para 98.

[44] *Bivolaru and Moldovan* (n 43) para 103.

[45] ibid, paras 338–40.

[46] Fink (n 24) 95.

[47] *Avotiņš v Latvia* (n 43) para 113.

the automatic and mechanical application of mutual-recognition mechanisms.[48] Rather, the Court requires, as a minimum, a review commensurate with the gravity of any serious allegation of human rights violations in order to ensure that the protection of those rights is not manifestly deficient.[49] In addition, the Court has also required Member States to correctly apply EU law, and in case of doubt on its application, they should refer the case to the CJEU.[50]

The EIBM is a shared competence of the EU and its Member States; in particular, the EU operates in this context through its agency Frontex, which coordinates the activities of Member States, other EU agencies and third countries. Significantly, the increased power of the agency does not affect the division of competences between the Union and the Member States regarding their international obligations.[51] It follows that Member States are responsible for their conduct during the agency's operations in breach of the ECHR. This, however, should be established on a case-by-case basis, with due regard to the circumstances of each situation.

The EIBM rests on instruments of secondary EU law that include human rights guarantees as included in the CFR, the ECHR, and other relevant international law instruments, such as the Refugee Convention or the CRC.[52] Where one of these instruments refers only to the CFR, by virtue of its Article 52(3), such protection should be interpreted as at least equivalent to that of the ECHR. Furthermore, the most recent Frontex Operational Plans also refer to relevant international law and fundamental rights guarantees.[53] All Member States participating in Frontex operations are thus bound by these obligations, including non-EU Schengen Member States. The latter, although not bound by the CFR, remain bound by relevant international human rights law instruments, such as the ECHR, the ICCPR and the Refugee Convention. All these instruments ensure the human rights compliance of all the actors participating in Frontex activities and in the management of the EU borders.

However, Fink rightly observes that the obligations of border officers participating in Frontex operations may originate not only in the mentioned legal instruments but also in the instructions received from the host state's authorities and from the agency.[54] The Operational Plans or the agency's Regulation do not provide any indication as to the ability of border guards to contravene instructions incompatible with the international obligations of the relevant authority.

[48] ibid, para 116.
[49] ibid, para 114.
[50] ECtHR, *Spasov v Romania*, Appl No 27122/14, 6 December 2022, para 97.
[51] Recital 20, Regulation (EU) 2019/1896 [2019] OJ L 295. See also Recital 25, Regulation (EU) 1052/2013 [2013] OJL 295/11.
[52] Art 4, SBC; Recitals 22–24, Arts 1 and 8(4), Directive 2008/115/EC; Arts 2(4), 20 (3) Regulation 1052/2013; Arts 1, 5(4), Art 46, 72(3), 80, 108–11, Annex 5, (3)(b), Regulation 2019/1896.
[53] OPLAN, *Joint Coordination Points, Sea*, 2018, para 2.3; OPLAN, *Join Operation Themis*, Amendment 1, 2018, paras 2.2 and 2.3; OPLAN, *Joint Coordination Points, Land*, LBS/03, 2016, para 3.1; OPLAN, *Joint Operation EPN Triton*, 2015/SBS/05, 2015, para 3.1 [On file with the author].
[54] Fink (n 24).

Regulation 2019/1896 introduced the duty of the coordinating officer to report to the executive director cases where instructions issued to teams by host Member States are not in compliance with fundamental rights and, where appropriate, to suggest the suspension or termination of an operation.[55] Nonetheless, it is not clear to what extent the executive director is under an obligation to terminate or suspend an operation in cases of human rights violations.

The ECtHR could hold that those operational instructions should, at any rate, comply with the human rights guarantees included in the legal or quasi-legal instruments from which they originate – that is, from the agency's regulation and operational plans. Yet, as highlighted in the previous parts of this study, those instruments suffer from several deficiencies in terms of human rights protection, not least with regard to the complaints mechanism recently included in the agency's legal framework.

All in all, it remains doubtful whether the legal framework surrounding Frontex activities would be considered as offering protection that is substantially and procedurally 'at least equivalent to that for which the Convention provides'.[56] Consequently, it seems conceivable that states' conduct during Frontex operations would require full scrutiny before the ECtHR.

IV. The Rules Governing the Attribution of an Internationally Wrongful Act in the Implementation of the EIBM

International responsibility arises from any conduct attributable to a state or international organisation that constitutes a breach of their international obligations. By and large, collective entities such as states and international organisations can only act with the intermediation of individuals. Attribution is therefore the legal operation aimed at imputing the conduct of an individual or group of individuals to a state or international organisation for the purposes of international law. An international wrongful act can be imputed directly to a state or international organisation that violates its international obligations, or it can be indirectly attributed to a state or international organisation that facilitated such a violation. The first case is often referred to as attribution of conduct, from which direct responsibility derives, while the second is labelled attribution of responsibility, from which indirect responsibility originates.[57]

Direct and indirect responsibilities differ as to the determination of these two constitutive elements of international responsibility. The fundamental difference

[55] Art 44(3)(d), Regulation 2019/1896.

[56] *Bosphorus* (n 38) para 155.

[57] For a clear differentiation of the two notions, see: JD Fry, 'Attribution of Responsibility' in André Nollkaemper and Ilias Plakokefalos (eds), *Principles of Shared Responsibility in International Law: An Appraisal of the State of the Art*, vol 1 (Cambridge, Cambridge University Press, 2014).

lies in the connection between the responsibility bearer and the breach of its international obligations. Namely, when it comes to direct responsibility, the international obligation breached pertains to the same entity breaching it. Therefore, direct responsibility implies the direct attribution of an actor's conduct in breach of its international obligations. Indirect responsibility, by contrast, is characterised by the distancing of these two elements, which are not linked straightforwardly.

In the following sections, I will explore the rules on attribution of international responsibility as included in the ILC's ARS and ARIO; I will then apply those general rules to the specific case of the EIBM as implemented by Frontex and the Member States during the agency's joint operations.

A caveat is in order. Given that the EU has not yet acceded to the ECHR and is not subject to any external human rights treaty body, all these observations are tentative. Hopefully, they will become useful in a more concrete fashion in the near future.

A. Direct Attribution of Conduct

The general assumption regarding responsibility for human rights violations occurring in the context of Frontex joint operations is that the principal responsibility rests on the Member State hosting an operation. As the host Member State retains primary responsibility for the management of its external borders, it is also primarily responsible for the potential wrongful outcomes of an operation. Notably, members of Frontex's border management teams are border guards of the host Member State, but more importantly, the degree of authority and control exercised by host states over an operation is substantial; this allows the attribution of conduct by deployed border management teams to the host state.

This section will show that Frontex joint operations are more intricate than is generally suggested by the abovementioned assumption. As seen in the previous part of this study, Frontex operates in a complex network of actors exercising various degrees and forms of control over border control activities. This complexity can be reflected in the legal framework governing international responsibility, which provides for the possibility of multiple attribution of conduct.

i. Exclusive Attribution of Responsibility to States

States, as autonomous legal persons, are only responsible for conduct which is attributable to them. In this respect, the most basic rule on attribution stipulates that acts or omissions of persons exercising a public function are attributed to the state, whereas the acts or omissions of private persons acting in their private capacity are not.[58] Under Article 4 ARS, the conduct of an organ of the state is attributable

[58] Olivier de Frouville, 'Attribution of Conduct to the State: Private Individuals' in James Crawford, Alain Pellet and Simon Olleson (eds), *The Law of International Responsibility* (Oxford, Oxford University Press, 2010).

to that state, irrespective of the formal status or the specific function (legislative, executive or judicial) that the organ is exercising within the state.[59] This is generally considered the most common basis for attribution established in the ARS, and it covers conduct by de jure organs.[60] This provision applies to border guards of a Member State or a third state hosting one of Frontex's joint operations; these officers would clearly be considered organs of the host state pursuant to Article 4 ARS.

The general rule of Article 4 knows, however, certain exceptions. There are situations where persons not officially identified as state organs may be authorised to exercise a public function, and therefore their conduct would be attributed to the state that conferred that authority to them. The first of these situations concerns private persons or entities that are not formally recognised as state organs but are empowered to exercise public functions. This is the case for persons or entities exercising elements of governmental authority as envisaged by Article 5 ARS.[61] Second, Article 6 ARS considers the conduct of organs of a state placed at the disposal of another state as imputable to the latter. A further exception to the general rule set in Article 4 is Article 7 ARS, which concerns the attribution to the state of conduct by de jure organs acting ultra vires. The common denominator of all these situations is the de iure relationship between the state and the person or entity, which is formally or at least effectively incorporated within the state's apparatus.[62] While these rules have in common the normative control of the state over the conduct of a person or entity,[63] Article 8 ARS provides for the attribution of conduct that does not result from a specific juridical connection to the state. This provision represents the main exception to the general rule providing for the non-imputability of private conduct to a state as it concerns the conduct of de facto organs of a state acting under its instruction, direction or control.[64]

For the present purposes, the most relevant of these rules is Article 6 ARS, concerning state organs placed at the disposal of other states. Following Article 6, the conduct of border guards of participating states is also attributable to the host state provided that three cumulative requirements are met.[65] First, the seconded

[59] Art 4, ARS, Commentary, para 5.

[60] de Frouville (n 58); Condorelli and Kress (n 17).

[61] Djamchid Momtaz, 'State Organs and Entities Empowered to Exercise Elements of Governmental Authority' in James Crawford, Alain Pellet and Simon Olleson (eds), *The Law of International Responsibility* (Oxford, Oxford University Press, 2010); Luigi Condorelli, 'L'imputation à l'État d'un Fait Internationalement Illicite: Solutions Classiques et Nouvelles Tendances' (1984) 189 *Collected Courses of the Hague Academy of International Law*.

[62] Condorelli and Kress (n 17) 230.

[63] See Andrés Delgado Casteleiro, *The International Responsibility of the European Union: From Competence to Normative Control* (Cambridge, Cambridge University Press, 2016).

[64] Other exceptions concern the attribution of conduct of 'agents of necessity' (Art 9, ARS), or insurrectional movements (Art 10, ARS), and conduct recognised and adopted by a state as its own (Art 11, ARS). See: de Frouville (n 58); Gérard Cahin, 'Attribution of Conduct to the State: Insurrectional Movements' in James Crawford, Alain Pellet and Simon Olleson (eds), *The Law of International Responsibility* (Oxford, Oxford University Press, 2010).

[65] Art 6, ARS, Commentary paras 2–5. See also: ILC, Report of the International Law Commission on the work of its twenty-sixth session, 1974, 290, para 18.

border guards should be considered as organs of the seconding state. This includes state organs as defined in the municipal law of the sending state.[66] Second, the conduct of the transferred organ must involve the exercise of elements of the governmental authority of the receiving State.[67] Third, this organ should be 'placed at the disposal' of the receiving state. This means that the transferred organ is 'acting with the consent, under the authority of and for the purposes of the receiving State'.[68] In this line, the ILC clarified that 'not only must the organ be appointed to perform functions appertaining to the State at whose disposal it is placed, but in performing the functions entrusted to it by the beneficiary State, the organ must also act in conjunction with the machinery of that State and under its exclusive direction and control, rather than on instructions from the sending State'.[69] The decisive element for the purposes of Article 6 is the authority that was responsible for the conduct of the organ in question, rather than the state apparatus to which it formally belonged or that within which it actually operates.[70]

These conditions seem to be met in the context of Frontex's joint operations. First, the seconded border guards from Member States participating in the operations are organs of the seconding state. An similar reasoning would apply to Frontex's statutory staff deployed in the host Member State.[71] The possibility of an international organisation placing its organs or agents at the disposal of a state was considered residual during the drafting of Article 6 ARS and was not included in the final text.[72] Nevertheless, the provision can apply to this situation by analogy.[73] During Frontex joint operations, the host state retains civil liability for damages created by its own officers, as well those created by Frontex staff.[74] Moreover, in case of criminal liability, the agency's staff should be treated as officials of the host Member State.[75] Second, border officers act with the consent, under the authority and for the purposes of the host Member State. While Member States 'ensure the management of their external borders and the enforcement of return decisions, in their own interests and in the common interest of all Member States',[76] they also bear 'the primary responsibility for the management of their sections of the external borders'.[77] Team members deployed

[66] Art 4(2), ARS.
[67] Art 6, ARS, Commentary, para 5.
[68] ibid, para 2.
[69] ibid, para 2. See also: Ago's Third Report on State Responsibility (n 14) 269, para 209.
[70] ibid, 269, paras 201–02.
[71] Art 55, Regulation 2019/1896.
[72] Cf: ILC, Report of the International Law Commission on the work of its twenty-sixth session, 1974, 286, para 1; ILC, First report on State responsibility, by Mr James Crawford, Special Rapporteur, UN Doc A/CN.4/490 and Add. 1–7, 46, para 231.
[73] See Francesco Francesco Messineo, 'Attribution of Conduct' in Andre Nollkaemper and Ilias Plakokefalos (eds), *Principles of Shared Responsibility in International Law: An Appraisal of the State of the Art* (Cambridge, Cambridge University Press, 2014); Fink (n 24) 122–23.
[74] Except in cases of gross negligence or willful misconduct. Art 84(2), Regulation 2019/1896.
[75] ibid, Art 85.
[76] ibid, Art 7(3).
[77] ibid, Art 7(1).

to host Member States are, therefore, essentially acting for the purposes of the host Member State. Yet, when team members from Frontex or its Member States are deployed in a third country, the answer to the question about the purposes of their activities is less straightforward. The agency's regulations and the model status agreements concluded between Frontex and third states are silent in this respect. However, the aim of their cooperation is 'to strengthen border management and enhance security at the EU's external borders'.[78] In this light, it is not clear whether team members deployed to a third country act for the purposes of the receiving state. Third, according to Regulation 2019/1896, deployed team members should always act under the instructions of the host Member State.[79] In the performance of their tasks, team members from Frontex and participating states must comply not only with international and EU law, but with the national law of the host Member State.[80]

The authority of the host state over Frontex joint operations may be limited in three main ways. First, the operational command over military assets remains with the Member State that contributed them.[81] Second, participating Member States retain disciplinary powers over their seconded team members.[82] Frontex statuary staff are also subject to the agency's disciplinary measures and provisions on the use of force.[83] Third, instructions issued by the host Member State should comply with the operational plan previously agreed upon by the host state and Frontex. The agency may communicate its views on these instructions, and the host Member State is bound to follow them 'to the extent possible'.[84]

Despite that, it seems overall possible to conclude that team members are generally 'placed at the disposal' of the host state. The responsibility for any human rights violations by team members is, therefore, ordinarily attributable to the host state.[85] As acknowledged by the ILC, however, there can also be situations where the organ of one state acts simultaneously on the instructions of its own and another state, or there may be a single entity which is a joint organ of several states.[86] In such cases, the conduct of the transferred organ could be attributed to both the sending and receiving state.

[78] Commission, European Border and Coast Guard: Launch of first ever joint operation outside the EU, Press Release, 21 May 2019, https://ec.europa.eu/commission/presscorner/detail/en/IP_19_2591.

[79] Art 43, Regulation 2019/1896.

[80] ibid, Art 82(3).

[81] See eg: OPLAN (Main Part), Joint Operation Themis, 2018, 23; OPLAN (Main Part), Joint Operation EPN Triton, 2015/SBS/05, 2015, 11; OPLAN (Main Part), Joint Operation EPN Poseidon Sea, 2015/SBS/07, 2015, 10; OPLAN (Main Part), Joint Operation EPN Hera, 2014/SBS/03, 2014, 9.

[82] Arts 43(5) and 51(5), Regulation 2019/1896.

[83] ibid, Art 55(5)(a).

[84] ibid, Art 43(2).

[85] Fink further differentiates between regular team members and those deployed on large assets. The latter are subject to the authority of both the host and the home states, and this would trigger the shared responsibility of both states. See: Fink (n 24) 125.

[86] Art 6, ARS, Commentary para 3; Ago's Third Report on State Responsibility (n 14) 201.

ii. Exclusive Attribution of Responsibility to the EU

Attribution of responsibility in the context of the EU has generated doctrinal controversies that are not yet firmly settled.[87] During the drafting process of the ARIO, the European Commission proposed to differentiate among various kinds of international organisations and supported the view according to which the special features of the EU called for the application of a lex specialis.[88] According to this view, the conduct of states implementing EU law should be considered as that of the EU since the organisation exercises normative control over its Member States. While the ILC rejected the Commission's position, it eventually adopted a lex specialis provision in Article 64 ARIO, probably with the EU in mind.[89]

That notwithstanding, the presence of a special rule of attribution for the EU seems objectionable from multiple angles. First, it seems incorrect to rely on the internal rules of an international organisation to establish the responsibility for a wrongful act, which should be determined according to international law. Second, in practice, such an interpretation would lead to the substantial impunity of all the actors involved in potential human rights violations, since the EU is not a party to most of the human rights treaties to which its Member States are subject. In this vein, the ECtHR has asserted that states cannot circumvent their ECHR obligations by transferring power to an international organisation.[90] However, as already observed, the Court also established that an action flowing from a state's membership to the EU could be justified to the extent that the organisation ensured a level of protection of fundamental rights considered equivalent to that of the ECHR, and in so far as the state was strictly implementing EU law.[91] On the other hand, states remain fully responsible where they are left with a margin of discretion in implementing their international obligations. For the purposes of the present discussion, it is worth remembering that a degree of discretion is left to Member States in implementing the EIBM. Member States retain the primary responsibility for the control of their borders and are free to conduct border control operations beyond the aegis of Frontex.[92] It seems therefore sensible to argue that they should

[87] Among the copious literature, see: Esa Paasivirta and Pieter Jan Kuijper, 'Does One Size Fit All?: The European Community and the Responsibility of International Organizations' (2005) 36 *Netherlands Yearbook of International Law* 169; Frank Hoffmeister, 'Litigating against the European Union and Its Member States–Who Responds under the ILC's Draft Articles on International Responsibility of International Organizations?' (2010) 21 *European Journal of International Law* 723; Andrés Delgado Casteleiro, *The International Responsibility of the European Union: From Competence to Normative Control* (Cambridge, Cambridge University Press, 2016); Jed Odermatt, *International Law and the European Union* (Cambridge, Cambridge University Press, 2021) ch 6.

[88] Comments and observations received from international organizations, UN Doc A/CN.4/637 and Add.1, 2011, 167.

[89] Art 64 ARIO, Commentary, para 2.

[90] *Matthews* (n 37) para 32; *Waite and Kennedy* (n 37) para 67.

[91] *Bosphorus* (n 39) paras 122 and 159–65.

[92] For instance, SAR activities are outside the remit of Frontex operations. See ch 3, s IV.C.i.

also retain the direct international responsibility flowing from their actions or omissions in the context of their border control operations.

In elaborating the ARIO, the ILC largely followed the model provided by the ARS. Mirroring Article 4 ARS, the general rule on the attribution of conduct in the ARIO is Article 6. Yet, this provision is more comprehensive than its correspondent in the ARS. Article 6 ARIO provides that the conduct of an organ or agent should be regarded as 'an act of that organisation under international law whatever position the organ or agent holds in respect of the organization'.[93] Article 2(c) ARIO identifies the 'organs' of an international organisation with 'any person or entity which has that status in accordance with the rules of the organization'; and Article 2(d) further specifies that the 'agents' of an international organisation are the officials or other persons or entities other than organs, who are 'charged by the organization with carrying out, or helping to carry out, one of its functions, and thus through whom the organization acts'. As the ARS, the ARIO leave it to the international organisation to define its own organs, whose conduct is attributable regardless of their position within the organisation itself.[94] The ICJ interpreted the term 'agent' in the 'most liberal sense' as 'any person through whom [the international organisation] acts'.[95] This broad definition, therefore, extends the scope of Article 6 ARIO to situations where the conduct of an agent is de iure or de facto connected to the organisation – corresponding respectively to Articles 5 and 8 ARS.[96]

In addition to Article 6, Article 7 ARIO governs the attribution of conduct to organs or agents placed at the disposal of an international organisation. According to this provision:

> The conduct of an organ of a State or an organ or agent of an international organization that is placed at the disposal of another international organization shall be considered under international law an act of the latter organization if the organization exercises effective control over that conduct.

While the expression 'placed at the disposal of' suggests a common element of control over the conduct of the transferred organ or agent, there are significant differences between Article 7 ARIO and its corresponding provision, Article 6 ARS. First, attribution under Article 7 ARIO is not limited to a specific kind of action. The provision does not require that the receiving organisation exercises 'elements of governmental authority', as such reference is unsuitable to international organisations.[97] Second, while Article 6 ARS requires exclusive direction and control over the seconded organ or agent, Article 7 ARIO refers to situations where the seconding state or organisation maintains to some extent a connection with the seconded agent or organ.[98] The conduct of organs or agents placed at the

[93] Art 6, ARIO.

[94] Art 6(2), ARIO; Art 2, ARIO, Commentary, paras 21–22.

[95] ICJ, *Reparation for Injuries Suffered in the Service of the United Nations*, Advisory Opinion of 11 April 1949, ICJ Reports 237, 177. Cited in Art 2 ARIO, Commentary, para 23.

[96] Art 6, ARIO, Commentary, paras 10–11.

[97] ibid, para 4.

[98] Art 7, ARIO, Commentary, para 1.

disposal of an international organisation is attributable to the latter where it exercises 'effective control' over them. In this sense, it is conceivable that both entities could exercise effective control over a given wrongful act, thus triggering their dual responsibility.[99] It follows – and this is the third difference – that the question to which Article 7 ARIO responds is not whether a conduct is attributable to an entity *vel non*, but *to which* of them it should be attributed and whether it could be attributed to both.

In sum, while the general rule set in Article 6 ARS covers the situation of organs or agents fully (de iure or de facto) seconded to an international organisation, Article 7 ARIO refers to situations where the seconding state or organisation maintains to some extent a connection with the seconded agent or organ, for instance by retaining disciplinary power or jurisdiction over criminal matters.[100] In this vein, the conduct of agents or organs over which an organisation exercises 'effective control' is attributable to the latter.

During Frontex joint operations, both the host state and the agency exercise a degree of influence over deployed personnel. The question is thus whether that influence reaches a degree of control sufficient to trigger the attribution of direct responsibility not only to the host state, but also to the agency. It is therefore necessary to look at who controls the actions of the various components of the border management teams deployed during Frontex operations.

Frontex's operational staff comprises statutory staff, staff seconded to the agency by the Member States for long- or short-term deployments and staff forming part of the reserve for rapid reaction for border interventions. First, since the entry into force of regulation 2019/1896, Frontex statutory staff deployed as members of border management teams are entrusted with executive powers.[101] Significantly, the regulation provides for the agency's liability in case of damages caused by its statutory staff in the performance of these powers.[102] Yet, some ambiguities remain, as all members of the teams are mandated to 'only perform tasks and exercise powers under instructions from and, as a general rule, in the presence of border guards or staff involved in return-related tasks of the host Member State'.[103] This rule is without prejudice to the Staff Regulations of Officials and the Conditions of Employment of Other Servants of the EU, which clarify that EU officials, such as Frontex staff, should 'neither seek nor take instructions from any government, authority, organisation or person outside this institution'.[104] This, in line with Article 6 ARIO, suggests that the conduct of its own agents is attributable to Frontex, and therefore to the EU. Second, team members seconded by Member

[99] ILC, Second report on responsibility of international organizations, by Mr Giorgio Gaja, Special Rapporteur, UN Doc A/CN.4/541, 2 April 2004, 14, para 48.

[100] Art 7, ARIO, Commentary, para 1.

[101] Art 55(7), Regulation 2019/1896.

[102] ibid, Recital 59, Art 97(4).

[103] ibid, Art 82(4).

[104] ibid, Art 95(1); Art 11, Regulation No 31 (EEC), 11 (EAEC) laying down the Staff Regulations of Officials and the Conditions of Employment of Other Servants of the European Economic Community and the European Atomic Energy Community, [1962] OJ 45, (as amended).

States receive instructions from and act in the presence of the host Member State's authorities. Therefore, where effective control is interpreted as exclusive command and control, the responsibility for any wrongful conduct performed by team members seconded from participating Member States is attributable to the host Member State, which retains the power to instruct them at the operational level.[105] The fact that participating Member States and Frontex retain disciplinary powers over their deployed personnel does not prevent the host state from exercising effective control over them.

Nonetheless, it has been pointed out that the Frontex's regulation does not explicitly exclude the agency's staff from instructing border management teams, nor does it include a reference to the exclusive obligation of host states' authorities to issue instructions.[106] Furthermore, Frontex has significant operational and decision-making powers relating to joint operations at the EU external borders. The agency's executive director draws up operational plans, which should receive the ex post facto agreement of the host Member State. The agency is also tasked with ensuring the efficient implementation and monitoring of these operational plans. This would suggest that Frontex could, to some extent, be involved in the command-and-control structure of the joint operations that it coordinates. Yet, a closer look at Frontex's operational plans suggests a different conclusion, for at the operational level, the command and control of team members remain with the host state.[107] It follows that effective control, traditionally understood as the power to give orders, remains with the host Member State, as does the ensuing responsibility. By contrast, Frontex's influence on the overall management of the EU's external borders may correspond to ultimate authority and control over the border management teams.

In sum, human rights violations resulting from the conduct of Frontex statutory staff are attributable to the agency, in so far as they are not seconded to the host Member State and they follow exclusively the agency's instructions. But violations occasioned by the conduct of Frontex border management teams' members are attributable to the host Member State, which retains the power to give orders to the teams. Finally, where a violation occurs as a result of the conduct of both a member of Frontex statutory staff and a team member deployed from a participating Member State, the ensuing responsibility could be attributed to each sending entity.

[105] Various scholars have reached this conclusion: Fink (n 24) 137–38; Roberta Mungianu, *Frontex and Non-Refoulement: The International Responsibility of the EU* (Cambridge, Cambridge University Press, 2016) 68–70; Efthymios Papastavridis, 'The EU and the Obligation of Non-Refoulement at Sea' in Francesca Ippolito and Seline Trevisanut (eds), *Migration in the Mediterranean: Mechanisms of International Cooperation* (Cambridge, Cambridge University Press, 2016) 256–57.

[106] Izabella Majcher, 'Human Rights Violations During EU Border Surveillance and Return Operations: Frontex's Shared Responsibility or Complicity?' [2015] *Silesian Journal of Legal Studies* 45, 61.

[107] Joint Operation Themis, 2018 para 8.1; Joint Coordination Points, Sea, 2018, para 8.1; Joint Coordination Points, Land, LBS/03, 2017, para 8.1; Joint Operation EPN Triton, 2015/SBS/05, 2015, para 8.1 [On file with the author].

iii. Effective Control and Multiple Attribution of Conduct

Besides the exclusive attribution of conduct or direct responsibility, international law also allows the possibility to attribute responsibility for wrongful acts to multiple entities.[108] This leads to a number of different interactions between the various rules of attribution previously identified in relation to independent subjects. Conduct can be attributed simultaneously to an individual, a state and an international organisation. This has been explained in terms of spheres of competence, layers of responsibility or, by analogy with quantum physics and the concept of complementarity.[109]

Multiple attribution of conduct mainly arises in two situations. First, the act or omission of one person or entity may be imputed to more than one subject simultaneously. This occurs, for instance, when a person or entity acts on behalf or under the instructions, direction or control of more than one state or international organisation at the same time, or it acts on behalf of one subject and under the instructions, direction, or control of another. Second, certain conduct may be jointly carried out by two or more persons or entities, each acting on behalf of a separate state or international organisation.[110] In this case, the joint conduct of different actors entails the responsibility of each of them as co-perpetrators.

The possibility of multiple attribution arises from the importance ascribed to the issue of effective control over certain wrongful conduct. Despite the acknowledgements of scholars[111] and the explicit recognition of the ILC,[112] the proper basis for such dual attribution is still a matter of debate, for it is unclear whether and in which circumstances effective control over specific conduct can be exercised simultaneously by two actors.[113]

While the legal framework seems to depict the host Member State as the scapegoat for all potential wrongs occurring during border control activities at its borders, Frontex and the other participating entities should not be relieved of all responsibilities. Besides situations where a potential human rights violation is caused by both Frontex's statutory staff and the host state's authorities, dual

[108] Art 47, ARS; Art 48, ARIO.

[109] Andrew Clapham, 'The Subject of Subjects and the Attribution of Attribution' in M Kohen, L Boisson de Chazournes and V Gowlland-Debbas (eds), *International Law and the Quest for Its Implementation: Liber Amicorum Vera Gowlland-Debbas* (Leiden, Brill, 2010) 57–58.

[110] See Messineo (n 73); Christian Dominicé, 'Attribution of Conduct to Multiple States and the Implication of a State in the Act of Another State' in James Crawford, Alain Pellet and Simon Olleson (eds), *Oxford Commentaries on International Law* (Oxford, Oxford University Press, 2010).

[111] Luigi Condorelli, 'De La Responsabilité Internationale de l'ONU et/Ou de l'État d'envoi Lors d'actions de Forces de Maintien de La Paix: L'écheveau de l'attribution (Double?) Devant Le Juge Néerlandais' (2014) 1 *QIL* 3; Tom Dannenbaum, 'Public Power and Preventive Responsibility: Attributing the Wrongs of International Joint Ventures' in Andre Nollkaemper and Jacobs Dov (eds), *Distribution of Responsibilities in International Law* (Cambridge, Cambridge University Press, 2015); André Nollkaemper, 'Dual Attribution Liability of the Netherlands for Conduct of Dutchbat in Srebrenica' (2011) 9 *Journal of International Criminal Justice* 1143.

[112] See Art 47, ARS; Art 48, ARIO. See also: Art 6, ARS, Commentary, para 3; Art 2, ARIO, Commentary, para 10; ARIO, Part V, Commentary, para 2.

[113] Nollkaemper (n 111) 1152–53.

attribution may also result from the conduct of an officer subject to the effective control of both the host state and Frontex simultaneously.

The effective control standard is relevant, in various ways, for the secondary rules of attribution of responsibility.[114] Nonetheless, given its ambiguous nature and scope of application, this test received multiple applications.[115] The effective control test first employed by the ICJ in relation to Article 8 ARS in the *Nicaragua* case,[116] as reaffirmed in the *Bosnia-Genocide* case,[117] requires the direction or the enforcement of the perpetration of a wrongful act.[118] Despite the apparent correspondence, this requirement should not be conflated with the 'effective control' required in the context of Article 7 ARIO. While both provisions require factual control over the impugned conduct, Article 8 ARS implies the exclusive attribution either to the state or to the non-state actor concerned, whereas Article 7 ARIO may give rise to concurrent attribution where both entities exercise operational control.[119]

The notion of effective control has most frequently been employed in the context of peace-keeping operations.[120] A prominent example is the now-infamous *Behrami* decision of the ECtHR.[121] The case concerned alleged human rights violations by both ECHR contracting states and troop-contributing countries to the UN and North Atlantic Treaty Organisation (NATO) operations in Kosovo. While purportedly applying the effective control test, it has been widely chronicled that the ECtHR employed the lower 'ultimate authority and control test'. The Court found that the UN Security Council exercised ultimate authority and control and that NATO retained effective command over the relevant operational matters, and therefore declared the case inadmissible for lack of competence.[122]

[114] James Crawford, *State Responsibility: The General Part* (Cambridge, Cambridge University Press, 2013) 244.

[115] Kristen E Boon, 'Are Control Tests Fit for the Future: The Slippage Problem in Attribution Doctrines' (2014) 15 *Melbourne Journal of International Law* 330.

[116] ICJ, *Case Concerning Military and Paramilitary Activities in and Against Nicaragua (Nicaragua v United States of America)*, Judgment of 27 June 1986, ICJ Reports 14.

[117] ICJ, *Application of the Convention on the Prevention and Punishment of the Crime of Genocide (Bosnia and Herzegovina v. Serbia and Montenegro)*, Judgment of 26 February 2007, ICJ Reports 43, para 413. See also: ICJ, *Armed Activities on the Territory of the Congo (DRC v Uganda)*, 19 December 2005, ICJ Reports 116, para 160. These cases famously dismissed the 'overall authority and control test' put forward by the ICTY in *The Prosecutor v Tadić*, Case No IT-94-1-A, Appeals Chamber, 15 July 1999. See most notably: Antonio Cassese, 'The Nicaragua and Tadić Tests Revisited in Light of the ICJ Judgment on Genocide in Bosnia' (2007) 18 *European Journal of International Law* 649.

[118] *Military and Paramilitary Activities in and Against Nicaragua* (n 116) para 115.

[119] Francesco Messineo, 'Attribution of Conduct' in Andre Nollkaemper and Ilias Plakokefalos (eds), *Principles of Shared Responsibility in International Law: An Appraisal of the State of the Art* (Cambridge, Cambridge University Press, 2014).

[120] ILC, Seventh report on responsibility of international organizations, by Mr Giorgio Gaja, Special Rapporteur, UN Doc A/CN.4/610, 27 March 2009, para 25.

[121] ECtHR, *Behrami and Behrami v France and Saramati v France, Germany and Norway*, Appl Nos 71412/01, 78166/01, 2 May 2007.

[122] ibid, para 140.

Many commentators criticised this decision,[123] and even the ILC distanced itself from the ECtHR interpretation of its rules on attribution.[124] The ECtHR had the occasion to partially correct its stance in the subsequent *Al-Jedda* case,[125] where the Court found that neither the 'ultimate authority and control' nor the 'effective control' tests were met and the alleged human rights violation was not attributable to the UN.[126] Significantly, this decision confirmed, a contrario, that dual attribution is possible under Article 7 ARIO.[127]

The possibility of dual attribution was, in fact, confirmed by the Dutch Supreme Court in the *Mustafic-Mujic*[128] and *Hasan Nuhanovic* cases,[129] in which the Netherlands was held responsible in relation to acts of Dutchbat seconded to the UN in the days following the fall of Srebrenica. These judgments, supported by various scholarly views,[130] determined that the responsibility for a given wrongful act lies with the entity best positioned to effectively and legally act to prevent the harmful result in question. Yet, it is too early to definitively conclude that effective control lies with the entity that has the power to prevent a given wrongful act. In particular, the relationship between Article 7 ARIO and Article 8 ARS remains particularly intricate. This complexity emerged more recently in the *Mothers of Srebrenica* case, where the Dutch Supreme Court rejected the previously established 'power to prevent' interpretation of effective control, and determined that 'effective control only exists in the event of "*actual participation of and directions given by that State*"'.[131]

In the context of the EIBM, the competences and responsibilities of various entities are intertwined and may be difficult to disentangle. This is due not only to the intricacy of the interaction between various layers of the EU administrative

[123] Pierre Klein, 'Responsabilité Pour Les Faits Commis Dans Le Cadre d'opérations de Paix et Étendue Du Pouvoir de Contrôle de La Cour Européenne Des Droits de l'homme: Quelques Considérations Critiques Sur l'arrêt Behrami et Saramati' (2007) 53 *Annuaire français de droit international* 43; Guglielmo Verdirame, 'Breaches of the European Convention on Human Rights Resulting from the Conduct of International Organisations' (2008) 2 *European Human Rights Law Review* 209; Pasquale De Sena and Maria Chiara Vitucci, 'The European Courts and the Security Council: Between Dédoublement Fonctionnel and Balancing of Values' (2009) 20 *European Journal of International Law* 193.

[124] Art 7, ARIO, Commentary, para 10.

[125] ECtHR, *Al-Jedda v the United Kingdom*, Appl No 27021/08, 11 July 2011.

[126] ibid, para 80.

[127] Francesco Messineo, 'Things Could Only Get Better: Al-Jedda beyond Behrami Agora: The Al-Jedda & Al-Skeini Cases before the European Court of Human Rights' (2011) 50 *Military Law and Law of War Review* 321.

[128] Supreme Court of the Netherlands, *The State of the Netherlands v Mustafic-Mujic*, Case No 12/03329, 6 September 2013.

[129] Supreme Court of the Netherlands, *The State of the Netherlands v Hasan Nuhanovic*, Case No 12/03324, 6 September 2013.

[130] See Tom Dannenbaum, 'Translating the Standard of Effective Control into a System of Effective Accountability: How Liability Should Be Apportioned for Violations of Human Rights by Member State Troop Contingents Serving as United Nations Peacekeepers' (2010) 51 *Harvard International Law Journal* 113; Dannenbaum (n 111).

[131] Supreme Court of the Netherlands, *Mothers of Srebrenica Association et al v The Netherlands*, Supreme Court, 19 July 2019, para 3.5.3. For further comments, see: Cedric Ryngaert and Otto

system, but also to the lack of transparency in which many of these activities take place. Given this complexity, the formal command-and-control structure in which EU agencies, Member States, and third countries cooperate should not be the only element to consider while assessing their responsibilities. According to the ILC, 'the factual control that is exercised over the specific conduct taken by the organ or agent placed at the receiving organization's disposal' is the main criterion for attribution of responsibility.[132] Put differently, effective control is triggered not only by the general and abstract possibility that Frontex or a state intervenes to order border guards to perform their tasks in a particular way. Rather, it is the specific factual situation in which the agency and the Member States are involved with the EIBM that triggers effective control. In this sense, effective control is understood here as the normative and factual ability to prevent a wrongful outcome.

Frontex's influence over the EIBM and its concrete implementation are far from negligible. From this influence may emerge the ability of the agency (and the EU) to prevent potential human rights violations occurring during border control operations. First and foremost, the agency has the ability (and to some extent the legal duty) to prevent human rights violations potentially occurring during its operations, for instance, through a decision by its executive director to terminate, suspend, or not launch activities.[133] This ability to prevent is further supported by the fact that the agency controls the selection and training of border management teams. While Member States should contribute a certain number of staff, the agency's management board decides on the specific profiles and the numbers of operational staff needed.[134] Furthermore, the executive director draws up a list of technical equipment and staff profiles required for each joint operation. This should be done in cooperation with the host Member State, but it is not sure whether this is a concerted decision or a decision requiring the final approval of the host state.[135] The agency is also mandated to develop specific training programmes tailored to the functions of border guards deployed during its activities.[136] This may result in a significant degree of control over the conduct of team members. In this respect, effective control on the part of Frontex may be understood as the ability to ensure compliance with EU and international law in the execution of legitimate orders.

The impact of Frontex's operational and administrative activities on the overall implementation and supervision of the EIBM should not be overlooked. It is Frontex's executive director who draws up each operational plan for joint operations.[137] Based on its vulnerability assessments, moreover, the agency may

Spijkers, 'The End of the Road: State Liability for Acts of UN Peacekeeping Contingents After the Dutch Supreme Court's Judgment in Mothers of Srebrenica (2019)' (2019) 66 *Netherlands International Law Review* 537.

[132] Art 7, ARIO, Commentary, para 4.
[133] Regulation 2019/1896, Art 46.
[134] ibid, Art 100(2)(i).
[135] ibid, Art 38(2).
[136] ibid, Art 62.
[137] ibid, Art 38.

also recommend that a Member State requests the launch or adjustment of joint operations, rapid border interventions or any other relevant actions.[138] Frontex enjoys a large margin of appreciation in relation to its vulnerability assessments, which in turn significantly impact the implementation of the EIBM in general, and individual operations more precisely. Suppose the concerned Member State does not comply with the agency's recommendations within the prescribed time limit. In that case, the Frontex management board will adopt a binding decision setting out the necessary measures to be taken by the Member State concerned, as well as the time limit for their implementation. If, again, the Member State does not duly implement such measures, the management board shall notify the Council and the Commission,[139] which in turn may take further action, including deploying Frontex teams and – as a last resort – reintroducing border controls at EU internal borders in accordance with Article 29 of the SBC.[140]

In terms of supervision, the agency is mandated to 'ensure proper and effective monitoring not only through situational awareness and risk analysis, but also through the presence of experts from its own staff in Member States'.[141] Significantly, concerning the protection of fundamental rights, Frontex coordinating officers monitor the correct implementation of each operational plan in cooperation with the fundamental rights monitors and report to the executive director.[142] The presence of Frontex liaison officers in Member States to monitor their border control activities and their reporting duties in connection to the vulnerability assessment further supports the view according to which the agency has gained important leverage in the overall configuration of the management of Member States' borders.[143] The agency's ability to take preventive actions in human rights protection is buttressed by the concomitant supervision of the FRO.[144]

Frontex's control of the planning and implementation of joint operations at the EU external borders and its supervision capabilities go well beyond mere overall influence. Rather, they are often framed in terms of binding decisions requiring a certain level of legal authority.[145] Frontex's decisions may also have a concrete impact on the specific conduct of border guards on the ground. This suggests that the agency is both normatively and concretely capable of preventing potential human rights violations from occurring during the implementation of the EIBM. That said, if one accepts the 'power to prevent' approach in establishing effective control, one may also find that human rights violations occurring during Frontex operations could, in some circumstances, be attributable to both the host Member State and the agency simultaneously.

[138] ibid, Art 41.
[139] ibid, Art 32.
[140] ibid, Art 42(3) and (10).
[141] ibid, Recital 42.
[142] ibid, Arts 44(3)(b) and 110.
[143] ibid, Art 31.
[144] ibid, Arts 108 and 109.
[145] Ch 2, s IV.C.

In conclusion, dual or multiple attributions of the same wrongful conduct emerge as the most appropriate solution to fairly allocate responsibility to each participating entity in the kind of multi-actor situations in which the EIBM is implemented, particularly Frontex joint operations. Yet, the legal basis for such a multiple attribution, concerning more specifically the effective control requirement, remains open to different interpretations.

B. Indirect Attribution of Responsibility

The bilateral paradigm requiring a direct connection between the responsibility bearer and the conduct in breach of its international obligations is no longer the dominant feature of international responsibility. Increasingly, the breach of an international obligation results from a network of relations between various international actors operating in complex and often opaque schemes and arrangements.[146] In this context, the bearer of responsibility does not correspond to the actor whose conduct directly caused the wrongful outcome.[147] The idea of holding a subject of international law responsible for wrongful acts not directly linked to its own conduct is relatively recent and is mainly due to the growing interdependence of the international society.[148]

There are two main forms of implication of a state or an international organisation in the internationally wrongful act of another. The first is the facilitation of the wrongful act (complicity); the second is the direction or coercion of another state or international organisation to commit an international wrong (derivative responsibility). Articles 16 ARS and 14 and 58 ARIO establish responsibility for aid or assistance provided in the commission of an internationally wrongful act by another entity. Articles 17 ARS and 15 and 59 ARIO determine responsibility for direction or control of another entity. Articles 18 ARS and 16 and 60 ARIO concern coercion in the commission of an internationally wrongful act.

These forms of indirect responsibility may be relevant to the integrated management of the EU external borders implemented by EU Member States under the

[146] André Nollkaemper and Dov Jacobs, 'Shared Responsibility in International Law: A Conceptual Framework' (2012) 34 *Michigan Journal of International Law* 359.

[147] Cf, Art 1, ARS; Art 1, ARIO. According to Nedeski and Nollkaemper, the ILC intended to broaden the scope of Art 1, ARIO, compared to Art 1 ARS, in order to include situations of responsibility of international organisations for acts other than their own. See Nataša Nedeski and André Nollkaemper, 'Responsibility of International Organizations "in Connection with Acts of States"' (2012) 9 *International Organizations Law Review* 33, 41–42; Bernhard Graefrath, 'Complicity in the Law of International Responsibility' (1996) 29 *Revue Belge de Droit International* 370, 371; Nikolaos Voulgaris, *Allocating International Responsibility Between Member States and International Organisations* (Oxford, Hart Publishing, 2019) 90.

[148] Georges Abi-Saab, 'Whither the International Community?' (1998) 9 *European Journal of International Law* 248; Pierre-Marie Dupuy, 'International Law: Torn between Coexistence, Cooperation and Globalization. General Conclusions' (1998) 9 *European Journal of International Law* 278; Nollkaemper and Jacobs (n 146).

aegis of Frontex. The agency, EU Member States, or third states may facilitate the wrongful acts of one another during border control joint operations. At the same time, the EU or Frontex may be found to direct or control the actions of states participating in joint operations at the EU external borders. The following sections will discuss the circumstances under which Frontex or EU Member States may be indirectly responsible for conduct associated with human rights violations occurring during border control activities.

i. Derivative Responsibility

The first form of indirect responsibility is that of 'direction and control' or 'coercion' over the wrongful act of another entity.[149] The concepts of direction and control are closely related to each other. Control refers to cases of 'domination over the commission of wrongful conduct' and not simply the exercise of influence or supervision. Similarly, the term direction does not encompass mere incitement or suggestion, but rather denotes the 'actual direction of an operative kind'.[150] Coercion, on the other hand, refers to 'conduct which forces the will of the coerced State … giving it no effective choice but to comply with the wishes of the coercing State'.[151]

The common feature of both the provisions on direction and control and coercion is the restriction of freedom imposed by a state or international organisation over another. Hence, the ILC's Special Rapporteur Roberto Ago proposed a single provision combining both instances of direction and control and coercion,[152] which here are analysed together under the label 'derivative responsibility', to distinguish them from situations of complicity where the responsibility bearer is to some extent involved in the offence.[153] Indeed, the dividing line between complicity and other instances of indirect responsibility lies with the freedom of the entity carrying out the internationally wrongful conduct and the participation of the responsibility bearer. Participation in the commission of a wrongful act freely perpetrated by another state or international organisation underlies the complicity model. In the case of direction and control or coercion, while the wrongful conduct remains that of the directed or coerced entity, the latter is no longer free to choose the course of action to be taken in a given situation.

Therefore, the crucial question is what constitutes an impairment of freedom for derivative responsibility. In the ARS, it seems that the restriction of freedom must create a factual relationship of domination so that one state is effectively dependent on another.[154] The responsibility of the dominant state can only be

[149] See respectively: Arts 17, ARS and 15 and 59, ARIO; Arts 18, ARS and 16 and 60, ARIO.
[150] Art 17, ARS, Commentary, para 7.
[151] Art 18, ARS, Commentary, para 2.
[152] Eighth Report on State Responsibility by Mr Roberto Ago, Special Rapporteur, Yearbook of the International Law Commission, 1979, 2(1) A/CN.4/SER.A/1979/Add.l, Part Two, paras 25–26.
[153] For a similar approach, see: Voulgaris (n 147) 108–23.
[154] Art 17, ARS, Commentary, para 7.

engaged if its direction and control played a decisive role in the commission of the internationally wrongful act by another state. This rigorous requirement seems warranted as in principle a state is responsible for its own acts, while the transfer of responsibility to others is the exception to the general rule. With international organisations, not only the factual but also legal relationships of direction and control may give rise to derivative responsibility. In this sense, the binding decisions of international organisations may represent a form of direction and control insofar as they do not leave any margin of discretion to Member States.[155]

As previously discussed, Frontex exercises a considerable influence on the overall implementation of the EIBM, while border guards act under the instructions of the host Member State. Concretely, the officers of the host Member State instruct guest officers from participating states and Frontex. Thus, based on the specific provisions on command and control included in each Operational Plan, it might be possible to argue that the host state, in some specific situations, could direct the activities of guest officers. It might, however, be challenging to argue that Frontex or participating states were severely impaired in the exercise of their freedom.

In turn, Frontex may, in specific circumstances, impose the implementation of certain measures on a Member State it considers unable to carry out all border management tasks.[156] Yet, those measures are generally taken in consultation with the state concerned, and where there is no cooperation on its part, the Commission may reintroduce border control at internal borders.[157] In this sense, the EU and its agency, Frontex, can effectively guide Member States in their management of the EU external borders – yet these remain national borders over which each Member State retains its sovereignty and primary responsibility.[158]

ii. Complicity

Given the peculiarity of situations where one entity can limit another entity's freedom, questions of derivative responsibility may arise only in exceptional circumstances. Thus, in the context of Frontex joint operations, the most relevant question revolves around the attribution of responsibility for complicity in a wrongful act occurring during border control activities performed by another actor.

Namely, two main situations can be identified in which the participation of states and the EU agency become relevant for questions of aid or assistance. The first concerns cases in which Frontex can be considered as assisting a state (an EU Member State or a third state) hosting its joint operations or receiving its technical or financial aid. The second and third scenarios concern the

[155] Art 15, ARIO, Commentary, para 4.
[156] Arts 32 and 42, Regulation 2019/1896.
[157] See ibid, Art 42(10) and SBC, Art 29.
[158] Art 7(1), Regulation 2019/1896. See also Arts 72, 73 and 77(3), TFEU.

complicity of states either hosting or participating in Frontex's joint operations at the external borders of the EU.

According to the ILC, a state or an international organisation that aids or assists another state or an international organisation in the commission of an internationally wrongful act is internationally responsible for doing so if: (a) it does so with knowledge of the circumstances of the internationally wrongful act; and (b) the act would be internationally wrongful if committed by the assisting state or international organisation.[159]

The scope of application of the 'aid and assistance' provisions in the ARS and ARIO is circumscribed in a threefold way. First, 'the aid or assistance must be given with a view to facilitating the commission of the wrongful act, and must actually do so'.[160] Second, the aid or assistance must be given with knowledge or intent to facilitate the commission of the internationally wrongful act.[161] Third, the provisions on aiding and assistance apply only where both the assisting and the assisted state or international organisation are bound by the same international obligation.[162] The strict requirements of complicity in the ILC's formulation have been the subject of abundant doctrinal discussion.[163] It is not the objective of this section to delineate a complete theory of complicity, but it is worth recollecting how the doctrine has interpreted Articles 16 ARS and 14 and 58 ARIO and the trends that tried to temper the stringency of the abovementioned requirements.

First, it is generally considered that the aid or assistance provided must be material, rather than merely psychological, for incitement of any kind is, in principle, regarded as a permissible interference under international law.[164] The nature of the aid or assistance, however, is not explicitly specified in the ILC's ARS or ARIO. It follows that whether material, political, legal or otherwise, the aid or assistance triggers responsibility as far as it can be determined that it facilitates the commission of the internationally wrongful act by another international legal person.[165] Furthermore, for international responsibility to arise, aid or assistance

[159] See Arts 16, ARS and 14, ARIO.

[160] Art 16, ARS, Commentary, para 3.

[161] Art 16(a), ARS.

[162] Art 16, ARS (b) and 14, ARIO (b).

[163] Helmut Philipp Aust, *Complicity and the Law of State Responsibility*, vol 81 (Cambridge, Cambridge University Press, 2011); Vladyslav Lanovoy, *Complicity and Its Limits in the Law of International Responsibility* (Oxford, Bloomsbury Publishing, 2016); Miles Jackson, *State Complicity in the Internationally Wrongful Act of Another State* (Oxford, Oxford University Press, 2015); Giuseppe Puma, *Complicità di Stati nell'illecito internazionale* (Turin, Giappichelli, 2018).

[164] ILC, Seventh report on State Responsibility by Mr Roberto Ago, Special Rapporteur – the internationally wrongful act of the State, source of international responsibility, UN Doc A/CN.4/307 and Add.1 & 2 and Corr.1 & 2, vol I (1) 1978, paras 62–63; Second report on State responsibility, by Mr James Crawford, Special Rapporteur, UN Doc A/CN.4/498 and Add.1–4, 1999, para 213. This assumption has been challenged, however. See: Miles Jackson, 'State Instigation in International Law: A General Principle Transposed' (2019) 30 *European Journal of International Law* 391.

[165] See generally: Vladyslav Lanovoy, 'Complicity in an Internationally Wrongful Act' in André Nollkaemper and Ilias Plakokefalos (eds), *Principles of Shared Responsibility in International Law: An Appraisal of the State of the Art* (Cambridge, Cambridge University Press, 2014).

should 'contribute significantly' to the commission of the wrongful act.[166] In this sense, the degree and extent of aid and assistance are particularly relevant: on one hand, if an entity's involvement is too scarce it would result in mere incitement; on the other hand, if its level of contribution exceeds, the same entity stops being an accomplice and becomes a co-perpetrator of the wrongful conduct, jointly and severally responsible for it.[167]

Second, the ILC has limited the scope of the provision on aid or assistance by adding a mental element that informs the relationship between the assisting state and the occurrence of the internationally wrongful outcome. Namely, the aid or assistance must be given 'with knowledge of the circumstances of the internationally wrongful act'.[168] The ILC explained that although the contribution should not be indispensable to the commission of an internationally wrongful act, it must be given 'with a view to facilitating the commission of the wrongful act, and must actually do so'.[169] This expression has proven particularly controversial, for in principle the ARS and the ARIO do not include any fault element.[170] Some commentators favour the prescription of wrongful intent, for a more comprehensive standard might deter beneficial forms of international cooperation.[171] Nevertheless, it has been pointed out that it is difficult, if not impossible, to establish the intentions of collective entities such as states or international organisations.[172] If states and international organisations 'have no wills except the wills of the individual human beings who direct their affairs',[173] their intentions, as the expression of their wills, are deprived of any subjective volition to commit an internationally wrongful act. In this line, the requirement of intent seems unnecessary and overly restrictive.[174] Palchetti has argued that the ILC's commentary simply means that aiding and assisting must be a deliberate act, without necessarily requiring that the complicit state be aware of the ultimate purpose of the assisted entity.[175] Recently, the Guiding Principles on Shared Responsibility in International Law proposed an even more flexible mental element, where the requirement of knowledge should be considered 'satisfied

[166] Art 16, ARS, Commentary, para 5; Art 14 ARIO, Commentary, para 4.

[167] Jackson (n 163) 158.

[168] Art 16(a), ARS.

[169] Art 16, ARS, Commentary, para 5.

[170] Art 2, ARS, Commentary, para 10.

[171] See most notably: Georg Nolte and Helmut Philipp Aust, 'Equivocal Helpers – Complicit States, Mixed Messages and International Law' (2009) 58 *International & Comparative Law Quarterly* 1, 31; Graefrath (n 147); Crawford (n 114) 407–08; Voulgaris (n 147) 94.

[172] The proof of intentionality would establish that a state not only knew that its assistance would be used to infringe upon an international obligation of another state, but that it provided assistance precisely for that purpose. See: Lanovoy (n 163), 102; Jackson (n 163) 160.

[173] Andrew Clapham, *Brierly's Law of Nations: An Introduction to the Role of International Law in International Relations* (Oxford, Oxford University Press, 2012) 52.

[174] Jackson (n 163) 160–61; Lanovoy (n 163) 102–03.

[175] Paolo Palchetti, 'State Responsibility for Complicity in Genocide' in Paola Gaeta (ed), *The UN Genocide Convention: A Commentary* (Oxford, Oxford University Press, 2009) 347.

when an international person knew or should have known the circumstances of the internationally wrongful act'.[176]

Third, the scope of application of the provisions on aiding and assistance is delimited by the requirement that both the assisting and the assisted state or international organisation are bound by the same international obligation.[177] The inclusion of an opposability requirement has been criticised, for it would allow the impunity of an otherwise complicit state on the basis that it is bound by a different rule from the one infringed by the assisted state.[178] Moreover, the opposability requirement runs the risk of encouraging third states to abuse their rights in breach of the principle of good faith. In fact, while a treaty is *res inter alios acta* for third parties who remain free to behave as they please,[179] this discretion is not absolute. The arbitrary or unreasonable exercise of rights and discretions may infringe upon the rights of others, and this may result in an abuse of rights when state sovereignty is exercised in bad faith.[180] As such, the 'bilateralisation of complicity' imposed by the opposability requirement fails to capture the social needs of the international legal system.[181] In this respect, Crawford considered that, without the inclusion of the opposability requirement, the provisions on aid or assistance 'could become a vehicle by which the effects of well-publicized bilateral obligations are given universal extension'.[182] Yet he clarified that what is required by Article 16(b) ARS is not the identity of the norm breached, but rather that the impugned conduct would have constituted a wrongful act for both the assisted and the assisting state, irrespective of the source of the international obligation breached.[183]

Finally, concerning Member States' complicity in the internationally wrongful acts of international organisations of which they are members, Article 58(2) ARIO establishes that '[a]n act by a State member of an international organisation done in accordance with the rules of the organisation does not *as such* engage the international responsibility of that State'.[184] Significantly, the fact that a state does not per se incur indirect responsibility for acting in accordance with the rules of the international organisation to which it belongs does not exclude its direct responsibility, for that state is not absolved from its international obligations.

[176] André Nollkaemper and others, 'Guiding Principles on Shared Responsibility in International Law' (2020) 31 *European Journal of International Law* 15, Principle 6.
[177] Art 16, ARS (b) and 14, ARIO (b).
[178] Aust (n 163) 264–65.
[179] Vienna Convention on the Law of Treaties, 155 UNTS 331, 22 May 1969.
[180] Georg Schwarzenberger, 'Uses and Abuses of the "Abuse of Rights" in International Law' (1956) 42 *Transactions of the Grotius Society* 147; Graham DS Taylor, 'The Content of the Rule Against Abuse of Rights in International Law' (1972) 46 *British Yearbook of International Law* 323; Alexandre Kiss, 'Abuse of Rights' (1992) 1 *Encyclopedia of Public International Law* 4; Michael Byers, 'Abuse of Rights: An Old Principle, A New Age' (2001) 47 *McGill Law Journal* 389.
[181] Lanovoy (n 163) 157–60; Voulgaris (n 147) 96.
[182] Crawford (n 114) 410.
[183] ibid.
[184] Emphasis added.

a. EU Complicity

In the case of Frontex, the three requirements for complicity to arise may be fulfilled, depending on the circumstances of the case and the international obligations of the state the agency is supporting. First, it should be proven that Frontex (the EU) aided or assisted a state in the commission of an offence. The state can be a Member State or a third state hosting a joint operation. Typically, aid or assistance involves material, logistical, technical, or financial support.[185] The aid provided should not be essential, but significant for the commission of the offence. While Jackson proposes to extend the application of the prohibition of complicity to instances of instigation,[186] Lanovoy observes that complicity may originate both from explicit treaty obligations and less formal cooperation.[187] This cooperation may encompass exchanges of intelligence, operational collaboration, common training and the provision of technical equipment used to commit human rights violations by the receiving state. The logistical, financial and technical aid provided by Frontex represents an incentive for Member States to participate in its joint operations.[188] The same holds with regard to working arrangements and status agreements with third states.[189] The aid provided should contribute significantly to the commission of the offence, but it does not need to be essential. The support provided by Frontex to host states may facilitate human rights violations in cases of their occurrence during a joint operation. The financial support of the EU and its Member States to third states, most notably Libya, Turkey and other countries,[190] coupled, for instance, with the common training of the Libyan coast guard developed by EUBAM, Frontex and the Italian authorities,[191] may also amount to aid or assistance in the event of human rights violations occurring in the context of the border control activities of the receiving states.[192]

Second, it should be proven that Frontex officers were aware of the human rights violations that would take place during the specific activity in which it was involved. Importantly, the answer to this question depends on the interpretation of the expression 'with knowledge of the circumstances of the internationally wrongful act'. Den Heijer noted that without a high threshold of knowledge, 'practically

[185] Art 14, ARIO, Commentary para 6; ILC, Third report on responsibility of international organizations, by Mr Giorgio Gaja, Special Rapporteur, UN Doc A/CN.4/553, 13 May 2005, para 28.

[186] Miles Jackson, 'State Instigation in International Law: A General Principle Transposed' (2017) 30 *European Journal of International Law* 391.

[187] Lanovoy (n 165) 141.

[188] Majcher (n 106) 67–68.

[189] See ch 2, s VI.D.

[190] The EU Emergency Trust Fund for Africa is a notable example in this sense. See Commission, Update on state of play of external cooperation in the field of migration policy, Council doc 9132/22, LIMITE, 20 May 2022.

[191] Bilateral Mission of Assistance and Support in Libya (MIASIT), 2018; Joint Pilot Project EUBAM – FRONTEX – Italy for the Libyan General Administration for Coastal Security (GACS), 21 February 2019, https://eeas.europa.eu/delegations/togo/58534/joint-pilot-project-eubam-%E2%80%93-frontex-%E2%80%93-italy-libyan-general-administration-coastal-security_it.

[192] See generally Fazzini Anna, *L'esternalizzazione delle frontiere e la responsabilità degli stati europei. Il caso Italia-Libia* (Naples, Editoriale Scientifica, 2023).

every form of contact with another state which is engaged in human rights violations may be labeled as assistance'.[193] The link between the aid and the wrongful conduct should thus be clear and unequivocal.[194] Arguably, however, the required knowledge or intention could be inferred from the cooperation between the relevant actors. Along these lines, the cognitive element requires, at a minimum, that the complicit state or organisation is aware of the circumstances of the wrongful act.

The presence of the coordinating officer in Frontex joint operations ensures that the agency has appropriate knowledge of the circumstances in which each operation is carried out. The awareness of the circumstances in which potential human rights violations may occur is buttressed by the coordinating officer's obligation to report to the executive director in case of non-compliance with the operational plan, especially regarding fundamental rights.[195] In turn, the executive director may decide to suspend or terminate the operation.[196] Furthermore, the fundamental rights officer monitors and investigates the agency's fundamental rights compliance. In doing so, it is assisted by fundamental rights monitors assigned to each operation and any relevant operational activity.[197] Consequently, it would be difficult to maintain that the agency was unaware of the circumstances of a wrongful act occurring during one of its activities.

More problematic would be to substantiate the required level of knowledge with respect to the EU financial assistance or training of third states' border guards.[198] One possibility would be to rely on the information concerning the general situation of the receiving country and that of the potential victims. As noted by the ECtHR in *Hirsi* regarding the absolute prohibition of torture and *refoulement*, the available information provided by multiple reliable sources may prove that the situation in the receiving country was known or ought to have been known to the EU authorities.[199] Yet, this level of knowledge, typically required by due diligence obligations, seems too low when it comes to complicity, which requires positive knowledge of the circumstances.[200]

Third, the opposability requirement implies that both Frontex and the assisted state breached the same international obligation. As discussed above, this

[193] Maarten den Heijer, *Europe and Extraterritorial Asylum* (Oxford, Hart Publishing, 2012) 106–07.
[194] Art 16 ARS, Commentary, para 5.
[195] Regulation 2019/1896, Art 44.
[196] ibid, Art 46.
[197] ibid, Arts 109 and 110 (3).
[198] With regard to the EU training of the Libyan Coast Guard, it has been observed that as it is impossible to prove that the EU training aimed at facilitating the commission of a wrongful act, no EU responsibility would ensue. Pierre d'Argent and Melinda Kuritzky, 'Refoulement by Proxy? The Mediterranean Migrant Crisis and the Training of Libyan Coast Guards by EUNAVFOR MED Operation Sophia' (2017) 47 *Israel Yearbook on Human Rights* 233. With regard to the Italian support to Libya, however, see: Giuseppe Pascale, 'Is Italy Internationally Responsible for the Gross Human Rights Violations against Migrants in Libya?' [2019] *QIL* 35.
[199] ECtHR, *Hirsi Jamaa and Others v Italy*, Appl No 27765/09, 23 February 2012, para 131.
[200] See below, s IV.D.

requirement may be questionable from both policy and legal perspectives. Frontex is bound by EU law and the CFR, but not by the ECHR or any other international human rights treaty that could be relevant in the context of border control measures. Thus, in joint operations launched by Frontex in the territory of EU Member States, all participating entities are bound by EU law and the CFR – but only Member States are bound by the major international human rights treaties as well as by the ECHR, for Frontex (the EU) is not yet party to them. Nonetheless, the obligations included in the EU treaties and the CFR correspond to a large extent to the international human rights law obligations of Member States.[201] Furthermore, both the EU and its Member States are bound by customary international law, most notably by the prohibition of torture and *refoulement*, the right to life and the prohibition of collective expulsion. As the complicit conduct would entail a violation of an international obligation of both the EU and the Member States hosting or participating in a joint operation, the opposability requirement would be fulfilled. Similarly, when Frontex operates in the territory of third states, as most of them are members of the Council of Europe, both the host and participating states are bound by the same international obligations. In practice, however, as the EU is not yet a party to the ECHR, it is not certain that the ECtHR would extend its competence to judge the indirect responsibility generated by a non-contracting entity.

When it comes to cooperation with third states that are parties neither to the ECHR nor to the Refugee Convention, such as Libya, it might be more difficult to substantiate the fulfilment of the opposability requirement before the ECtHR. However, Libya is a party to the ICCPR, the CAT and the CRC,[202] and norms of customary international law also bind it, therefore, the opposability requirement could be fulfilled with respect to many human rights obligations. The most promising litigation venue seems to lead to UN Treaty Bodies. Against this background, two main recommendations can be drawn from these observations. First, the EU should accede to the ECHR; second, in the meantime, the EU should refrain from concluding status agreements with countries that are not parties to the Council of Europe.

b. State Complicity

The indirect responsibility of the host state for a breach committed by Frontex or participating states depends on the three elements set out above. Regarding the material element, it seems sufficient to note that the host state provides logistical

[201] See ch 3, s II.

[202] While Libya is a party to eight of the core international human rights treaties (ICERD, ICCPR, ICESCR, CEDAW, CAT, CRC, ICRMW and CRPD) it is a party only to the ICCPR optional protocol, which means that an individual can bring a claim against Libya only before the HRC. See: OHCHR, *Ratification Status*, https://tbinternet.ohchr.org/_layouts/15/TreatyBodyExternal/Treaty.aspx?CountryID=99&Lang=EN.

and technical structures to run the operation. In relation to participating states, even though their contribution is not essential, it may still be significant for the concrete implementation of Frontex operations. Yet, where their contribution is minimal and has no relevant impact on the discharge of operational activities, the material requirement would not be fulfilled, and the ensuing indirect responsibility could not be attributed to participating states.

Second, the host Member State has the requisite knowledge of the circumstances, for it is required to agree on the operational plan drawn by the agency; but it also directs and controls the operational implementation of the joint operation. Presumably, the same could be true for participating states, with national officials reporting back to their home state on their activities.[203] Yet, the element of participating states' knowledge may be more difficult to prove in practice, especially where their contribution is limited, and there is no evidence of structural or inherent deficiencies in the human rights protection system of the host state. Again, more problematic would be to substantiate the required level of knowledge with respect to the Member States' financial assistance or training of third states' border guards.[204]

Third, with respect to the opposability requirement, the same considerations outlined above in the opposite situation would apply to cases of the host or participating state's complicity with Frontex. Only where the complicit conduct would facilitate a violation of an international obligation of both the EU and the complicit Member State, the opposability requirement would be fulfilled. The same can be presumed in the case of participating states' complicity with the host state – given that they are all bound by the ECHR and major human rights treaties.

c. Complicity by Omission

Frontex joint operations display the *géometrie variable* of indirect responsibility, where a number of international actors contribute to border control activities with different levels and forms of support. Let's imagine that Frontex and other Member States participating in a joint operation at sea contribute to the commission of a violation of the principle of *non-refoulement* by the host Member State. Following Article 14 ARIO, Frontex would incur responsibility for aiding the host Member State in the commission of the wrongful act. In the same vein, under Article 16 ARS, participating states would be held responsible for their assistance to the host state, to the extent that they contributed significantly to the offence, and they were at least aware of it through the reports of national officers deployed in the border management teams. Yet, Articles 16 ARS and 14 ARIO limit the scope of indirect responsibility for complicity in various ways. Most importantly, the cognitive requirement seems difficult to substantiate when the relevant information was

[203] Fink (n 24) 165.
[204] d'Argent and Kuritzky (n 198).

gained during the implementation of a joint operation, and nothing was done to avoid the harmful outcome.

The crucial question is therefore whether complicity can arise out of a failure to act, that is, from an omission. Most notably, in the *Bosnia Genocide* case, the ICJ clarified that 'complicity always requires that some positive action has been taken to furnish aid or assistance'.[205] Accordingly, Crawford has concluded that the complicit 'contribution must be in the form of a positive act: neither active incitement nor a mere omission will suffice to ground responsibility'.[206] Despite the soundness of the ICJ decision in the *Bosnia Genocide* case, it should be noted that the Court was mainly focusing on the interpretation of the Genocide Convention and its specific complicity provision.[207] Along these lines, scholars have suggested that complicity should not be generally excluded from the range of application of international responsibility.[208] Undeniably, neither Article 16 ARS nor Article 14 ARIO seems to explicitly exclude the possibility of establishing responsibility for omissions. Besides, cases of responsibility for omission 'are at least as numerous as those based on positive acts, and no difference in principle exists between the two'.[209] In sum, it should not be *a priori* excluded that responsibility for complicity could arise from wrongful acts and omissions.

If one accepts this interpretation in the context of Frontex joint operations, a participating state or the agency could be held responsible for having facilitated a wrongful omission under three conditions. First, the state should have at least positive knowledge of the circumstances of the principal wrongful act. In this regard, Frontex and the host Member States are the best-placed entities to gain knowledge about human rights violations occurring during border control activities performed by border management teams coordinated by the agency. Second, there should be a link between the aid or assistance provided by omission and the principal wrongful act. Frontex or the Member States should at least be aware of the consequences of their failure to act. This requirement seems the most controversial in theory and demanding to substantiate in practice. Third, the primary breach and the complicit omission should both infringe on an international obligation of the responsibility bearer. This means that there should be an underlying obligation to act for complicity by omission to arise. In the case of Frontex joint operations, human rights law imposes on states and the agency positive duties to protect people involved in their activities. Frontex's duty to act is unequivocally supported by regulation 1896/2019, which explicitly recognises

[205] *Application of the Convention on the Prevention and Punishment of the Crime of Genocide* (n 117) para 432.

[206] Crawford (n 114) 405. See also, Fink (n 24) 165–66.

[207] Alexander AD Brown, 'To Complicity … and Beyond! Passive Assistance and Positive Obligations in International Law' (2016) 27 *Hague Yearbook of International Law / Annuaire de La Haye de Droit International* 133.

[208] Aust (n 163) 227; Lanovoy (n 163) 210–12.

[209] Art 2, ARS, Commentary, para 4.

the possibility of submitting a complaint to every individual directly affected by the agency's 'actions or *failure to act*'.[210]

Frontex and the Member States may incur indirect responsibility if they fail to take appropriate and reasonable measures to prevent human rights violations from occurring during their joint border control activities as soon as they gain knowledge thereof. The same could hold with respect to the implementation of informal cooperation schemes with third countries, provided that the opposability requirement is fulfilled. Yet, where their contribution to a joint operation is general and not engaged in any specific human rights violation, Member States cannot be held responsible for assisting in the misconduct. Similarly, in the case of Frontex's support to states participating in its operations where the required level of knowledge is not reached, the agency's responsibility cannot arise.

These conclusions are tentative and depend on a 'softened' interpretation of the strict requirements of the ARS and ARIO provisions on complicity. Notably, while the possibility of establishing responsibility for omissions cannot be *a priori* excluded, in such situations, the cognitive element remains rather daunting to prove before a court, even where it is limited to positive knowledge of the violations. The opacity surrounding Frontex's serious incidents reports adds another layer of practical hurdles.

C. Responsibility for Negligence

An alternative way to establish the responsibility for human rights violations occurring during Frontex joint operations relies on the doctrine of positive obligations.[211] The doctrine of positive obligations under human rights law would allow difficult questions of the attribution of wrongful acts to be obliterated.[212] Yet, as we shall see, potential victims might need to overcome other procedural obstacles, such as the issue of extraterritorial jurisdiction.

[210] Art 111, Regulation 1896/2019 (emphasis added).

[211] Maïté Fernandez, 'The EU External Borders Policy and Frontex-Coordinated Operations at Sea: Who Is in Charge? Reflections on Responsibility for Wrongful Acts' in Violeta Moreno-Lax and E Papastavridis (eds), *'Boat Refugees' & Migrants at Sea: A Comprehensive Approach. Integrating Maritime Security with Human Rights* (Leiden, Brill, 2016); Melanie Fink, 'A "Blind Spot" in the Framework of International Responsibility? Third Party Responsibility for Human Rights Violations: The Case of Frontex' in Thomas Gammeltoft-Hansen and Jens Vedsted-Hansen (eds), *Human Rights and the Dark Side of Globalisation: Transnational Law Enforcement and Migration Control* (Abingdon, Routledge, 2016).

[212] Maarten den Heijer, 'Shared Responsibility Before The European Court of Human Rights' (2013) 60 *Netherlands International Law Review* 411; Anja Seibert-Fohr, 'From Complicity to Due Diligence: When Do States Incur Responsibility for Their Involvement in Serious International Wrongdoing?' (2017) 60 *German Yearbook of International Law* 667; Helen Keller and Reto Walther, 'Evasion of the International Law of State Responsibility? The ECtHR's Jurisprudence on Positive and Preventive Obligations under Article 3' (2020) 24 *The International Journal of Human Rights* 957.

Human rights treaty bodies have long considered both acts and omissions to be sources of state responsibility for breaches of human rights obligations.[213] In the same vein, the ECtHR regularly condemns contracting states' passivity before the actions of third parties.[214] Relying on the principle of effectiveness, the Court established that state authorities are obliged to adopt legislation that safeguards the rights enshrined in the ECHR,[215] or to implement reasonable and appropriate measures to protect the right in question.[216]

What is deemed reasonable and appropriate is defined in light of the specific circumstances of each case;[217] nonetheless, two essential factors of this due diligence standard are (1) the capacity to prevent or respond to human rights violations and (2) the foreseeability of the risk.[218] The latter in particular, entails a less demanding mental element compared to complicity. While complicity requires actual knowledge of the circumstances of the assisted offence (or even intent), due diligence obligations entail the constructive knowledge that the breach will occur.[219] The responsibility of a state is therefore engaged if it knew or ought to have known of a violation but failed to take appropriate measures that would reasonably have prevented or mitigated it.[220] In this respect, the duty of due diligence implies an obligation of means. In contrast, the duty not to aid or assist the wrongful conduct of other entities entails an obligation of result.

In addition, a failure to act with due diligence to protect against violations of third parties constitutes unlawful conduct per se, while an omission analysed through the complicity frame should not necessarily be independently wrongful; it becomes so in connection with the primary breach. Moreover, positive obligations may be triggered by the conduct of private persons, while the responsibility for complicity can arise only with respect to the conduct of states or international organisations. Finally, and perhaps most importantly for the present purposes, compliance with a positive obligation requires the exercise

[213] IACtHR, *Velasquez-Rodriguez*, (Ser C) No 4, 29 July 1988, paras 166 et seq; CESCR, General Comment No 3: The Nature of States Parties' Obligations, 14 December 1990, UN Doc E/1991/23, 14 December 1990; HRC, General Comment No 31: *The Nature of the General Legal Obligation Imposed on States Parties to the Covenant*, UN Doc CCPR/C/21/Rev.1/Add.13, 26 May 2004, para 8; HRC, Article 6 Right to Life, General Comment No 36, CCPR/C/GC/36, 30 October 2018, paras 7 and 21. See generally: Dinah Shelton and Ariel Gould, 'Positive and Negative Obligations' in Dinah Shelton (ed), *The Oxford Handbook of International Human Rights Law* (Oxford, Oxford University Press, 2013).

[214] See eg: ECtHR, *Osman v United Kingdom*, Appl No 23452/94, 28 October 1998, para 115.

[215] ECtHR, *Vgt Verein Gegen Tierfabriken v Switzerland*, Appl No 24699/94, 28 September 2001, para 45.

[216] ECtHR, *X and Y v the Netherlands*, Appl No 8978/80, 26 March 1985, para 23; ECtHR, *López-Ostra v Spain*, Appl No 16798/90, 9 December 1994, para 55.

[217] Olivier Corten, 'La "complicité" dans le droit de la responsabilité internationale : un concept inutile ?' (2011) 57 *Annuaire Français de Droit International* 57.

[218] *Velasquez-Rodriguez* (n 213) para 172.

[219] Lanovoy (n 163) 146.

[220] *Application of the Convention on the Prevention and Punishment of the Crime of Genocide* (n 119) para 430; ILA Study Group on Due Diligence in International Law Second Report July 2016.

of jurisdiction, and therefore some degree of power or effective control to be exercised over territories or people.

Member States are not discharged from their positive obligations when they cooperate during Frontex's joint operations. In EU law and policy there are clear indications regarding the particular human rights sensitivity of such activities, which require a heightened standard of diligence. Namely, in the context of Frontex activities, Member States and the agency should

> apply fundamental rights due diligence to all of their activities, ensuring the highest standard of performance, assessing and mitigating the risk of violating fundamental rights from planning through monitoring and evaluation, and respecting human dignity and the principle of 'do no harm' with regard to the rights of those on the move.[221]

During Frontex joint operations, the host Member States will generally have the required level of knowledge about the risks of human rights violations and dispose of the appropriate practical and legal capacities to prevent or mitigate those risks. The exercise of executive powers by Frontex officers, for example, should be in accordance with the national law of the host Member State and depends on its previous authorisation. The actions of the agency's staff are therefore attributable to the host state,[222] but they also require the latter to exercise particular vigilance over them.[223] Any incident during such operations should be reported to the agency and the host state's authorities.[224] Given their leading position during joint operations, it can be generally assumed that the authorities of host Member States have the required knowledge about the human rights risks of a given manoeuvre, as well as the capacity to react in case of an actual violation promptly. Generally, the host state's failure to protect the rights of people involved in a joint operation could therefore entail its responsibility for breaching its positive obligations. But only a case-by-case assessment would allow accurate conclusions.

Attributing responsibility for negligence to states participating in Frontex joint operations is more complex. This is because they might not have the required level of knowledge, they might not be in a position to influence a given situation significantly, and – most importantly – they act extraterritorially.[225] Yet, there are circumstances where their contribution to a human rights violation might entail their responsibility for breach of positive obligations. This is the case where (1) there are structural deficiencies in the border control system of a host state or where the operational plan is inherently problematic;[226] (2) the authorities of participating Member States have the capacity to prevent or mitigate the harmful event;

[221] Frontex, Management Board Decision 12/2021 adopting the Fundamental Rights Strategy, 14 February 2021, 6.
[222] See above, s V.A.i.
[223] Annex V to Regulation 2019/1896.
[224] Regulation 2019/1896, Art 38(3)(h).
[225] For a similar conclusion, see: Fink (n 24) 155.
[226] Regulation 2019/1896, Art 38(1).

and (3) their participation in the agency's activities involves a certain degree of exercise of state power.[227]

In principle, the necessary degree of knowledge is met where there are objective deficiencies in the operational plan upon which every participating state agrees. Yet, the power participating Member States have over the course of a joint operation seems particularly limited. First, while they are under an obligation to issue a serious incident report when they witness, are involved in, or suspect the occurrence of human rights violations, they might not be able to influence its follow-up procedure.[228] Significantly, under the current legal framework, participating states can withdraw their officers or equipment from a joint operation only in 'exceptional situations' that would 'substantially affect the discharge of national tasks'.[229] Taken to the extremes, this means that EU law could oblige Member States to breach their international human rights obligations. Second, and related, officers from participating Member States exercise their powers on behalf of the host state – with its previous authorisation and on its territory. Hence, in principle, they do not exercise jurisdiction over individuals involved in joint operations. In this respect, Fink has accurately observed that participating states contributing large military assets retain a certain authority over them, mainly through a commanding officer responsible for the asset.[230] This might entail the concurrent jurisdiction of both the host and the participating Member State. Yet this possibility remains to be tested in practice and depends on the specific circumstance of each case.[231]

In turn, Frontex's responsibility for negligence rests on the power and influence that the agency has over its joint operations. More precisely, the agency has the required level of knowledge about and capacity to prevent human rights violations that may occur during those operations. Frontex is explicitly required to 'follow high standards for border management allowing for transparency and public scrutiny in full respect of the applicable law and ensuring respect for, and protection and promotion of fundamental rights'.[232] The agency's due diligence duties is further corroborated by its obligation to terminate, suspend or not launch a joint operation where there are risks of serious human rights violations,[233] as well as by its duty to develop an 'independent and effective complaints mechanism'.[234] In addition, prior to entering into any formal cooperation with third states, the agency should identify any potential human rights challenge by 'undertak[ing] a due diligence assessment of fundamental rights risks and the impacts of such cooperation'.[235] Not only should Frontex abstain from direct violations, but it

[227] Fink distinguishes between participating states contributing large assets and those who are not. Only the latter are considered to exercise 'public powers' and, therefore, jurisdiction. Fink (n 24).

[228] See ch 2, s VII.A.

[229] Arts 51(3), 57(9), 64(9), Regulation 2019/1896.

[230] Fink (n 24) 155.

[231] Ch 4, s V.C.

[232] Art 10(1)(ad), Regulation 2019/1896.

[233] ibid, Art 46.

[234] ibid, Art 111(1).

[235] Frontex, Fundamental Rights Strategy, 14.

should also exercise a certain vigilance so that human rights violations do not take place during its activities, and when they do, the agency should conduct an investigation and take appropriate measures.

Ultimately, both the EU (via Frontex) and its Member States could be held responsible for a failure to protect migrants against the human rights violations perpetrated by the other actors participating in the EU integrated border management. However, the question of human rights jurisdiction over these positive obligations remains open. While it is true that jurisdiction is not a relevant criterion for ascertaining complicity in an internationally wrongful act, the determination of positive obligations is subordinated to the establishment of jurisdiction over given conduct. In other words, jurisdiction is the precondition for the very existence of the obligation breached. In the context of extraterritorial migration control measures, a breach of positive obligations necessitates the extraterritorial exercise of jurisdiction.

D. Complicity and Positive Obligations: Differences, Overlaps or Parallel Functions?

To counter the difficulties related to the ECHR's jurisdictional threshold, in the specific case of Frontex joint operations, Fink has advanced the possibility of complementing the doctrine of positive obligations with the concept of complicity.[236] In this respect, some authors have argued that complicit states may be held responsible for the breach of positive obligations.[237] This approach would have several advantages. On the one hand, complicity does not require the complicit state to exercise jurisdiction over the victim of the primary breach. This would allow the establishment of responsibility for human rights violations occurring during extraterritorial border control operations – that is, from the perspective of participating states, any Frontex joint operation. On the other hand, positive obligations have a less demanding mental element requirement as compared to complicity, for they entail merely the constructive knowledge of a risk that the breach will occur. Furthermore, the horizontal application of human rights obligations could overcome the potential difficulty of the opposability requirement when the harmful event takes place on the territory of a third country.

In this context, the difference between primary and secondary rules of international law is easily blurred.[238] The differences and overlaps between positive obligations and the indirect attribution of responsibility for complicity are subject to intense discussion;[239] they become less visible where the strict requirements for

[236] Fink (n 24) 166–67.

[237] See Jackson (n 163) 129. Anna Liguori, 'Overlap between Complicity and Positive Obligations: What Advantages in Resorting to Positive Obligations in Case of Partnered Operations' (2022) 27 *Journal of Conflict and Security Law* 229.

[238] John Cerone, 'Re-Examining International Responsibility: Inter-State Complicity in the Context of Human Rights Violations' (2007) 14 *ILSA Journal of International & Comparative Law* 525.

[239] Corten (n 217).

complicity to arise are 'softened' by capacious interpretations. Nonetheless, it is not clear how one set of rules would complement the other in practice. It is worth remembering that, in practice, this form of indirect attribution has seldom been applied.[240]

To provide for more effective protection against third parties' involvement in human rights violations, human rights bodies have tried to develop their own rules of attribution of responsibility.[241] Along these lines, human rights treaties were claimed to constitute lex specialis with respect to the general rules of state responsibility.[242] The ECtHR's decisions on extraordinary rendition cases are relevant examples.[243] Notably, in *El-Masri*, the Court's Grand Chamber developed a standard based on 'acquiescence or connivance' to hold a third state responsible for acts committed on its territory by another state.[244] The Court's reasoning is not always indicative of its conceptual basis. Nonetheless, the decision can hardly be based on the rules of attribution of responsibility for complicity.[245] It can therefore be presumed that the Court applied the doctrine of positive obligations.[246] This approach allows the Court, first, to overcome the difficulty of the opposability requirement set by the rules on complicity and its lack of competence to adjudicate over the conduct of a state that was not party to the ECHR. Second, with regard to the cognitive requirement, the ECtHR considers sufficient that the respondent state 'knew or ought to have known' about the risk of serious human rights violations.[247] Although the Court generally employs the threshold of constructive knowledge with regard to states' positive obligations, the authorities' awareness of the risk usually concerns the specific situation of the victim.[248] In situations of particularly dangerous activities, such as SAR operations, for example, requiring a higher degree of care, the requirement that state authorities should have been aware of the risk to a specific individual is generally presumed.[249]

[240] Samantha Besson, 'La Due Diligence En Droit International' [2020] *Recueil des cours de l'Académie du droit international de La Haye*.

[241] James Crawford and Amelia Keene, 'The European Convention on Human Rights and General International Law' in Iulia Motoc and Anne van Aaken (eds), *The Structure of State Responsibility under the European Convention on Human Rights* (Oxford, Oxford University Press, 2018).

[242] *Velasquez-Rodriguez* (n 213); IACtHR, *Mapiripán Massacre v Colombia*, (Ser C) No 134, Judgment of 15 September 2005. See also: Jackson (n 163) 189–200.

[243] ECtHR, *El-Masri v The Former Yugoslav Republic of Macedonia*, Appl No 39630/09, 13 December 2012. See also: ECtHR, *Husayn (Abu Zubaydah) v Poland*, Appl No 7511/13, Judgment of 24 July 2014; ECtHR, *Al Nashiri v Poland*, Appl No 28761/11, 24 July 2014; ECtHR, *Nasr and Ghali v Italy*, Appl. No. 44883/09, Judgment of 23 February 2016; ECtHR, *Al Nashiri v Romania*, Appl No 33234/12, 31 May 2018.

[244] ECtHR, *El-Masri* (n 243) para 206.

[245] The Court referred to Art 16 ARS, but did not base its findings on this provision.

[246] Keller and Walther (n 212) 961.

[247] *El-Masri* (n 243) para 198.

[248] Vladislava Stoyanova, 'Fault, Knowledge and Risk within the Framework of Positive Obligations under the European Convention on Human Rights' [2020] *Leiden Journal of International Law* 1, 9–10.

[249] ECtHR, *Öneryildiz v Turkey*, Appl No 48939/99, 30 November 2004, para 90. Joint partly dissenting opinion of Judges Vučinić and Lemmens, ECtHR, *Sakine Epőzdemir and Others v Turkey*, Appl

Ultimately, states' positive obligations under the ECHR offer more far-reaching protection than the rules on attribution for complicity.[250] Nonetheless, while the existence of positive obligations is incontrovertible for potential violations occurring within a state's jurisdiction, the *vexata quaestio* about their extraterritorial reach remains open. The applicability of positive obligations in extraterritorial settings depends on the relationship between the individual and the duty bearer, that is, on the exercise of jurisdiction over the potential victim of a human rights violation. Both universal and regional human rights bodies have recognised extraterritorial positive obligations in relation to third-party actions beyond the exercise of effective control over territory or individuals.[251] Even beyond situations of effective control over territories or people, there may be instances in which a state may nevertheless influence a particular entity because of the extraterritorial reach of its normative power.[252] If one espouses the approach to extraterritorial jurisdiction advanced in chapter four, jurisdiction will arise whenever a state exercises its power over people in a sufficiently effective and normative manner. Hence, the entire range of substantive rights set out in the ECHR would apply, including positive obligations.[253]

It remains to be seen whether the ECtHR will espouse this relational approach to human rights jurisdiction. Thus far, the Strasbourg Court's case law on the Convention's extraterritorial application has been far from coherent.[254] Nevertheless, there have been few instances in which the Court decided to apply its doctrine of positive obligations in extraterritorial contexts.[255] How the ECtHR will further shape its jurisprudence on extraterritorial jurisdiction is vital for questions of shared responsibility in the domain of border control.

V. Legal Consequences for the Responsible Actors

The notion of international responsibility 'covers the new legal relations which arise under international law by reason of the internationally wrongful act' of a state or international organisation.[256] The legal relationship between the injured

No 26589/06, 1 December 2015. See also: Thomas Spijkerboer, 'Moving Migrants, States, and Rights Human Rights and Border Deaths' (2013) 7 *The Law & Ethics of Human Rights* 213, 230.

[250] For a similar conclusion, see: Fink (n 24) 167.

[251] See ch 4.

[252] Carla Ferstman, 'Human Rights Due Diligence Policies Applied to Extraterritorial Cooperation to Prevent "Irregular" Migration: European Union and United Kingdom Support to Libya' (2020) 21 *German Law Journal* 459.

[253] ECtHR, *Al-Skeini v UK*, Appl No 55721/07, 7 July 2011, para 138.

[254] Judge Bonello Concurring Opinion in *Al-Skeini* (n 253) para 4.

[255] See eg: ECtHR, *Ilaşcu and Others v Moldova and Russia*, Appl no 48787/99, 8 July 2004, para 331; ECtHR, *Manoilescu and Dubrescu v Romania and Russia* Appl no 60861/00, 3 March 2005, para 101; ECtHR, *Treska v Albania and Italy* Appl no 26937/04, 29 June 2006.

[256] Art 1, ARS, Commentary, para 5.

party and the wrongdoer does not cease to exist but continues and adapts to the new situation created by the wrongful conduct. The obligations breached by the wrongdoer continues to bind it.[257] As a corollary, the entity responsible for a wrongful conduct must cease it, if it is continuing; and offer appropriate assurances and guarantees of non-repetition, if circumstances so require.[258] In addition, Articles 31 ARS and 31 ARIO require the responsible entity to make full reparation for the injury caused by their internationally wrongful act.

Despite the rather solid appearance of these provisions, they are not exempt from uncertainties in their concrete application – especially when one applies them to the case of human rights violations occurred during Frontex activities. First, regarding the obligation of cessation, it should be established whether the breach of the relevant international obligation has a continuing character. In this respect, the ILC stressed that 'while the obligation to cease wrongful conduct will arise most commonly in the case of a continuing wrongful act, Article 30 also encompasses situations where a State has violated an obligation on a series of occasions, implying the possibility of further repetitions'.[259] The ECtHR considers that 'an accumulation of identical or analogous breaches which are sufficiently numerous and inter-connected to amount not merely to isolated incidents or exceptions but to a pattern or system' constitutes a practice incompatible with the Convention.[260]

Establishing the existence of such a practice in the context of Frontex joint operations seems rather unlikely, not least because of several preventive measures put in place to avoid systematic violations of migrants' rights. Namely, Frontex has an obligation not to launch or to suspend or terminate activities entailing serious or persistent human rights violations.[261] Similarly, in the context of cooperation with third states, the agency must suspend or terminate its operational activities, if the executive director considers that serious or persistent fundamental rights violations could take place during the agency's activities.[262] Yet, this obligation is undercut by the executive director's wide discretion over decisions to suspend or terminate an activity.[263] An obligation that is not envisaged,

[257] Arts 29, ARS and ARIO. See also: James Crawford and Simon Olleson 'The Nature and Forms of International Responsibility', in J Crawford, A Pellet and S Olleson (eds), *The Law of International Responsibility* (Oxford, Oxford University Press, 2010).

[258] Arts 30 ARS and 31, ARIO.

[259] Art 30 ARS, Commentary, para 3.

[260] ECtHR, *Ireland v UK*, Appl No 5310/71 18 January 1978, para 159; See the revision judgment on the same case: ECtHR, *Ireland v UK*, Appl no 5310/71, 20 March 2018. See also: ECtHR, *Cyprus v Turkey*, Appl No 25781/94, 10 May 2001, para 115; ECtHR, *Georgia v Russia (I)*, Appl No 13255/07, 3 July 2014, para 123.

[261] Art 46(4), Regulation 2019/1896.

[262] See eg: Art 18(4), Agreement between the European Union and the Republic of North Macedonia on Operational Activities Carried Out by the European Border and Coast Guard Agency in the Republic of North Macedonia [2023] OJ L 61. See also Art 73, Regulation (EU) 2019/1896.

[263] It is worth noting that newer status agreements generally employ the verb 'shall' instead of 'may' as in older ones. This is in line with Frontex amended legal framework. Cf Art 6(3), Status Agreement between the European Union and Montenegro [2020]; Art 46(4), Regulation 2019/1896; Art 18(1), Status agreement between the European Union and North Macedonia [2023].

for instance, in the Memorandum of Understanding between Italy and Libya, which does not include a provision on suspension or termination for breaches human rights obligations.[264]

In addition, whereas cessation is concerned with 'securing an end to continuing wrongful conduct',[265] assurances and guarantees of non-repetition serve a preventive function.[266] Appropriate assurances and guarantees have an exceptional character and should be afforded only when 'circumstances so require'.[267] Under human rights law, important forms of guarantees of non-repetition are the adoption of appropriate legislative measures or the training of law enforcement officers.[268] Applied to Frontex joint operations, this rule would require a state responsible for human rights violations to guarantee that they would not occur in the future. In this respect, while the IACtHR has developed an innovative and articulated jurisprudence;[269] beyond granting interim measures in a number of cases ordering the provisional stay of expulsion procedures,[270] the ECtHR has traditionally interpreted rather restrictively non-pecuniary measures of reparation, leaving a large margin of discretion to national judges.[271]

Second, while the obligation to make full reparation for the injury caused has a firm standing in the legal framework for the consequences of an internationally wrongful conduct, situations of shared or indirect responsibility are

[264] Memorandum of understanding on cooperation in the fields of development, the fight against illegal immigration, human trafficking and fuel smuggling and on reinforcing the security of borders between the State of Libya and the Italian Republic, 2 February 2017.

[265] Commentary Art 30, ARS, para 1.

[266] ICJ, *LaGrand Case (Germany v United States of America)*, Judgment of 27 June 2001, ICJ Reports 466; ICJ, *Avena and Other Mexican Nationals (Mexico v United States of America)*, Judgment of 31 March 2004, ICJ Reports 12.

[267] Art 30(b) ARS. On reparation, cessation, assurances and guarantees in multi-actor situations, see most notably: Pierre d'Argent, 'Reparation, Cessation, Assurances and Guarantees of Non-Repetition' in A Nollkaemper and I Plakokefalos (eds), *Principles of Shared Responsibility in International Law: An Appraisal of the State of the Art* (Cambridge, Cambridge University Press, 2014).

[268] Basic Principles and Guidelines on the Right to a Remedy and Reparation for Victims of Gross Violations of International Human Rights Law and Serious Violations of International Humanitarian Law, adopted by the United Nations General Assembly, Resolution 60/147, UN Doc A/RES/60/147 (2005), 16 December 2005.

[269] See in particular: Hélène Tigroudja, 'La satisfaction et les garanties de non-répétition de l'illicite dans le contentieux interaméricain des droits de l'homme', in E Lambert and K Martin-Chenut (eds), *Réparer les violations graves et massives des droits de l'homme: La Cour interaméricaine, pionnière ou modèle ?* (Société de législation comparée, 2010); Gabriella Citroni, 'Measures of Reparation for Victims of Gross Human Rights Violations: Developments and Challenges in the Jurisprudence of Two Regional Human Rights Courts' (2012) 5 *Inter-American & European Human Rights Journal* 49.

[270] Andrea Saccucci, 'Interim Measures at the European Court of Human Rights: Current Practice and Future Challenges' in Fulvio Maria Palombino, Roberto Virzo and Giovanni Zarra (eds), *Provisional Measures Issued by International Courts and Tribunals* (Berlin, Springer, 2021).

[271] For further discussion, see: Veronika Fikfak, 'Non-Pecuniary Damages before the European Court of Human Rights: Forget the Victim; It's All about the State' (2020) 33 *Leiden Journal of International Law* 335. More specifically on reparations afforded by the ECtHR for migrants' rights violations: Marie-Benedicte Dembour, *When Humans Become Migrants* (Oxford, Oxford University Press, 2015) ch 10.

more complex.[272] Namely, with regard to the legal consequences of complicity, it is not clear to what extent the aiding or assisting state would be required to make reparation for the injury caused. Indeed, 'consideration must be given to cases in which the injuries are not caused exclusively by an unlawful act but have been produced also by concomitant causes among which the unlawful act plays a decisive but not exclusive role'.[273] In this respect, what seems to be required is that the violation would not have occurred *but for* the contribution of the complicit state.[274] While the aiding or assistance provided by the complicit entity is not necessarily wrongful *per se*, the aid or assistance should contribute significantly to the commission of the wrongful act.[275] In addition, the complicit entity should indemnify the injury that it caused, but this does not necessarily exclude its obligation to make full reparation for the indivisible injury suffered by the victims of human rights violations.[276] This interpretation is however controversial, and could lead to potentially inequitable solutions, where the complicit state bears all the consequences of the principal perpetrator's wrongdoing.[277]

In the context of a plurality of states or international organisations causing the same wrongful act, the ARS and ARIO provide for their joint and several responsibility. Yet, the requirements of these rules are stringent.[278] In particular, the presence of the same wrongful act poses a significant obstacle to the victims. It requires both responsible actors to be bound by the same international obligations and, most importantly for the present purposes, to be subject to the jurisdiction of the same judicial body. This is certainly different from the case of the EU Member States and Frontex (and the EU), which, contrary to the Member States, is not a party to the ECHR nor any other relevant human rights instrument. It is problematic for a victim to bring both Frontex and the Member States before the same judicial body. Even where this would be procedurally possible, it would be difficult to distribute the consequent reparation among them, given the complex causality of many human rights violations. The ECtHR, for example, on many occasions determined the responsibility of multiple states. Yet, the Court's case law reveals that it not only separates the distinct states' conduct contributing to the injury but

[272] Alexander Orakhelashvili, 'Division of Reparation between Responsible Entities' in J Crawford, A Pellet and S Olleson (eds), *The Law of International Responsibility* (Oxford, Oxford University Press, 2010).

[273] Second Report on State Responsibility, by Mr Gaetano Arangio-Ruiz, UN Doc A/CN.4/425 1989, 14, para 44.

[274] Art 16, ARS, Commentary, paras 1 and 10. See also: Lanovoy (n 163) 276.

[275] Art 16, ARS, Commentary, para 5; Art 14 ARIO, Commentary, para 4.

[276] See: André Nollkaemper and others, 'Guiding Principles on Shared Responsibility in International Law' (2020) 31 *European Journal of International Law* 15, Principle 10.

[277] See eg, Aust (n 163) 281–83; Christine Chinkin, 'The Continuing Occupation?: Issues of Joint and Several Liability and Effective Control' in P Shiner and A Williams (eds), *The Iraq War and International Law* (Oxford, Hart Publishing, 2008).

[278] Art 47, ARS; Art 48, ARIO. For further discussion, see: Samantha Besson, 'La pluralité d'États responsables: vers une solidarité internationale ?' (2007) 1 *Revue suisse de droit international et de droit européen* 13; Orakhelashvili (n 272).

that it also allocates the ensuing reparations independently, based on the contribution of each responsible actor to the injury,[279] even in cases where there the injury is indivisible.[280]

Perhaps, once again, a solution to the problems of distribution of responsibility and its consequences in the context of Frontex joint operations relies on the doctrine of positive obligations. On the one hand, positive obligations may represent the best method to individuate multiple violations, thus eschewing questions of shared responsibility. On the other hand, a solution to coordinate the allocation of concurrent human rights responsibilities is to identify a general positive duty of all states of concurrent jurisdiction to distribute human rights duties among themselves. This implies that all states exercising concurrent jurisdiction over a specific situation bear a general positive duty to establish institutions or procedures to coordinate the distribution of their concurrent ECHR duties.[281] This coordination duty would apply when the violation occurs in the institutional context of an international organisation like the EU and Frontex joint operations more specifically. In these cases, the institutional setting already exists and it 'could not only coordinate the implementation of the concurrent human rights duties of States … but also the allocation of their concurrent responsibilities'.[282] But again, this would concern only the Member States, as the EU is not a party to the ECHR yet.

Finally, it is worth mentioning that a special regime of legal consequences is foreseen for serious breaches of obligations under peremptory norms of general international law.[283] Under Articles 41 ARS and 42 ARIO, states and international organisations are required to cooperate to end the serious breach of a

[279] See eg: ECtHR, *Rantsevv Cyprus and Russia*, Appl No 25965/04, 7 January 2010, paras 341–43; *M.S.S.* (n 31) paras 403–23.

[280] Eg: *Ilaşcu* (n 255). For further references and discussion, see: M den Haijer, 'Shared Responsibility before the European Court of Human Rights' (2013) 60 *Netherlands International Law Review* 411. The HRC has also not taken a clear position with regard to the distribution of responsibilities and reparations among multiple states. See most recently: HRC, *A.S., D.I., O.I. and G.D. v Italy*, Comm No 3042/2017, UN Doc CCPR/C/130/D/3042/2017, 27 January 2021; HRC, *A.S., D.I., O.I. and G.D. v Malta*, Comm No3043/2017, UN Doc CCPR/C/128/D/3043/2017, 27 January 2021.

[281] See generally: Samantha Besson, 'La Responsabilité Solidaire Des États et/Ou Des Organisations Internationales: Une Institution Négligée' in *Face à l'irresponsabilité: la dynamique de la solidarité* (Collège de France, Paris 2018). For a similar argument, see also: J d'Aspremont, 'Abuse of the Legal Personality of International Organizations and the Responsibility of Member States' (2007) 4 *International Organizations Law Review* 91.

[282] Samantha Besson, 'Concurrent Responsibilities under the European Convention on Human Rights: The Concurrence of Human Rights Jurisdictions, Duties, and Responsibilities' in Iulia Motoc and Anne van Aaken (eds), *The European Convention on Human Rights and General International Law* (Oxford, Oxford University Press, 2018).

[283] Art 53, VCLT. See also: ILC Draft Conclusions on Peremptory Norms of General International Law (*Jus Cogens*) (with commentaries), Report of the International Law Commission, Seventy-First Session, UN Doc A/74/10. For further comments, see Daniel Costelloe, *Legal Consequences of Peremptory Norms in International Law* (Cambridge, Cambridge University Press, 2017); Helmut Philipp Aust, 'Legal Consequences of Serious Breaches of Peremptory Norms in the Law of State Responsibility: Observations in the Light of the Recent Work of the International Law Commission' in Dire Tladi (ed), *Peremptory Norms of General International Law: Perspectives and Future Prospects* (Leiden, Brill Nijhoff, 2021).

peremptory norm;[284] and not to recognise as lawful a situation created by a serious breach or render aid or assistance in maintaining that situation.[285] Significantly, Articles 41(2) ARS and 42(2) ARIO provide for a duty of non-assistance similar to the prohibition of complicity. Yet, in contrast to Articles 16 ARS and 14 ARIO, the elements of opposability and knowledge are not required here.[286] For the present purposes, while the *ius cogens* character of the principle of *non-refoulement* is still a matter of debate,[287] arguably, the customary norms prohibiting slavery, racial discrimination, and torture have peremptory status.[288] Accordingly, the EU and its Member States should abstain from cooperating with third states where violations of these peremptory norms are occurring, nor should they recognise such situations as lawful.[289]

VI. The Concurrence between Individual Criminal Responsibility and the Responsibility of States and International Organisations

As already discussed, states and international organisations act only through their organs or representatives. But in legal terms, international responsibility originates not from the conduct of an individual, but from that of a state or international organisation.[290] In this sense, state responsibility is independent of and does not entail that of individuals. Yet, 'the moral effect of the law is vastly reduced if the human agents involved are able to separate themselves personally both from the duties the law imposes and from the responsibility which it entails'.[291] In this line, international criminal law has removed the veil of states' acts, and it no longer leaves adjudicating the crimes of individuals exclusively to state discretion, even when they are acting as states' agents. Therefore, in a limited set of circumstances, certain state acts can lead to the concurrent attribution of responsibility to a state and an individual.[292]

Against this background, in certain situations, like that of refugees in Greek detention centres or the European and Italian cooperation with Libya, the recourse

[284] Arts 41(1), ARS and 42(1), ARIO.

[285] Arts 41(2), ARS and 42(2), ARIO.

[286] Art 16, ARS, Commentary, para 11. See also: G Nolte and HP Aust, 'Equivocal Helpers – Complicit States, Mixed Messages and International Law' (2009) 58 *International & Comparative Law Quarterly* 1.

[287] See ch 3, s IV.A.

[288] Art 40, ARS, Commentary, paras 4 and 5.

[289] For a similar argument in relation to the Italy-Libya cooperation, see Pascale (n 198) 58.

[290] Pierre-Marie Dupuy, 'Dionisio Anzilotti and the Law of International Responsibility of States' (1992) 3 *European Journal of International Law* 139.

[291] Philip Allott, 'State Responsibility and the Unmaking of International Law' (1988) 29 *Harvard International Law Journal* 1, 14.

[292] For a detailed discussion see: André Nollkaemper, 'Concurrence between Individual Responsibility and State Responsibility in International Law' (2003) 52 *International & Comparative Law Quarterly* 615.

to international criminal law may address the systematic violence perpetrated against migrants at the border of the EU.[293] This situation may lead to the concurrence of individual and state responsibility. The International Criminal Court potentially has jurisdiction to investigate allegations of crimes against humanity committed by heads of governments of the EU Member States and other high-ranking EU officials. This would not displace the responsibility of the EU and its Member States. On the contrary, the concurrence between international responsibility and individual responsibility may have a meaningful practical impact. For instance, findings pertaining to individual responsibility may influence subsequent determinations on state responsibility.

The question of concurrence of responsibilities is also relevant from a theoretical perspective, for it bears the question about the very nature of international responsibility and its unity.[294] This emerges most notably with regard to remedies. Remedies for individual responsibility and state or international organisations' responsibility are different in that the former leads to an obligation to punish criminals and the latter results in various forms of reparation.[295] Contrary to remedies ensuing state responsibility, the obligation to prosecute and punish individuals is a matter of primary norms. Yet, an obligation to punish may be part of a remedy. In this sense, '[a] synergy between individual and state responsibility may then occur, as the implementation of an obligation to punish is at the same time a remedy against both the state and the individual'.[296] Accordingly, a potential finding regarding the criminal responsibility of an individual in the context of the EIBM may imply the obligation of the state to punish the individual concerned; and, vice versa, the punishment of individual perpetrators may be considered as (part of) the remedy against a Member State or the EU.

VII. Implementing Responsibility

As its final step, this analysis now turns to the actual implementation of the rules discussed thus far. Under which circumstances can victims seek to enforce these

[293] See most notably: Omer Shatz, Juan Branco and others, *EU Migration Policies in the Central Mediterranean and Libya (2014–2019)*, Communication to the Office of the Prosecutor of the International Criminal Court Pursuant to the Article 15 of the Rome Statute, 2019; SJAC, 'Communiqué to the Office of the Prosecutor of the International Criminal Court regarding Crimes against Humanity Committed by Greek and Frontex Officials against Refugees' 28 January 2021; UpRights, Adala For All and StraLi, 'Article 15 Communication on War Crimes and Crimes Against Humanity Committed Against Migrants and Asylum Seekers in Libya', 17 January 2022. See also: Ioannis Kalpouzos and Itamar Mann, 'Banal Crimes against Humanity: The Case of Asylum Seekers in Greece' (2015) 16 *Melbourne Journal of International Law* 1; Giulia Raimondo, 'Invisible Crimes: Accountability for Crimes Against Migrants in Libya' (2023) 25 *European Journal of Migration and Law* 328.

[294] André Nollkaemper, 'Concurrence between Individual Responsibility and State Responsibility in International Law' (2003) 52 *International & Comparative Law Quarterly* 615.

[295] James Crawford, *Brownlie's Principles of Public International Law* New edn, 9th edn (Oxford, Oxford University Press, 2019) 566–89; Dinah Shelton, 'Righting Wrongs: Reparations in the Articles on State Responsibility' (2002) 96 *American Journal of International Law* 833.

[296] Nollkaemper (n 294) 638.

rules? How can they seek redress for human rights violations occurring during Frontex's activities? As has already been discussed, contrary to the case with Member States, the implementation of Frontex and the EU's international responsibility is rather cumbersome, as it is not a party to the ECHR, nor can it be held responsible before universal human rights treaty bodies. In this sense, the accountability of international organisations such as the EU may become particularly relevant. For the present purposes, the notion of accountability is understood to be broader than that of (legal) responsibility and therefore may offer a better avenue for potential victims to seek redress. Furthermore, non-judicial scrutiny can also serve as an instrument of democratic control and participation and an important prevention tool for human rights advocates. Accordingly, the next sections will explore the available judicial remedies and the non-judicial accountability mechanisms available to victims of human rights violations occurring in the context of the EIBM.

A. Domestic Courts of Member States

The most obvious legal route an individual can take against a decision taken in the context of the EIBM and infringing its fundamental rights is to bring a claim before a national court. This is because national authorities often execute the final action in the chain of events leading to a human rights violation in the context of integrated border controls. Moreover, one of the conditions of admissibility before supranational judicial bodies is the exhaustion of domestic remedies.[297] At the same time, Member States retain the primary responsibility for the management of their sections of the external border, the detention of returnees and issuing of return decisions.[298]

In principle, while Frontex is responsible for the conduct of its staff before the CJEU, the civil and criminal liability of border guards deployed during its operations, including the agency's statutory staff, rests on the host Member State.[299] Insofar as criminal liability is concerned, moreover, team members should be treated in the same way as officials of the host Member State. In addition, Frontex regulation does not offer any guidance regarding the agency's executive director's criminal responsibility. By analogy, the executive director could be held responsible before the Member State where the violation occurred.

Furthermore, while Frontex statutory staff is subject to the disciplinary measures provided for in the Staff Regulations and the Conditions of Employment, border officers deployed from Member States remain subject to the disciplinary or other measures regarding human rights violations of their home Member State.[300]

[297] Art 35, ECHR; Art 41(1)(c), ICCPR.
[298] Art 7, Regulation 1896/2019.
[299] ibid, Arts 84 and 85.
[300] ibid, Art 43(5).

Significantly, however, members of Frontex's statutory staff do not have a home state. This creates a critical lacuna, which is only partially alleviated by the provision requiring the agency to reimburse any sums the host Member State would pay the victims where damage is caused by 'gross negligence or wilful misconduct' by the statutory staff.[301]

In the context of model status agreements concluded with third countries, team members and statutory staff of the agency benefit from immunity from the criminal, civil and administrative jurisdiction of the third country hosting the agency's joint operations.[302] In this respect, Frontex executive director determines whether the conduct of the agency's team member in question was performed in the exercise of their official functions.[303] Yet both Frontex regulation and status agreements remain silent as to the conditions and criteria that the executive director should follow to reach such a determination. Privileges and immunities from the jurisdiction of third states do not exempt team members seconded to the agency from the jurisdiction of their home Member State. However, in the absence of a sending Member State, this would result in impunity for crimes committed by Frontex statutory staff during operations on the territory of third countries. Besides, status agreements differ in many respects regarding procedural rules. For example, some older agreements provide an obligation of team members to provide evidence before the courts of third states, while more recent ones explicitly exclude it.[304]

A final and more general observation is in order. Traditionally, domestic courts decline to adjudicate complaints against international organisations based on their immunity from jurisdiction. The underlying logic is to ensure the independence and effective functioning of international organisations.[305] The EU is no exception.[306] Frontex, as an EU agency enjoys the same privileges

[301] ibid, Art 84(2).

[302] Art 7, Status Agreement between the European Union and the Republic of Albania on actions carried out by the European Border and Coast Guard Agency in the Republic of Albania [2019] OJ L 46/3; Art 6, Status Agreement between the European Union and the Republic of Serbia on actions carried out by the European Border and Coast Guard Agency in the Republic of Serbia [2020] OJ L 202; Art 12, Agreement between the European Union and the Republic of Moldova on operational activities carried out by the European Border and Coast Guard Agency in the Republic of Moldova [2022] OJ L 91/4; Art 12, Agreement between the European Union and the Republic of North Macedonia on operational activities carried out by the European Border and Coast Guard Agency in the Republic of North Macedonia [2023] OJ L 61; Art 12, Status Agreement between the European Union and Montenegro on actions carried out by the European Border and Coast Guard Agency in Montenegro [2023] OJ L 140.

[303] Laura Letourneux, 'Protecting the Borders from the Outside: An Analysis of the Status Agreements on Actions Carried Out by Frontex Concluded between the EU and Third Countries' (2022) 24 *European Journal of Migration and Law* 330.

[304] Cf, Art 6(6), Status Agreement between the EU and Montenegro (n 302); Art 12(8), Status Agreement between the EU and the Republic of Moldova (n 302).

[305] Among the abundant literature, see most notably: August Reinisch, *The Privileges and Immunities of International Organizations in Domestic Courts* (Oxford, Oxford University Press, 2013); Jan Klabbers, 'The EJIL Foreword: The Transformation of International Organizations Law' (2015) 26 *European Journal of International Law* 9.

[306] Protocol No 7 on the privileges and immunities of the European Union, 26 October 2012, OJ C 326/1, as amended.

and immunities.[307] While this may compromise the exercise of the right to an effective remedy and a fair trial, the ECtHR has established that the immunities of international organisations are permissible, providing that the claimants have access to reasonable alternative remedies, including internal review mechanisms.[308] As explained in previous parts of this work, despite the presence of a complaints mechanism within Frontex's structure, its deficiencies do not consent to regard it as an effective remedy.[309] Yet, regulation 2019/1896 transferred to the CJEU the competence to adjudicate on the legality of Frontex's conduct.[310] This, as the next section will discuss, may result in an additional obstacle to overcome for potential victims seeking access to justice.

B. Court of Justice of the European Union

The EU legal order encompasses a system of judicial remedies against breaches of EU law. This system occurs at two levels: before national courts and the CJEU. Under EU law, Frontex is responsible for human rights violations committed by its staff.[311] The CJEU is competent to decide on disputes arising from such violations.[312] In general, the CJEU exercises its control over the legality of acts of EU institutions by virtue of the reference preliminary ruling,[313] the actions for annulment,[314] the action for failure to act[315] and the action for damages.[316]

The action for annulment concerns the judicial review of the legality of acts intended to produce legal effects towards third parties. This remedy might however entail some burdensome obstacles for individuals bringing a claim before the CJEU against border control measures taken in the context of the EIBM. First, the impugned measure must have legal effects that are binding on the applicant and bring about a change in their legal situation.[317] Second, while Article 263(1) TFEU, accords passive legitimation to EU institutions, bodies, offices or agencies; active legitimation is recognised to two categories of applicants: privileged applicants, encompassing Member States and EU institutions,[318] and non-privileged applicants, that is, natural or legal persons which must be the addressees of the impugned act, or prove that it is of 'direct and individual concern' to them.[319] With

[307] Art 96, Regulation 1896/2019.
[308] See, most notably, *Waite and Kennedy* (n 37) para 68.
[309] Ch 3, s IV.H.iii.
[310] Art 98, Regulation 2019/1896.
[311] ibid, Art 97(4).
[312] ibid.
[313] Art 267, TFEU.
[314] Art 263, TFEU.
[315] Art 265, TFEU.
[316] Art 340, TFEU.
[317] Case 60/81, *IBM v Commission*, 11 November 1981, ECLI:EU:C:1981:264, para 9.
[318] Art 263(2)(3), TFEU.
[319] Art 263(4), TFEU.

regard to the first condition, Frontex operational plans are binding on the agency, the host and participating Member States.[320] Yet it is not clear whether the measures adopted by Frontex staff are to be considered legally binding on individuals. Regulation 2019/1896 recognises to Frontex statutory staff extensive executive powers, including, for instance, the ability to issue admission or refusal of entry decisions, which are measures clearly producing legal effects on the concerned individual.[321] But the performance of tasks and the exercise of powers by members of the border management teams, in particular those entailing executive powers, require the authorisation of the host Member State.[322] As for the second requirement, individual applicants must show that the act in question was of direct and individual concern to them. The general understanding is that a measure is of direct concern where it directly affects the legal situation of the applicant, leaving no discretion to the authorities entrusted with its implementation.[323] The individual concern of a measure requires the applicant to prove that impugned measure 'affects them by reason of certain attributes which are peculiar to them or by reason of circumstances in which they are differentiated from all other persons and by virtue of these factors distinguishes them individually just as in the case of the person addressed'.[324]

The same procedural hurdles apply to the action for failure to act.[325] This procedure applies to situations where the defendants have the duty to perform specific actions in accordance with EU law. It would therefore offer individuals the possibility of challenging Frontex's omissions. Namely, this procedure could represent an important remedy against the failure of the agency's executive director to terminate or suspend joint operations where there are serious and persistent human rights violations in accordance with Article 46 of Frontex regulation.[326] In this procedure, the agency should have been first called upon to act, and only after its inaction, the applicants can introduce a complaint before the CJEU.[327] However, it is sufficient that the agency defines its position on the call to act for the action to be considered inadmissible.[328] This was precisely the case of a minor and a woman who were victims of several pushbacks in the Aegean Sea while seeking asylum in Greece.[329] Assisted by two NGOs, they sent a letter to Frontex executive director asking to suspend or terminate the agency's operations in Greece.

[320] Art 38(3), Regulation 2019/1896.
[321] ibid, Art 55(7)(b)(c).
[322] ibid, Art 82.
[323] Paul Craig and Gráinne De Búrca, *EU Law: Text, Cases, and Materials* (Oxford, Oxford University Press, 2020) 548.
[324] Case 25/62, *Plaumann & Co v Commission*, ECLI:EU:C:1963:17, 15 July 1963, 107.
[325] Art 265, TFEU.
[326] Art 46, Regulation 2019/1896. See Front-Lex, *Preliminary Action Pursuant to Article 265 TFEU*, 15 February 2021.
[327] Case T-832/14, *Nutria v Commission*, not published, EU:T:2016:428, 21July 2016, para 45 and references therein.
[328] Case T-245/17, *ViaSat v Commission*, 10 March 2021, ECLI:EU:T:2021:128, para 59.
[329] Case T-282/21, *SS and ST v Frontex*, 7 April 2022, ECLI:EU:T:2022:235.

The executive director replied that Frontex's actions in the Aegean Sea had strictly complied with the applicable legal framework. In particular, the agency recalled Article 46 of Regulation 2019/1896 requires incidents of a certain level of seriousness or likely to persist, and 'isolated incidents' such as those concerning the applicants cannot constitute a condition for the applicability of that provision.[330] The CJEU accepted this statement of reasons without questioning the executive director's discretion, and considered it sufficient to define the agency's position, thus bringing the failure to act to an end.[331]

At the same time, the Court suggested that a separate action for annulment under Article 263 TFEU could have challenged Frontex ambiguous reply to the applicants' request.[332] In an action for annulment, the applicant must prove that she is individually and directly concerned by the measure, that is, she has attributes or characteristics that distinguish her from all other persons and mark her out as the addressee of the measure. Victims of human rights violations could more easily meet these requirements occurred during an operation that Frontex should have suspended or terminated or that the agency should not have launched to begin with. Notably, while the applicants in this procedure must be the same as the parties of the pre-contentious procedure, nothing seems to hinder the possibility of natural persons being represented by civil society organisations.

All in all, the status of non-privileged applicants before the CJEU considerably reduces their chances of starting a review procedure.[333] A possible way to move beyond this difficulty would be for applicants to rely on EU institutions, such as the Parliament, which could bring their claim before the CJEU without being subject to these stringent criteria.[334] Nevertheless, the most promising judicial remedy currently available for potential applicants is the action for damages established pursuant to Articles 268 and 340 TFEU and replicated in Frontex Regulation.[335] The action for damages aims to establish the responsibility and award compensation to the victims. The expression 'EU public liability' denotes the non-contractual responsibility of public authorities under EU law,[336] which should be distinguished from international liability.[337] While the liability of Frontex is

[330] ibid, para 26.
[331] ibid, para 31.
[332] ibid, para 33. This was the object of an alternative claim included in the applicants' observations on Frontex Plea of Inadmissibility, available at: www.statewatch.org/media/3022/procedural-document-observations-regularalized-091221_redacted.pdf.
[333] Craig and De Búrca (n 323) 546 et ss.
[334] Gkliati and Rosenfeldt (n 1); Majcher (n 106).
[335] Art 97(4), Regulation 2019/1896. See also: Case T-600/21, *WS and Others v Frontex*, 6 September 2023, ECLI:EU:T:2023:492; Case T-136/22, *Hamoudi v Frontex* (application), 10 March 2022.
[336] For a comprehensive and clear analysis of the case law underlying EU public liability and its application to Frontex joint operations, see: Melanie Fink, 'The Action for Damages as a Fundamental Rights Remedy: Holding Frontex Liable' (2020) 21 *German Law Journal* 532; Fink (n 24) 180–316.
[337] Michael B Akehurst, 'International Liability for Injurious Consequences Arising Out of Acts Not Prohibited By International Law' (1985) 16 *Netherlands Yearbook of International Law* 3.

explicit in EU law, the liability of the Member States was developed by the CJEU starting with the leading case *Francovich*.[338] Irrespective of the implication of the Union or the Member States, liability presupposes (1) a serious breach, (2) of a rule conferring rights on individuals and (3) the existence of a causal link between the conduct and the damage alleged.[339]

While, at first glance, the first two requirements do not seem difficult to establish, the procedural and substantive hurdles persist. First, the burden of proof concerning the damage, which must be actual and certain, lies with the applicant.[340] The defendant EU body should assist the applicant by producing the relevant documentation and information.[341] However, in the case of Frontex's activities, this might be a daunting task, as access to the relevant information is often denied on the grounds of public security protection.[342] Any rule breached in the context of the EIBM and of Frontex joint operations specifically confers rights on the individuals concerned and may result in sufficiently serious breaches. Yet, the existence of a causal link between the conduct and the damage should be 'direct, immediate and exclusive'.[343] This, again, might represent a burdensome obstacle for individual applicants in a case concerning human rights violations occurring during border control operations performed cooperatively by multiple actors. Finally, an important lacuna in the remedial avenue offered by the CJEU is the lack of guidance regarding the joint responsibility of both the EU and its Member States.

Those difficulties emerged in *WS and Others v Frontex*, a case concerning the deportation of a Syrian family from Greece to Türkiye, including four young children.[344] The applicants arrived in Greece in 2016 and expressed their intention to seek international protection, yet a joint return operation conducted by Frontex and Greece led to their transfer to Türkiye. The applicants were prevented from applying for international protection, without access to any individual procedure, and during the return flight they were separated from their children. Afraid of being returned to Syria by the Turkish authorities, they eventually moved to Iraq, where they have resided ever since. By their action for damages, they sought compensation for the material and non-material damage they have suffered as a result of Frontex's alleged unlawful conduct before, during and after the return operation.[345] Nonetheless, the CJEU found that Frontex's alleged conduct could

[338] Joined Cases Nos C-6/90 and 9/90, *Francovich*, ECR I-5357, 19 November 1991.

[339] Cases C–46 and 48/93, *Brasserie du Pêcheur*, 5 March 1996, ECLI:EU:C:1996:79, para 51; Case C–352/98, *Bergaderm*, 4 July 2004, ECLI:EU:C:2000:361, para 42.

[340] *WS and Others v Frontex* (n 335) para 56.

[341] Joined Cases 29, 31, 36, 39–47, 50 and 51/63, *Usines de la Providence*, 9 December 1965, ECLI:EU:C:1965:120, 943–44.

[342] See Case T-31/18, *Izuzquiza*, 27 November 2019, ECLI:EU:T:2019:815. See also: Case T-205/22, *Naass and Sea Watch* (application), 15 April 2022.

[343] AG Toth, 'The Concepts of Damage and Causality as Elements of Non-Contractual Liability' in Henry G Schermers, Ton Heukels and J Philip Mead (eds), *Non-Contractual Liability of the European Communities* (Leiden, Brill, 1988).

[344] *WS and Others v Frontex* (n 335).

[345] ibid, para 28.

not have directly caused the damage allegedly suffered. The Court noted that while Frontex plays an ancillary role in return operations, providing technical and operational support to the Member States, it is the Member States alone that are competent to assess the merits of return decisions and examine applications for international protection.[346] Consequently, the Court found that there was no sufficiently direct causal link between the damage suffered and the agency's alleged wrongful conduct.[347]

The Court did not determine the legality of Frontex's conduct, despite that being the first of the three cumulative requirements for the EU to incur non-contractual liability under Article 340 TFEU.[348] Instead, it implied that because the agency had no competence either as regards the assessment of the return decisions or as regards applications for international protection, it also had not breached its fundamental rights obligations. However, while Frontex cannot enter into the merits of return decisions or asylum claims, it has broad monitoring and supervisory obligations during joint operations. In particular, Frontex, together with the Member States, shall ensure that the respect for fundamental rights, in particular the principle of *non-refoulement* and the proportionate use of means of constraints, are guaranteed during their return operations.[349] By focusing on Frontex competences over the return decisions, the Court disregarded the agency's monitoring and supervisory obligations (and its competence) in the execution of those decisions. This confusion of competences with causes eluded the issue of Frontex and Member States' joint responsibility.[350] The Court ignored whether the expulsion decision was unlawful under international and EU law and, as a consequence, it overlooked the question of Frontex contribution to the Greek authorities' ostensibly unlawful conduct.

At any rate, Frontex omissions should also directly have caused the harm suffered. In this case, Frontex's alleged omissions were closely connected to the unlawful conduct of the Greek authorities. This raises the question whether the Greek authorities' conduct could be considered as the unique and immediate cause of the alleged damage thus breaking the causal chain of causation. The Court had already expressed the view that the cause of the damage may lie not in a single cause but in several causes that decisively contributed to its occurrence.[351] In this case, Frontex could have contributed to the damage by not preventing Greece from breaching EU law. Yet, the conflation between attribution and causation virtually precluded the Court from considering the agency's responsibility for any breach

[346] ibid, paras 64–65.
[347] ibid, para 66.
[348] ibid, para 52.
[349] Art 28(3), Regulation 2016/1624; Art 50(3), Regulation 2019/1896.
[350] Joyce De Coninck, 'Shielding Frontex' (Verfassungsblog, 9 September 2023); See also: Gareth Davies 'The General Court finds Frontex not liable for helping with illegal pushbacks: it was just following orders' (European Law Blog, 11 September 2023).
[351] Case T-401/11 P, *Lusignano*, 7 December 2017, ECLI:EU:T:2017:874, para 71; Case C-229/84 *Sommerlatte v Commission*, 12 June 1986, ECLI:EU:C:1986:241, paras 26–27.

of its monitoring and supervisory obligations.[352] In *WS and Others v Frontex*, the General Court avoided these issues;[353] it remains to be seen if and how the Court of Justice will resolve them upon appeal.

C. European Court of Human Rights and Other Human Rights Bodies

As already discussed,[354] Article 6(2) of the TEU requires that the EU should accede to the ECHR, and Protocol No 14 to the ECHR provides for such a possibility within the ECHR legal framework.[355] The accession will open the possibility of external scrutiny of the EU's compliance with human rights obligations under the ECHR. However, the CJEU's *Opinion 2/13* postponed this opportunity to the distant future.[356] At the time of writing, negotiations have been resumed and it remains to be seen whether they will find a compromise capable of leading to the accession of the EU to the Convention.[357]

Other human rights treaty bodies cannot scrutinise EU compliance with human rights. Hence, the implementation of the EU's (via Frontex) international responsibility for human rights violations appears as a rather improbable perspective, at least in the foreseeable future. In this light, the increased powers of the agency's statutory staff may exacerbate the legal vacuum in which its responsibility cannot be implemented.

As for the Member States, individual applicants can bring a claim before the ECtHR. This also opens up the possibility for multiple attribution of responsibility where the wrongful act results from the joint conduct of host and participating states during Frontex joint operations. Less clear is whether the Court will be ready to decide on cases of aid or assistance provided by an EU Member State to a third country. Despite the ECtHR's reluctance to decide on issues of indirect attribution of responsibility, its expansive application of the doctrine of positive obligations may render the question superfluous. Another litigation route remains open for potential claimants before universal human rights bodies.[358] The HRC, for instance, could receive a complaint from an individual whose rights have been infringed during border control operations. On one hand, this would offer a

[352] De Coninck (n350); Melanie Fink, *Expert Opinion: Case T-600/21 WS and Others v Frontex* (2022).

[353] Note that the Court recently dismissed a similar case as manifestly unfounded. See *Hamoudi* (n 335); Press Release No 188/23, 13 December 2023.

[354] Ch 3, s II.A.

[355] Art 17, Protocol No 14 amending the control system of the Convention, CETS No 194, 13 May 2004.

[356] *Opinion 2/13*, 18 December 2014, ECLI:EU:C:2014:2454.

[357] Jean Paul Jacqué, 'Encore un effort camarades … L'adhésion de l'Union à la Convention européenne des droits de l'homme est toujours à votre portée' (2020) 1 *Europe des droits et libertés* 27.

[358] Başak Çalı, Cathryn Costello and Stewart Cunningham, 'Hard Protection through Soft Courts? Non-Refoulement before the United Nations Treaty Bodies' (2020) 21 *German Law Journal* 355.

faster and simpler remedy to the victims, as compared to the ECtHR; on the other hand, the Committee's individual communication procedure is binding only to state parties that have ratified the First Optional Protocol to the ICCPR. Finally, the turn to international criminal law to frame and address violations of migrant rights in the context of border control may open new litigation routes at both the domestic and international levels.[359]

D. Other Accountability Routes

Where legal responsibility is difficult to attain, less formal accountability mechanisms represent the last resort and the most effective tool to respond to the victims' demand for justice. Regulation 2019/1896 establishes that Frontex should be 'fully responsible and accountable for any decision it takes and for any activity for which it is solely responsible'.[360] This suggests not only that the agency should respond to its wrongs and remedy them; it should also give a transparent account of its activities to the EU institutions and to the general public.

Accountability is a broader concept than responsibility. By and large, the term accountability is employed as a conceptual umbrella that covering various ideas, such as transparency, efficiency, good governance, democracy, responsiveness and responsibility.[361] In a narrower sense, accountability has been famously defined as 'a relationship between an actor and a forum, in which the actor has an obligation to explain and to justify his or her conduct, the forum can pose questions and pass judgement, and the actor may face consequences'.[362] Accountability, moreover, can have a retrospective or a prospective nature. It is devoted to respond to past events; but it also encompasses participatory and standard-setting processes and mechanisms. In this sense, 'the grounds on which someone can be held accountable are much less demanding than the grounds on which they can be held responsible'.[363]

Depending on the forum exercising its oversight on a given actor, accountability can be defined as administrative, political, or social. Administrative accountability refers to supervision by quasi-legal and quasi-independent supervisory authorities. Since the inception of Frontex, important improvements have been realised to foster its administrative accountability. The establishment of the consultative forum

[359] Kalpouzos and Mann (n 293); Kalpouzos (n 293); Elspeth Guild, 'Serious International Crimes, Human Rights, and Forced Migration' in *When Border Control Operations Become Crimes Against Humanity* (Abingdon, Routledge, 2022).

[360] Art 7(4), Regulation 2019/1896.

[361] See International Law Association, Berlin Conference 'Accountability of International Organizations' (2004) 1 *International Organizations Law Review* 221; Mark Bovens, 'Two Concepts of Accountability: Accountability as a Virtue and as a Mechanism' in *Accountability and European Governance* (Abingdon, Routledge, 2012).

[362] Mark Bovens, 'Analysing and Assessing Accountability: A Conceptual Framework' (2007) 13 *European Law Journal* 447.

[363] Philip Pettit, 'Responsibility Incorporated' (2007) 117(2) *Ethics* 171, 173.

and the FRO, assisted by FRMs, certainly enhanced the scrutiny of the agency's activities. Soft-law instruments, such as Frontex Fundamental Rights Strategy, can play an important role in accountability processes. The most important promise to realise Frontex's administrative accountability lies with its complaint mechanism, which, however, is still inadequate.[364] Oftentimes, the confusion between monitoring and complaint procedures generates a flagrant lack of independence. Better monitoring, administered by an independent body such as the FRA, could contribute to improving the level of consistency of national oversight exercised by national human rights bodies.

The European Ombudsman, which is already opened several investigations on the agency, represents another independent scrutiny venue for Frontex's activities. Significantly, while only EU citizens or a resident in the EU can place a complaint before the European Ombudsman, her office can open investigations *motu proprio*.[365] The European Court of Auditors is another administrative forum to oversee Frontex activities. In 2021, for example, the ECA published a special report shedding light on the limited effectiveness of Frontex support to external border management and the lack of information on its actual cost and performance.[366] Yet, decisions and audits of the European Ombudsman and the ECA are not legally binding and cannot be enforced, thus requiring either the cooperation of the institution concerned.[367] A further option is that of the European Anti-Fraud Office, which opened an investigation after receiving information referring to possible irregularities affecting the agency. While the report of the investigation, remained classified for months, and – beyond the resignation of the Frontex executive director – did not result in any legal consequence for the moment; when the secretiveness over it was broken by media organisations,[368] the European Parliament voted against Frontex budget discharge.[369]

In turn, political accountability requires each public institution to explain and justify its conduct to the body that gives it power.[370] Frontex is accountable to the European Parliament and the Council and should fully report on its activities to the EU institutions.[371] The agency, moreover, should transmit its annual activity

[364] See ch 3, s IV.H.iii.

[365] Art 43, CFR.

[366] ECA, *Frontex's support to external border management: not sufficiently effective to date*, Special Report 08/2021.

[367] Anchrit Wille and Mark Bovens, 'Watching EU Watchdogs Assessing the Accountability Powers of the European Court of Auditors and the European Ombudsman' (2022) 44 *Journal of European Integration* 183.

[368] Giorgos Christides and Steffen Lüdke, 'Why DER SPIEGEL Is Publishing the OLAF Report on Frontex's Complicity in Pushbacks' (*Der Spiegel*, 13 October 2022), www.spiegel.de/international/europe/why-der-spiegel-is-publishing-the-eu-investigative-report-on-pushbacks-a-5218398a-5c1e-414e-a477-b26515353fce>.

[369] European Parliament decision on discharge in respect of the implementation of the budget of the European Border and Coast Guard Agency for the financial year 2020 (2021/2146(DEC)) 4 May 2022.

[370] Bovens (n 361).

[371] Art 6, Regulation 2019/1896.

report to the national parliaments.[372] National parliaments, and interparliamentary cooperation, are as critical as overlooked venues to enhance transparency and human rights oversight in the implementation of the EIBM.[373]

While in the past, the role of the European Parliament was merely that of a budgetary authority, today it has a more general overview of the agency's activities.[374] Most notably, it should be kept fully informed about the deployment of liaison officers to third states.[375] The executive director should provide timely answers to any question from members of the European Parliament.[376] The executive director is also required to report regularly to the European Parliament and may be invited to report on the carrying out of the agency's activities.[377] Significantly, in all these circumstances, the executive director is under obligation to provide the information requested. The classification of relevant information does not preclude its availability to the Parliament.[378]

Following several reports alleging Frontex involvement in illegal pushbacks in the Aegean Sea,[379] the European Parliament's LIBE Committee has established a scrutiny working group on Frontex to oversee all the aspects of the agency's activities.[380] After numerous reports of human rights violations during the agency's operations, this move was long overdue. The working group started its work in February 2021 and was mandated to permanently monitor Frontex activities. In July of the same year, the working group published its report on the alleged involvement of Frontex in fundamental rights violations at the external borders.[381] It found that while Frontex was not directly involved in fundamental rights violations, the agency was aware of allegations of fundamental rights violations in Member States with which it had a joint operation, 'but failed to address and follow-up on these violations promptly, vigilantly and effectively'.[382] Frontex did not prevent these violations, nor did it reduce the risk of future violations. Such negligent inaction may breach the agency's positive obligations – most notably the obligation to suspend or terminate an operation where there are serious and persistent human rights concerns.[383]

[372] ibid, Art 112 (3).

[373] Laura Salzano, 'Unexploited Monitoring Opportunities: Exercising oversight on Frontex through National Parliaments' (VerfBlog, 28 October 2022) https://verfassungsblog.de/unexploited-monitoring-opportunities/.

[374] See ch 2, s VIII.

[375] Art 76(5), Regulation 2019/1896.

[376] ibid, Art 106 (2).

[377] ibid, Arts 50(7) and 106.

[378] ibid, Art 92(3).

[379] See most notably: 'Scandals Plunge Europe's Border Agency into Turmoil' (*Der Spiegel International*, 5 February 2021) www.spiegel.de/international/europe/missteps-and-mismanagement-at-frontex-scandals-plunge-europe-s-border-agency-into-turmoil-a-d11ae404-5fd4-41a7-b127-eca47a00753f.

[380] LIBE Committee Frontex Scrutiny Working Group (FSWG) Draft mandate, 29 January 2021.

[381] European Parliament, Report on the fact-finding investigation on Frontex concerning alleged fundamental rights violations, 14 July 2021.

[382] ibid, 5.

[383] Art 46, Regulation 2019/1896.

Whereas the first steps towards the political accountability of the agency have been taken, some gaps remain. The principal body to which the executive director is accountable is Frontex's management board. Only the management board has the power to take disciplinary measures against the actions of the executive director.[384] The director is therefore not directly accountable before national ministers or members of the European Parliament; instead, the director responds to civil servants who, in turn, are accountable to their ministers.[385] Frontex's management board may invite an expert on the European Parliament to attend its meetings, but there is no obligation to do so.[386] Further, when the Commission begins negotiations of a status agreement with a third country, it should assess its fundamental rights situation and inform the Parliament thereof. In this context, EU law requires Parliament's consent to conclude these agreements.[387] This is apparently not the case for Frontex's working arrangements with third countries, where the agency should inform the European Parliament regarding the parties to these arrangements and their envisaged content.[388] The human-rights-sensitive activities that Frontex's working arrangements entail mandate stronger parliamentary oversight.

Finally, social accountability is mainly exercised by NGOs and civil society organisations. In the case of Frontex, the Consultative Forum provides independent advice in fundamental rights matters. Members of the Forum have access to all information relevant to the agency's human rights compliance and can conduct visits during its activities. The Consultative Forum's principal task is to foster the creation and improvement of human-rights-related documents. Yet, the Forum's recommendations are not limited to the agency's main fundamental rights documents but expand to several areas of Frontex activity, such as risk analysis, training, strategic planning and joint operations.[389]

The organisations and agencies represented in the Consultative Forum ensure so-called inside lobbying aimed at influencing policymakers and administrators. In contrast, other grassroots organisations exercise outside lobbying, directed to the media and, therefore, the public.[390] At least since 2008, grassroots organisations advocating against Frontex's alleged human rights violations at the EU borders have been organising campaigns.[391] Frontex is not directly influenced by these external advocacy strategies so long as they do not gain access to the Consultative Forum. However, they raise awareness about the impact of the

[384] ibid, Art 100(2)(n).
[385] ibid, Art 101.
[386] ibid, Art 104 (7).
[387] Art 218(6)(a), TFEU.
[388] Art 76(4), Regulation 2019/1896.
[389] Leila Giannetto, 'More than Consultation: Civil Society Organisations Mainstreaming Fundamental Rights in EU Border Management Policies. The Case of Frontex and Its Consultative Forum' (PhD Thesis, University of Trento 2018) [On file with the author].
[390] Leila Giannetto, 'Lobbying EU Agencies from Within: Advocacy Groups in Frontex Consultative Forum on Fundamental Rights', in *Lobbying in the European Union* (Cham, Springer, 2019).
[391] See eg the 'Frontexit' campaign, available at: www.frontexit.org/fr/.

EIBM, which is essential for better protecting migrant rights and preventing potential violations.

Lastly, the migrant rights violations at the borders of Europe are becoming an important issue addressed by people's tribunals. Following the model of the Russell-Sartre Tribunal, these initiatives aim at preventing 'the crime of silence',[392] by providing a forum in which the actions of governments and other actors are scrutinised against legal and non-legal norms. Along these lines, for example, the Permanent People's Tribunal held several sessions on the rights of 'migrant people along externalised and internal European borders'.[393] This civil society tribunal, composed of members of civil society organisations, jurists and intellectuals, found that Italy and the EU were 'co-responsible' for the violations of migrant rights occasioned by their cooperation with Libya and Egypt, as well as by the retreat of Frontex operations in the Mediterranean Sea.[394] It invited the Italian and the European Parliament to urgently convene Commissions of inquiry on their migration policies and on the use of funds allotted for international cooperation. Importantly, the Tribunal also recalled 'the specific responsibility of communicators and mass media to ensure correct information on migration issues, recognising migrants not as a threat but as holders of fundamental human rights'.[395]

The same aim of spectacle and publicity can be – perhaps even more efficiently – achieved by theatre performances, films, novels and other forms of art. Nonetheless, what seems to distinguish people's tribunals from other forms of social accountability is their adherence to existing legal norms and the victims' central role in the proceedings. Those informal tribunals 'seek to harness the power and legitimacy of law and claim for themselves a role in interpreting it and holding its addressees accountable in a public albeit informal way'.[396] In a sense, they represent a 'popular' form of international law that claims the authority to speak in the name of the people it governs and affects, thus constituting a jurisdiction beyond international law's institutional architecture structured around states' borders.[397]

[392] John Duffett (ed), *Against the Crime of Silence, Proceedings of the International War Crimes Tribunal* (New York, Simon and Schuster, 1968).

[393] Permanent People's Tribunal, 'The Human Right to Health of Migrant and Refugee Peoples', Berlin, 23–25 October 2020, 4.

[394] Permanent People's Tribunal, Sessione sulla violazione dei diritti delle persone migranti e rifugiate (2017–2018), Palermo, 18–20 December 2017, 19 http://permanentpeoplestribunal.org/wp-content/uploads/2018/01/TPP_PALERMO_MIGRANTI_SENTENZA_DEF_ITA.pdf.

[395] ibid, 20 (author's translation).

[396] Andre Byrnes and Gabrielle Simm, 'International Peoples' Tribunals: Their Nature, Practice and Significance' in A Byrnes and G Simm (eds), *Peoples' Tribunals and International Law* (Cambridge, Cambridge University Press, 2018) 13.

[397] Sara Dehm, 'Accusing Europe' in A Byrnes and G Simm (eds), *Peoples' Tribunals and International Law* (Cambridge, Cambridge University Press, 2018) 179–81.

VIII. Conclusion: The Many Roads to Responsibility in the EIBM

This chapter examined the international legal responsibility of the EU and its Member States when they act concertedly to control the European borders, most notably during Frontex's joint operations. The analysis was based on the ILC's ARS and the ARIO, mainly applied to the context of the ECtHR, the principal judicial body overseeing the human rights compliance of EU Member States (and hopefully, in the future, also of the EU). The ECtHR's scrutiny over EU Member States' conduct during the strict implementation of EU law may be limited, following the *Bosphorus* doctrine. Yet, Member States involved in the EIBM, and specifically in Frontex joint operations, maintain a considerable degree of discretion that allows the full scrutiny of the Strasbourg Court. When it comes to the responsibility of Frontex, and therefore of the EU, the organisation is not yet subject to the judicial review of the ECtHR; moreover, individual victims' access to the CJEU is hindered by a number of procedural obstacles. In addition, the possibility of holding Frontex responsible before national courts of Member States (provided that it waived its immunity from jurisdiction) seems to be ruled out by the agency's regulation that transferred this competence to the CJEU. Of course, this does not exclude individual border guards' criminal or civil responsibility. However, this will not solve the problem of Frontex's responsibility under international and EU law.

The EIBM and Frontex joint operations offer a perfect illustration of the complexity and the opacity surrounding multilateral cooperation in the field of border control. The EIBM encompasses the cooperative action of multiple state and non-state actors, which in the event of human rights violations, might shield themselves with the veil of legal uncertainty created by such cooperation. The 'many hands' involved in the management of the EU's borders make individuating those actors who should be held responsible particularly challenging.

In such a context, international law contributes to structure and confront this complexity. Regarding direct responsibility for the primary breach, the basic rule is that conduct by members of the border management teams is generally attributed to the entity that seconded them. This rule, however, has some exceptions. First, where a state places its border guards at the disposal of another state hosting the joint operation, the conduct of those border guards should be attributed to the host state insofar as they act for the purposes, with the consent and under the authority of the latter. Second, where Frontex, places its own staff at the disposal of the host state, their conduct is attributed to the entity exercising effective control over them. If effective control is interpreted as the power to give operational orders, the conduct of Frontex staff placed at the disposal of the host Member State would therefore be attributed exclusively to the latter. If, however, the notion of effective control is understood more progressively, as the lawful power to prevent a violation, both Frontex and the host Member State could be held directly responsible. In this sense, multiple attribution of conduct seems the most appropriate solution to fairly distribute the responsibility for human rights violations occurring in the context of Frontex activities.

These findings leave open the question of whether those entities not directly responsible for a violation of migrant rights during a Frontex joint operation might be held indirectly responsible for it. Indirect responsibility might arise from the facilitation of a breach committed by another actor, or by the failure to prevent it. While derived responsibility is not of immediate relevance to this study (besides exceptional circumstances of direction and control), the concepts of complicity, extraterritorial jurisdiction and positive obligations are potentially powerful tools to answer questions of indirect responsibility in the context of the EIBM.

While the doctrine has progressively interpreted the strict requirements of complicity, some difficulties in applying this notion remain to be tested in practice. The main challenge to the indirect attribution of responsibility in the context of Frontex joint operations consists in proving the required mental element. Moreover, with respect to cooperation with third states, the opposability requirement might further complicate the attribution question.

What emerges from the foregoing analysis is that in several situations, neither the host state nor Frontex should and could be held exclusively and independently responsible for the human rights violations occurring during Frontex joint operations. The concept of due diligence inherent in the doctrine of positive obligations may serve as a potential way forward for allocating responsibility for human rights violations occurring where the control over a given situation is diffused among a plurality of actors, provided that each of them is exercising jurisdiction over the victims of the alleged violations. This would enable victims of human rights violations occurring during Frontex joint operations to reach a remedial solution that would otherwise be impaired by the dispersal of border control practices and by the opacity surrounding them.

An important aspect in need of further clarification in theory and practice is the content of the responsibility shared by the various actors involved in Frontex joint operations. How should reparations be apportioned between the states and/or international organisations contributing to the same indivisible injury? In this respect, Article 3 of the Draft Agreement on the Accession of the EU to the ECHR supported the institution of a co-respondent mechanism between the EU and its Member States involving their joint responsibility.[398] It remains to be seen whether this solution will be confirmed during the negotiations of the future agreement.

The struggle for migrant rights takes many forms, encompassing a range of tactics and articulations. Formal litigation is just part of it. In the face of the current limitations regarding the possibility to held Frontex (and the EU) responsible before an independent human rights court, existing accountability mechanisms should be strengthened, and the agency's transparency improved so that democratic scrutiny could better oversee its actions.

[398] Art 3(7), Consolidated version of the draft Accession Instruments (as of 7 October 2022), 46+1 (2022)28REV, 9 November 2022. Cf: Art 3(7), Draft Agreement on the Accession of the European Union to the Convention for the Protection of Human Rights and Fundamental Freedoms, CM(2013)93add1, 9 July 2013.

Conclusion

> Les droits apparaissent toujours comme liés à certaines conditions. L'obligation seule peut être inconditionnée. Elle se place dans un domaine qui est au-dessus de toutes conditions, parce qu'il est au-dessus de ce monde.
>
> Simone Weil, *L'Enracinement* (Paris, Gallimard, 1943).

I. Recapitulation

Border management is a human rights-sensitive activity. Borders define collective identities and some of the most basic individual rights. Yet, human rights are held to be universal and applicable irrespective of borders and migration status. The tension between the universality and relativity of human rights is brought into sharp relief by the EIBM. On the one hand, the extraterritorial propagation of migration control measures that Frontex and the Member States perform beyond their borders ostensibly reduces their international obligations towards migrants. On the other hand, the multiplicity of actors implementing the EIBM contributes to diffusing their responsibility for any violation of migrant rights, rendering their justiciability extremely difficult.

The management of the European borders is increasingly integrated into a complex network of multiple actors and technologies, often operating in an extraterritorial setting. In this context, Frontex plays a pivotal role: it shapes and operationalises the project of European borders integration. The agency reinforces, assesses and coordinates Member States' border control activities. Its actions complement those of Member States to ensure the effectiveness of the EU's migration policy. This supposedly subsidiary role exacerbates problems related to the attribution of responsibility for migrant rights violations occurring in complex situations involving a multiplicity of actors cooperating at various operational and administrative levels.

Against this background, it is hardly surprising that persistent claims against Frontex's human rights compliance have dogged the agency. Since its inception, Frontex's activities have been controversial and surrounded by legal ambiguity. In 2020, media reports alleged the involvement of Frontex and its Member States in pushback operations at the Greek maritime border.[1] This prompted long

[1] See Bellingcat, 'Frontex at Fault: European Border Force Complicit in 'Illegal' Pushbacks', 23 October 2020, www.bellingcat.com/news/2020/10/23/frontex-at-fault-european-border-force-complicit-in-illegal-pushbacks/.

overdue scrutiny of the agency's role and obligations during its joint border control operations.[2] Still, the agency remained present in many operational scenes where flagrant human rights violations were occurring. For example, Frontex keeps patrolling the Aegean Sea, where migrants are routinely intercepted, or taken from reception centres, and then pulled out into the sea and abandoned in inflatable boats,[3] and where the Pylos shipwreck occurred in circumstances yet to be clarified, while state authorities requested the agency to leave the accident site.[4]

Many questions remain unanswered by the agency and the EU.[5] They concern both the content and scope of Frontex's international obligations (and those of the States it assists and coordinates), as well as the distribution of responsibility for potential breaches of those international obligations among the various public actors involved in Frontex's activities. This work has attempted to address these questions using the grammar of international law. The main legal argument developed in this study is that Frontex (via the EU) and its Member States are bound by a chain of interlinked and complementary yet distinct – and therefore concurrent – obligations deriving from both international and EU law. This chain of protection connects the public actors involved in the integrated management of the European external borders. The breach of one of these interconnected obligations may thus entail the concurrent responsibility of multiple actors.

The border control activities of Frontex and the Member States are guided by the concept of EIBM. The EIBM is based on a diffused control model encompassing measures in neighbouring and third countries, border control measures at the external borders, risk analysis, measures within the Schengen area and return.[6] Border controls are increasingly integrated, yet they shift in space and time, and in how they are experienced. They are enforced across different jurisdictions by a plurality of actors. Tangled in an 'assemblage' of coercive and surveillance practices, border controls are expanding and deepening their reach to stem migratory movements towards Europe. Articulated in this continuum of control, the EIBM intends to facilitate mobility; while enhancing the internal security of Member States by precluding access to Europe and preventing the departure of undocumented migrants.

Frontex is a key enabler of the continuum of control underlying the administration of EU borders. Not only does it contribute to the transformation of

[2] Frontex, Fundamental Rights and Legal Operational Aspects of Operations in the Aegean Sea, Final Report of the Frontex Management Board Working Group, 1 March 2021.

[3] Matina Stevis-Gridneff and others, 'Greece Says It Doesn't Ditch Migrants at Sea. It Was Caught in the Act' (*The New York Times*, 19 May 2023), www.nytimes.com/2023/05/19/world/europe/greece-migrants-abandoned.html; Niamh Keady-Tabbal and Itamar Mann, 'Weaponizing Rescue: Law and the Materiality of Migration Management in the Aegean' (2023) 36 *Leiden Journal of International Law* 61.

[4] Frontex statement following tragic shipwreck off Pylos (Frontex, 16 June 2023), https://frontex.europa.eu/media-centre/news/news-release/frontex-statement-following-tragic-shipwreck-off-pylos-dJ5l9p.

[5] For a detailed comment on the EU's response to the reported incidents at the Greek borders see: Meijers Committee, Frontex and pushbacks: obligations and accountability, CM2105, April 2021.

[6] Recital 11, Regulation (EU) 2019/1896 [2019] OJ L 295.

European border control practices, but it also considerably influences the policies it is mandated to implement. Overall, the agency holds a central position within the EIBM, and since its inception, its powers have increasingly been enhanced. Despite its significant autonomy, however, as an EU agency, Frontex does not enjoy a discrete international legal personality separate from its parent organisation. Thus, under international law, its conduct may entail the EU's international responsibility. Incontrovertibly, over the years, the agency's legal framework has made considerable improvements regarding human rights standards. However, Frontex's heightened technical and operational capacities appear to remain paired with inadequate human rights safeguards and independent monitoring.

Chapter two has shown how Frontex catalyses the diffusion of border controls underlying the EIBM. The agency cooperates with third countries, training their border guards, sharing information with them and enforcing border controls in their own territories. In addition, it fosters a solid information and surveillance network to prevent potential arrivals. In doing so, it challenges the conception of the border as a technology of state-territorial power. On the one hand, the agency's pervasive influence over border management enables it to gradually erode Member States' powers in that area, without formally undermining their sovereignty. On the other hand, by operating beyond the territory of Schengen Member States and cooperating with third countries, Frontex also trespasses on their territorial jurisdiction. This may result in the frustration of the human rights obligations binding the EU and its Member States.

The EIBM concomitantly reduces and intensifies the significance of borders within and beyond the Schengen area. This poses several challenges to both the applicability of the migrant rights obligations binding Frontex and its Member States and the identification of the actor(s) responsible for their violation. This book is an attempt to address these difficulties.

Chapter three identified the international obligations binding the EU, Frontex and the Member States in the management of European borders. In doing so, it explored the complex interplay of diverse norms and institutions directly or indirectly involved in the EIBM. Frontex (and therefore the EU) and the Member States are bound by various obligations deriving from both international and EU law. These obligations form a chain of protection that started from refugee law and developed into international and EU human rights law. This chain of protection results from a complex network of relationships, each entailing rights and duties. The level of protection accorded to any given individual within the chain depends on these relationships.

The chain of protection binding the EU and its Member States encompasses positive and negative obligations towards migrants at their borders. Member States have a duty to ensure that third parties, such as the EU and its agency Frontex, whose action they are in a position to influence, do not breach their human rights obligations. In turn, Frontex is bound by a positive duty to ensure the respect of human rights during all its activities.[7] Significantly, this study also observed the relevant role that the agency may play in promoting human rights while implementing the EIBM. Where migrant rights violations occur, the negligence of the Member States or the agency may, in certain circumstances, entail their responsibility.

This chain of protection connects the public actors involved in the control of the European external borders. The breach of one of its obligations by different public actors may thus entail their concurrent responsibility. In this respect, a salient question concerns the allocation of responsibilities for migrant rights violations occurring during concerted action taken by Frontex and various state authorities. The multiplicity of actors involved in Frontex operations may imply the concurrent exercise of jurisdiction by different entities over the same situation. This, in turn, may result in Frontex and the Member States' shared responsibility.

While this normative chain can provide solid legal protection to migrants in vulnerable situations at the border, there are situations escaping the reach of the chain of protection, situations where the gaps between its chain's links leave open spaces of legal uncertainty. To escape any responsibility, the EU and its Member States leverage the uncertainty within the interstices of the chain. For example, by impeding any physical contact with the individuals concerned, extraterritorial and cooperative border control measures might allow for the circumvention of Frontex and the Member States' obligations.

All Member States have an obligation to secure the human rights of everyone within their jurisdiction.[8] This study has observed, however, that the absence of any direct control over the individual concerned may preclude jurisdiction, and therefore, the very legal existence of human rights obligations. For example, neither the territorial nor the personal model of jurisdiction developed under human rights law would apply to the situation of individuals blocked in third countries with Member States' or the EU's support. Beyond highlighting the broad scope of applicability of EU fundamental rights, Chapter four examined some alternative constructions of human rights jurisdiction and advanced a more flexible interpretation thereof. Namely, jurisdiction has been defined in relational terms: it arises from a relationship of power between a public authority and an individual.

This position is controversial, however, especially regarding the jurisdictional reach of the European Convention on Human Rights, which has been strictly interpreted thus far. Some would also comment that, albeit commendable, a generous approach to human rights jurisdiction is strategically questionable. Indeed, expansively interpreting jurisdiction as a relationship of power between public actors and individuals could risk exacerbating the current backlash against human rights norms and institutions. Consequently, international courts may take a step back and return to more rigid positions.

[7] Frontex Fundamental Rights Strategy, 2021.
[8] Art 1, ECHR.

Admittedly, approaching jurisdiction as a mere exercise of power remains vague and open to contradictory interpretations. Nonetheless, this study proposed to conceptualise jurisdiction as a relationship of (public) power combining legal, administrative and factual elements; a power relationship that is manifested in complex governance mechanisms implementing border controls across multiple borders and actors. The relational approach to jurisdiction proposed in chapter four offers a coherent interpretation of the scope of applicability of human rights obligations regardless of their nature and allows for contextualised applications, including the possibility of concurrent jurisdictions. Ultimately, the relational understanding of jurisdiction appears to be the most faithful to the complex realities to which this notion must apply.

At any rate, interpreting jurisdiction in a relational sense as an exercise of public powers is only one element in evaluating whether the states participating in Frontex operations have contravened their human rights obligations. Beyond the difficulties related to the jurisdictional reach of migrant rights, chapter five underlined the legal issues related to the multiple actors cooperating in the integrated management of European borders. In this respect, 'the profusion of agents obscures the location of agency', and the concomitant responsibility for its harmful results.[9] The uncertainties regarding the attribution of responsibilities for migrant rights violations during the implementation of the EIBM, together with the practical obstacles that migrants must overcome to invoke them, contribute to deepening the gap between theoretical legal assertions and their practical implementation. All in all, what seems most problematic for protecting migrant rights at the borders of Europe is not the dearth of legal solutions, but their difficult implementation.

International law was found to provide some important mechanisms to respond to the problem of diffused responsibility at the European borders. At the same time, this study observed the limitations of positive rules of attribution of responsibility under international law and offered a reflection on alternative solutions. To this end, the analysis drew a distinction between direct and indirect responsibility. With regard to direct responsibility, where a state places its border guards at the disposal of another state hosting a Frontex joint operation, the conduct of its officers should be attributed to the host state insofar as they act to the purposes, with the consent, and under the authority of the latter. By analogy, where Frontex places its own staff at the disposal of a host state exercising effective control over them – interpreted as the power to give operational orders – their conduct should be attributed to the latter. However, if the notion of effective control is progressively understood as the lawful power to prevent a violation, both Frontex and the host Member State should be held directly and concurrently responsible.

[9] Dennis Thompson, 'Designing Responsibility: The Problem of Many Hands in Complex Organizations' in Jeroen van den Hoven, Seumas Miller and Thomas Pogge (eds), *The Design Turn in Applied Ethics* (Oxford, Oxford University Press, 2017) 32.

These findings leave open the question of whether those entities not directly responsible for a violation of migrant rights during a Frontex joint operation might be held indirectly responsible for it. Indirect responsibility might arise from the facilitation of a breach committed by another actor, or by the failure to prevent it. In this respect, the concepts of complicity and positive obligations provide the tools to answer questions of indirect responsibility in the context of Frontex joint operations.

In principle, complicity can be established under three cumulative conditions. First, 'the aid or assistance must be given with a view to facilitating the commission of the wrongful act, and must actually do so'.[10] Second, the aid or assistance must be given with knowledge or intent to facilitate the commission of an internationally wrongful act.[11] Third, the provisions on aiding and assistance apply only where the wrongful conduct would have been such if committed by the assisting state or international organisation.[12] The strict requirements of complicity under international law have sparked abundant academic discussions.[13] Nevertheless, despite several progressive doctrinal interpretations, some difficulties in applying the notion of complicity remain to be tested in practice. The main challenge to the indirect attribution of responsibility in the context of Frontex joint operations consists in proving the required mental element. In addition, with respect to cooperation with third states, the opposability requirement might further complicate the question of indirect attribution of responsibility.

The doctrine of positive obligations can help in moving beyond these difficulties.[14] States hosting Frontex joint operations generally know about the risks of migrant rights violations and dispose of the appropriate practical and legal capacities to prevent or mitigate those risks. Hence, generally, the host state's failure to protect the rights of people involved in a joint operation could entail responsibility for breaching its positive obligations. The responsibility for negligence by other states participating in Frontex joint operations is less straightforward to substantiate, as they act extraterritorially and might not have the required knowledge or power to significantly influence a given situation. Yet, there are circumstances where their knowledge about and contribution to a violation might entail their responsibility for breach of positive obligations.[15] Likewise, Frontex's responsibility for negligence mainly depends on the required level of knowledge of human

[10] Art 16, ARS, Commentary, para 3.
[11] Art 16(a), ARS.
[12] Arts 16, ARS (b) and 14, ARIO (b).
[13] See, most notably: Helmut Philipp Aust, *Complicity and the Law of State Responsibility* (Cambridge, Cambridge University Press, 2011); Miles Jackson, *State Complicity in the Internationally Wrongful Act of Another State* (Oxford, Oxford University Press, 2015); Vladyslav Lanovoy, *Complicity and Its Limits in the Law of International Responsibility* (Oxford, Hart Publishing, 2016); Giuseppe Puma, *Complicità di Stati nell'illecito internazionale* (Turin, Giappichelli, 2018).
[14] Ch 5, s IV.D.
[15] For a similar conclusion, see: Melanie Fink, *Frontex and Human Rights: Responsibility in 'Multi-Actor Situations' under the ECHR and EU Public Liability Law* (Oxford, Oxford University Press, 2018) 155.

rights risks as well as the power and influence the agency has over its joint operations. This study has shown that these requirements could potentially be met, for the agency generally has an adequate level of knowledge about, and the capacity to prevent or mitigate migrant rights violations during its joint operations.

Ultimately, both Frontex (the EU) and the Member States could be held concurrently responsible for migrant rights violations occurring during their concerted actions. Under EU law, this is corroborated by Article 7 of regulation 2019/1896, according to which the agency and the Member States share the responsibility of the EIBM. Nonetheless, for positive obligations to apply, it would be necessary to establish jurisdiction over certain conduct – a particularly daunting task in the context of extraterritorial border control operations. In this sense, the way international jurisprudence will shape and apply the concept of extraterritorial jurisdiction is vital for questions of shared responsibility in the domain of border control.

An important issue in need of further research concerns the content and consequences of the responsibility shared by the various actors involved in Frontex joint operations.[16] In this respect, Article 3 of the Draft Agreement on the Accession of the EU to the ECHR supports the institution of a co-respondent mechanism between the EU and its Member States involving their joint and several responsibilities.[17] It remains to be seen whether this solution will be confirmed by future negotiations of the agreement.[18]

Frontex's activities involve a number of legal questions, from the issue of establishing jurisdiction over extraterritorial operations to issues of attribution of responsibility among multiple actors operating under different legal frameworks. This study explored the possible answers that international law might offer to such questions, as well as the many ways in which international law frames the policy choices underlying them. Despite the different answers the law may have, one of the greatest obstacles confronting individuals whose rights have been infringed by the concerted action of Frontex and Member States is the scarcity of legal remedies.

This study has observed the various difficulties in implementing Frontex's responsibility before relevant human rights bodies and tribunals. Implementing international responsibility on Frontex (and the EU) for human rights violations is virtually impossible. It's not simply that the competence to adjudicate the legality of Frontex's conduct was transferred to the CJEU;[19] the agency also enjoys

[16] See generally : Samantha Besson, 'La Responsabilité Solidaire Des États et/Ou Des Organisations Internationales : Une Institution Négligée', in Alain Supiot (ed), *Face à l'irresponsabilité : la dynamique de la solidarité* (Paris, Collège de France, 2018).

[17] Arti 3(7), Consolidated version of the draft Accession Instruments (as of 7 October 2022), 46+1(2022)28REV, 9 November 2022.

[18] See Przemyslaw Tacik, 'Attribution of Responsibility after the EU Accession to the ECHR and the "Co-Respondent Mechanism"' (2018) 16 *Baltic Yearbook of International Law Online* 29.

[19] Art 98, Regulation 2019/1896.

immunity before national courts.[20] Moreover, unlike its Member States, the EU is not a party to the ECHR, nor can it be held responsible before universal human rights treaty bodies, which have no competence with regard to the EU. Against this background, the future accession of the EU to the ECHR is crucial.

Yet, other accountability mechanisms are available and represent not only the last resort, but also an effective tool to respond to victims' demands for justice.[21] Strengthening these mechanisms is indispensable for the victims and for the credibility of supranational agencies like Frontex. In addition, Frontex's obligation to suspend or terminate or withdraw the financing for any of its activities should be effectively implemented and the executive director's discretion clearly defined.[22] Contrary to what is sometimes assumed, where human rights violations occur systematically, the agency's presence can have a legitimising influence instead of having a 'deescalating and preventive effect'.[23]

In the face of the limits of the current legal framework and all the complications for its effective implementation, the law is but one of the means to realise the promise of human rights. As the law is often but a reflection of the structural inequalities underlying the political system, social action is needed to try to change the current reality of migration control in Europe. Among the many forms that social action could take, education is perhaps one of the most basic. It marks 'the point at which we decide whether we love the world enough to assume responsibility for it'.[24] Of course, this is a daunting task; yet it is crucial to remain faithful not just to the EU's founding values but to our shared humanity. This does not necessarily mean dismantling borders; but abolishing their violence, with a culture of respect for the dignity of others that, in turn, entails the disavowal of unfettered discretionary power over national borders. Litigation may function as a catalyst for change, but it is not the only or even the primary means to attain it.

II. Epilogue: The Borders of Responsibility

When I started this research, people in Europe were still shocked by images and reports of tragedies at sea costing the lives of hundreds of people – fathers, sons, mothers and their babies.[25] The image of two-year-old Alan Kurdi, whose body,

[20] Art 96, Regulation 1896/2019; Protocol No 7 on the privileges and immunities of the European Union [2012] OJ C 326/1, as amended.

[21] Ch 5, s VI.D.

[22] Art 46, Regulation 2019/1896.

[23] Frontex Management Board, 'Fundamental Rights and Legal Operational Aspects of Operations in the Aegean Sea', 1 March 2021, 17.

[24] Hannah Arendt, 'The Crisis in Education' in *Between Past and Future. Eight Exercises in Political Thought* (New York, The Viking Press, 1993), 14.

[25] Lizzy Davis, 'Lampedusa victims include mother and baby attached by umbilical cord' (The Guardian, 10 October 2013), www.theguardian.com/world/2013/oct/10/lampedusa-victims-mother-baby-umbilical-cord.

washed up ashore after he drowned with his mother and brother in an attempt to reach Europe, became the most poignant symbol of the profound crisis in the European response to people on the move and in need of protection.

A few years later, fatigue and detachment replaced shock. In the first six months of 2023, more than a thousand people lost their lives in the Mediterranean Sea.[26] This news does not cause a sensation. We have become used to hearing about migrants' deaths and struggles; we simply do not register the information anymore, or we absolve ourselves with a momentary feeling of compassion and go on with our daily occupations. Something similar happened with the deaths and suffering created by the COVID-19 pandemic.[27] The victims of the uncontrollable became an indistinct mass of people, numbers. Analogously, during the war in Ukraine, with the passing of time, sympathy, compassion and even curiosity about individual stories – the victims' names, their lives and the families they leave – have disappeared. The outrage that once was so sharp has dulled into resignation, somehow replaced by a measure of numbness.[28]

Elias Canetti would explain this as a mechanism linked to our survival instinct and with the removal of death and disease, with the terror they provoke in everyone.[29] Or maybe numbers are to blame. Perhaps a single tragedy inspires individual action, while – paradoxically – collective human suffering registers as an abstraction.[30] An abstraction eliciting transient sympathy allows us to bypass any serious reconsideration of the state of things. This is because, as Susan Sontag observed: '[s]o far as we feel sympathy, we feel we are not accomplices to what caused the suffering. Our sympathy proclaims our innocence as well as our impotence'.[31] Any attempt to explain the human tragedy of a pandemic, a war or of border deaths and violence, presupposes the possibility that things could be different, that we could recover from the pandemic, that peace could be reached and that our borders could be managed humanely. Unable to change the state of things, we have adapted to it, defending ourselves with disillusionment and disconnection: 'compassion is an unstable emotion. It needs to be translated into action, or it withers'.[32] The question remains of what to do with compassion, especially where one has the impression that there is nothing we *can* do; especially, where it is not clear who that 'we' includes. At best, impotence and tepid sympathy towards migrants' struggles confirm our

[26] UNHCR, Operational Portal, Refugee Situation, https://data2.unhcr.org/en/situations/mediterranean.

[27] Annalisa Camilli, *Frontiere* (Internazionale, 25 January 2021), https://us16.campaign-archive.com/?u=9606152151dbc9a1003b9d59b&id=280d8b31eb.

[28] Andrew Mitrovica, *Russia-Ukraine war at 100 days: Compassion fatigue is here* (*Aljazeera*, 3 June 2022), www.aljazeera.com/opinions/2022/6/3/russia-ukraine-war-at-100-days-compassion-fatigue-is-here.

[29] Elias Canetti, *Potere e sopravvivenza* 8th edn (F Jesi tr, Milan, Adelphi, 1974).

[30] Khaled Hosseini, 'Refugees are still dying. How do we get over our news fatigue?' (The Guardian, 17 August 2018), www.theguardian.com/books/2018/aug/17/khaled-hosseini-refugees-migrants-stories.

[31] Susan Sontag, *Regarding the Pain of Others* (London, Picador, 2003) 74.

[32] ibid.

clean conscience. At worst, the widespread thoughtless indifference to distant human suffering allows us to ignore questions about our responsibility towards those distant others. Every European citizen can be petrified before migrants' deaths and suffering, but an unassailable 'common sense' also allows many to justify the policies at the root of these tragedies.[33] Yet, migrants' deaths at sea and their mistreatment at the borders are not natural catastrophes nor inevitable side effects of legitimate policies. Not only are these tragedies avoidable, but the very legitimacy of the policy choices underlying them should be questioned.

Ultimately, the EIBM is not merely the responsibility of European states and Frontex. It is not merely the responsibility of European governments, EU institutions or executive directors. Every European citizen has a stake in the management of the European borders. Hence, all of us have a responsibility in something that goes so wrong as to leave, year after year, the European borders covered by a thicker, yet invisible, blanket of despair. What matters, ultimately, is not only that public authorities respect the law and are held responsible if they fail to do so; what matters, too, is that we evaluate their conduct and correct it if needed.

Transparency is the necessary, yet not sufficient, condition to enable any meaningful corrective action; when it comes to the implementation of the EIBM, it is a condition that is still not adequately met. In addition, many migrant rights violations occur far from public attention.[34] Meanwhile, migrants adapt and react to a generally hostile environment. They change with it and demand – compellingly – to be heard and have their rights respected. Any sincere effort to alleviate the many problems migrants face at the borders of Europe should thus indubitably start with listening to them.

The responsibility for the management of the European borders does not stop with the legal and administrative framework outlined above; instead, as Hannah Arendt would put it, all of us (citizens and non-citizens) need to assume the responsibility to act in our common world.[35] Certainly, this is easier said than done, not least because of the permanent political and ethical crisis we live in. There is no magic – let alone legal – formula to solve this crisis. But any serious attempt in that direction presupposes acknowledging and reminding our unconditioned obligation towards others.[36]

[33] The rhetoric of 'common sense' allows the interlocutor to have racist and xenophobic purposes and support lies with the excuse that they seem sensible because shared by the majority. See: Laura Cervi, Santiago Tejedor and Mariana Alencar Dornelles, 'When Populists Govern the Country: Strategies of Legitimization of Anti-Immigration Policies in Salvini's Italy' (2020) 12 *Sustainability* 10225.

[34] See generally: Cathryn Costello and Itamar Mann, 'Border Justice: Migration and Accountability for Human Rights Violations' (2020) 21 *German Law Journal* 311.

[35] Hannah Arendt, *The Human Condition* (Chicago, University of Chicago Press, 1958); Hannah Arendt, *Responsibility and Judgment* (ed J Kohn, Berlin, Schocken Books, 2003) 147–58. See also: Jan Klabbers, 'Possible Islands of Predictability: The Legal Thought of Hannah Arendt' (2007) 20 *Leiden Journal of International Law* 1.

[36] Simone Weil, *L'Enracinement* (Paris, Gallimard, 1943) 4.

SELECTED BIBLIOGRAPHY

Aaken, A van and Motoc, I (eds), *The European Convention on Human Rights and General International Law* (Oxford, Oxford University Press, 2018)

Aalto, P, *Public Liability in EU Law: Brasserie, Bergaderm and Beyond* (Oxford, Bloomsbury, 2011)

Abi-Saab, G, 'Whither the International Community?' (1998) 9 *European Journal of International Law* 248

Achiume, ET, 'Governing Xenophobia' (2018) 51 *Vanderbilt Journal of Transnational Law* 333

—— 'Migration as Decolonization' (2019) 71 *Stanford Law Review* 1509

—— 'Digital Racial Borders' (2021) 115 *American Journal of International Law* 333

—— 'Racial Borders' (2022) 110 *Georgetown Law Journal* 445

Ago, R, 'Le Délit International' (1939) 68 *Recueil des cours de l'Academie de droit international de la Haye* 415

Ahlborn, C, 'The Rules of International Organizations and the Law of International Responsibility' (2011) 8 *International Organizations Law Review* 397

Ahmed, T and de Jesús Butler, I, 'The European Union and Human Rights: An International Law Perspective' (2006) 17 *European Journal of International Law* 771

Aleinikoff, TA and Zamore, L, *The Arc of Protection: Toward a New International Refugee Regime* (Stanford, Public Seminar Books, 2018)

Allen, J, 'Powerful Assemblages?' (2011) 43 *Area* 154

Allen, S and others (eds), *The Oxford Handbook of Jurisdiction in International Law* (Oxford, Oxford University Press, 2019)

Allott, P, 'State Responsibility and the Unmaking of International Law' (1988) 29 *Harvard International Law Journal* 1

Alston, P (ed), *The EU and Human Rights* (Oxford, Oxford University Press, 1999)

Altwicker, T, 'Transnationalizing Rights: International Human Rights Law in Cross-Border Contexts' (2018) 29 *European Journal of International Law* 581

Amerasinghe, CF, 'The Essence of the Structure of International Responsibility' in Maurizio Ragazzi (ed), *International Responsibility Today: Essays in Memory of Oscar Schachter* (Leiden, Martinus Nijhoff, 2005)

Andrade, PG, 'The External Dimension of the EU Immigration and Asylum Policies Before the Court of Justice' (2022) 7 *European Papers* 109

Ansems de Vries, L and Guild, E, 'Seeking Refuge in Europe: Spaces of Transit and the Violence of Migration Management' (2019) 45 (12) *Journal of Ethnic and Migration Studies* 2156

Arendt, H, 'The Rights of Man: What Are They?' (1949) 3 *Modern Review* 24

—— 'Communicative Power' in Steven Lukes (ed), *Power: A Radical View* (New York, New York University Press, 1986)

—— 'The Crisis in Education' in *Between Past and Future. Eight Exercises in Political Thought* (New York, The Viking Press, 1993)

—— *Responsibility and Judgment* (ed J Kohn, Berlin, Schocken Books, 2003)

Aust, HP, *Complicity and the Law of State Responsibility* (Cambridge, Cambridge University Press, 2011)

Azoulai, L, 'Europe Is Trembling. Looking for a Safe Place in EU Law' (2020) 57 *Common Market Law Review* 1675

Azoulai, L, Places, SB des and Pataut, E (eds), *Constructing the Person in EU Law: Rights, Roles, Identities* (Oxford, Bloomsbury, 2016)

Baldaccini, A, 'Extraterritorial Border Controls in the EU: The Role of FRONTEX in Operations at Sea' in *Extraterritorial Immigration Control: Legal Challenges* (Leiden, Martinus Nijhoff, 2010)
Balibar, É, 'The Borders of Europe' in P Cheah and B Robbins (eds), *Cosmopolitics: Thinking and Feeling Beyond the Nation* (Minneapolis, University of Minnesota Press, 1998)
—— 'Europe at the Limits' (2016) 18 *Interventions* 165
Bańkowski, Z and Christodoulidis, E, 'The European Union as an Essentially Contested Project' (1998) 4 *European Law Journal* 341
Barnidge, RP, 'The Due Diligence Principle under International Law' (2006) 8 *International Community Law Review* 81
Bartels, L, 'The EU's Human Rights Obligations in Relation to Policies with Extraterritorial Effects' (2014) 25 *European Journal of International Law* 1071
Basilien-Gainche, M-L, 'Live and Let Die: The EU Banopticon Approach to Migrants at Sea' in V Moreno-Lax and E Papastavridis (eds), *'Boat Refugees' and Migrants at Sea: A Comprehensive Approach: Integrating Maritime Security with Human Rights* (Leiden, Brill, 2016)
Battjes, H, 'The Soering Threshold: Why Only Fundamental Values Prohibit Refoulement in ECHR Case Law' [2009] *European Journal of Migration and Law* 205
—— 'Territoriality and Asylum Law: The Use of Territorial Jurisdiction to Circumvent Legal Obligations and Human Rights Law Responses' in M Kuijer and W Werner (eds), *Netherlands Yearbook of International Law 2016: The Changing Nature of Territoriality in International Law* (The Hague, TMC Asser Press, 2017)
Baxewanos, F, 'Relinking Power and Responsibility in Extraterritorial Immigration Control: The Case of Immigration Liaison Officers' in T Gammeltoft-Hansen and J Vedsted-Hansen (eds), *Human Rights and the Dark Side of Globalisation* (Abingdon, Routledge, 2016)
Bengoetxea, J, 'The EU as (More Than) an International Organization' in J Klabbers and A Wallendahl (eds), *Research Handbook on the Law of International Organizations* (Cheltenham, Edward Elgar, 2011)
Benhabib, S, *The Rights of Others: Aliens, Residents, and Citizens* (Cambridge, Cambridge University Press, 2004)
—— 'The End of the 1951 Refugee Convention? Dilemmas of Sovereignty, Territoriality, and Human Rights' (2020) 2 *Jus Cogens* 75
Benvenisti, E, *The Law of Global Governance* (Leiden, Brill, 2014)
Besson, S, 'Human Rights, Institutional Duties and Cosmopolitan Responsibilities' (2003) 23 *Oxford Journal of Legal Studies* 507
—— 'The Extraterritoriality of the European Convention on Human Rights: Why Human Rights Depend on Jurisdiction and What Jurisdiction Amounts To' (2012) 25 *Leiden Journal of International Law* 857
—— 'The Bearers of Human Rights Duties and Responsibilities for Human Rights – A Quiet (R)Evolution.' (2015) 32 *Social Philosophy and Policy* 244
—— 'La Responsabilité Solidaire Des États et/Ou Des Organisations Internationales: Une Institution Négligée' in *Face à l'irresponsabilité : la dynamique de la solidarité* (Paris, Collège de France, 2018)
—— 'Concurrent Responsibilities under the European Convention on Human Rights: The Concurrence of Human Rights Jurisdictions, Duties, and Responsibilities' in I Motoc and A van Aaken (eds), *The European Convention on Human Rights and General International Law* (Oxford, Oxford University Press, 2018)
—— 'La Due Diligence En Droit International' (2020) 409 *Recueil des cours de l'Académie du droit international de La Haye*
—— *Theories of International Responsibility Law* (Cambridge, Cambridge University Press, 2022)
Besson, S and Tasioulas, J, *The Philosophy of International Law* (Oxford, Oxford University Press, 2010)
Bianchi, A, 'Reflexive Butterfly Catching: Insights from a Situated Catcher' in J Pauwelyn, J Wouters and RA Wessel (eds), *Informal International Lawmaking* (Oxford, Oxford University Press, 2012)
Bigo, D, 'The Möbius Ribbon of Internal and External Security(Ies)' in M Albert, D Jacobson and Y Lapid (eds), *Identities, Borders, Orders* (Minneapolis, University of Minnesota Press, 2001)

Bigo, D and Guild, E, *Controlling Frontiers: Free Movement Into and Within Europe* (Farnham, Ashgate, 2005)

Binder, C and Hofbauer, JA, 'Applicability of Customary International Law to the European Union as a Sui Generis International Organization: An International Law Perspective' in A Th Müller, FL Bordin and F Pascual-Vives (eds), *The European Union and Customary International Law* (Cambridge, Cambridge University Press, 2022)

Byrnes, A and Simm, G (eds), *Peoples' Tribunals and International Law* (Cambridge, Cambridge University Press, 2018)

Blokker, N, 'International Organizations and Their Members. "International Organizations Belong to All Members and to None" – Variations on a Theme' (2004) 1 *International Organizations Law Review* 139

—— 'Member State Responsibility for Wrongdoings of International Organizations: Beacon of Hope or Delusion?' (2015) 12 *International Organizations Law Review* 319

—— 'International Legal Personality of the European Communities and the European Union: Inspirations from Public International Law' [2016] 35 *Yearbook of European Law* 471.

Boon, KE, 'Are Control Tests Fit for the Future: The Slippage Problem in Attribution Doctrines' (2014) 15 *Melbourne Journal of International Law* 330

Bordin, FL, *The Analogy between States and International Organizations* (Cambridge, Cambridge University Press, 2018)

Bordin, FL, Müller, ATh and Pascual-Vives, F (eds), *The European Union and Customary International Law* (Cambridge, Cambridge University Press, 2022)

Bosworth, M, Fili, A and Pickering, S, 'Women and Border Policing at the Edges of Europe' (2018) 44 *Journal of Ethnic and Migration Studies* 2182

Boutin, B, 'Responsibility of the Netherlands for the Acts of Dutchbat in Nuhanović and Mustafić: The Continuous Quest for a Tangible Meaning for "Effective Control" in the Context of Peacekeeping' (2012) 25 *Leiden Journal of International Law* 521

Bovens, M, *The Quest for Responsibility: Accountability and Citizenship in Complex Organisations* (Cambridge, Cambridge University Press, 1998)

—— 'Analysing and Assessing Accountability: A Conceptual Framework' (2007) 13 *European Law Journal* 447

Brouwer, E, *Digital Borders and Real Rights: Effective Remedies for Third-Country Nationals in the Schengen Information System* (Leiden, Brill, 2008)

—— 'Extraterritorial Migration Control and Human Rights: Preserving the Responsibility of the EU and Its Member States' (2010) 21 *Extraterritorial Immigration Control: Legal Challenges* 199

—— 'Legal Boundaries and the Use of Migration Technology' in H Dijstelbloem and A Meijer (eds), *Migration and the New Technological Borders of Europe* (London, Palgrave Macmillan UK, 2011)

Brouwer, E and Borgesius, FZ, 'Access to Personal Data and the Right to Good Governance during Asylum Procedures after the Cjeu's YS. and M. and S. Judgment (C-141/12 and C-372/12)' (2015) 17 *European Journal of Migration and Law* 259

Brown, AAD, 'To Complicity … and Beyond! Passive Assistance and Positive Obligations in International Law' (2016) 27 Hague Yearbook of International Law 133

Busuioc, M, Curtin, D and Groenleer, M, 'Agency Growth between Autonomy and Accountability: The European Police Office as a "Living Institution"' (2011) 18 *Journal of European Public Policy* 848

Caflisch, L, 'Attribution, Responsibility and Jurisdiction in International Human Rights Law' (2017) 10 *ACDI – Anuario Colombiano de Derecho Internacional* 161

Çalı, B and others (eds), *Migration and the European Convention on Human Rights* (Oxford, Oxford University Press, 2021)

Çalı, B, Costello, C and Cunningham, S, 'Hard Protection through Soft Courts? Non-Refoulement before the United Nations Treaty Bodies' (2020) 21 *German Law Journal* 355

Camilli, A, *La legge del mare* (Milan, Rizzoli, 2019)

Campesi, G, *Polizia della frontiera: Frontex e la produzione dello spazio europeo* (Rome, DeriveApprodi, 2015)

—— 'European Border and Coast Guard (Frontex): Security, Democracy, and Rights at the EU Border' [2018] *Oxford Research Encyclopedia of Criminology and Criminal Justice*

Cannizzaro, E, 'The Neo-Monism of the European Legal Order' in E Cannizzaro, P Palchetti and R A Wessel (eds), *International Law as Law of the European Union* (Leiden, Brill, 2012)

—— 'Beyond the Either/Or: Dual Attribution to the European Union and to the Member State for Breach of the ECHR' in *The International Responsibility of the European Union* (Oxford, Hart Publishing, 2013)

—— 'The EU's Human Rights Obligations in Relation to Policies with Extraterritorial Effects: A Reply to Lorand Bartels' (2014) 25 *European Journal of International Law* 1093

—— 'Disintegration Through Law?' (2016) 1 *European Papers* 3

—— 'Fundamental Values and Fundamental Disagreement in Europe' (2018) 3 *European Papers* 469

Cannizzaro, E, Palchetti, P and Wessel, RA, *International Law as Law of the European Union* (Leiden, Martinus Nijhoff, 2011)

Cantor, D and others, 'Externalisation, Access to Territorial Asylum, and International Law' (2022) 34 *International Journal of Refugee Law* 120

Carlier, J-Y, 'Droit d'asile et Des Réfugiés: De La Protection Aux Droits' (2008) 332 *Collected Courses of the Hague Academy of International Law*

Carrera, S and Geddes, A (eds), *The EU Pact on Migration and Asylum in Light of the United Nations Global Compact on Refugees* (Florence, EUI, 2021)

Carrera, S, den Hertog, L and Parkin, J, 'The Peculiar Nature of EU Home Affairs Agencies in Migration Control: Beyond Accountability versus Autonomy?' (2013) 15 *European Journal of Migration and Law* 337

Carrera, S, den Hertog, L, Panizzon, M and Kostakopoulou, D, *The EU External Policies on Migration, Borders and Asylum in an Era of Large Flows: Policy Transfers or Intersecting Policy Universes?* (Leiden, Brill, 2018)

Carrera, S and Stefan, M, *Fundamental Rights Challenges in Border Controls and Expulsion of Irregular Immigrants in the European Union: Complaint Mechanisms and Access to Justice* (Abingdon, Routledge, 2020)

Carrera, S, Vara, JS and Strik, T (eds), *Constitutionalising the External Dimensions of EU Migration Policies in Times of Crisis* (Cheltenham, Edward Elgar, 2019)

Cassese, S, *Territori e potere. Un nuovo ruolo per gli Stati?* (Bologna, Il Mulino, 2016)

Chetail, V, 'Le Droit Des Réfugiés à l'épreuve Des Droits de l'homme: Bilan de La Jurisprudence de La Cour Européenne Des Droits de l'homme Sur l'interdiction Du Renvoi Des Étrangers Menacés de Torture et de Traitements Inhumains Ou Dégradants' [2004] *Revue Belge de Droit International* 155

—— 'Théorie et Pratique de L'Asile En Droit International Classique: Etude Sur Les Origines Conceptuelles et Normatives Du Droit International Des Réfugiés' (2011) 115 *Revue Générale de Droit International Public* 625

—— 'Are Refugee Rights Human Rights? An Unorthodox Questioning of the Relations between Refugee Law and Human Rights Law' in R Rubio-Marin (ed), *Human Rights and Immigration* (Oxford, Oxford University Press, 2014)

—— 'The Legal Personality of Multinational Corporations, State Responsibility and Due Diligence: The Way Forward' in D Alland and others (eds), *Unité et Diversité du Droit international: Ecrits en l'Honneur du Professeur J-M Dupuy* (Leiden, Martinus Nijhoff, 2014)

—— 'The Common European Asylum System: Bric-à-Brac or System?' in P De Bruycker, F Maiani and V Chetail (eds), *Reforming the Common European Asylum System: The New European Refugee Law* (Leiden, Brill, 2016)

—— 'Sovereignty and Migration in the Doctrine of the Law of Nations: An Intellectual History of Hospitality from Vitoria to Vattel' (2016) 27 *European Journal of International Law* 901

—— *International Migration Law* (Oxford, Oxford University Press, 2019)

—— 'Crisis Without Borders: What Does International Law Say About Border Closure in the Context of Covid-19?' (2020) 2 *Frontiers in Political Science*

—— 'The International Organization for Migration and the Duty to Protect Migrants: Revisiting the Law of International Organizations' in Jan Klabbers (ed), *The Cambridge Companion to International Organizations Law* (Cambridge, Cambridge University Press, 2022)

Chetail, V, Bruycker, PD and Maiani, F (eds), *Reforming the Common European Asylum System: The New European Refugee Law* (Leiden, Brill Nijhoff, 2016)

Chimni, BS, 'The Geopolitics of Refugee Studies: A View from the South' (1998) 11 *Journal of Refugee Studies* 350

—— 'Aid, Relief, and Containment: The First Asylum Country and Beyond' (2002) 40 *International Migration* 75

—— 'The International Law of Jurisdiction: A TWAIL Perspective' [2021] *Leiden Journal of International Law* 1

Chinkin, C, 'The Challenge of Soft Law: Development and Change in International Law' (1989) 38 *The International and Comparative Law Quarterly* 850

Cholewinski, R, 'Family Reunification and Conditions Placed on Family Members: Dismantling a Fundamental Human Right' (2002) 4 *European Journal of Migration and Law* 271

—— 'The Need for Effective Individual Legal Protection in Immigration Matters' (2005) 7 *European Journal of Migration and Law* 237

Clapham, A, *Human Rights Obligations of Non-State Actors* (Oxford, Oxford University Press, 2006)

Collins, R and White, ND, *International Organizations and the Idea of Autonomy: Institutional Independence in the International Legal Order* (Abingdon, Routledge, 2011)

Coman-Kund, F, *European Union Agencies as Global Actors: A Legal Study of the European Aviation Safety Agency, Frontex and Europol* (Abingdon, Routledge, 2018)

Combacau, J, 'Obligations de résultat et obligations de comportement: quelques questions et pas de réponse' in *Mélanges offerts à Paul Reuter: le droit international: unité et diversité* (Paris, Pedone, 1981)

Cormack, BT, *A Power to Do Justice* (Chicago, The University of Chicago Press, 2008)

Cornelisse, G, *Immigration Detention and Human Rights* (Leiden, Brill, 2010)

—— 'Territory, Procedures and Rights: Border Procedures in European Asylum Law' (2016) 35 *Refugee Survey Quarterly* 74

Cornelisse, G and Reneman, M, 'Border Procedures in the European Union: How the Pact Ignored the Compacts' (2022) 11 *Laws* 38

Corten, O, 'La "complicité" dans le droit de la responsabilité internationale: un concept inutile ?' (2011) 57 *Annuaire Français de Droit International* 57

Costello, C, 'The Bosphorus Ruling of the European Court of Human Rights: Fundamental Rights and Blurred Boundaries in Europe' (2006) 6 *Human Rights Law Review* 87

—— *The Human Rights of Migrants and Refugees in European Law* (Oxford, Oxford University Press, 2015)

—— 'Immigration Detention: The Grounds Beneath Our Feet' (2015) 68 *Current Legal Problems* 143

—— 'The Search for the Outer Edges of Non-Refoulement in Europe: Exceptionality and Flagrant Breaches' [2016] *Human Rights and the Refugee Definition* 180

Costello, C and Foster, M, 'Non-Refoulement as Custom and Jus Cogens? Putting the Prohibition to the Test' in M den Heijer and H van der Wilt (eds), *Netherlands Yearbook of International Law. Jus Cogens: Quo Vadis?* (The Hague, T.M.C. Asser Press, 2016)

Costello, C and Mann, I, 'Border Justice: Migration and Accountability for Human Rights Violations' (2020) 21 *German Law Journal* 311

Craig, P and De Búrca, G, *EU Law: Text, Cases, and Materials* (Oxford, Oxford University Press, 2020)

Crawford, J, *Brownlie's Principles of Public International Law* (Oxford, Oxford University Press, 2019)

Crawford, J, Pellet, A and Olleson, S (eds), *The Law of International Responsibility* (Oxford, Oxford University Press, 2010)

Cremona, M and Scott, J, *EU Law Beyond EU Borders: The Extraterritorial Reach of EU Law* (Oxford, Oxford University Press, 2019)

Csernatoni, R, 'Constructing the EU's High-Tech Borders: FRONTEX and Dual-Use Drones for Border Management' (2018) 27 *European Security* 175
Curtin, D and Nollkaemper, A, 'Conceptualizing Accountability in International and European Law' (2005) 36 *Netherlands Yearbook of International Law* 3
Curtin, D and van Ooik, R, 'The Sting Is Always in the Tail. The Personal Scope of Application of the EU Charter of Fundamental Rights' [2001] *Maastricht Journal of European and Comparative Law* 102
Cusumano, E, 'Straightjacketing Migrant Rescuers? The Code of Conduct on Maritime NGOs' (2019) 24 *Mediterranean Politics* 106
Cusumano, E and Gombeer, K, 'In Deep Waters: The Legal, Humanitarian and Political Implications of Closing Italian Ports to Migrant Rescuers' (2018) 25 *Mediterranean Politics* 245
Cuttitta, P and Last, T (eds), *Border Deaths: Causes, Dynamics and Consequences of Migration-Related Mortality* (Amsterdam, Amsterdam University Press, 2019)
d'Aspremont, J, 'Abuse of the Legal Personality of International Organizations and the Responsibility of Member States' (2007) 4 *International Organizations Law Review* 91
—— 'Softness in International Law: A Self-Serving Quest for New Legal Materials' (2008) 19 *European Journal of International Law* 1075
—— 'The Multifaceted Concept of the Autonomy of International Organizations and International Legal Discourse' in R Collins and N D White (eds), *International Organizations and the Idea of Autonomy* (Abingdon, Routledge, 2011)
Da Costa, K, *The Extraterritorial Application of Selected Human Rights Treaties* (Leiden, Martinus Nijhoff, 2012)
Dagan, H and Dorfman, A, 'Interpersonal Human Rights' (2018) 51 *Cornell International Law Journal* 361
Daugirdas, K, 'How and Why International Law Binds International Organizations' (2016) 57 *Harvard International Law Journal* 325
—— 'Member States' Due Diligence Obligations to Supervise International Organizations' in H Krieger, L Kreuzer and A Peters (eds), *Due Diligence and Structural Change in the International Legal Order* (Oxford, Oxford University Press, 2020)
Daugirdas, K and Schuricht, S, *Breaking the Silence: Why International Organizations Should Acknowledge Customary International Law Obligations to Provide Effective Remedies* (Leiden, Brill, 2020)
Davitti, D, 'Beyond the Governance Gap: Accountability in Privatized Migration Control' (2020) 21 *German Law Journal* 487
De Búrca, G, 'The Road Not Taken: The European Union as a Global Human Rights Actor' (2011) 105 *American Journal of International Law* 649
De Coninck, J, 'Effective Remedies for Human Rights Violations in EU CSDP Military Missions: Smoke and Mirrors in Human Rights Adjudication?' (2023) 24 *German Law Journal* 342
de Frouville, O, 'Attribution of Conduct to the State: Private Individuals' in J Crawford, A Pellet and S Olleson (eds), *The Law of International Responsibility* (Oxford, Oxford University Press, 2010)
De Schutter, O, 'Human Rights and the Rise of International Organisations: The Logic of Sliding Scales in the Law International Responsabilité' in J Wouters and E Brems (eds), *Accountability for Human Rights Violations by International Organizations* (Antwerp, Intersentia, 2011)
De Witte, B, 'The European Union as an International Legal Experiment' [2012] *The Worlds of European Constitutionalism* 19
Delgado Casteleiro, A, *The International Responsibility of the European Union: From Competence to Normative Control* (Cambridge, Cambridge University Press, 2016)
den Heijer, M, 'Whose Rights and Which Rights? The Continuing Story of Non-Refoulement under the European Convention on Human Rights' (2008) 10 *European Journal of Migration and Law* 277
—— *Europe and Extraterritorial Asylum* (Oxford, Hart Publishing, 2012)
—— 'Shared Responsibility Before The European Court of Human Rights' (2013) 60 *Netherlands International Law Review* 411
den Heijer, M, Rijpma, J and Spijkerboer, T, 'Coercion, Prohibition, and Great Expectations: The Continuing Failure of the Common European Asylum System' (2016) 53 *Common Market Law Review* 607

Desautels-Stein, J, *The Right to Exclude: A Critical Race Approach to Sovereignty, Borders, and International Law* (Oxford, Oxford University Press, 2023)
Di Pascale, A, 'Migration Control at Sea: The Italian Case' in Bernard Ryan and Valsamis Mitsilegas (eds), *Extraterritorial Immigration Control* (Leiden, Brill, 2010)
Dominicé, C, 'Attribution of Conduct to Multiple States and the Implication of a State in the Act of Another State' in J Crawford, A Pellet and S Olleson (eds), *Oxford Commentaries on International Law* (Oxford, Oxford University Press, 2010)
Duez, D, 'A Community of Borders, Borders of the Community The EU's Integrated Border Management Strategy' in E Vallet (ed), *Borders, Fences and Walls. State of Insecurity?* (Farnham, Ashgate, 2014)
Dupuy, P-M, 'Reviewing the Difficulties of Codification: On Ago's Classification of Obligations of Means and Obligations of Result in Relation to State Responsibility' (1999) 10 *European Journal of International Law* 371
—— 'L'obligation En Droit International' (2000) 44 *Archives de philosophie du droit* 217
Eckes, C and Wessel, RA, 'An International Perspective' in R Schütze and T Tridimas (eds), *Oxford Principles Of European Union Law: The European Union Legal Order* (Oxford, Oxford University Press, 2018)
Egan, S, 'Mapping State Responsibility for Complicity in Extraordinary Rendition' in S Egan (ed), *Extraordinary Rendition and Human Rights: Examining State Accountability and Complicity* (Cham, Springer, 2019)
Ekelund, H, 'The Establishment of FRONTEX: A New Institutionalist Approach' (2014) 36 *Journal of European Integration* 99
Evans, MD and Koutrakos, P (eds), *The International Responsibility of the European Union: European and International Perspectives* (Oxford, Hart Publishing, 2013)
Faist, T, 'Contested Externalisation: Responses to Global Inequalities' (2019) 7 *Comparative Migration Studies* 45
Fasterling, B and Demuijnck, G, 'Human Rights in the Void? Due Diligence in the UN Guiding Principles on Business and Human Rights' (2013) 116 *Journal of Business Ethics* 799
Fazzini, A, *L'esternalizzazione delle frontiere e la responsabilità degli stati europei. Il caso Italia-Libia* (Naples, Editoriale Scientifica, 2023)
Fernandez, M, 'Multi-Stakeholder Operations of Border Control Coordinated at the EU Level and the Allocation of International Responsibilities' in T Gammeltoft-Hansen and J Vedsted-Hansen (eds), *Human Rights and the Dark Side of Globalisation: Transnational Law Enforcement and Migration Control* (Abingdon, Routledge, 2016)
—— 'The EU External Borders Policy and Frontex-Coordinated Operations at Sea: Who Is in Charge? Reflections on Responsibility for Wrongful Acts' in V Moreno-Lax and E Papastavridis (eds), *'Boat Refugees' & Migrants at Sea: A Comprehensive Approach. Integrating Maritime Security with Human Rights* (Leiden, Brill, 2016)
Ferraro, F and De Capitani, E, 'The New European Border and Coast Guard: Yet Another "Half Way" EU Reform?' (2016) 17 *ERA Forum* 385
Ferstman, C, 'Human Rights Due Diligence Policies Applied to Extraterritorial Cooperation to Prevent "Irregular" Migration: European Union and United Kingdom Support to Libya' (2020) 21 *German Law Journal* 459
Fikfak, V and Izvorova, L, 'Language and Persuasion: Human Dignity at the European Court of Human Rights' (2022) 22 *Human Rights Law Review* ngac018
Fink, M, 'Frontex Working Arrangements: Legitimacy and Human Rights Concerns Regarding "Technical Relationships"' (2012) 28 *Merkourios–Utrecht Journal of International and European Law* 20
—— *Frontex and Human Rights: Responsibility in 'Multi-Actor Situations' under the ECHR and EU Public Liability Law* (Oxford, Oxford University Press, 2018)
—— 'The Action for Damages as a Fundamental Rights Remedy: Holding Frontex Liable' (2020) 21 *German Law Journal* 532
Fischer-Lescano, A, Löhr, T and Tohidipur, T, 'Border Controls at Sea: Requirements under International Human Rights and Refugee Law' (2009) 21 *International Journal of Refugee Law* 256
Ford, RT, 'Law's Territory (A History of Jurisdiction)' (1998) 97 *Michigan Law Review* 843

Franko, K, 'The Two-Sided Spectacle at the Border: Frontex, NGOs and the Theatres of Sovereignty' (2021) 25 *Theoretical Criminology* 379

Franko, K and Gundhus, HO, 'Policing Humanitarian Borderlands: Frontex, Human Rights and the Precariousness of Life' (2015) 55 *British Journal of Criminology* 1

Frenzen, N, 'The Legality of Frontex Operation Hera-Type Migration Control Practices in Light of the Hirsi Judgment' in T Gammeltoft-Hansen and J Vedsted-Hansen (eds), *Human Rights and the Dark Side of Globalisation: Transnational Law Enforcement and Migration Control* (Abingdon, Routledge, 2016)

Fry, JD, 'Attribution of Responsibility' in A Nollkaemper and I Plakokefalos (eds), *Principles of Shared Responsibility in International Law: An Appraisal of the State of the Srt*, vol 1 (Cambridge, Cambridge University Press, 2014)

Gammeltoft-Hansen, T, 'The Refugee, the Sovereign, and the Sea: European Union Interdiction Policies' in *Sovereignty Games* (New York, Springer, 2008)

—— *Access to Asylum: International Refugee Law and the Globalisation of Migration Control* (Cambridge, Cambridge University Press, 2011)

—— 'The Perfect Storm: Sovereignty Games and the Law and Politics of Boat Migration' in V Moreno-Lax and E Papastavridis (eds), *'Boat Refugees' and Migrants at Sea: A Comprehensive Approach: Integrating Maritime Security with Human Rights* (Leiden, Brill Nijhoff, 2016)

—— 'Extraterritorial Human Rights Obligations in Regard to Refugees and Migrants' in M Gibney, Krajewski and W Vandenhole (eds), *Routledge Handbook on Extraterritorial Human Rights Obligations* (Abingdon, Routledge, 2021)

Gammeltoft-Hansen, T and Hathaway, JC, 'Non-Refoulement in a World of Cooperative Deterrence' (2014) 53 *Columbia Journal of Transnational Law* 235

Gammeltoft-Hansen, T and Vedsted-Hansen, J (eds), *Human Rights and the Dark Side of Globalisation: Transnational Law Enforcement and Migration Control* (Abingdon, Routledge, 2016)

Ganesh, A, 'The European Union's Human Rights Obligations Towards Distant Strangers' (2016) 37 *Michigan Journal of International Law* 475

Gardner, J, 'Complicity and Causality' (2007) 1 *Criminal Law and Philosophy* 127

Garelli, G and Tazzioli, M, 'The Humanitarian War against Migrant Smugglers at Sea' (2018) 50 *Antipode* 685

Gatta, F, 'Migration and Rule of (Human Rights) Law in the EU: A "Constitutional" Crisis' (2022) Forum Transregionale Studien Working Paper

Gattini, A, 'Smoking/No Smoking: Some Remarks on the Current Place of Fault in the ILC Draft Articles on State Responsibility' (1999) 10 *European Journal of International Law* 397

Gerards, J and Brems, E, *Procedural Review in European Fundamental Rights Cases* (Cambridge, Cambridge University Press, 2017)

Gianelli, A, 'Customary International Law in the European Union' in E Cannizzaro, P Palchetti and R Wessel (eds), *International Law as Law of the European Union* (Leiden, Martinus Nijhoff, 2011)

Giannetto, L, 'More than Consultation: Civil Society Organisations Mainstreaming Fundamental Rights in EU Border Management Policies. The Case of Frontex and Its Consultative Forum' (PhD Thesis, University of Trento 2018)

—— 'CSOs and EU Border Management: Cooperation or Resistance? The Case of Frontex Consultative Forum' [2019] *American Behavioral Scientist* 0002764219882988

—— 'Lobbying EU Agencies from Within: Advocacy Groups in Frontex Consultative Forum on Fundamental Rights' in D Dialer and M Richter (eds) *Lobbying in the European Union* (Cham, Springer, 2019)

Giuffré, M, 'Watered-down Rights on the High Seas: Hirsi Jamaa and Others V Italy (2012)' (2012) 61 *International & Comparative Law Quarterly* 728

—— 'State Responsibility Beyond Borders: What Legal Basis for Italy's Push-Backs to Libya?' (2012) 24 *International Journal of Refugee Law* 692

—— *The Readmission of Asylum Seekers Under International Law* (Oxford, Hart Publishing, 2020)

Giuffré, M and Moreno Lax, V, 'The Raise of Consensual Containment: From "Contactless Control" to "Contactless Responsibility" for Forced Migration Flows' in SS Juss (ed), *Research Handbook on International Refugee Law* (Cheltenham, Edward Elgar, 2019)

Gkliati, M, 'The EU Returns Agency: The Commissions' Ambitious Plans and Their Human Rights Implications' (2022) 24 *European Journal of Migration and Law* 545

—— 'The Next Phase of The European Border and Coast Guard: Responsibility for Returns and Push-backs in Hungary and Greece' (2022) 7 *European Papers* 171

Gkliati, M and Kilpatrick, J, 'Crying Wolf Too Many Times: The Impact of the Emergency Narrative on Transparency in FRONTEX Joint Operations' (2022) 17 *Utrecht Law Review* 57

Gkliati, M and Nicolosi, SF, 'External Solidarity in Integrated Border Management: The Role of EU Migration Agencies' in E Kassoti and N Idriz (eds), *The Principle of Solidarity: International and EU Law Perspectives* (The Hague, TMC Asser Press, 2023)

Gkliati, M and Rosenfeldt, H, 'Accountability of the European Border and Coast Guard Agency: Recent Developments, Legal Standards and Existing Mechanisms' (School of Advanced Studies, Refugee Law Initiative 2018) Working Paper 30

Goodwin-Gill, GS, 'The Right to Leave, the Right to Return and the Question of a Right to Remain' in *International Law and the Movement of Persons Between the States* (Oxford, Oxford University Press, 1978)

—— 'Non-Refoulement and the New Asylum Seekers Commentary' (1985) 26 *Virginia Journal of International Law* 897

—— 'The Right to Leave, the Right to Return and the Question of a Right to Remain' in V Gowlland-Debbas (ed), *The Problem of Refugees in the Light of Contemporary International Law Issues* (The Hague, Martinus Nijhoff, 1995)

—— 'Article 31 of the 1951 Convention Relating to the Status of Refugees: Non-Penalization, Detention and Protection' in E Feller, V Türk and F Nicholson (eds), *Refugee Protection in International Law* (Cambridge, Cambridge University Press, 2003)

—— 'State Responsibility and the "Good Faith" Obligation in International Law' in M Fitzmaurice and D Sarooshi, *Issues of State Responsibility before International Judicial Institutions* (Oxford, Hart Publishing, 2004)

—— 'Migrants Rights and Managed Migration' in V Chetail (ed), *Mondialisation, migration et droits de l'homme: le droit international en question* (Brussels, Bruylant, 2007)

—— 'The Right to Seek Asylum: Interception at Sea and the Principle of Non-Refoulement' (2011) 23 *International Journal of Refugee Law* 443

Goodwin-Gill, GS and McAdam, J, *The Refugee in International Law* (Oxford, Oxford University Press, 2021)

Goldner Lang, I, 'Towards "Judicial Passivism" in European Union Migration and Asylum Law?' in T Capeta, I Goldner Lang and T Perišin (eds) *The Changing European Union* (Oford, Hart Publishing, 2022)

Goldner Lang, I and Nagy, B, 'External Border Control Techniques in the EU as a Challenge to the Principle of Non-Refoulement' (2021) 17 *European Constitutional Law Review* 442

Graefrath, B, 'Complicity in the Law of International Responsibility' (1996) 29 *Revue Belge de Droit International* 370

Groenendijk, K, 'Reinstatement of Controls at the Internal Borders of Europe: Why and Against Whom?' (2004) 10 *European Law Journal* 150

Grześkowiak, M, 'The "Guardian of the Treaties" Is No More? The European Commission and the 2021 Humanitarian Crisis on Poland–Belarus Border' (2023) 42 *Refugee Survey Quarterly* 81

Guild, E, 'Discretion, Competence and Migration in the European Union' (1999) 1 *European Journal of Migration and Law* 61

—— 'Who Is an Irregular Immigrant' in B Bogusz and others (eds), *Irregular Migration and Human Rights: Theoretical, European and International Perspectives* (Leiden, Martinus Nihjoff, 2004)

—— *Moving the Borders of Europe*, Inaugural Lecture (University of Nijmegen 2001)

—— 'The Legal Framework: Who is Entitled to Move?' in D Bigo and E Guild (eds), *Controlling Frontiers* (Farnham, Ashgate, 2005)

—— (ed), *Monitoring Border Violence in the EU: Frontex in Focus* (Abingdon, Taylor & Francis, 2023)

Guild, E and Bigo, D, 'The Transformation of European Border Controls' in Bernard Ryan and Valsamis Mitsilegas (eds), *Extraterritorial Immigration Control: Legal Challenges* (Leiden, Martinus Nijhoff, 2010)

Guild, E and Stoyanova, V, 'The Human Right to Leave Any Country: A Right to Be Delivered' [2018] *European Yearbook on Human Rights* 373

Haggerty, KD and Ericson, RV, 'The Surveillant Assemblage' (2000) 51 *The British Journal of Sociology* 605

Hailbronner, K, 'Non-Refoulement and "Humanitarian" Refugees: Customary International Law or Wishful Legal Thinking?' (1986) 26 *Virginia Journal of International Law* 857

Hakimi, M, 'State Bystander Responsibility' (2010) 21 *European Journal of International Law* 341

Hanke, P and Vitiello, D, 'High-Tech Migration Control in the EU and Beyond: The Legal Challenges of "Enhanced Interoperability"' in E Carpanelli and N Lazzerini (eds), *Use and Misuse of New Technologies: Contemporary Challenges in International and European Law* (Cham, Springer, 2019)

Hart, HLA, *Punishment and Responsibility: Essays in the Philosophy of Law (1968)* 2nd edn (John Gardner ed, Oxford, Oxford University Press, 2008)

Hathaway, JC, *The Rights of Refugees under International Law* (Cambridge, Cambridge University Press, 2021)

Hernández i Sagrera, R, 'Exporting EU Integrated Border Management beyond EU Borders: Modernization and Institutional Transformation in Exchange for More Mobility?' (2014) 27 *Cambridge Review of International Affairs* 167

Heschl, L, *Protecting the Rights of Refugees Beyond European Borders: Establishing Extraterritorial Legal Responsibilities* (Antwerp, Intersentia, 2018)

Herwig C.H. Hofmann, 'Article 47 – Right to an Effective Remedy' in S Peers and others (eds), *The EU Charter of Fundamental Rights: A Commentary* (Oxford, Hart Publishing, 2021)

Herwig C.H. Hofmann, Vos, E and Chamon, M, *The External Dimension of EU Agencies and Bodies: Law and Policy* (Cheltenham, Edward Elgar, 2019)

Horii, S, 'It Is about More than Just Training: The Effect of Frontex Border Guard Training' (2012) 31 *Refugee Survey Quarterly* 158

—— 'Accountability, Dependency, and EU Agencies: The Hotspot Approach in the Refugee Crisis' (2018) 37 *Refugee Survey Quarterly* 204

Huysmans, J, *The Politics of Insecurity: Fear, Migration and Asylum in the EU* (Abingdon, Routledge, 2006)

Iglesias Sánchez, S and González Pascual, M (eds), *Fundamental Rights in the EU Area of Freedom, Security and Justice* (Cambridge, Cambridge University Press, 2021)

Ioffe, Y, 'The Right to Family Reunification of Children Seeking International Protection under the Convention on the Rights of the Child: Misplaced Reliance on Travaux?' (2022) 34 *International Journal of Refugee Law* 215

Ippolito, F and Trevisanut, S, *Migration in the Mediterranean: Mechanisms of International Cooperation* (Cambridge, Cambridge University Press, 2016)

Jackson, M, *State Complicity in the Internationally Wrongful Act of Another State* (Oxford, Oxford University Press, 2015)

Jacobs, D, Nollkaemper, A and Schechinger, JNM (eds), *Distribution of Responsibilities in International Law* (Cambridge, Cambridge University Press, 2015)

Kalpouzos, I, 'International Criminal Law and the Violence against Migrants' (2020) 21 *German Law Journal* 571

Kamminga, MT and Scheinin, M, *The Impact of Human Rights Law on General International Law* (Oxford, Oxford University Press, 2009)

Karageorgiou, E and Noll, G, 'What Is Wrong with Solidarity in EU Asylum and Migration Law?' (2022) 4 *Jus Cogens* 131

Karamandidou, L and Kasparek, B, 'From Exception to Extra-Legal Normality: Pushbacks and Racist State Violence against People Crossing the Greek-Turkish Land Border' (2022) 11 *State Crime Journal* 12

Keady-Tabbal, N and Mann, I, 'Weaponizing Rescue: Law and the Materiality of Migration Management in the Aegean' (2023) 36 *Leiden Journal of International Law* 61

Keller, H and Walther, R, 'Evasion of the International Law of State Responsibility? The ECtHR's Jurisprudence on Positive and Preventive Obligations under Article 3' (2020) 24 *The International Journal of Human Rights* 957

Kellerbauer, M, Klamert, M and Tomkin, J (eds), *The EU Treaties and the Charter of Fundamental Rights: A Commentary* (Oxford, Oxford University Press, 2019)

Klabbers, J, 'Presumptive Personality: The European Union in International Law' in Martti Koskenniemi (ed), *International Law Aspects of the European Union* (Leiden, Martinus Nijhoff, 1998)

—— '(I Can't Get No) Recognition: Subjects Doctrine and the Emergence of Non-State Actors' in J Petman and J Klabbers (eds), *Nordic Cosmopolitanism: Essays in International law for Martti Koskenniemi* (Leiden, Brill, 2003)

—— 'The Paradox of International Institutional Law' (2008) 5 (2008) *International Organizations Law Review* 151

—— *Treaty Conflict and the European Union* (Cambridge, Cambridge University Press, 2009)

—— 'Völkerrechtsfreundlich? International Law and the Union Legal Order' in P Koutrakos (ed), *European Foreign Policy: Legal and Political Perspectives* (Cheltenham, Edward Elgar, 2011)

—— *The European Union in International Law* (Paris, Pedone, 2012)

—— 'Law, Ethics and Global Governance: Accountability in Perspective' (2013) 11 *New Zealand Journal of Public and International Law* 309

—— 'Unity, Diversity, Accountability: The Ambivalent Concept of International Organisation' (2013) 14 *Melbourne Journal of International Law* 149

—— 'Straddling the Fence: The European Union and International Law' in D Chalmers and A Arnull (eds), *The Oxford Handbook of European Union Law* (Oxford, Oxford University Press, 2015)

—— 'The EJIL Foreword: The Transformation of International Organizations Law' (2015) 26 *European Journal of International Law* 9

—— 'Sui Generis? The European Union as an International Organization' in Dennis Patterson and Anna Södersten (eds), *A Companion to European Union Law and International Law* (Oxford, John Wiley & Sons, 2016)

—— 'Sources of International Organizations' Law: Reflections on Accountability' in S Besson and J d'Aspremont (eds), *The Oxford Handbook of the Sources of International Law* (Oxford, Oxford University Press, 2017)

—— (ed), *The Cambridge Companion to International Organizations Law* (Cambridge, Cambridge University Press, 2022)

Klabbers, J, Peters, A and Ulfstein, G, *The Constitutionalization of International Law* (Oxford, Oxford University Press, 2009)

Kochenov, D, 'The Right to Leave Any Country Including Your Own in International Law' (2012) 28 *Connecticut Journal of International Law* 43

Koivurova, T, 'What Is the Principle of Due Diligence' in J Petman and J Klabbers (eds), *Nordic Cosmopolitanism: Essays in International Law for Martti Koskenniemi* (Leiden, Martinus Nijhoff, 2003)

Kolb, R, *The International Law of State Responsibility: An Introduction* (Cheltenham, Edward Elgar, 2017)

Komp, L-M, *Border Deaths at Sea under the Right to Life in the European Convention on Human Rights* (Abingdon, Routledge, 2023)

Koskenniemi, M, 'International Law in Europe: Between Tradition and Renewal' (2005) 16 *European Journal of International Law* 113

—— *From Apology to Utopia: The Structure of International Legal Argument* (Cambridge, Cambridge University Press, 2006)

Krieger, H, Peters, A and Kreuzer, L, *Due Diligence in the International Legal Order* (Oxford, Oxford University Press, 2020)

Krisch, N, 'Jurisdiction Unbound: (Extra)Territorial Regulation as Global Governance' (2022) 33 *European Journal of International Law* 481

Kube, V, *EU Human Rights, International Investment Law and Participation: Operationalizing the EU Foreign Policy Objective to Global Human Rights Protection* (Cham, Springer, 2019)

Kuijper, PJ, 'Attribution – Responsibility – Remedy. Some Comments on the EU in Different International Regimes' (2013) 46 *Revue Belge de Droit International* 57

Kuşkonmaz, EM, 'Border Management and Technology: A Challenge to the Right to Privacy' in *Migration, Security, and Resistance* (Abingdon, Routledge, 2021)

Landau, LB, 'A Chronotope of Containment Development: Europe's Migrant Crisis and Africa's Reterritorialisation' (2019) 51 *Antipode* 169

Lanovoy, V, 'Complicity in an Internationally Wrongful Act' in A Nollkaemper and I Plakokefalos (eds), *Principles of Shared Responsibility in International Law: An Appraisal of the State of the Art* (Cambridge, Cambridge University Press, 2014)

—— *Complicity and Its Limits in the Law of International Responsibility* (London, Bloomsbury, 2016)

Laube, L, 'The Relational Dimension of Externalizing Border Control: Selective Visa Policies in Migration and Border Diplomacy' (2019) 7 *Comparative Migration Studies* 29

Lavenex, S, 'Shifting up and out: The Foreign Policy of European Immigration Control' (2006) 29 *West European Politics* 329

Lavrysen, L, *Human Rights in a Positive State: Rethinking the Relationship Between Positive and Negative Obligations Under the European Convention on Human Rights* (Antwerp, Intersentia, 2016)

Léonard, S, 'EU Border Security and Migration into the European Union: FRONTEX and Securitisation through Practices' (2010) 19 *European Security* 231

Léonard, S and Kaunert, C, 'The Securitisation of Migration in the European Union: Frontex and Its Evolving Security Practices' (2020) 48 *Journal of Ethnic and Migration Studies* 1417

Letourneux, L, 'Protecting the Borders from the Outside: An Analysis of the Status Agreements on Actions Carried Out by Frontex Concluded between the EU and Third Countries' (2022) 24 *European Journal of Migration and Law* 330

Liguori, A, *Migration Law and the Externalization of Border Controls: European State Responsibility* (Abingdon, Routledge, 2019)

Lukes, S (ed), *Power: A Radical View* (New York, New York University Press, 1986)

Majcher, I, 'Human Rights Violations During EU Border Surveillance and Return Operations: Frontex's Shared Responsibility or Complicity?' [2015] *Silesian Journal of Legal Studies* 45

—— *The European Union Returns Directive and Its Compatibility with International Human Rights Law: Analysis of Return Decision, Entry Ban, Detention, and Removal* (Leiden, Brill, 2020)

Mann, I, *Humanity at Sea: Maritime Migration and the Foundations of International Law* (Cambridge, Cambridge University Press, 2016)

—— 'Maritime Legal Black Holes: Migration and Rightlessness in International Law' (2018) 29 *European Journal of International Law* 347

—— 'The Right to Perform Rescue at Sea: Jurisprudence and Drowning' (2020) 21 *German Law Journal* 598

Marin, L, 'The Cooperation Between Frontex and Third Countries in Information Sharing: Practices, Law and Challenges in Externalizing Border Control Functions' (2020) 26 *European Public Law* 157

Markard, N, 'The Right to Leave by Sea: Legal Limits on EU Migration Control by Third Countries' (2016) 27 *European Journal of International Law* 591

McCorquodale, R, 'International Law, Boundaries and Imagination' in D Miller and S.H Hashmi (eds), *Boundaries and Justice: Diverse Ethical Perspectives* (Princeton, Princeton University Press, 2001)

Melin, P, 'The Global Compact for Migration: Lessons for the Unity of EU Representation' (2019) 21 *European Journal of Migration and Law* 194

Messineo, F, 'Non-Refoulement Obligations in Public International Law: Towards a New Protection Status' in *The Ashgate Research Companion to Migration Law, Theory and Policy* (Farnham, Ashgate, 2013)

—— 'Attribution of Conduct' in Andre Nollkaemper and Ilias Plakokefalos (eds), *Principles of Shared Responsibility in International Law: An Appraisal of the State of the Art* (Cambridge, Cambridge University Press, 2014)

Mezzadra, S and Neilson, B, *Border as Method, or, the Multiplication of Labor* (Durham, Duke University Press, 2013)

Milanović, M, 'From Compromise to Principle: Clarifying the Concept of State Jurisdiction in Human Rights Treaties' (2008) 8 *Human Rights Law Review* 411

—— *Extraterritorial Application of Human Rights Treaties: Law, Principles and Policy* (Oxford, Oxford University Press, 2011)

—— 'Al-Skeini and Al-Jedda in Strasbourg' (2012) 23 *European Journal of International Law* 121

—— 'Human Rights Treaties and Foreign Surveillance: Privacy in the Digital Age' (2015) 56 *Harvard International Law Journal* 81

—— 'Jurisdiction and Responsibility: Trends in the Jurisprudence of the Strasbourg Court' in Iulia Motoc and Anne van Aaken (eds), *The ECHR and General International Law* (Oxford, Oxford University Press, 2018)

Milanović, M and Papić, T, 'As Bad as It Gets: The European Court of Human Rights's Behrami and Saramati Decision and General International Law' (2009) 58 *International and Comparative Law Quarterly* 267

Mitsilegas, V, Moreno-Lax, V and Vavoula, N, *Securitising Asylum Flows: Deflection, Criminalisation and Challenges for Human Rights* (Leiden, Brill, 2020)

Molnár, T, 'The EU Shaping the Global Compact for Safe, Orderly and Regular Migration: The Glass Half Full or Half Empty?' (2020) 16 *International Journal of Law in Context* 321

Monar, J, 'The External Shield of Internal Security: The EU's Emerging Common External Border Management' in David Brown and Alistair Shepherd (eds), *The Security Dimensions of EU Enlargement* (Manchester, Manchester University Press, 2018)

Moreno-Lax, V, 'The EU Regime on Interdictions, Search and Rescue, and Disembarkation: The Frontex Guidelines for Intervention at Sea' (2010) 25 *The International Journal of Marine and Coastal Law* 621

—— 'Seeking Asylum in the Mediterranean: Against a Fragmentary Reading of EU Member States' Obligations Accruing at Sea' (2011) 23 *International Journal of Refugee Law* 174

—— 'Hirsi Jamaa and Others V Italy or the Strasbourg Court Versus Extraterritorial Migration Control?' (2012) 12 *Human Rights Law Review* 574.

—— *Accessing Asylum in Europe: Extraterritorial Border Controls and Refugee Rights under EU Law* (Oxford, Oxford University Press, 2017)

—— 'The EU Humanitarian Border and the Securitization of Human Rights: The "Rescue-Through-Interdiction/Rescue-Without-Protection" Paradigm' (2018) 56 *JCMS: Journal of Common Market Studies* 119

—— 'The Axiological Emancipation of a (Non-) Principle: Autonomy, International Law and the EU Legal Order' in Sacha Garben and Inge Govaere (eds), *The Interface Between EU and International Law* (Oxford, Hart Publishing, 2019)

—— 'The Architecture of Functional Jurisdiction: Unpacking Contactless Control – On Public Powers, S.S. and Others v. Italy, and the "Operational Model"' (2020) 21 German Law Journal 385

—— 'Protection at Sea and the Denial of Asylum' in *The Oxford Handbook of International Refugee Law* (Oxford, Oxford University Press, 2021)

Moreno-Lax, V and Costello, C, 'The Extraterritorial Application of the EU Charter of Fundamental Rights: From Territoriality to Facticity, the Effectiveness Model' in Steve Peers and others (eds), *The EU Charter of Fundamental Rights* (Oxford, Hart Publishing, 2014)

Moreno-Lax, V and Lemberg-Pedersen, M, 'Border-Induced Displacement: The Ethical and Legal Implications of Distance-Creation through Externalization' (2019) 56 *Questioni di Diritto Internazionale* 5

Moreno-Lax, V and Papastavridis, E, *'Boat Refugees' and Migrants at Sea: A Comprehensive Approach: Integrating Maritime Security with Human Rights* (Leiden, Brill, 2016)

Morriss, P, *Power: A Philosophical Analysis* (Manchester, Manchester University Press, 2002)

Müller, A Th, 'The Direct Effect of Customary International Law: The "Treaty Analogy" and Its Limits' in A Th Müller, FL Bordin and F Pascual-Vives (eds), *The European Union and Customary International Law* (Cambridge, Cambridge University Press, 2022)
Mungianu, R, *Frontex and Non-Refoulement: The International Responsibility of the EU* (Cambridge, Cambridge University Press, 2016)
Neal, AW, 'Securitization and Risk at the EU Border: The Origins of FRONTEX' (2009) 47 *Journal of Common Market Studies* 333
Nedeski, N and Nollkaemper, A, 'Responsibility of International Organizations "in Connection with Acts of States"' (2012) 9 *International Organizations Law Review* 33
Nesi, G, 'Boundaries' in MG Kohen, M Hébié and G Nesi (eds), *Research Handbook on Territorial Disputes in International Law* (Cheltenham, Edward Elgar, 2018)
Nicolosi, SF, 'Refashioning the EU Visa Policy: A New Turn of the Screw to Cooperation on Readmission and to Discrimination?' (2020) 22 *European Journal of Migration and Law* 467
Noll, G, *Negotiating Asylum: The EU Acquis, Extraterritorial Protection and the Common Market of Deflection* (Leiden, Martinus Nijhoff, 2000)
—— 'Seeking Asylum at Embassies: A Right to Entry under International Law?' (2005) 17 *International Journal of Refugee Law* 542
Nollkaemper, A, 'Concurrence between Individual Responsibility and State Responsibility in International Law' (2003) 52 *International & Comparative Law Quarterly* 615
—— 'Constitutionalization and the Unity of the Law of International Responsibility' (2009) 16 *Indiana Journal of Global Legal Studies* 535
—— 'Dual Attribution Liability of the Netherlands for Conduct of Dutchbat in Srebrenica' (2011) 9 *Journal of International Criminal Justice* 1143
—— 'Responsibility' in J d'Aspremont and S Singh (eds), *Fundamental Concepts for International Law* (Cheltenham, Edward Elgar, 2017)
Nollkaemper, A and others, 'Guiding Principles on Shared Responsibility in International Law' (2020) 31 *European Journal of International Law* 15
Nollkaemper, A and Jacobs, D, 'Shared Responsibility in International Law: A Conceptual Framework' (2012) 34 *Michigan Journal of International Law* 359
Nollkaemper, A and Plakokefalos, I, *The Practice of Shared Responsibility in International Law* (Cambridge, Cambridge University Press, 2017)
Nolte, G and Aust, HP, 'Equivocal Helpers – Complicit States, Mixed Messages and International Law' (2009) 58 *International & Comparative Law Quarterly* 1
Odermatt, J, 'Brexit and International Law: Disentangling Legal Orders' (2017) 31 *Emory International Law Review* 1051
—— 'Unidentified Legal Object: Conceptualising the European Union in International Law' (2017) 33 *Connecticut Journal of International Law* 215
—— *International Law and the European Union* (Cambridge, Cambridge University Press, 2021)
Okada, Y, 'Effective Control Test at the Interface between the Law of International Responsibility and the Law of International Organizations: Managing Concerns over the Attribution of UN Peacekeepers' Conduct to Troop-Contributing Nations' (2019) 32 *Leiden Journal of International Law* 275
Ollino, A, *Due Diligence Obligations in International Law* (Cambridge, Cambridge University Press, 2022)
Orakhelashvili, A, 'Restrictive Interpretation of Human Rights Treaties in the Recent Jurisprudence of the European Court of Human Rights' (2003) 14 *European Journal of International Law* 529
Orator, A and Griller, S, 'Everything under Control? The "Way Forward" for European Agencies in the Footsteps of the Meroni Doctrine' (2010) 35 *European Law Review* 3
Orford, A, 'Jurisdiction without Territory: From the Holy Roman Empire to the Responsibility to Protect Symposium: Territory without Boundaries – Universal Jurisdiction' [2008] *Michigan Journal of International Law* 981
—— 'International Law and the Populist Moment: A Comment on Martti Koskenniemi's Enchanted by the Tools? International Law and Enlightenment' in *Proceedings of the ASIL Annual Meeting* (Cambridge, Cambridge University Press, 2019)

Ott A, Vos, E and Coman-Kund, F, *EU Agencies and Their International Mandate: A New Category of Global Actors?* (The Hague, TMC Asser Institute, 2013)

Paasivirta, E, 'The European Union: From an Aggregate of States to a Legal Person' (1997) 2 *Hofstra Law and Policy Symposium* 37

Paasivirta, E and Kuijper, PJ, 'Does One Size Fit All?: The European Community and the Responsibility of International Organizations' (2005) 36 *Netherlands Yearbook of International Law* 169

Palchetti, P, 'Unità, Pluralità o Inutilità Dei Regimi Di Responsabilità Internazionale Applicabili Alle Organizzazioni' in Michele Vellano (ed), *Il futuro delle organizzazioni internazionali: prospettive giuridiche* (Naples, Editoriale Scientifica, 2015)

—— 'Applying the Rules of Attribution in Complex Scenarios: The Case of Partnerships among International Organisations' (2016) 13 *International Organizations Law Review* 37

Pallister-Wilkins, P, 'The Humanitarian Politics of European Border Policing: Frontex and Border Police in Evros' (2015) 9 *International Political Sociology* 53

Panebianco, S, 'The EU and Migration in the Mediterranean: EU Borders' Control by Proxy' (2020) 48 *Journal of Ethnic and Migration Studies* 1398

Papachristodoulou, A, 'The Recognition of a Right to Be Rescued at Sea in International Law' (2022) 35 *Leiden Journal of International Law* 337

Papanicolopulu, I, *International Law and The Protection of People at Sea* (Oxford, Oxford University Press, 2018)

Papastavridis, E, '"Fortress Europe" and FRONTEX: Within or Without International Law?' (2010) 79 *Nordic Journal of International Law* 75

—— *The Interception of Vessels on the High Seas: Contemporary Challenges to the Legal Order of the Oceans* (Oxford, Hart Publishing, 2013)

—— 'Is There a Right to Be Rescued at Sea? A Skeptical View' [2014] *Questions of International Law* 17

—— 'The European Convention of Human Rights and Migration at Sea: Reading the "Jurisdictional Threshold" of the Convention Under the Law of the Sea Paradigm' (2020) 21 *German Law Journal* 417

Pascale, G, 'Is Italy Internationally Responsible for the Gross Human Rights Violations against Migrants in Libya?' [2019] *Questions of International Law* 35

Paul, R, 'Harmonisation by Risk Analysis? Frontex and the Risk-Based Governance of European Border Control' (2017) 39 *Journal of European Integration* 689

Paz, M, 'Between the Kingdom and the Desert Sun: Human Rights, Immigration, and Border Walls' (2016) 34 *Berkeley Journal of International Law* 1

Peers, S and others, *The EU Charter of Fundamental Rights: A Commentary* (Oxford, Bloomsbury, 2021)

Perkowski, N, 'Frontex and the Convergence of Humanitarianism, Human Rights and Security' (2018) 49 *Security Dialogue* 457

Pijnenburg, A, 'From Italian Pushbacks to Libyan Pullbacks: Is Hirsi 2.0 in the Making in Strasbourg?' (2018) 20 *European Journal of Migration and Law* 396

—— 'Containment Instead of Refoulement: Shifting State Responsibility in the Age of Cooperative Migration Control?' (2020) 20 *Human Rights Law Review* 306

—— *At the Frontiers of State Responsibility: Socio-economic rights and cooperation on migration* (Antwerp, Intersentia 2021)

Pijnenburg, A and Pas, K van der, 'Strategic Litigation against European Migration Control Policies: The Legal Battleground of the Central Mediterranean Migration Route' (2022) 24 *European Journal of Migration and Law* 401

Pollak, J and Slominski, P, 'Experimentalist but Not Accountable Governance? The Role of Frontex in Managing the EU's External Borders' (2009) 32 *West European Politics* 904

Pollozek, S, 'Turbulences of Speeding up Data Circulation. Frontex and Its Crooked Temporalities of "Real-Time" Border Control' [2020] *Mobilities* 1

Portmann, R, *Legal Personality in International Law* (Cambridge, Cambridge University Press, 2010)

Prescott, JRV, *Boundaries and Frontiers* (Abingdon, Taylor & Francis, 1978)

Progin-Theuerkauf, S, 'Defining the Boundaries of the Future Common European Asylum System with the Help of Hungary?' (2021) 2021 6 *European Papers* 7

Puma, G, *Complicità di Stati nell'illecito internazionale* (Turin, Giappichelli, 2018)
Quigley, J, 'Complicity in International Law: A New Direction in the Law of State Responsibility' (1987) 57 *British Yearbook of International Law* 77
Quintel, T, 'Interoperable Data Exchanges Within Different Data Protection Regimes: The Case of Europol and the European Border and Coast Guard Agency' (2020) 26 *European Public Law* 205
Raible, L, 'The Extraterritoriality of the ECHR: Why Jaloud and Pisari Should Be Read as Game Changers' [2016] *European Human Rights Law Review* 161
—— *Human Rights Unbound: A Theory of Extraterritoriality* (Cambridge, Cambridge University Press, 2020)
Ramji-Nogales, J, 'Undocumented Migrants and the Failures of Universal Individualism' [2014] *Vanderbilt Journal of Transnational Law* 699
Reinisch, A, 'Securing the Accountability of International Organizations' (2001) 7 *Global Governance* 131
—— *The Privileges and Immunities of International Organizations in Domestic Courts* (Oxford, Oxford University Press, 2013)
Rijpma, JJ, 'Frontex: Successful Blame Shifting of the Member States?' [2010] *Análisis del Real Instituto Elcano (ARI)* 1
—— 'Hybrid Agencification in the Area of Freedom, Security and Justice and Its Inherent Tensions: The Case of Frontex' in M Busuioc, M Groenleer and J Trondal (eds), *The Agency Phenomenon in the European Union: Emergence, Institutionalisation and Everyday Decision-Making* (Manchester, Manchester University Press, 2012)
—— 'Brave New Borders: The EU's Use of New Technologies for the Management of Migration and Asylum' in *New Technologies and EU Law* (Oxford, Oxford University Press, 2017)
Rijpma, JJ and Fink, M, 'The Management of The European Union's External Borders' in Evangelia (Lilian) Tsourdi and Philippe De Bruycker (eds), *Research Handbook on EU Asylum and Migration Law* (Cheltenham, Edward Elgar, 2022)
Rijpma, J and Vermeulen, M, 'EUROSUR: Saving Lives or Building Borders?' (2015) 24 *European Security* 454
Rosas, A, 'Exclusive, Shared and National Competence in the Context of EU External Relations: Do Such Distinctions Matter?' [2014] *The European Union in the World* 17
Ruffert, M, 'Personality under EU Law: A Conceptual Answer towards the Pluralisation of the EU' (2014) 20 *European Law Journal* 346
Ryngaert, C, 'The European Court of Human Rights' Approach to the Responsibility of Member States in Connection with Acts of International Organizations' (2011) 60 *The International and Comparative Law Quarterly* 997
Ryngaert, C and Spijkers, O, 'The End of the Road: State Liability for Acts of UN Peacekeeping Contingents After the Dutch Supreme Court's Judgment in Mothers of Srebrenica (2019)' (2019) 66 *Netherlands International Law Review* 537
Salmon, J, 'Le fait étatique complexe – une notion contestable' (1982) 28 *Annuaire Français de Droit International* 709
Salomon, S and Rijpma, J, 'A Europe Without Internal Frontiers: Challenging the Reintroduction of Border Controls in the Schengen Area in the Light of Union Citizenship' (2023) 24 *German Law Journal* 281
Sánchez, MAA, 'An Analysis of Integrated Management of the External Borders of the European Union' [2020] *Paix et sécurité internationales: Journal of International Law and International Relations* 121
Sassen, S, *Territory, Authority, Rights: From Medieval to Global Assemblages* (Princeton, Princeton University Press, 2008)
Scheinin, M, 'Extraterritorial Effect of the International Covenant on Civil and Political Rights' in F Coomans and M Kamminga (eds), *Extraterritorial Application of Human Rights Treaties* (Antwerp, Intersentia, 2004)
Schermers, HG and Blokker, NM, *International Institutional Law* 6th edn (Leiden, Brill, 2018)

Seibert-Fohr, A, 'From Complicity to Due Diligence: When Do States Incur Responsibility for Their Involvement in Serious International Wrongdoing?' (2017) 60 *German Yearbook of International Law* 667

Shany, Y, 'Taking Universality Seriously: A Functional Approach to Extraterritoriality in International Human Rights Law' (2013) 7 *The Law & Ethics of Human Rights* 47

—— 'The Extraterritorial Application of International Human Rights Law' (2020) 409 *Collected Courses of the Hague Academy of International Law*

Shelton, D and Gould, A, 'Positive and Negative Obligations' in D Shelton (ed), *The Oxford Handbook of International Human Rights Law* (Oxford, Oxford University Press, 2013)

Sicilianos, L-A, 'Preventing Violations of the Right to Life: Positive Obligations under Article 2 of the ECHR' (2014) 3 *Cyprus Human Rights Law Review* 117

Smith, KE, 'Speaking with One Voice? European Union Co-Ordination on Human Rights Issues at the United Nations' (2006) 44 *JCMS: Journal of Common Market Studies* 113

Spijkerboer, T, 'The Human Costs of Border Control' (2007) 9 *European Journal of Migration and Law* 127

—— 'Moving Migrants, States, and Rights Human Rights and Border Deaths' (2013) 7 *The Law & Ethics of Human Rights* 213

—— 'Wasted Lives. Borders and the Right to Life of People Crossing Them' (2017) 86 *Nordic Journal of International Law* 1

—— 'Bifurcation of People, Bifurcation of Law: Externalization of Migration Policy before the EU Court of Justice' (2018) 31 *Journal of Refugee Studies* 216

Stachowitsch, S and Sachseder, J, 'The Gendered and Racialized Politics of Risk Analysis. The Case of Frontex' (2019) 7 *Critical Studies on Security* 107

Stefan, M and Hertog, L den, 'Frontex: Great Powers but No Appeals' in M Chamon, A Volpato and M Eliantonio (eds), *Boards of Appeal of EU Agencies: Towards Judicialization of Administrative Review?* (Oxford, Oxford University Press, 2022)

Stern, B, 'The Elements of an Internationally Wrongful Act' in J Crawford, A Pellet and S Olleson (eds), *The Law of International Responsibility* (Oxford, Oxford University Press, 2010)

Stoyanova, V, 'The Disjunctive Structure of Positive Rights under the European Convention on Human Rights' (2018) 87 *Nordic Journal of International Law* 344

—— 'Fault, Knowledge and Risk within the Framework of Positive Obligations under the European Convention on Human Rights' [2020] *Leiden Journal of International Law* 1

Stoyanova, V, *Positive Obligations under the European Convention on Human Rights: Within and Beyond Boundaries* (Oxford, Oxford University Press, 2023)

Tan, NF and Gammeltoft-Hansen, T, 'A Topographical Approach to Accountability for Human Rights Violations in Migration Control' (2020) 21 *German Law Journal* 335

Tazzioli, M and Walters, W, 'The Sight of Migration: Governmentality, Visibility and Europe's Contested Borders' (2016) 30 *Global Society* 445

Terpan, F, 'Soft Law in the European Union – The Changing Nature of EU Law' (2015) 21 *European Law Journal* 68

Thym, D, *European Migration Law* (Oxford, Oxford University Press, 2023)

Topolski, A, 'Relationality as a "Foundation" for Human Rights: Exploring the Paradox with Hannah Arendt and Emmanuel Levinas' (2014) 2 *Theoria and Praxis: International Journal of Interdisciplinary Thought*

Toth, AG, 'The Concepts of Damage and Causality as Elements of Non-Contractual Liability' in HG Schermers, T Heukels and J Philip Mead (eds), *Non-Contractual Liability of the European Communities* (Leiden, Brill, 1988)

Thomas, C, 'What Does the Emerging International Law of Migration Mean for Sovereignty?' (2013) 14 *Melbourne Journal of International Law* 392

Thompson, D, 'Designing Responsibility: The Problem of Many Hands in Complex Organizations' in J van den Hoven, S Miller and T Pogge (eds), *The Design Turn in Applied Ethics* (Oxford, Oxford University Press, 2017)

Trevisanut, S, 'Is There a Right to Be Rescued at Sea?: A Constructive Overview' [2014] *Questions of International Law* 3
—— 'The Principle of Non-Refoulement and the De-Territorialization of Border Control at Sea International Law and Practice' [2014] *Leiden Journal of International Law* 661
—— 'The Interception of Vessels on the High Seas, Contemporary Challenges to the Legal Order of the Oceans' (2014) 25 *European Journal of International Law* 616
Van Den Meerssche, D, 'Virtual Borders: International Law and the Elusive Inequalities of Algorithmic Association' (2022) 33 *European Journal of International Law* 171
Van Ooik, RH, 'The Growing Importance of Agencies in the EU. Shifting Governance and the Institutional Balance' in D Curtin and RA Wessel (eds), *Good Governance and the European Union. Reflections on Concepts, Institutions and Substance* (Antwerp, Intersentia, 2005)
Vara, JS and Sánchez-Tabernero, SR, 'In Deep Water: Towards a Greater Commitment for Human Rights in Sea Operations Coordinated by Frontex?' (2016) 18 *European Journal of Migration and Law* 65
Vaughan-Williams, N (ed), *Border Politics. The Limits of Sovereign Power* (Edinburgh, Edinburgh University Press, 2009)
Verdirame, G, *The UN and Human Rights: Who Guards the Guardians?* (Cambridge, Cambridge University Press, 2011)
Violi, F, 'The Function of the Triad "Territory", "Jurisdiction" and "Control" in Due Diligence Obligations' in H Krieger, A Peters and L Kreuzer (eds), *Due Diligence in the International Legal Order* (Oxford, Oxford University Press, 2020)
Vitiello, D, 'Agencification as a Key Component of the EU Externalisation Toolkit. Observations on a Silent Escape from the Rule of Law' [2018] *EU External Migration Policies in an Era of Global Mobilities: Intersecting Policy Universes* 125
Vogiatzis, N, 'Frontex: Human Rights Obligations and the Role of the European Ombudsman' in A Karatzogianni, D Nguyen and E Serafinelli (eds), *The Digital Transformation of the Public Sphere* (London, Palgrave Macmillan, 2016)
Voulgaris, N, *Allocating International Responsibility Between Member States and International Organisations* (Oxford, Hart Publishing, 2019)
Wagner, J, 'The European Union's Model of Integrated Border Management: Preventing Transnational Threats, Cross-Border Crime and Irregular Migration in the Context of the EU's Security Policies and Strategies' (2021) 59 *Commonwealth & Comparative Politics* 424
Waldron, J, 'Is Dignity the Foundation of Human Rights?' in R Cruft, SM Liao and M Renzo (eds), *Philosophical Foundations of Human Rights* (Oxford, Oxford University Press, 2015)
Walters, W, 'Border/Control' (2006) 9 *European Journal of Social Theory* 187
—— 'Rethinking Borders Beyond the State' (2006) 4 *Comparative European Politics* 141
Wessel, RA, 'Revisiting the International Legal Status of the EU' (2000) 5 European Foreign Affairs Review 507
Wilde, R, 'Legal Black Hole-Extraterritorial State Action and International Treaty Law on Civil and Political Rights' (2004) 26 *Michigan Journal International Law* 739
——, 'Compliance with Human Rights Norms Extraterritorially: "Human Rights Imperialism"?' in M Kohen and L Boisson de Chazournes (eds), *International Law and the Quest for its Implementation* (Leiden, Brill, 2010)
—— 'The Unintended Consequences of Expanding Migrant Rights Protections' (2017) 111 *AJIL Unbound* 487
Wille, A and Bovens, M, 'Watching EU Watchdogs Assessing the Accountability Powers of the European Court of Auditors and the European Ombudsman' (2022) 44 *Journal of European Integration* 183
de witte, B, 'The European Union as an International Legal Experiment' in G de Búrca and JHH Weiler (eds), *The Worlds of European Constitutionalism* (Cambridge, Cambridge University Press, 2011)
Wittgenstein, L, *Philosophical Investigations (1958)* (Oxford, Wiley-Blackwell, 2009)
Wolff, S and Schout, A, 'Frontex as Agency: More of the Same?' (2013) 14 *Perspectives on European Politics and Society* 305

Wyler, E and Castellanos-Jankiewicz, L, 'Serious Breaches of Peremptory Norms' in A Nollkaemper and I Plakokefalos (eds), *Principles of Shared Responsibility in International Law: An Appraisal of the State of the Art* (Cambridge, Cambridge University Press, 2014)

Zaiotti, R, *Cultures of Border Control: Schengen and the Evolution of European Frontiers* (Chicago, University of Chicago Press, 2011)

Ziegler, KS, 'International Law and EU Law: Between Asymmetric Constitutionalisation and Fragmentation' in A Orakhelashvili (ed), *Research Handbook on the Theory and History of International Law* (Cheltenham, Edward Elgar, 2011)

—— 'Piecing the Puzzle Together Beyond Pluralism and Autonomy: Systemic Harmonization as a Paradigm for the Interaction of EU Law and International Law' (2016) 35 *Yearbook of European Law* 667

—— 'The Relationship between EU Law and International Law' in D Patterson and A Södersten (eds), *A Companion to European Union Law and International Law* (Oxford, John Wiley & Sons, 2016)

Ziegler, KS, Neuvonen, PJ and Moreno Lax, V (eds), *Research Handbook on General Principles in EU Law: Constructing Legal Orders in Europe* (Cheltenham, Edward Elgar, 2022)

Zolberg, AR, 'The Archeology of "Remote Control"' in A Fahrmeir, O Faron and P Weil (eds), *Migration Control in the North Atlantic World: The Evolution of State Practices in Europe and the United States from the French Revolution to the Inter-War Period* (Oxford, Berghahn Books, 2003)

INDEX

www.ingramcontent.com/pod-product-compliance
Ingram Content Group UK Ltd.
Pitfield, Milton Keynes, MK11 3LW, UK
UKHW020237290926
15470UKWH00002B/592

9 781509 964543